Restructuring Law and Practice

Restructuring Law and Practice

Chris Howard
Partner, Freshfields Bruckhaus Deringer LLP

Bob Hedger
Director, Corporate Restructuring Unit, Specialised Lending Services, Royal Bank of Scotland

LexisNexis®

Members of the LexisNexis Group worldwide

United Kingdom	LexisNexis, a Division of Reed Elsevier (UK) Ltd, Halsbury House, 35 Chancery Lane, London, WC2A 1EL, and London House, 20–22 East London Street, Edinburgh EH7 4BQ
Australia	LexisNexis Butterworths, Chatswood, New South Wales
Austria	LexisNexis Verlag ARD Orac GmbH & Co KG, Vienna
Benelux	LexisNexis Benelux, Amsterdam
Canada	LexisNexis Canada, Markham, Ontario
China	LexisNexis China, Beijing and Shanghai
France	LexisNexis SA, Paris
Germany	LexisNexis Deutschland GmbH, Munster
Hong Kong	LexisNexis Hong Kong, Hong Kong
India	LexisNexis India, New Delhi
Italy	Giuffrè Editore, Milan
Japan	LexisNexis Japan, Tokyo
Malaysia	Malayan Law Journal Sdn Bhd, Kuala Lumpur
New Zealand	LexisNexis NZ Ltd, Wellington
Poland	Wydawnictwo Prawnicze LexisNexis Sp, Warsaw
Singapore	LexisNexis Singapore, Singapore
South Africa	LexisNexis Butterworths, Durban
USA	LexisNexis, Dayton, Ohio

© Reed Elsevier (UK) Ltd 2008

Reprinted August 2008

Published by LexisNexis

A CIP Catalogue record for this book is available from the British Library.

ISBN 978-1-4057-3502-5

9 781405 735025

Typeset by Letterpart Ltd, Reigate, Surrey

Printed and bound in Great Britain by CPI Antony Rowe, Chippenham, Wiltshire

Visit LexisNexis at www.lexisnexis.co.uk

About the authors

Chris Howard has 15 years experience in restructurings. He is a partner at Freshfields Bruckhaus Deringer LLP and is a member of the firm's acclaimed restructuring team which is a consistent winner of the major industry awards.

In relation to financial restructurings, Chris advises the leading investment and commercial banks on multi-creditor cross border restructuring transactions. He has recently advised a syndicate of banks and funds on the £1.2bn restructuring of Polestar, the senior lenders on the restructuring of TMD GmbH and steering committees of banks on the restructuring of Johnson Services Group plc and Uniq plc.

Further restructuring transactions for senior and subordinated creditors include Whistlejacket (the Structured Investment Vehicle) Nightfreight, MyTravel, Primacom, Marconi, Laing, AEA Technology, and Jarvis. Chris was also admitted to the New York Bar in 1999 and he has particular experience in US Chapter 11 restructurings, previously advising institutional financial creditors on APW (which was simultaneously reorganised through a provisional liquidation in Bermuda), Peguform, Enron and Comdisco.

Bob Hedger is a well-known restructuring banker having been involved in many high profile situations. He is Director in the Corporate Restructuring Unit, Specialised Lending Services, at Royal Bank of Scotland. This role sees him head the Large Corporate and Leveraged Finance restructuring team. Bob has been in banking for 34 years and is highly regarded and experienced in his field having specialised in Corporate Restructurings/Workouts since first becoming involved in a number of high profile Distressed Corporate problems during the last major UK recession of the early 1990s. He has since been involved, most often as lead Banker performing the role of Co-ordinator, in a significant number of complex, well publicised, UK and cross border restructurings, involving a variety of different stakeholders.

Having joined the Special Situations Group within NatWest in 1990 and moved into the equivalent unit (Corporate Restructuring Unit) in RBS upon the takeover of NatWest in 2000, Bob has 18 years of continual relevant experience. Bob was nominated for and awarded the Society of Turnaround Professionals (STP) 'Turnaround Financier of the Year' in 2005 for his work in respect of the MyTravel restructuring.

About the authors

Examples of experience – the majority as lead banker – include:

- Waterford Wedgwood
- Rosehaugh Stanhope
- Mountleigh
- Vesty Family (Frederick Leyland)
- Memorex Telex (Chapter 11)
- Wace Group
- McCarthy Stone
- Costain
- YJ Lovell
- Queens Moat Houses
- Booker
- Dunlop Slazenger
- Harnischfeger (Chapter 11)
- Unipart
- Iceland/Big Food Group
- John Laing
- Telewest
- Uniq
- British Energy
- HP Bulmer
- MyTravel
- Mowlem
- Global Automotive Logistics

Acknowledgements

The authors would like to thank numerous partners and associates at Freshfields Bruckhaus Deringer LLP for their insight and contribution. The firm's restructuring practice led by Ken Baird continues to be the leader in its field and the unprecedented transactional experience of the firm has been of enormous assistance to this publication.

Tim Wilmot has made a major contribution to the rights issue chapter and has been of enormous assistance on all aspects of UK public company law. Sarah Falk and Mark Boyle have been enormously helpful in all matters relating to taxation and David Pollard continues to be the fountain of all knowledge in relation to pensions and restructuring.

Helen Howard deserves a special mention for her patience and support.

Simon Brodie's assistance with the chapter on credit derivatives is also noted.

Contents

Table of Statutes

Table of Statutes

Table of Statutory Instruments

Table of European Legislation

Table of European Legislation

Table of Cases

Chapter 1

INTRODUCTION TO RESTRUCTURING

A SCOPE

1.1–1.2 This chapter analyses what a consensual restructuring actually is and explores how a financially impaired company can be the subject of a contractual financial restructuring with a view to preserving both the company and its business. The chapter will initially explore the informal regulatory framework within which such consensual restructurings are executed. This will be followed by an insight into why certain corporates undergo a restructuring.

B MEANING OF RESTRUCTURING

1.3 Restructurings, workouts and corporate rescue are interchangeable terms which describe the process by which the liabilities of a company in financial difficulties are restructured so as to enable the company, and therefore value, to be preserved and for its business to be carried on as a going concern. Preservation of a company and its business can be achieved by use of a statutory procedure or can be undertaken on an informal non-statutory and contractual basis. The company need not be solvent at the time the rescue is implemented, but the extent of the rescue and the nature of the restructuring which results from it will largely be determined by the seriousness of the company's financial difficulties, the economic and credit climate at the relevant time, the nature of the obligations in question and the attitude of the company's creditors to the proposals put to them.

1.4 Whether or not a restructuring should be entertained at all is principally a commercial judgment although other factors may be relevant. Commercial factors include the value of the security cover enjoyed by lenders at the time the company's difficulties became apparent, the prospects from, and timeliness of, recovery through a receivership, administration or liquidation, the ease with which other creditor constituencies can be brought into a restructuring and their willingness to participate in it and the nature of the problems

1

experienced by the company and whether they are soluble at all. Other factors include the size of the company concerned and whether its shares are publicly traded, the sensitivity of its lenders to publicity which may be associated with an insolvency (which will be more acute if the company has a high profile or is located in an area suffering high levels of local unemployment), and whether the relationship enjoyed by the company with its lenders is sufficiently close and historically profitable to encourage the lenders to take a long-term view of its prospects.

1.5 This chapter principally deals with the rescue of companies undertaken on an informal non-statutory and contractual basis.

C INFORMAL ARRANGEMENTS COMPARED TO STATUTORY PROCEDURES

1.6 Where a corporate restructuring is undertaken outside of a statutory procedure, it will be regulated by a contract which will invariably require the agreement of all financial creditors affected by it.

1.7 A corporate rescue of a company registered under the Companies Act 1985 or of a company incorporated under one of the previous Companies Acts (as described in the Companies Act 1985, s 735[1]) may also be undertaken under the auspices of a statutory procedure. Particular considerations apply in the case of insurance companies, banks and building societies, to which Part VII of the Financial Services and Markets Act 2000 will apply. Relevant statutory procedures include schemes of compromise or arrangement under the Companies Act 1985, ss 425[2] and 427[3] (as amended by the Companies Act 1989), a voluntary arrangement under the Insolvency Act 1986, ss 1–7 or, in the case of a winding up, an arrangement under the Insolvency Act 1986, s 110.

[1] The Companies Act 1985, s 735(1)(a) and (b) is to be replaced by the Companies Act 2006, s 1(1), which is not yet in force but which is expected to be brought into force on 1 October 2009. The Companies Act 1985, s 735(1)(c) and (3) is to be replaced (with some changes) by the Companies Act 2006, s 1171, which will come into force at the same time as s 1(1).

[2] The Companies Act 1985, s 425(1) is to be replaced by the Companies Act 2006, ss 895(1) and 896(1) and (2). The Companies Act 1985, s 425(2) is to be replaced by the Companies Act 2006, ss 899(1) and (3), 907(1) and 922(1). The Companies Act 1985, s 425(3) is to be replaced (with some changes) by the Companies Act 2006, ss 899(4), 901(3) and (4). The Companies Act 1985, s 425(4) is to be replaced by the Companies Act 2006, s 901(5) and (6). The Companies Act 1985, s 425(6) is to be replaced by the Companies Act 2006, s 895(2). The Companies Act 2006, ss 895–935 are to come into force on 6 April 2008 (SI 2007/3495). For transitional provisions and savings, see SI 2007/3495, arts 6, 9, 12, Schs 1, 4.

[3] The Companies Act 1985, s 427 is to be replaced by the Companies Act 2006, s 900 on 6 April 2008 (SI 2007/3495). For transitional provisions and savings, see SI 2007/3495, arts 6, 9, 12, Schs 1, 4.

1.8 A rescue using a statutory procedure can be undertaken during the period of an out of court administration order (made under Part II of the Insolvency

Act 1986). The statutory moratorium which is imposed on the enforcement of obligations of a company in administration creates a favourable environment in which a rescue may be planned and implemented. Under the Insolvency Act 1986, s 8 the objectives for the achievement of which an administration order may be made include the survival of a company as a going concern (subsection (3)(a)), the approval of a voluntary arrangement (subsection (3)(b)), and the sanctioning under the Companies Act 1985, s 425 of a scheme of arrangement (subsection (3)(c)[1]).

[1]   See para 1.7, footnote 2.

1.9 The option of using administrative receivership as a device for salvaging parts of a business has diminished with the implementation of the Enterprise Act 2002. The Enterprise Act 2002, s 250 inserts a new Chapter IV into Part III of the Insolvency Act 1986. Section 72A of the new Chapter IV sets out the general prohibition on floating charge holders from appointing administrative receivers. Section 72A(1) states that: 'the holder of a qualifying floating charge in respect of a company's property may not appoint an administrative receiver of the company'. This general prohibition is subject to eight exceptions so that the appointment of an administrative receiver is permitted in the following circumstances and industries:

(a)   the capital markets;
(b)   public private partnerships;
(c)   utilities;
(d)   urban regeneration projects;
(e)   project finance;
(f)   certain financial markets;
(g)   registered social landlords (housing associations); and
(h)   protected railway companies; water and sewerage undertakers; air traffic services.

1.10 Whilst the legacy provisions contained in the Insolvency Act 1986 continue to apply to lending arrangements that are secured by a floating charge entered into before 15 September 2003 so as to permit the appointment of an administrative receiver under such instruments and notwithstanding the various exceptions outlined above, it is clear that in the vast majority of circumstances administrative receivership will cease to be an option for creditors dealing with a distressed company. This has not caused undue concern within the financial markets because, in an era where typically there are a plethora of financial creditors in a layered capital structure, the limitations of administrative receivership have become increasingly apparent. Even if administrative receivership had proven to be successful in terms of salvaging remnants of the business via a business sale implemented by a receiver, experience had shown that flexibility is invariably lost and value for creditors as a whole is usually diminished.

Provisions of the Insolvency Act 2000

1.11 The Insolvency Act 2000 received the Royal Assent on 30 November 2000. It contains a new moratorium procedure for small companies. This is designed to provide a framework in which 'small companies' can evaluate whether they can sort out their financial problems.

1.12 'Small companies' that can avail themselves of this moratorium option include those companies with up to 50 employees, those with a turnover of up to £5.6m, or balance sheet of not more than £2.8m. The Act contains powers for the eligibility criteria to be amended by statutory instrument.

1.13 A small company wishing to propose a company voluntary arrangement (CVA) will have the option of a moratorium of up to 28 days (extendable for up to two more months), to put together a CVA. The moratorium will begin with the filing of certain prescribed documents at court, including a statement from a professional acting as a 'nominee' that in the nominee's opinion the CVA has a reasonable prospect of success.

1.14 During the moratorium the directors will continue to manage the company while the nominee monitors its affairs. The nominee should ensure that the proposed CVA continues to have a reasonable prospect of success and that the company has sufficient funds available to carry on its business. In order to have any realistic prospect of success, any moratorium would need to be accompanied by a willingness by banks to finance companies through the moratorium period.

1.15 A moratorium is generally not available to insurance companies or authorised credit institutions. Also, the new regime does not affect the special insolvency provisions which protect participants in the financial markets.

Informal arrangement preferred

1.16 Depending upon which procedure is used it is possible to implement a corporate rescue using a statutory regime without the consent of all the parties who will be affected by it. Both a scheme of arrangement and a voluntary arrangement require the support of 75% in value of each class of affected creditors to implement a rescue. However, both regimes have drawbacks. A scheme may only be implemented if it is also approved by a majority in number of each class of affected creditors. Equally, voluntary arrangements may not deal at all with certain categories of creditors, eg secured, preferential creditors.

1.17 Although a panoply of statutory techniques can be deployed when a company is in financial difficulties, the principal reason for undertaking an informal consensual restructuring is the potential for improved value recovery, flexibility, lower cost and expediency of the arrangements, both as to how the rescue is planned and implemented. Ultimately, it may not be just a question of losing flexibility: if the business of that company is based around the skills of the individuals who work within it then the public nature of a formal insolvency procedure will probably destroy value almost instantaneously. An informal restructuring avoids the need to adhere to a statutory timetable and the procedural formalities laid down by the statutory regimes which operate in a public goldfish-bowl. If publicity will impede implementation of a rescue, or further damage the trading position of a company, it will be preferable to use an informal arrangement as it should be easier to control disclosure of information.

1.18 Although one can try to gauge the impact of publicity, it is not easy for creditors to establish whether a contractual restructuring or an insolvency is the best option. The key driver here is the nature of the information available to financial creditors at the outset: without detailed information financial creditors may have no idea whether it is sensible for the company to go into some form of insolvency or not. The company may be completely beyond redemption or it may merely require additional funding to meet short-term cashflow problems. In the latter example, if the financial creditors decided to place the company into administration in order to take advantage of the moratorium that would be like using a sledgehammer to crack a nut – it would hardly be a sensible or cost-effective way of achieving the objectives of preserving value and avoiding bad debt provisions. In fact, it might have the opposite effect by eroding the reputation of the business and consequently ruining any prospects of a restructuring in the medium term. The problem is that creditors may not know that initially. So information is vital.

1.19 The purpose of a contractual restructuring, at least initially, is to enable financial creditors to agree to continue to provide limited financial support for a defined period. Note both the vagueness and precision of that purpose; vagueness because the definition gives no real explanation as to why or how the creditors should be doing that; precision because the support will be limited and provided for a defined period only. By providing interim support, financial creditors are in essence, buying time. During that time they may conclude that they need to move towards an insolvency or enforcement procedure, but at least the creditors have not pre-empted their options by jumping to that conclusion at too early a stage.

D THE LONDON APPROACH

1.20 The 'London Approach' is a phrase which has been around since the large restructurings of the early 1990s and, in some ways, it has caused confusion. Its origins go back a long way: the Bank of England (both in its former role as banking regulator and in its ongoing role as monetary controller) has obvious concerns about the systemic implications of bad debts if they are owed by a large corporate with a high profile.

1.21 The Bank of England has been involved informally in discussions in relation to large restructurings for many years, often acting in recent years in a consultative role in order to help tackle them. In the 1970s, at the time of the secondary banking crisis, that tended to take the form of heavy intervention because the Bank organised and co-ordinated the rescue of secondary banks which were running into difficulties and ensured that the larger commercial banks were there providing support. In the early 1980s following the fallout of the previous decade and the recession, the Bank again was involved, but this time largely with major corporates that were in difficulties, consulting with the banks and giving directions as to what they should be doing to resolve matters. At that stage too, it adopted a high-profile interventionist role. If a deal had not been done, then people would be locked into a meeting room with the Bank until they came out with one. The atmosphere had changed again by the time of the last major recession in the early 1990s when the Bank's attitude was much more informal and it left the banks to themselves to sort out these problems. Its attitude was that it was prepared to discuss the principles, to act as a sounding board in relation to particular cases and to be involved, but it would not tell the banks how to proceed since that was a matter for them to resolve (see Euromoney, November 1998 for a discussion of the collapse of the LTCM hedge fund and the Bank of England's approach).

1.22 Sometimes the London Approach is referred to as the 'London Rules' even though the Bank of England has never favoured that term. These are a set of principles which codify an approach; they are not rules and they are not prescriptive. If they were rules, then they would be the territory of lawyers which is not the case; lawyers tend to be involved but only as specific advisers in relation to the nature of the workout contract; there is certainly no requirement for them to interpret a set of rules with which the terms of that contract must conform. There is also no regulatory aspect to this activity and the London Approach is no more than a set of helpful but general principles.

1.23 During the recession of the 1990s institutions and advisory firms talked of the 'London Approach', but far fewer knew what the term actually meant perhaps with the exception of a minority of restructuring professionals employed by the UK's leading clearing and investment banks. The Bank of England had circulated a document to major UK banks which was highly confidential and set out the relevant principles. The document merely enunciated the sensible, albeit high level thinking on the matter, but it was not in wide circulation. The principles became articulated more fully at after-dinner speeches and conferences by representatives from the Bank of England. They gave their thoughts as to the nature of the London Approach and articulated its terms. This well illustrates the informality of the regime.

1.24 Informality did however create a degree of confusion: by way of example people would say 'in accordance with the London Approach we are going to follow liquidation principles', a phrase which will be explained later on. In fact there is nothing set forth in the London Approach itself that tells creditors that they have to use liquidation principles, let alone what those principles actually are.

1.25 So the London Approach is not prescriptive and it is not formal. It is however the pioneering regime for managing multi-creditor restructuring that articulates a number of high level general principles that stop short of prescribing specific details and rules as to what should be done in any given context. Whilst the Bank of England has never had the authority to interfere in commercial relations between banks and their customers, it has clearly made its support of the London Approach widely known and adherence to the guidelines has historically been regarded as good London market practice.

So what are the tenets of the London Approach?

1 Banks should remain supportive when they receive bad news

1.26 This is a very bland general statement. It does not tell banks what they have to do or what is supportive and what is not supportive. It merely reminds banks not to panic. It can perhaps be distilled to mean that bank creditors should remain supportive of a company in financial difficulties at least while a full assessment of the company's position is made and plans agreed for its future.

2 Make decisions based on accurate information that is shared with other creditors

1.27 Financial creditors will usually encounter two big problems in a work-out: one is lack of control and even in the new information age the other handicap is, invariably, a lack of information. These two problems are very closely related and many large companies which fall into difficulties do so because, in part, their finance function is not performing adequately. Recent cases like MyTravel and Mayflower continue to highlight how a prolonged inability to produce accurate trading and financial information inevitably pre-empts a restructuring. This makes it difficult to measure the size of the problem – if the finance function is not doing its job then not only will there be a degree of chaos in the way in which the company deals with its creditors, but also it will be difficult to retrieve the information needed in order to make a reasonable judgment. Should bankers be placing the company into adminis-tration or lending it new money on an unsecured basis? A key tenet of the London Approach is to ensure that financial creditors obtain full, shared information in order to help them make that decision.

3 Working together to a collective view

1.28 The tenet of sharing information in order to reach a collective position is another general yet sensible principle. The advantages of this are obvious – co-ordinated collective action between a group of bank creditors helps to avoid duplication of costs. Additionally, if they all work together to create the same pool of information it should help to improve the collective decision-making process and to ensure that the wiser counsels prevail. Indeed, the London Approach encourages constructive co-operation amongst bank credi-tors on the assumption that the interests of all creditors will be better served through co-operation, rather than by the premature appointment of an administrator on the instigation of other isolated creditors seeking an insolvency. In particular, this aspect of the London Approach encourages the exchange of information to the company's broader constituency of financial creditors.

4 Equal treatment for equal ranking

1.29 This is the nearest that the London Approach gets to promulgating that banks should follow liquidation principles. The principle here is that different levels of seniority of debt should be recognised in the structure of any workout. This is entirely sensible. There should be some principle of shared pain with equivalent tiers of a group's capital structure which is again entirely rational. However, it's sometimes difficult to apply the good sense of this principle when faced with the practical problems of a workout and the shameless protection of self-interests.

E THE LONDON APPROACH IN A MODERN CONTEXT – THE INSOL PRINCIPLES

1.30 During the last economic downturn of the early millennium broad adherence by financial creditors to the London Approach was maintained. In many ways the tenets of the London Approach still hold good today, but with the ever increasing complexity of the capital structures of major corporates, the global nature of their business and capital raising and their exposure to a diverse range of financial creditors based in a myriad of jurisdictions it was logical and indeed inevitable that the sensible principles of the London Approach be articulated in an international context.

1.31 The proliferation of debt trading, the emergence of a somewhat opportunistic distressed M&A market, the relentless globalisation of capital markets and an increasing tendency for financial constituents of all creeds to manage out their risk on a bilateral basis have irrevocably altered the rules of engagement, but the co-operative behaviour sponsored by the London Approach has become embedded in the 'INSOL Principles' which have proven to be compatible with a co-ordinated and managed process even though certain constituencies of financial creditors including banks may have paid only lip service to their various tenets and principles.

1.32 Whilst the Bank of England has reiterated its role as 'keepers of the London Approach' it has publicly acknowledged that its 'direct participation as a mediator in corporate workouts has declined'. (See speech by David Clementi, Deputy Governor, at the INSOL International Sixth World Congress at the Hilton Metropole Hotel London, 19 July 2001 at www.bankofengland.co.uk/publications/speeches/2001/speech136.htm). The declining influence of the Bank of England may in part also be due to its evolving role which has become more commonly associated with the Monetary Policy Committee and the pursuit of financial stability. The emergence of the Financial Services Authority as a super regulator and its increasing interest in the efficiency of corporate restructuring has also arguably blurred the role of the Bank of England.

1.33 Not surprisingly the Bank of England has responded by taking a lead in developing an international framework governing corporate restructurings and most notably it has been supportive of INSOL but also a number of variants such as the Hong Kong Approach to Corporate Difficulties, the Framework for Corporate Debt Restructuring in Thailand and the Jakarta Initiative in Indonesia. More recently David Clementi the Deputy Governor of the Bank of England (in conjunction with multilateral institutions such as the World Bank and the International Monetary Fund) has specifically signalled his support for the INSOL Lenders Group's mission to take a leadership role in international insolvency and credit issues and to bring about greater international co-operation among the influential financial creditor groups by endorsing the INSOL Lenders Group's core principles governing international corporate restructurings at the pre-insolvency stage, known as the 'Statement of Principles for a Global Approach to Multi-Creditor Workouts' (the INSOL Principles).

1.34 By comparison these Principles by their international nature have perhaps been perceived less suspiciously and like an international treaty they are seen as inherently more neutral. Their acceptance across a wider universe has also been achieved in part by the fact that discussions and indeed negotiations on the enunciation of the Principles involved not only the largest global banks, but also an array of other finance providers including insurance companies, pension funds and institutional investors, credit insurers, securities houses, fund managers, hedge funds and even secondary market debt traders. The INSOL Principles are set out below and it is no surprise that they bear a strong resemblance to the tenets of the London Approach.

The INSOL Principles

1.35 FIRST PRINCIPLE: Where a debtor is found to be in financial difficulties, all relevant creditors should be prepared to co-operate with each other to give sufficient (though limited) time (a 'Standstill Period') to the debtor for information about the debtor to be obtained and evaluated and for proposals for resolving the debtor's financial difficulties to be formulated and assessed, unless such a course is inappropriate in a particular case.

1.36 SECOND PRINCIPLE: During the Standstill Period, all relevant creditors should agree to refrain from taking any steps to enforce their claims against or to reduce their exposure to the debtor (otherwise than by disposal of their debt to a third party) but are entitled to expect that during the Standstill Period their position relative to other creditors and each other will not be prejudiced.

1.37 THIRD PRINCIPLE: During the Standstill Period, the debtor should not take any action which might adversely affect the prospective return to relevant creditors (either collectively or individually) as compared with the position at the date of commencement of the Standstill Period.

1.38 FOURTH PRINCIPLE: The interests of relevant creditors are best served by co-ordinating their response to a debtor in financial difficulty. Such co-ordination will be facilitated by the selection of one or more representative co-ordination committees and by the appointment of professional advisers to advise and assist such committees and, where appropriate, the relevant creditors participating in the process as a whole.

1.39 FIFTH PRINCIPLE: During the Standstill Period, the debtor should provide, and allow relevant creditors and/or their professional advisers reasonable and timely access to, all relevant information relating to its assets, liabilities, business and prospects, in order to enable proper evaluation to be made of its financial position and any proposals to be made to relevant creditors.

1.40 SIXTH PRINCIPLE: Proposals for resolving the financial difficulties of the debtor and, so far as practicable, arrangements between relevant creditors relating to any Standstill should reflect applicable law and the relative positions of relevant creditors at the Standstill Commencement Date.

1.41 SEVENTH PRINCIPLE: Information obtained for the purposes of the process concerning the assets, liabilities and business of the debtor and any proposals for resolving its difficulties should be made available to all relevant creditors and should, unless already publicly available, be treated as confidential.

1.42 EIGHTH PRINCIPLE: If additional funding is provided during the Standstill Period or under any rescue or restructuring proposals, the repayment of such additional funding should, so far as practicable, be accorded priority status as compared to other indebtedness or claims of relevant creditors.

1.43 As well as potentially appealing to a wider universe, it is arguable that the INSOL Principles (compared to the London Approach) also offer a more detailed and formal framework for conducting an international restructuring. They also formally enshrine three fundamental concepts that over time had been reflected in the evolving London Approach and the London restructuring market generally, namely that creditors should expressly refrain from taking any action to reduce their exposure, debtors should not take any action that would adversely affect the returns of creditors as compared with the position of the Standstill date and perhaps most importantly that new money is to have priority.

1.44 It should still be noted however that like the London Approach that preceded them, the INSOL Principles have no legal status in the UK. In many of the large restructurings in the UK where bondholders and private placement holders consistently take aggressive bilateral positions against the debtor and other creditor constituencies it remains the case that the INSOL Principles only constitute informal guidelines which in certain cases are paid no more than minimal lip service.

F RESTRUCTURING PRACTICE

1.45 This section moves from restructuring theory, ideology and dogma to practice. In this regard it is productive, at least initially, to identify some of the warning signs that indicate that a company is about to spiral into financial difficulty. Early detection is key and whilst it may not guarantee the debtor's viability it may well mitigate against significant value erosion.

1.46 Early detection becomes even more important in the case of leveraged companies. Focusing exclusively on gearing at the expense of other operational dynamics and business fundamentals may actually conceal the core problems in a business which may ultimately undermine the debtor's long-term viability and value.

1.47 Notwithstanding the reasons for the company's distress the fact that the management team is often in denial will compound many of the problems cited below. Having quality information and early detection systems in place and a strong relationship with management is critical to ensure that uncorrected problems do not evolve into chronic demise.

Warning signs

1.48 What are the signs? Transactional lawyers and deal originators within banks are quite adept at anticipating and implementing new transactions, but where do workouts originate from? A restructuring is not something that a corporate or its financial creditors actually seek or volunteer or subscribe to and, therefore, invariably a restructuring only happens because a corporate runs out of money. It sounds banal but that is the common position. Corporates do, however, become illiquid for a variety of reasons and it is worthwhile considering some of these causes.

1.49 There are three major causes of financial distress and they can be broadly categorised as follows:

(i)   specific problems in the debtor's operations, business, management, finances and capital structure;
(ii) sectoral declines that affect the debtor's industry generally; and
(iii) recessionary cycles and the state of the economy generally.

Factors and symptoms that fall within these three broad categories are considered below.

General state of the economy

1.50 Economists can always point to the underlying economic fundamentals and indicators. Recently, expectations of steady increases in interest rates (which will reduce disposable income) have generated much greater prudence amongst consumers and this has been attributable to a spate of restructurings in the retail and leisure sectors such as Courts, Unwins, Allders, Holmes Place, MFI, Focus and Regent Inns.

Peer group analysis – sector fundamentals

1.51 Corporate Information services such as Debtwire info@debtwire.com, City Webwatch Daily Feed info@citywebwatch.com, the credit departments of major banks, hedge funds and advisory firms in the restructuring and insolvency industry are conducting detailed peer group analysis to identify the restructuring candidates of tomorrow. Given the earlier travails of John Laing and Amey which were established PFI and construction businesses, it was perhaps no surprise that the application of a sector analysis to similar businesses ensured that those tipping Jarvis for financial difficulty were eventually vindicated.

Regulatory framework

1.52 Specific sector and regulatory trends can also operate as a useful indicator of financial demise. Changes to pricing regulation and the reorganisation of the electricity industry along distribution and supply channels combined with the demise of a global player like Enron ensured that the restructurings of Teeside Power, TXU, Drax and others in the power sector were reasonably predictable. Similarly, the over supply in the telecoms sector and the huge leverage multiples incurred in a raft of telco transactions at the end of the 1990s and beyond precipitated a number of high-profile restructurings across Europe and the US such as NTL, Telewest, Kirsch, Marconi, Jazztel, Calahan Ish and Energis.

1.53 If this all sounds like reflective wisdom, many commentators are predicting an avalanche of restructurings of leveraged buyouts over the next two years. Leverage multiples of seven to ten times are undoubtedly a recipe for a number of corporate collapses and restructuring transactions such as Meridien Hotels, Vantico, Gate Gourmet, Welcome Break, Swissport, Polestar, Ontex and TMD Friction are predicted to be the tip of an enormous iceberg.

Pension deficits

1.54 The impact of the Pensions Act 2004 has been extremely far-reaching. Under the Pensions Act 2004, ss 221–223 the historic minimum funding requirement (MFR) was replaced with a scheme-specific funding requirement. Much of the detail of the new regime is set out in the Occupational Pension Schemes (Scheme Funding) Regulations 2005, SI 2005/3377 (referred to as the Funding Regulations). The Funding Regulations came into force on 30 December 2005. In addition to the Funding Regulations, the Pensions Regulator (TPR) has issued a code of practice to facilitate adequate funding of defined benefit occupational pension schemes. The Funding Regulations have applied to schemes with effect from the date of their first actuarial valuation after 22 September 2005.

1.55 Every scheme is now subject to a statutory funding objective (SFO): a scheme must have sufficient and appropriate assets to cover its 'technical provisions' (the term used in the EU pensions directive which means, broadly, the amount of assets a scheme needs to hold now, on the basis of the actuarial methods and assumptions used, in order to pay its accrued benefits as they fall due in the future). Inevitably this has placed a great deal of financial pressure on UK corporates that have defined benefit schemes.

1.56 The Funding Regulations give more detail on how the technical provisions of a scheme are to be calculated, but a key change under the Funding Regulations has been the need for trustees to determine the actuarial methods and assumptions to be used, having obtained advice from the scheme actuary. The Funding Regulations provide that:

(i)   an accrued benefits funding method must be used (described in the code of practice);
(ii) in calculating the technical provisions the trustees must take into account the actuary's estimate of the solvency of the scheme on a buyout basis and act in accordance with a set of formulaic principles; and
(iii) the principles require a large degree of 'prudence' to be used in, for example, choosing the actuarial assumptions and the discount rates (but unhelpfully prudence is not defined).

1.57 Within 15 months of the date of the first valuation under the new regime, trustees of defined benefit schemes have had to prepare a statement of funding principles (SFP). This is the written statement of their policy for ensuring that the SFO is met. The statement must record the methods and assumptions used in calculating the scheme's technical provisions.

1.58 Actuarial valuations must also be prepared at least every three years. These must be based on a funding approach consistent with the strategy set out in the scheme's SFP and annual reports. The Funding Regulations provide that actuarial valuations must contain the actuary's certification of the calculation of the technical provisions and the actuary's estimate of the solvency of the scheme. Again the regularity with which the solvency of schemes is assessed has led to periodic financial pressure on a number of large UK corporates.

1.59 In addition to triennial valuations there must be annual actuarial reports, and following each actuarial valuation or report, members and beneficiaries must be sent a summary funding statement. If the valuation shows that the SFO is not met, the trustees must put in place a recovery plan, setting out the period over which the deficit is to be remedied. A copy of each recovery plan must be sent to TPR. These must similarly be in place within 15 months of the effective date of the actuarial valuation. Schedules of contributions for five-year periods must also be in place within 15 months of the effective date of the actuarial valuation. The need for a recovery plan, increased schedules of contributions and the overall requirement to address underfunding have led to a number of high-profile restructurings since April 2005 including MFI, Heath Lambert, AEA Technology plc and Uniq plc.

1.60 To put the new pensions regime into context, as at 1 January 2004 some 89 companies in the FTSE 100 index offered defined benefit pensions schemes. The total deficit under FRS17 for those companies' UK defined benefit pension schemes was £42bn in July 2004 (see Lane Clark & Peacock LLP, Accounting For Pensions: UK and Europe Annual Survey 2004). The projected deficit for all FTSE 350 companies as at 31 December 2004 was £71bn; the total deficit for all UK pension schemes is estimated at £128bn (see Mercer Human Resource Consulting, FTSE 350 – UK Pension Scheme Deficits and Trends (9 February 2005)). It is clear that pension obligations under UK law will continue to precipitate a raft of major corporate restructurings.

Poor management

1.61 Warning signs can also be seen on a micro-level in individual corporates. Poor management in the case of certain companies will always give restructurings an air of predictability whilst the large-scale fraud that becomes evident in certain cases means that their restructuring destiny is often predetermined. Episodic causes can also be discerned on a micro-level and the integration of problematic IT systems by certain companies has been the trigger for their rather unfortunate lapse into a short-term financial and corporate restructuring.

Litigation

1.62 Litigation can also be identified as a common cause of a restructuring. One only needs to look at the industrial companies such as Cape, which had a significant exposure to asbestos litigation, to understand why it had to undergo a prolonged restructuring. Turner & Newell quickly lurched from a consensual restructuring to administration for the same reason.

Unsuccessful acquisitions

1.63 Not surprisingly a number of major corporate restructurings have been triggered by an ill-advised acquisition strategy. On reflection the strategy of Marconi to become an acquisitive player in the Telco sector partially explains its demise. The acquisitions by Mayflower and APW (a New York Stock Exchange listed multinational) of a number of engineering and industrial companies at a premium in circumstances where there may not have been an appreciation of the difficulties confronting the target companies did not assist their financial stability.

1.64 MyTravel is another case in point. In the late 1990s the company pursued an acquisitive strategy that was debt funded. In the face of intensive competition, the 9/11 terrorist atrocities and SARS epidemic, the business acquired did not yield sufficient returns to service the indebtedness of the MyTravel group. At a time when demand was slowing, the group continued to increase capacity and operate volume businesses. This culminated in a substantial restructuring and an alternative strategy of controlling capacity and improving the margins on each holiday sold.

Flawed business strategy

1.65 Occasionally a flawed business strategy will be a precursor to a corporate restructuring. John Laing undoubtedly regrets the fixed price construction contracts it entered into on the Millennium Stadium and the National Physical Laboratory projects and the decision of Alldays Plc to support its franchises in the way it did, led to a certain credit guru at one of the UK's major clearing banks predicting its financial difficulties one year before its first all-bank meeting.

Breach of financial covenants

1.66 Given the improvements in modelling and forecasting and the progression of accounting standards in terms of sophistication, transparency and stringency it is rare for a corporate not to negotiate sufficient headroom in its financial covenants, or to otherwise avoid a deterioration in performance or a credit downgrade constituting a default or an increase in pricing under a margin ratchet which in time will lead to financial pressure and an eventual default. It is the experience of the authors that a poorly negotiated covenant package or a credit downgrade can be a reliable indicator of a pending financial crisis.

Irregular purchasing patterns

1.67 The loss of important and historic suppliers and/or an accompanying tightening of credit insurer limits may well result in a churn of suppliers and changes to a company's supply chain that provides an illuminating insight into a company's declining liquidity and the use of the supply chain as a source of working capital.

1.68 Once a company acknowledges its financial difficulties or the early warning signs translate themselves into a financial crisis a restructuring process is imminent. Typically the restructuring process can be divided into three stages: a pre-contractual phase, a contractual phase and an exit.

Chapter 2

THE RESTRUCTURING PROCESS

A   The pre-contractual phase
B   The contractual phase
C   Distributions pre and post insolvency

A THE PRE-CONTRACTUAL PHASE

Introduction

2.1 The pre-contractual phase is the phase during which financial creditors try to put in place the foundations of the restructuring. A restructuring is a non-statutory contractual arrangement so obviously there is a period during which that contract is being negotiated and drafted. In practice, this can often go on for a very long time. In fact, in a number of recent restructurings, agreement on even a short form interim stabilisation document took six months to negotiate. Criticism is often levelled at restructuring co-ordinators and their advisers when they attempt to put together an elaborate restructuring document which is the whole object of the pre-contractual phase, but which is never actually signed. In the first Gate Gourmet restructuring which arose out of the insolvency of its parent Swissair, it was two years before any form of document was signed. This shows that perseverance can sometimes be rewarded. In circumstances where these negotiations are protracted, or as with MyTravel, where it was impossible to procure a Standstill due to the phasing of defaults in the various facilities and the complexity of the capital structure, restructuring co-ordinators will endeavour to maintain a de facto Standstill whereby creditors are persuaded not to take unilateral action. There are, however, many other cases where a formal Standstill genuinely works very well indeed and responsible creditors acting in a manner that is consistent with the London Approach and the INSOL Principles sign up to relevant Standstill documentation quickly.

Information gathering

2.2 The pre-contractual phase is essentially an information gathering stage during which a strategy needs to be developed. It is a time when the size of the problem is ascertained, the lending, asset and group structure charts are being prepared, the strategy of the business is re-evaluated, recent trading is assessed, cashflow is analysed, a schedule of banking facilities is prepared, the recourse of creditors and the maturity of their credit lines are established, other non-bank creditors are contacted and intra-group positions are analysed.

2.3 *The restructuring process*

The first all bank meeting

2.3 Crucial to information gathering is the first all bank meeting. Given that one of the tenets of the London Approach and the INSOL Principles is information sharing, it is vital to identify which bank creditors should attend that meeting.

Attendees

2.4 Formulating a list of attendees sounds simpler than it sometimes is in practice. If a particular bank is only lending to part of an international conglomerate and its exposure reflects no more than some local lending in a remote jurisdiction for a relatively small amount, then does that mean that you invite them to London for discussions? Probably not, especially as confidentiality and speed are going to be key issues in managing the process.

2.5 Are there entities other than banks who should be involved in this process; sureties, bonding providers, asset financiers, export credit agencies or credit insurers, for example, and in particular bondholders? The factors that might determine an invitation are the maturity of a debt instrument (ie will the instrument mature or otherwise need to be dealt with during the anticipated life-span of the restructuring?) and whether the instrument is likely to be subject to a default (particularly a cross-default). In circumstances where taking security is envisaged or a disposal programme is to be implemented, an invitation might be needed if a creditor has a negative pledge or other covenants in its facility (such as a disposals restriction) that will impede this strategy.

Identifying bondholders

2.6 A major problem with bondholders in restructuring discussions is actually identifying them. In a recent case a bondholders' meeting had been convened so that the issuer could try to persuade the bondholders to waive potential events of default under the bonds. There had been a change to the nature of the proposals that the issuer wished to put to those bondholders, but 21 days' notice was required to be given in order to convene a meeting to discuss those changes. This meant that consent to short notice was needed in order to ensure that a default would not arise within the notice period. How do you find these constituents, particularly within such a short space of time? It may be that there is a bondholder trustee which you can use to locate them, but even then you need to think carefully about how to involve that trustee. In many cases lead banks are vastly experienced in dealing with security trustees and syndicate members under syndicated loan agreements, but bondholder trustees are very different, both in the way that they operate and in the nature of their duties. Recognition should perhaps be conveyed to certain bondholder advisers who routinely track Bloomberg, Reuters, Debtwire and a whole host of other corporate news services and who seem to have a clear ability in identifying the main holders and forming ad hoc bondholder committees or working groups at very short notice.

Scope of the first meeting

2.7 When the company and its advisers have decided which institutions to invite, what actually happens at the meeting? The company and its advisers usually make a presentation to explain the nature of the problem and what they are doing about it. There may well be an element of denial. The lead bank at this stage will also need to make a presentation to the assembled creditors explaining its perspective on events and its strategy for progressing discussions with the company. Professional advisers such as accountants and legal counsel will need to be appointed. If the lawyers have already been appointed by the lenders with the largest exposure (as can often be the case), they may also need to make a presentation reflecting their current identification of legal issues and the results of their initial due diligence.

2.8 By way of illustration of that last point, one of the major problems in the restructuring of a listed construction company was that the company had entered into a series of relatively one-sided construction contracts. Unfortunately, it transpired that the company was on the wrong side and had mispriced certain fixed price contracts. This became the source of most of its problems in that it hindered its attempts to spin-off its unprofitable construction division. However, the various constituencies of creditors needed to understand the whole construction division, its contracts, the processes and risks underlying those contracts and the basis of the planned disposal in order to ascertain the residual risks of supporting the disposal.

2.9 The prospective reporting accountants will probably also make a brief presentation dealing with the likely scope of their work. In particular in the first instance, they will need to determine the liquidity and cashflow pressures confronting the company in the short term.

Valuations

2.10 As the pre-contractual phase gathers pace, there may well be a necessity for the reporting accountants to conduct an analysis of going concern and liquidation values which will be made available to the participating creditors. In order to make an informed decision as to the appropriate strategy, it is very useful for the creditors to know and benchmark what the alternatives mean in monetary terms. If the business is to be placed into formal insolvency proceedings, what estimates do the accountants give of the creditors' likely recoveries?

2.11 Increasingly, valuations of businesses and companies in the context of their overall indebtedness are becoming ever more relevant to the feasibility of an exit and in particular a debt for equity swap. Valuation methodology and the development of jurisprudence in this important area are considered in more detail in Chapter 5.

Potential disposals

2.12 It may also be necessary to determine the impact on cashflow that a disposal programme would produce. The problem with such a programme is, of course, that the market will quickly conclude that a commercial party is under pressure to dispose of its assets on an expedited basis in order to repay its financial creditors, if its problems are widely known. Clearly this in itself can act as a price depressant since it signals a 'fire sale'. This is a key reason why confidentiality is of fundamental importance.

2.13 The impact of being a distressed seller can however be overstated in a buoyant M&A market: if more than one party is pursuing an asset then it is a gamble for a potential buyer to place too much significance on the fact that the disposal looks like a forced sale. If competitive tension is present the asset should still sell at the right price. The key to preserving value is the preservation of confidentiality and it is right and proper that the company and its advisers consistently remind their body of creditors of their duties in this regard.

2.14 Similarly, will the proposal reduce cashflow pressure by, for example, removing a division that is a significant consumer of cash or will it be detrimental in that a cash generative entity is cut loose from the group?

The role of the company's advisers

2.15 Corporate finance advisers to the company also need to indicate what a particular strategy might mean in terms of outcome for the creditors and the shareholders and their role in formulating and modelling this strategy with the company often in parallel with the lead bank or the steering committee and advisers to the financial creditors is of paramount importance. However, whatever the strategy, the company must always consider its own position and responsibilities under corporate and insolvency law: an ambitious disposal programme will need to be considered extremely carefully as it may well leave a large body of creditors with a shortfall. In this scenario the company's directors need to consider their duties very carefully, given their potential liability for wrongful trading and the possibility of disqualification, and the potential for suggestions that they have not acted in accordance with their fiduciary duties.

The need for stability

2.16 The atmosphere within which the initial meetings take place can be fraught. There is often a lot of fire fighting required as suppliers stop supplying goods or the attitudes of credit insurers harden. By way of example, if the company concerned is involved in the construction industry it will be bidding for work all the time and as part of that bidding process it will need to establish that it will continue as a going concern. The same is true of an advertising business where the confidence of clients and key individuals in the business is paramount.

2.17 To sum up, there are a lot of different issues to consider in this phase and the financial creditors and their advisers need to be able to deal rapidly with problems as and when they arise, whilst maintaining confidentiality and a professional approach – without panicking.

The scope of the restructuring and the opportunity for reducing debt service obligations

2.18 The scope and the extent of a restructuring will depend upon the difficulties experienced by the company. Ideally the restructuring should seek to remedy the source of the difficulties on a permanent basis. If the company's financial difficulties are to be remedied, there must be an attempt to match financial obligations with trading performance.

2.19 The financial commitments of a company may be reduced by:

(a)   a write-off of a proportion of its debt by the lenders;
(b)   a conversion of a proportion of its debt into permanent share capital by the issue of equity shares in consideration of the discharge of debt, usually referred to as a debt for equity swap;
(c)   the issue of shares in satisfaction of all or part of its financial obligations;
(d)   using the proceeds of a rights issue (or other capital issue) or disposal to discharge financial obligations;
(e)   the variation of terms governing existing facilities, for example, the resetting of covenants, the extension of repayment dates, the varying of interest rates or the deferral or accrual of interest payment obligations; or
(f)   a reorganisation of the company's financial obligations. For instance, a proportion of the debt may be transferred to another entity, possibly incorporated specifically for the purpose. The terms of repayment of this part of the debt will be varied so that payments on the debt will only be made if trading performance improves and the new entity receives income from the original debtor company.

B THE CONTRACTUAL PHASE

The Standstill

Key objective

2.20 Quite often, the most important aspect of a restructuring for a corporate is the protection from unilateral action by any of the financiers, and for the existing facilities to remain in place. The agreement not to take unilateral action is known as the 'Standstill'. The ancillary terms of Standstill arrangements vary according to the requirements of a particular case. However, it is a fundamental principle of all such arrangements that, pending full disclosure of the company's position and agreement on a rescue plan or other action, and subject to the occurrence of no other specified defaults set out in the Standstill agreement, lenders agree not to enforce obligations of the company on a unilateral basis and the company agrees in return not to prefer any one lender either by way of repayment or improved security.

Scope – maintenance of credit lines

2.21 In terms of the detail each financier must make available, it must declare its facilities at the drawn level (assuming defaults or impending defaults result in a downstop of commitments) on a given day which is usually the exposure at the close of business on the day before the first all creditor meeting. This is known as the 'maintenance of Day 1 positions' and creditors signing up to the Standstill will be required to preserve their facility availability at that level, notwithstanding anything that would otherwise enable them not to do so (for example, because the facility is uncommitted and revolving and could be withdrawn immediately on notice).

Replacement loans for maturing contingent liabilities

2.22 Where the facility provided is a guarantee, indemnity bonding or other contingent facility, and demand is made by the beneficiary of such instrument, the Standstill will usually provide that the financier shall not make demand on a group company under its counter indemnity but must make available an 'equivalent replacement loan'. The concept of a replacement loan is common in the restructuring market and it will typically have a maturity date that corresponds with the maturity of the Standstill period and any subsequent longer term restructuring period that is negotiated. Indeed, it is not uncommon for such a 'replacement loan' to feature as a term loan in the eventual restructuring.

2.23 Such a replacement loan will bear interest at the same rates as all other debt facilities with a similar ranking and usually the provider of such a facility will seek short interest periods so that there is a regular return on such loan. Equivalent fees and covenants will apply to such replacement loans as those facilities with a similar ranking and for all intents and purposes the replacement loan will have the same status, save for any obvious differences in the priority and security or guarantee package supporting the original contingent facility prior to its conversion to a replacement loan.

Duration of the Standstill and timing of the accountant's report

2.24 The initial Standstill period is usually determined by the length of time required by the reporting accountants to undertake their initial review and for the financiers to assimilate and discuss its contents before deciding on what action they wish to take. The length of time the accountants are usually given to undertake their investigations will be determined by the level of structuring and investigation required and the complexity of the group and will be balanced against the urgency of any new money required by the group so as to be able to continue to trade during such period. There may also be other pressing commercial reasons such as the tendering for or signing of a contract or for the company to be able to execute a planned disposal or publish its annual accounts. The usual practice is for the accountants to spend a short period focusing on short-term cash and therefore an assessment of any new money required in the short term and reporting to the bank co-ordinator as to whether they have discovered any immediate, unknown or unforeseen problems. The full report usually follows several weeks later obviously dependent on the nature and complexity of the business.

Decision making and the concept of 'majority institutions'

2.25 Whilst each case is governed by the agreement reached between the financiers, decision making during the Standstill and in particular the termination of the Standstill prior to its agreed maturity will be determined by a decision of the 'majority institutions'. This is typically based upon those institutions having $66\frac{2}{3}\%$ of the aggregate exposure for each layer of credit in the capital structure, although in many leveraged transactions the 'second lien' debt will typically vote with the overall senior debt unless the issue in question affects the second lien creditors only. For certain decisions unanimity and the consent of all lenders will be required. These so-called 'entrenched provisions' are designed to protect the integrity of the facilities entered into by the group and without limitation entrenched provisions will usually prevent extensions of the maturity date, amendments to the definition of 'majority creditors', a change in currency of payment of any amount under the finance documents, the order of priority or subordination provisions, reduction in the applicable margin, fees or commission payable, a change to the borrowers or guarantors, a reduction in the principal amount outstanding under any facility (except as a result of a repayment or prepayment) or an increase or reduction in any commitment.

2.26 Historically, the existence of entrenched provisions of the type outlined above have inevitably hampered restructuring efforts. As a consequence loan facility technology has developed over time in order to overcome these obstacles and in certain instances where there is multi-tiered debt the concept of 'facility change' has been developed such that in certain voting issues where the vote only impacts upon a certain constituency of lenders (such as the most senior facility A lenders in a leveraged loan agreement by way of example) a vote can be carried if all of the A lenders agree to the 'facility change' and a majority of all other lenders agree. This avoids the need for all lenders to carry the vote which might have otherwise have been the case.

2.27 Similarly, where there are certain so-called 'hold out' recalcitrant lenders who are withholding their consent in circumstances where a 66.677% or perhaps 80% majority have agreed to a facility amendment, it might be possible for the borrower to go through a so-called process of 'yanking' the dissentient banks by repaying them at par plus accrued interest either through a shareholder loan or any other cash reserves it has. This process of 'yank-the-bank' may prove to be a helpful device in procuring important consents, waivers or amendments that could facilitate a restructuring by those lenders who are supportive of the company.

2.28 In exceptional circumstances where there are only a few financiers, such as a small group of bilateral lenders, unanimity may be required or conceded by the financial creditors who are involved in the restructuring. Unanimity is obviously less attractive to the corporate as it means that each lender can extract hold-out value. As such this type of 'consensual/supportive unanimity' only works in small 'club' arrangements where the other creditors are well known to each other.

2.29 Where the concept of 'majority' is agreed, the number of financiers required to form a majority and/or the percentage of the facilities that they collectively provide is very much an issue of negotiation based on the circumstances. Where there are one or two financiers with large exposures, they will not want a large number of financiers with a smaller aggregate exposure either to be able to end the Standstill period and make demand or more usually to use the negotiating position that this would give them to extract other advantages for themselves. Likewise the financiers with smaller exposures will not wish to end up bound into a restructuring so that mechanically, unless the financier with the largest exposure wants to end the Standstill prematurely, it is not possible to do so. Negotiation of the voting provision can quite often be one of the most difficult issues to resolve.

2.30 The inclusion of bondholders and private placement noteholders in a voting majority is a further complicating factor. If voting and decision making is not already pre-ordained in a pre-existing inter-creditor agreement negotiated at the time of the original financings, this issue will be the subject of detailed negotiations with bondholders, private placement noteholders or for that matter any other creditor, including other subordinated creditors, which may mean that the majority threshold is modified to enable certain constituents in combination to have a degree of influence. For example, it may be adjusted in percentage terms to enable private placement noteholders to have a blocking vote on certain key issues. Similarly, a number of entrenched rights might be negotiated by certain creditor constituencies so that on certain issues such as an increase in exposure, a waiver of payments or an extension of the Standstill period, unanimity is required.

2.31 It is also possible for a constituency of private placement noteholders to retain the existing voting mechanisms in their documentation so as to reach a voting block and for this block to vote as one in any inter-creditor resolution involving all financial creditors.

2.32 Alternatively, certain issues may be subject to a qualified majority. In one major restructuring the concern of certain US private placement noteholders that they may be obliged to continue with their support in the event that the company became increasingly distressed was resolved by permitting a specified minority of institutions to accelerate and enforce if second tier financial covenants (adjusted by granting considerable headroom of 30% against the company's base case) were breached *and* such a minority still represented 25% of the total exposures of all institutions.

2.33 Similarly, it is not uncommon to see a secondary voting mechanism which requires a simple majority, but still requires a certain proportion of a constituency (eg 25% of noteholders) to endorse the decision. The fine tuning of voting arrangements is only limited by the imagination of the draftsmen and the parties, but as a general rule it is the aggregate of the Day 1 exposures that drives the calculation of a minority or a majority as a percentage of the total exposures including new money. For voting purposes hedging exposures add a further complication because of their volatility and the potentially bizarre decisions it can produce. The inclusion of hedging may depend upon the make-up and size of the exposure, but one common practice for dealing with such exposure in the London market in respect of voting and fee arrangement is to evaluate hedging exposure on a pre-determined percentage of notional principal to ensure consistency.

2.34 To minimise the impact of abstentions voting provisions may potentially be based on the decisions of voting institutions that actually register a vote – the so-called 'snooze and lose' provision.

2.35 To avoid certain constituencies organising themselves and presenting a united front it is possible to insert a contractual 'voting' representation that no unique or separate voting arrangements exist and a voting override provision that ensures that the voting arrangements in the Standstill document prevail over any competing voting provision in an original finance contract.

Majority voting – the decision in Redwood Master Fund Ltd v TD Bank Europe Ltd and its implications for restructurings

2.36 When confronted by a credit of declining quality or when navigating a restructuring, financial institutions inevitably identify and protect their own self interests. For those consistently involved in restructurings the legitimacy of such conduct in the specific context of majority voting arrangements had always been an issue that one considered, but essentially parked because it could not be easily resolved. There was no substantive precedent on the point but a rather troublesome analogy could be made to those historic decisions relating to majority voting under instruments constituting debenture security and judicial decisions relating to shareholder voting (specifically in the context of an amendment to the articles of association of a company).

2.37 Viscount Haldane in the case of *British American Nickel Corpn Ltd v M J O'Brien Ltd*[1] (a decision dealing with the powers of a majority of debenture holders to amend the underlying instrument constituting the security) resolved that there was an implied restriction on the powers of a majority of a special class of debenture holders to bind a minority – similar to the concept of 'unfair prejudice' towards the interests of minority shareholders. He held at p 371 that such powers 'must be subject to a general principle, which is applicable to all authorities conferred on majorities of classes to bind minorities; namely, that the power given must be exercised for the purpose of benefiting the class as a whole, and not merely individual members only. Subject to this, the power may be unrestricted'.

[1]   [1927] AC 369.

2.38 These principles had found similar expression in a number of subsequent authorities, including by Sir Raymond Evershed MR in the Court of Appeal in the case of *Greenhalgh v Arderne Cinemas Ltd*[1], which concerned the other analogous situation of a resolution by a majority purporting to validly alter the articles of association of a company at the expense of a minority class. The legal challenge was founded on the *British American* jurisprudent proposition that a resolution by a majority must be 'bona fide and for the benefit of the company as a whole'. Evershed MR clarifies the meaning of this principle when he states that 'bona fide for the benefit of the company as a whole' means two things not one[2]. It means that each shareholder must proceed upon what, in his honest opinion, is for the benefit of the company as a whole. The second is that the phrase 'the company as a whole' does not (at any rate in such a case as the present) mean the company as a commercial entity, distinct from its corporators: it means the company as a general body. That is to say, the case may be taken of an individual hypothetical member and it may be asked whether what is proposed is, in the honest opinion of those who voted in its favour, for that person's benefit.

[1]   [1951] Ch 286, [1950] 2 All ER 1120.
[2]   See [1951] Ch 286 at 291, [1950] 2 All ER 1120 at 1126.

2.39 The matter can, in practice, be more accurately and precisely stated by looking at the converse and by saying that a resolution of this kind would be liable to be impeached if the effect of it were to discriminate between the majority shareholders and the minority shareholders so as to give the former an advantage of which the latter were deprived. When the cases are examined in which the resolution has been successfully attacked, it is on that ground.

2.40 It is true that this line of cases only registered a cautionary note with practitioners because, with the possible exception of *British American*, they concerned (and in the case of *British American* were founded on) resolutions relating to an amendment of the articles of association of a company. In a restructuring scenario or a distressed syndicated loan there is no equivalent of the company in a comparable context, merely the economic interest of lenders in a pre-existing contract that had regulated the rights of those lenders inter-se. Accordingly, when the respective voting rights and obligations of lenders in the context of an agreement by a majority to amend a syndicated loan facility came to be considered by Rimer J in the Chancery Division in the case of *Redwood Master Fund Ltd v TD Bank Europe Ltd*[1], it caught the attention of the restructuring market.

[1]   [2002] EWHC 2703 (Ch), [2006] 1 BCLC 149.

2.41 The judgment in *Redwood*, while recognising that majority voting provisions exist precisely because there are likely to be conflicts of interest between different lenders, also empowers a majority to bind a dissentient minority even though the minority will be placed in a worse position than the majority.

2.42 In the *Redwood* case an international syndicate of banks agreed to make available a syndicated credit facility of €4bn to two Dutch telecoms borrowers, UPC Distribution Holding BV and UPC Financing Partnership, in a revolving 'A' credit facility and separate fixed term 'B' and 'C' facilities. When the syndicated credit agreement was signed, the lenders participated in the facilities pro rata so it would not have mattered that one was used to repay the other. Certain original lenders in the 'A' facility transferred their commitments to lend under the 'A' facility to various hedge funds. Clause 25 of the underlying facility agreement provided that changes which were capable of affecting and binding all of the lenders, would be implemented if the consent of a two-thirds majority (as to value) of the lenders was obtained. When the borrowers became financially distressed, the hedge funds, in this case the claimants, found that pursuant to the terms of a waiver letter agreed by the requisite majority, their commitments under the 'A' facility were being increased and that proceeds thereof were being used to pay back the loans of the holders of the 'B' facility and to reduce their commitments. The Facility 'B' lenders were in fact voting for the majority decision to reduce the 'B' facility from the 'A' facility.

2.43 The claimants contended that a substantial subjective lack of good faith on the part of the majority of the lenders had been exercised which was in breach of their duty to act in the interests of the lenders as a whole. It was argued that the waiver agreed between the banks, which required a two-thirds majority, subjected them to an unfair exposure to risk, and that any power conferred on a majority of a special class which enabled it to bind the minority had to be exercised bona fide for the benefit of the class as a whole.

2.44 Alternatively, the claimants contended that viewing the matter objectively, no reasonable lender could have concluded that the modified waiver letter was in the interests of the lenders as a whole applying the same logic as in the *British American* case and *Greenhalgh*, since the effect of the letter was to obligate a sub-class of the 'A' facility to advance a further €30.5m to what was perceived to be an impaired credit.

2.45 The court found that there was no evidence that the majority lenders had acted in bad faith, and that this was a commercial decision that the majority was entitled to take: there were benefits for all, an acceleration of a restructuring process and the potential survival of the group, the payment of a waiver fee and an increased interest rate.

2.46 On the alternative claim, Rimer J held that the waiver letter was not sufficiently discriminatory and unfair towards the minority to justify a finding that the waiver and amendments contained therein were not for the benefit of the lenders as a whole. Moreover the contention of *Redwood* that the changes to the terms of the facility agreement pursuant to Clause 25 of the facility agreement was subject to an implied term in the agreement that the voting powers would be exercised bona fide for the benefit of the lenders as a whole did not reflect the intention of the parties to the facility agreement. In particular in a restructuring context it was recognised by Rimer J that it would be virtually impossible for the majority to exercise its powers under the voting clause in a manner which, viewed objectively, could have been said to have been for the benefit of each of the lenders.

2.47 In this case the judge perfectly anticipated the expectations of the syndicated and restructuring markets by articulating that the starting point for the courts in assessing the validity of the exercise of any voting powers was to assess, by reference to the available evidence, whether the power was being exercised in good faith for the purpose for which it was conferred. He elaborated by suggesting that merely because a minority might be able to adduce evidence that it had been relatively disadvantaged as compared with the majority, it was not axiomatic that the voting power had been exercised improperly by the majority.

2.48 Had Rimer J found in favour of the funds, the syndicated loan market would have effectively been paralysed. A dissatisfied creditor would now be empowered to block an entire syndicate or a restructuring. The judgment is also for borrowers; companies undergoing a restructuring, or even merely seeking a lender consent, will want to know that negotiations with their creditors will be quick and binding when they become necessary. As far as distressed debt trading is concerned, those buying debt should know they will be bound by majority decisions in a restructuring, and will need to consider closely the terms of any ad hoc inter-creditor arrangements.

The duties and obligations of banks involved in restructurings

2.49 The case of *National Westminster Bank plc v Rabobank Nederland*[1] is the leading authority on the mutual duties and obligations of banks involved in restructurings. The case is of critical importance to restructuring practice and the conduct of workouts because the High Court held that in the absence of an express agreement to the contrary there was only a very limited duty of disclosure owed between banks engaged in a restructuring.

[1]   [2007] EWHC 1056 (Comm).

2.50 The litigation arose in the context of the involvement of both banks in the restructuring of their borrower, the Yorkshire Food Group. In March 1996, pursuant to the terms of a syndicated facility agreement under which NatWest were the agent, Rabobank and NatWest each agreed to lend Yorkshire Food Group US$50mn.

2.51 There then followed a sharp deterioration in Yorkshire Food Group's financial performance and by 30 July 1996 the company gave the agent notice that it might be in breach of the financial covenants in the facility agreement. The loan then became subject to intensive management by the respective restructuring teams at both banks and by September 1996, Price Waterhouse were appointed to conduct an independent business review. Further advances were made by the banks to enable Yorkshire Food Group to continue to trade and to support the sale of its US business. By September 1997, Rabobank had devised a structured refinancing of the Group and negotiated a purchase of NatWest's debt at a substantial discount pursuant to a deed of transfer (the DOT) which released NatWest as agent from any obligations, liabilities or responsibilities in respect of the facility. The financial performance of the Group continued to decline and by the time that administrative receivers had been appointed at the beginning of December 1997 Rabobank had incurred losses of around US$127mn.

2.52 The key aspect of Rabobank's complaint related to the fact that between the period of March 1996 and October 1997, NatWest (through a separate lending office) made significant personal loans to various directors and former directors and managers of Yorkshire Food Group. It was alleged that these loans were used in dealings which, Rabobank later argued, were 'the gateway to disclosure of a complex substructure of misconduct by the directors' and that a failure by NatWest to disclose to Rabobank the existence of these loans or the fact that they were in default was pivotal in that if NatWest had disclosed the information about the personal loans, Rabobank would not have advanced sums during the workout period or acquired NatWest's debt and consequently would not have suffered certain losses.

2.53 Rabobank commenced proceedings in California which were eventually dismissed, but as a result NatWest commenced proceedings in the High Court claiming that the litigation in California had been conducted in breach of the DOT which had released NatWest from liability and which had prohibited the commencement of proceedings. For its part Rabobank counterclaimed seeking rescission of the DOT for fraudulent misrepresentation, damages for misrepresentation under the Misrepresentation Act 1967, s 2(1), damages for deceit and damages for breach of an alleged agreement between NatWest and Rabobank that they would negotiate in good faith (the Good Faith Agreement).

2.54 The court held that whether a representation has been made and, if it has what its nature is, must be judged objectively according to the impact that whatever is said may be expected to have on a reasonable representee in the position and with the known characteristics of the representee. This aspect of the judgment constituted an endorsement of the recent decision of Mance LJ in *MCI Worldcom International Inc v Primus Telecommunications Inc*[1].

¹ [2004] 2 All ER 833.

2.55 The key question for the court was whether Rabobank was entitled to infer from NatWest's conduct that NatWest had agreed to disclose to Rabobank all facts material to the conduct of the workout. This inevitably required a detailed assessment by the court of the duties owed by NatWest and Rabobank as co-workout banks. In order to make this determination the court relied heavily on the expert evidence presented by the parties on the practice of co-workout banks in the 1990s. The court favoured the expert put forward by NatWest (whose experience was more recent and relevant than that of the expert put forward by Rabobank) and found that there was no established practice of co-workout banks disclosing to each other all material information, although it was good practice to disclose matters known to them which they honestly thought were material. In the absence of an express contractual obligation, there was no legal duty on banks to adhere to that practice or to exercise reasonable care to do so, but they normally followed it. In giving effect to such a practice, workout banks would typically make their own subjective assessment of what was important and would ordinarily disclose those facts which each considered to be material to the decisions of their fellow restructuring banks.

2.56 On the facts of the present case the court held that the parties expected the restructuring to be a conventional one to be conducted in accordance with usual practice. As such Rabobank as a participating restructuring bank should have been operating on the basis that most, but importantly not all, information known to NatWest which NatWest honestly considered would be significant to Rabobank would be disclosed. Importantly, there was therefore no justifiable reliance by Rabobank on an expectation of any wider disclosure (see generally paragraphs 110–114 of the judgment).

2.57 The court also held that in a restructuring scenario a bank is not entitled to assume that silence meant that no other material matters are known to other participants. In the instant case the court therefore held that such silence could mean that NatWest had no knowledge of any material matters, or that NatWest did not consider such matters to be material or that NatWest was not adhering to what was generally regarded as good practice among workout banks. The judge expressly stated that ... 'Although the last eventuality might be morally objectionable, it could not of itself, without more, give rise to a duty to speak'.

2.58 Having considered the evidence very carefully, the court dismissed all of Rabobank's claims in misrepresentation, both fraudulent and under the Misrepresentation Act 1967, s 2(1). The judge considered that there had been only five representations upon which Rabobank was entitled to rely. He then considered whether any were untrue. He found that in each case they were not. It was not therefore necessary for him to consider whether NatWest representatives knew the representation to be untrue or were reckless as to their truth.

2.59 The court dismissed the claims in deceit on the facts and the claim for breach of the Good Faith Agreement was dismissed as the court took a narrow construction of the clause whereby the parties had agreed to negotiate in good faith holding that it was directed at the parties making a genuine effort to arrive at common ground on the wording of the DOT and did not oblige the parties to put all their cards on the table as Rabobank had suggested. But in any event, even if the scope of the Good Faith Agreement had been as wide as Rabobank alleged it would have been unenforceable for uncertainty[1].

[1]   See *Walford v Miles* [1992] AC 128.

2.60 This case clearly demonstrates the importance in restructurings for those banks involved to avoid uncertainty as to what should and should not be disclosed between them by putting in place an express agreement covering disclosure and the flow of information.

Termination/expiry of the Standstill

2.61 Unless the Standstill is extended beyond its expiry each financier may at expiry or upon the occurrence of specifically identified defaults listed in the Standstill agreement terminate its support for the Standstill and take unilateral action against the company. Typically, the events or circumstances that will bring the Standstill to an end other than expiry are the failure to comply with the terms of the Standstill agreement, an insolvency event (for obvious reasons this is defined widely to include inter alia in any jurisdiction, petitions or applications for administration or a winding up of a material subsidiary or the appointment of a receiver of any kind), a change of control or illegality, a majority institution decision at any time to cease support, a breach of existing and newly negotiated covenants or representations in the original contract such as inter alia disposals, negative pledges, financial undertakings and breaches of specified representations (save for those existing defaults expressly waived as part of the Standstill). In essence the institutions are providing a limited waiver during the Standstill period, but only in relation to matters and defaults that they know about. For example, a waiver of a breach of an interest cover covenant will not exonerate a subsequent breach of a gearing or security cover covenant during the Standstill period.

2.62 It is important to note that the Standstill agreement will contain new obligations, undertakings and representations as to the 'price' for the Standstill. For example, security may have to be granted and invariably there will be a representation about the exposures of the institutions under the various facilities in addition to controls on the group as to the use of cash, payment of dividends, capital expenditure to be incurred and the pricing of ongoing facilities. Accordingly, care must be taken by the corporate and its advisers to ensure that the information represented in the Standstill is correct and that it can in fact conform with the new terms of the Standstill.

2.63 At the end of the Standstill (for whatever reason) institutions can take unilateral action. Recent practice has suggested that this is a concern to both creditors and the company as it may create an unseemly enforcement process upon expiry. Accordingly, it may be prudent to include a soft provision that upon expiry of the Standstill, institutions will consult with each other and the company to the extent reasonably practicable in order to ascertain the feasibility of an extension or the prospects of a more co-ordinated enforcement process.

Extensions and de facto Standstills

2.64 Extending the Standstill requires the unanimous agreement of all of the financiers. Quite often where a financier has an issue or grievance that it wants to have resolved it will delay extending the contractual Standstill period. Whilst this issue is being resolved the lead bank will endeavour to obtain a verbal (and not legally binding) assurance from the dissentient creditor that it will not take precipitous action without giving the lead bank prior warning. Any period such as this where a verbal assurance not to make a demand is given or a creditor does not take action when it is otherwise entitled to do so, is usually referred to as a 'de facto Standstill'.

'Day 1 positions'

Timing

2.65 As intimated a Standstill will typically commence at close of business on the day before the first all bank meeting and the whole basis of a restructuring contract between different creditors is the maintenance of their exposure positions vis-à-vis the company at this time and during the Standstill period.

Importance of the calculation

2.66 The identification of a creditor's Day 1 position is also crucial to the extrapolation of a creditor's relationship with other creditors, for example, in considering new money requirements, security sharing, equalisation and loss sharing and entitlement to distributions emanating from, for example, disposal proceeds. As we will see later all are driven by each creditor's Day 1 exposure and it is therefore a fundamental principle of consensual restructurings that the Day 1 positions are captured so that the creditors are not disadvantaged or indeed advantaged by the subsequent restructuring process.

Importance of the date of the first bank meeting in determining the 'Day 1 position'

2.67 Given that the Day 1 position is typically the position at close of business on the evening before the first bank meeting, the timing of this meeting can be critical, especially for those institutions providing overdrafts, or other revolving facilities where the periodic disparity in the limit and the actual amount drawn can be significant. Suspicion and scepticism will be expressed if the lead bank convening the first bank meeting does so at a time when its revolving credit lines are at their low point in a cycle perhaps days before an anticipated utilisation relating to a significant payment to suppliers or employees in respect of their salaries. Temptation should be resisted by lead banks to exploit the timing of the first all bank meeting, because the moment its integrity is questioned experience shows that the whole restructuring process becomes more protracted.

2.68 The other important consequence of establishing Day 1 positions is that it acts as a barometer and a starting point for identifying new money. This is critical because new money usually has priority status and will usually be repaid first pre and post a formal insolvency.

New moneys

A negotiating 'hot-spot'

2.69 Negotiations relating to the quantum and provision of any new money is as a matter of routine a negotiating 'hot spot' and because it is typically afforded priority status new money reinvigorates a detailed assessment of the corporate's underlying credit quality not only for those providing it, but also for those creditors who are effectively subordinated to it. Creditors effectively have to assess the likelihood of both the new money and the existing exposures ultimately being repaid. New money also raises questions relating to the credibility of the group and its ability to produce accurate cashflow forecasts budgets and other financial information. The creditors, in conjunction with their advisers, have to consider whether continuing support and providing new money will improve the prospect of generating an enhanced recovery overall. New money is effectively a device for buying time in order to assess the viability of the business and therefore the merits of the restructuring and a more orderly disposal of assets outside of a 'fire sale' that is triggered by an insolvency. The aspiration is that the provision of new money will reduce subsequent losses on old money.

Importance of the accuracy of the request

2.70 From the perspective of the corporate and its various advisers the accuracy of the new money request is critical. Underestimating the amount required will be received just as negatively as an excessive request designed to produce too much headroom. Once the financiers lose faith in the efficacy of financial information provided by the group and its advisers it becomes extremely difficult to retain faith in the group's analysis of its requirements and any proposed solution to its commercial problems. There is nothing more unnerving for a bank group to have inconsistent and/or repeated requests for new money.

Quantum

2.71 The quantum of new money can be minimised and the urgency of the requirement can be controlled by ensuring that the details of the restructuring remain confidential. Financial creditors are encouraged to be discreet because once it is common knowledge that a corporate has liquidity problems the attitudes of suppliers harden and the providers of credit insurance to suppliers of the corporate and the debt factoring facilities provided by financial institutions to those suppliers can be reduced, thereby intensifying the illiquidity of the group and increasing the new money requirement. In the Booker restructuring in late 1998/99, the banks resisted the temptation to request full debenture security since the public registration of that security would have been a signal to the group's suppliers and credit insurers of its financial difficulties, thereby alarming suppliers, credit insurers and invoice discounters to such an extent that the group and the institutions involved in the restructuring would have had a significantly greater new money problem than they already faced which would have exceeded 'pound for pound' the benefit of the perceived security value.

2.72 In situations where the security for the new money is deficient or inadequate the new money provider may require a full underwriting from other financial creditors.

Form of the new money

2.73 At the first meeting of the institutions their Day 1 positions are set and the exposure under their facilities is capped (defaults thereby creating draw-stops to existing commitments). The new money required by the group can include an additional overdraft, revolving credit, bonding, guarantee and hedging facilities. Quite often new money is made available by the relevant institutions permitting their existing facilities which are 'draw-stopped' to be utilised above their Day 1 position and quite often up to their pre-Standstill limits. Like actual new money this reinstatement of the original commitment (so as to create headroom) will be afforded priority both pre and post enforcement. Similarly, the Day 1 'mark to market position' under derivative facilities provided to the group will also be calculated and any increase in that mark to market position during the restructuring will also rank as priority new money. This is a useful device because it means that strategic and economically important hedging previously implemented by the group can be maintained.

Providers of the new money

2.74 In a small club deal new money is typically provided by each institution in proportion to its original Day 1 exposure. However, in larger, more complex, transactions, and given the problems faced by certain CDOs and insurance company investors active in the private placement markets in being permitted to make further investments in impaired credits, the entirety of the new money requirement is in many cases provided by the members of the 'steering committee' or more likely, by the lead bank co-ordinator exclusively. Delays in making the new money available can sometimes emerge because even those not providing the new money will require credit approval for ceding priority to or underwriting those providing it.

Return on the new money

2.75 It is normal for the economic return on new money to be higher than on existing facilities which is quite surprising given its priority status and the perception that it is less exposed to risk and therefore non-payment. The reality can be different to the perception and one only needs to look at US Chapter 11 precedents where 'DIP financiers' providing new money in a Chapter 11 restructuring have suffered shortfalls on a Chapter 7 liquidation and a number of UK restructurings where the new money has been under water during the turnaround process. Where there is a degree of competition to provide the new money it is not uncommon for certain institutions to request that the institution providing the new money shares the income generated given that the other participants are effectively underwriting it by ceding priority on the existing asset cover. In the face of such a request it is not uncommon or indeed unreasonable for the new money institution to request that the other institutions seeking a share of the income risk participate in the new money facility or underwrite it. In some ways this is a slight anomaly as the new money will usually enjoy priority over the existing exposures and therefore typically carry less risk. In cases where the new money needs to be made available as a matter of urgency, or there would be an undue administrative burden to put in place a risk sharing arrangement and to implement the actual mechanisms for distributing relatively small sums to risk participating institutions, it is preferable for the dissentient institutions to relent and to recognise one of the key tenets of the INSOL Principles that new money has priority.

2.76 For a detailed analysis of the impact of entity priority claims on the availability and repayment of new money see section C entitled 'Distributions pre and post insolvency' at para 2.98ff.

New security

Prospects of granting new security

2.77 It does not automatically follow that a Standstill or indeed the provision of new money will result in the grant of new security. In restructurings where financial creditors have been confronted by a booklet of negative pledges or there has been a significant volume of supplier credit insurance or debt factoring in the background, institutional creditors have refrained from taking full asset security that is registerable (even for their new money) so as to avoid a liquidity crunch posed by the relevant suppliers or their financiers having an adverse reaction to this news and terminating or at the least winding down their exposure.

2.78 It may be possible to grant a charge or a pledge of shares of a key subsidiary in these circumstances since such a security under the terms of the Financial Collateral Arrangements Directive (2002/47/EC) will still be valid notwithstanding any obligation to register such security under local applicable law. It then becomes a question of judgment as to whether the grant of such security for new money should be discussed with the credit insurers or any other stakeholders as a means of fostering trust.

Existing legacy security

2.79 If there is some existing legacy security that has previously been granted in favour of an institution this will have priority and the institution having such security will insist that only it is able to grant a release of that security or consent to a secondary security in order to realise its priority.

The form of the new security

2.80 The new security that is taken as part of the restructuring will usually take the form of all monies, cross guarantees and debentures. This means that each company granting such security will be guaranteeing all of the obligations (past, present, future, actual and contingent) of each company in the group to each of the institutions. It will be charging all of its assets in support of its own obligations as principal debtor to each relevant institution providing a facility directly to it and in respect of its guarantee of the liabilities of each other member of the group to all of the institutions.

2.81 As intimated where the security is being granted in support of new money it is possible that the security will be limited and confined to a specific asset or shares in a subsidiary having a value that broadly correlates with the quantum of the new money.

Timing of the grant of the new security

2.82 A corporate is unlikely to sanction such security merely as part of a Standstill and at the preliminary Standstill stage will almost certainly only grant limited scope security in support of any new money.

2.83 The directors may be advised that there is insufficient corporate benefit and justification for the grant of security in the absence of long-term financial support from its creditors. Equally, any floating charge will arguably be invalid under the Insolvency Act 1986, s 245, except to the extent of the aggregate of the value of the consideration granted by lenders at the same time as or after the creation of the charge. This position taken by a corporate is not always entirely correct given that the grant of the security is facilitating the continuation of the support to the group and the fact that the floating charge will be validated to the extent of any amounts that revolve and are re-advanced either under an overdraft, revolving credit or other working capital facility, but the directors will need to satisfy themselves as to their fiduciary and other duties, and may seek independent advice in this regard.

2.84 It is typically the case, however, that the more substantive security package will only realistically be granted as consideration for longer-term restructuring support provided by the institutions.

The importance of existing negative pledges

2.85 When considering the grant of new security in a restructuring context, due diligence will be required to establish whether or not the company may be bound by an existing 'negative pledge' – a contractual undertaking given to a third party by which the company is prohibited from creating security altogether, or is only entitled to do so only in restricted circumstances. A contractual undertaking of this nature is often given in a variety of finance documents and whilst the obvious places to look are existing loan and security documents more obscure instruments such as surety bonds, a schedule to an ISDA agreement or a debenture stock deed should also be diligenced. On occasion a similar undertaking may even be given in a commercial agreement (such as a shareholders' agreement) or the articles of the company itself. An appropriate waiver or release should be obtained from the beneficiary of the undertaking so as to prevent the company from being in breach of contract and exposing the lenders to a tortuous claim for inducement of a breach of contract. If security is created in contravention of a negative pledge contained in a floating charge, of which the lenders have notice, the considered view is that the new security will be subject to the priority of that floating charge. The only substantive question here is whether registration of a negative pledge at Companies House is sufficient to constitute constructive knowledge which satisfies the 'notice test' for these purposes. Given the propensity for professional lending institutions to register their negative pledges and for those seeking new security to similarly check the register it is the view of the authors that registration of such a pledge will constitute notice for these purposes[1].

[1] See also *Manchester Trust Ltd v Furness, Withy & Co Ltd* [1895] 2 QB 539, 1 Com Cas 39, CA.

Vulnerability of the new security

2.86 Even if the grant of the security may not be subject to a contractual prohibition restricting its grant, institutions seeking new security as part of a restructuring either to improve their position as an existing lender, or to secure an advance of new moneys will, in either case, need to ensure that the security is valid and not vulnerable to the claims of other parties on a liquidation.

Preferences

2.87 The main provision of concern which may render security granted as part of a restructuring process vulnerable to the claims of third parties is the Insolvency Act 1986, s 239 relating to the grant of unlawful preferences. The vulnerability of security created at the time of a rescue situation is increased because of the poor financial condition of the company. Section 239 applies in circumstances where a preference, meaning the doing of something which places a creditor in a better position than he would have been on a company's liquidation, is given at a 'relevant time'. Other than in the case of a connected person (as defined in the Insolvency Act 1986, ss 249 and 435) in which case the period is two years, it will be a relevant time if the preference is given within the period of six months prior to the onset of insolvency and at such time the company is unable to pay its debts within the meaning of the Insolvency Act 1986, s 123 or becomes unable to do so as a result of the transaction. Where a company has at a relevant time given a preference to a relevant person as defined in the Insolvency Act 1986, s 240, the administrator or liquidator may apply to the court for an order. The court will then make such order as it thinks fit to restore the position to what it would have been if the company had not given that preference. The court can also decline to make an order.

2.88 The court order may:

(a)   require any property transferred as part of the transaction, or in connection with the giving of the preference, to be vested in the company;

(b)   require any property to be so vested if it represents in any person's hands the application either of the proceeds of sale of property so transferred or of money so transferred;

(c)   release or discharge (in whole or in part) any security given by the company;

(d)   require any person to pay, in respect of benefits received by him from the company, such sums to the office-holder as the court may direct;

(e)   provide for any surety or guarantor whose obligations to any person were released or discharged (in whole or in part) under the transaction, or by the giving of the preference, to be under such new or revived obligations to that person as the court thinks appropriate;

(f)   provide for security to be provided for the discharge of any obligation imposed by or arising under the order, for such an obligation to be charged on any property and for the security or charge to have the same priority as a security or charge released or discharged (in whole or in part) under the transaction or by the giving of the preference; and

(g)   provide for the extent to which any person whose property is vested by the order in the company, or on whom obligations are imposed by the order, is to be able to prove in the winding up of the company for debts or other liabilities which arose from, or were released or discharged (in whole or in part) under or by, the transaction or the giving of the preference.

2.89 However, any order will not prejudice any interest in property which was acquired from a person other than the company in good faith for value, and will not require a person who was not a party to the transaction or preference to account to the administrator or liquidator for a benefit received under the preference in good faith and for value.

2.90 In considering whether a preference has been given it is necessary to show that the person granting security (or other potential preference) was influenced by the desire to put the person benefiting from the preference into a better position in the event of the company's liquidation than he would have been in had the preference not been given. Desire for this purpose is subjective and the company must be motivated by a desire to improve the lender's position as a creditor in the event of its liquidation. Millett J (as he was then) in *Re M C Bacon Ltd*[1] has made it clear that for the provision of security to be a preference the company must positively desire the effect described in the Insolvency Act 1986, s 239, namely to improve the position of a lender in the event of an insolvent liquidation. The company will not be deemed to desire the consequences of all of its actions. As a result, provided the desire of the company in providing security to an existing lender is not to improve that lender's position on a liquidation, but is motivated by some other factor – for instance the need to retain that lender's continued support or to obtain fresh moneys – the provision of security will not be a preference. For there to be a preference, the company must positively wish to improve the position of that lender in the event of its liquidation.

[1]   [1991] Ch 127, [1990] 3 WLR 646.

Void floating charges

2.91 The other main provision of concern is the Insolvency Act 1986, s 245 which provides that, in certain circumstances, floating charges created before the commencement of a winding up or the making of an administration order will be void. For this to happen the floating charge must have been given at a 'relevant time', which in the case of a charge given in favour of a person connected to the company is at any time within two years prior to the onset of insolvency. In the case of a charge in favour of any other person, the relevant time is any time within 12 months prior to the onset of insolvency, provided that at such time the company is unable to pay its debts within the meaning of the Insolvency Act 1986, s 123 or becomes unable to do so as a result of the transaction.

2.92 For the charge to be void it must have been given otherwise than for good consideration. A charge is given for good consideration only insofar as the consideration granted for it does not exceed the aggregate of:

(a) the value of money paid for goods or services supplied to the company at or after the creation of the charge;
(b) the value of the discharge or reduction, at or after the creation of the charge, of any debt of the company; and
(c) such interest as may be payable on these amounts as the result of any agreement under which the money was paid, the goods or services supplied, or the debt discharged or reduced.

2.93 Thus, a floating charge given to secure new money borrowed by the company giving the charge should not be vulnerable to adjustment, but a floating charge given by a third party or to secure pre-existing debt, even if paid to the company in consideration for the charge, may be set aside[1].

[1] *Re Shoe Lace Ltd* [1994] 1 BCLC 111, [1993] BCC 609.

Tacking – consolidation of advances

2.94 It may be possible for a lender to tack further advances onto secured advances with the result that new advances are secured to the same extent and with the same priority. The ability to tack this way is governed by the Law of Property Act 1925, s 94, which provides that the holder of security is entitled to tack further advances to it by arrangement with subsequent security holders, where he has not had notice of any subsequent security interest at the time the new advance is made, and where the lender is under an obligation contained in the original mortgage to make the new advance. As the lender is unlikely to be under an obligation to make further advances, tacking will usually require the agreement of all secured creditors. If, as part of the restructuring, there is a further security take-up it may be possible for the new money to be tacked on to the existing security with the consent of the other institutions that are to become subsequent security holders. This is a mechanism that would ensure that the new money is subject to existing security that may have 'hardened' in the sense that the time limits pursuant to which it is vulnerable under the Insolvency Act 1986, ss 239 and 245 have expired. This does not mean, of course, that the provider of the new money would not also take further security over additional assets and from other members of the group where this is available.

Third party security and transactions at an undervalue

2.95 Where a company gives a charge or guarantee in respect of another's liabilities, the transaction may appear gratuitous because no obvious benefit accrues to the company. It may be argued that such a transaction is a transaction at an undervalue for the purposes of the Insolvency Act 1986, s 238. If the provision of security or the giving of a guarantee in respect of the liabilities of a third party is found by the court to be a transaction at an undervalue, the court may make such order as it sees fit for the purpose of restoring the position to what it would have been if the transaction had not been entered into (Insolvency Act 1986, s 238(3)). The court also has the specific powers to adjust transactions at an undervalue contained in the Insolvency Act 1986, s 241.

2.96 For the transaction to be a transaction at an undervalue it must have been made at a 'relevant time', which means at any time during the period of two years prior to the onset of insolvency. This is the same period as for preferences involving connected persons (the period for preferences not involving connected persons is six months). The court will not make an order under the Insolvency Act 1986, s 238 if it is persuaded that the third party entered into the transaction in good faith and for the purpose of carrying on its own business, and that at the time the transaction was entered into there were reasonable grounds for believing that the transaction would benefit the company (Insolvency Act 1986, s 238(5)).

2.97 Transactions at an undervalue may also raise corporate issues such as unlawful returns of capital to shareholders[1], unlawful distributions and unlawful financial assistance. The company will need to ensure that it is properly advised in these circumstances.

[1]   See *Aveling Barford Ltd v Perion Ltd* [1989] BCLC 626.

C DISTRIBUTIONS PRE AND POST INSOLVENCY

General principles

2.98 Provisions regulating each creditor's entitlement to the proceeds of distributions resulting from a disposal of secured assets and/or assets of group companies that have granted guarantees to their institutional creditors are frequently the most contested provisions in any Standstill or restructuring agreement. The negotiations are just as intense irrespective of whether these proceeds arise as part of (i) a planned disposal pre enforcement and/or pre insolvency, or (ii) as part of an enforcement process post enforcement and/or post insolvency.

Contractual restrictions on disposals

2.99 Whilst it is obvious that a corporate can not deal with its secured assets without the consent of its relevant secured creditors, it is also very difficult for the directors of a corporate to deal with the disposal proceeds of its assets (including in particular a sale of shares in its subsidiaries) where it or that subsidiary has not granted security, but it has significant creditors including those with primary debt or guarantee claims. In the first instance this is because in a restructuring where it is highly likely to be a sale by a distressed corporate of varying degrees, the corporate is likely to have to account to its creditors for such proceeds in order to avoid a default especially if it is sufficiently resourced to discharge those liabilities from other sources. On this basis its creditors, including those having a guarantee claim ranking pari passu, are going to be in a strong position to argue over the proceeds unless the directors are prepared to dissipate those proceeds and incur potential personal liability in the process. Indeed, in a sale of shares on a debt-free basis where a purchaser will assume the trade liabilities of the target company, the purchaser will not complete unless it is satisfied that the claims of the financial creditors and any related guarantees have been released.

2.100 In the second instance (and more likely following a Standstill as part of a restructuring) the corporate will be prohibited as a matter of contract from disposing of its assets notwithstanding that they may not be secured. This is because the group will have granted a whole host of undertakings covenanting not to dispose of its assets without the consent of the institutions and/or without applying the proceeds in order of application pre-ordained by its institutional creditors.

The key issue – application of liquidation principles

2.101 The main focus of the negotiations between institutional creditors is how the proceeds of distributions resulting from a disposal are to be allocated. Both the London Approach and the INSOL Principles dictate that all creditors are to be treated equitably and in order to achieve this, most consensual restructurings remain cognisant of the Day 1 positions of each creditor and strive to preserve the relevant positions of creditors vis-à-vis each other when crafting the distribution and security sharing provisions. Mechanically, the lead bank, security trustee or distribution agent will look at each institution's proportion of the aggregate exposure and will (subject to any new money and entity priority claims – see below) ensure that both the pre-enforcement proceeds and the post-enforcement proceeds are distributed to each institution in accordance with agreed market convention. Pre-enforcement it is likely that there will be no distribution to creditors with contingent exposures (such as under bonding lines) or with hedging exposures directly to those exposures since this would be an inefficient allocation of the company's cash at a time of tightening liquidity.

2.102 In certain cases however institutions providing ancillary facilities have sought a pre-enforcement distribution from scheduled repayments, equity raising, surplus cash and disposal proceeds by requiring their exposure to be cash covered. This is not the common approach however and of course any distributions that have been made with respect to such contingent facilities will be subject to equalisation and adjustment post-enforcement in order to achieve a 'true-up' of losses across all institutions.

2.103 Conceptually, the emphasis on the Day 1 positions of institutions as the means of determining the interim and final distributions of institutional creditors is akin to calculating their claims in a notional liquidation and for this reason this approach is known as the application of 'liquidation principles'.

Existing security and guarantees and the principle of entity priority

The basic concept

2.104 In applying liquidation principles it is perfectly logical for an institution that had direct lending to an asset-owning subsidiary or security from or a guarantee claim against such an entity before the first all institution meeting to retain priority in relation to the proceeds of realisation of that lending/security, up to the limits of the facility that it was providing at Day 1.

2.105 If only one institution, or a minority of institutions have direct lending or guarantee claims/security from a member of the group it or they, as the case may be, are said to have an 'entity priority' claim which consistent with a liquidation, would enable them to prove for their claim with priority to those institutions that did not have a similar claim on Day 1. Those institutions will strive to preserve their entity priority claims. The only exceptions to this principle will occur where either an institution took security or a guarantee in contravention of a negative pledge imposed by another institution or in anticipation of the first institution meeting and cognisant of the distressed state of the group, that institution pre-emptively switched its lending to a new entity or took such security or a guarantee to improve its own position. In this situation peer group pressure will typically prevail and the opportunistic creditor will usually relent on the basis that the lead bank will highlight the position and the likelihood of challenge. On a more pragmatic level the institution in question will be reminded that this type of conduct is not conducive to a successful consensual restructuring where unanimity will be required.

Inter-company claims

2.106 In calculating the liquidation position of each creditor by reference to their Day 1 positions the unsecured claims of non-institutional creditors are usually disregarded. Conversely, the position of inter-company claims is not so easily resolved and the question as to whether they are to be included or excluded from the liquidation analysis is a difficult one with the answer largely predicated on the positions of the specific creditors and the size and impact of the relevant claims. If the creditors have the same or substantially the same recourse either in terms of primary claims or guarantee claims and there are no significant entity priority claims the position of inter-company claims is less likely to be an issue. However, it is quite common for one or more creditors to have advanced facilities to the parent, finance or 'treasury' company in a large group and for this borrower to then funnel the cash around the group on an inter-company basis to where it is actually needed. If those institutions are bereft of credit support in the form of group guarantees it is highly likely that they will seek to ensure that the inter-company claims, as assets of that parent or treasury company, be incorporated into any application of the liquidation principles. Given that the institution in question has recourse to the parent/treasury company and its assets in the form of inter-company debts, it will require recourse to the value of those inter-company claims on any liquidation analysis. This is perfectly equitable on the basis that its facility has been used to support the group and that on a liquidation of an English company an unsecured inter-company claim would still rank pari passu with other unsecured guarantee claims.

Distribution waterfalls

2.107 As intimated above, it is a common tenet of liquidation principles that where financial creditors do not have the same recourse across a debtor group and entity priority claims are indeed prevalent then the value of each creditor's claims and the precise nature of its recourse will need to be considered at each juncture where there is a distribution from that company whether this be pre or post insolvency. After reimbursing any outstanding costs of the administrative parties such as the agent and the security trustee from any distribution proceeds (and usually after repayment of any new monies – see below), the secured entity priority claims will be discharged before the reimbursement of any entity priority guarantee claims and any competing inter-company claims ranking at the same level. Other claims of the institutions will then be discharged pro rata from any surplus amounts.

The distorting effect of new money

2.108 Any application of the liquidation principles both pre and post insolvency will be distorted by the provision of new money. For this reason financial creditors making available the new money and any creditors with an entity priority position will consider extremely carefully where the new money is to be made available and how it is to be repaid. Invariably an institution with a fully covered entity priority position will be reluctant to see any modifications to the funding and recourse structure within a corporate group that disrupt its anticipated full repayment. Conversely, those creditors making the new money available will wish to see it repaid with priority out of any pre-payment including a disposal made by an entity priority company. If this is not the case they may well require an undertaking from the members of the group that are the recipients of the new money that they will not disburse it to the entity priority companies. One compromise might be for the new money to at least rank pari passu with the existing entity priority claims, but this may not always be achievable. All of this may be less of a problem if the entity priority company does not require new money although one should not underestimate the propensity for institutions to question their support of the main group by making available new money when this indirectly preserves value of a group member that is the subject of an entity priority claim from another institution. If the entity priority company does require new money the institutions with the entity priority claim will either have to fund the new money required by the entity priority group company themselves or enter into a compromise with the new money providers.

2.109 If entity priority claims do not disrupt the provision of new money or indeed a compromise is reached between the new money providers and the entity priority creditors as described above so that the new money will have priority in the conventional way, then it will be possible for the new money to be drawn by a designated company and then disbursed around the group to where it is needed.

The position of 'ancillary facilities'

2.110 It is inevitable that the maintenance of Day 1 positions within a notional liquidation can sometimes become impossible to achieve in a purely technical sense, particularly when there are 'ancillary' or contingent facilities such as letters of credit, performance bonds/guarantees and hedging facilities involved. It is a rather banal point, but in order to maintain an institution's Day 1 positions at a later point in time, one must be able to determine what the position at Day 1 actually was. In the case of a guarantee or performance bond this 'call amount' is not easy to discern. How can the potential liability of a guarantee of an uncompleted contract be realistically quantified? In relation to a guarantee of a profitable or strategically important contract even in an insolvency this contract is likely to be completed or transferred for value (often by way of a novation) to a third party purchaser as an asset of that company. In that situation the guarantee is unlikely to be called and so the exposure of an institution under this instrument in any liquidation model is debatable. It may therefore be necessary for the reporting accountants to value the exposure under such a performance bond in order that the creditors may agree to apply a deemed call amount, or alternatively use the regulatory capital weighting applicable to the facility in question.

2.111 Notwithstanding the difficulties of valuing exposure under ancillary facilities the market convention increasingly is to assume that there would be a maximum loss under the instrument on a subsequent insolvency. Accordingly, the institution in question would share pre-enforcement for the maximum possible loss under the instrument which invariably is its face value, and conversely if the institution in question does ultimately not suffer any loss on the facility and sees the quantum of its exposure decrease it will need to equalise its Day 1 position (see the section on 'Loss sharing and equalisation' at para 2.126ff). Where pre-payments or distributions are made, any allocation in relation to such ancillary facilities is therefore likely to be undertaken pro rata to the exposure on all facilities at the same point in the distribution waterfall (taking into account, of course, secured claims and any entity priority claims which rank ahead of it as outlined above), but the proceeds however are applied to the debt facilities.

2.112 In most restructurings however, the proceeds of distribution (pre-enforcement) in relation to such ancillary facility claims are not actually paid to the relevant facility. Instead, the distribution that the relevant institution was entitled to out of the disposal proceeds for its claim under the relevant ancillary facility may be placed in a suspense account by way of 'cash cover' and retained by the security trustee. As the liabilities under the instrument are reduced either pre or post insolvency (because, for example, the contract is completed and the guarantee is either wholly or partly released) the cash cover is released back to the lead bank co–ordinator for distribution to the institutions.

2.113 In most cases the pre-enforcement distribution proceeds may not even be deposited with a security trustee as cash cover for the ancillary facilities. Indeed, institutional creditors may agree to make a larger distribution with respect to lending facilities at the expense of providing cash cover for ancillary facilities so as to reduce financing costs and create financial efficiencies with an equalisation and adjustment of the relative positions of lending banks and ancillary providers being made post-enforcement when the amount of actual exposure under ancillary facilities is known.

2.114 If cash cover was provided with respect to any ancillary facilities pre-enforcement, then the release of that cash cover upon completion of the contract is synonymous to a disposal and the cash released will be applied on the basis of the current security sharing arrangements. If a claim is made on the instrument and the institution in question settles the liability the cash will be distributed to it. If the cash is insufficient to discharge the liability, the institution (pre insolvency) will have to convert part of its exposure under the instrument into a replacement loan.

2.115 Alternatively and again as a matter of prudent treasury management in order to avoid a corporate having substantial sums being held as cash cover which increases the group's working capital and therefore its new money requirements (unless full interest set-off is provided against debt facilities provided by that financier), it is possible that the institutions who are entitled to cash cover may be satisfied with interim bank indemnities from other financiers (with unequal positions being 'trued-up' upon any subsequent enforcement event through equalisation and loss sharing) who may receive such monies and whose lending to the group was reduced by it. However, there is a perception amongst institutions that if they have cash cover their negotiating position is improved and so such an arrangement may not be forthcoming.

The position of hedging facilities

2.116 Institutions providing certain particularly volatile hedging facilities (such as interest rate/currency swaps) may insist as part of negotiations that such positions are 'closed out' to crystallise an equivalent loan position. If, however, these facilities are strategically important and the company and the other institutions request that the hedging arrangements continue, the institution in question is likely to insist that it 'proves' in any pre-enforcement distributions for the mark to market exposure under the hedging at the time of the distribution, but such distribution is actually applied against its debt facilities to the extent that it has any. If an institution does not provide any debt facilities then rather than make a pre-enforcement distribution for hedging, the preferred and indeed the conventional approach is for lending facilities to be discharged pursuant to a so-called 'true-up' between lending institutions and hedge providers taking place post-enforcement if necessary.

2.117 The important concessions by the hedge providers for agreeing to this position will be the ceding of priority for any increase in the mark to market exposure under the hedges during the course of the restructuring. Due to the ongoing risk on such instruments, the 'profit' or 'loss' on which can move markedly even over short periods, the hedge providers will insist that any increase in its mark to market exposure under the hedging will be given new money priority treatment post enforcement.

Mechanical application of the liquidation principles as part of a distribution regime

The difficulties of making an application

2.118 As we have seen, the application of liquidation principles requires that the value of the claims of each institution are calculated across each member of the debtor group by reference to the Day 1 positions of each creditor so as to establish the competing claims of the institutions in what is a notional liquidation. As articulated, this process becomes even more difficult to complete when the value of existing security, entity priority claims, inter-company receivables, new money and hedging and guarantee facilities are incorporated. If one then incorporates the impact of currency fluctuations, different bases of calculating security values and the nuances of cross-border insolvency laws these calculations can become incredibly challenging. Mechanically there are a number of ways of achieving this.

The use of a liquidation model

2.119 Quite often the reporting accountants as part of their work-scope might be instructed to model the competing claims of the institutions based on the impact of the factors and variables mentioned in the preceding paragraph. The calculations in the model can then be referred to in the Standstill agreement and any more formal restructuring agreement that replaces it.

2.120 It should be noted that the construction of such a liquidation model can become a 'mini-industry' and can take an eternity to complete and agree. On the recent restructuring of MyTravel plc the process took approximately nine months to complete due to the complexity of the calculations and the need to reflect entity priority claims as part of the ultimate debt for equity conversion. It was even necessary to hold a series of workshops to explain the methodology and the results to the various institutions. It should be recognised by creditors that any model will have its imperfections but as long as the assumptions and guiding methodology are approved, experience has shown that creditors will tolerate a degree of imperfection.

Distribution percentages

2.121 In other cases the creditors have dispensed with a liquidation model and have simply looked at Day 1 exposures and established the percentage of each institution's realisation from each company without taking into account inter-company claims, currency fluctuations and other complicating factors. Depending on the facts of the case, the perceived overall value or recovery and the scope of the negotiations, the impact of guarantee and hedging claims together with entity priority claims and new money can still be factored in. As intimated earlier, new money can have a distorting effect and one of the weaknesses of this approach is the fact that the returns of creditors can be affected by the order in which enforcement takes place on insolvency and assets are disposed of and realised.

Combination of basic pro-rata sharing pre-enforcement and liquidation principles post-enforcement

2.122 Another mechanical solution involves having basic pro rata sharing for pre-enforcement distributions (post new money and entity priority distributions) with respect to lending facilities and following enforcement ensuring that the security agent corrects any inequities by subsequently recalculating the distributions based upon a notional liquidation applying the respective Day 1 positions of the institutions taking into account the actual relative claims of the institutions in their capacities as both principal debtors and via their claims under guarantees or inter-company loans and applying equalisation principles. The advantages of this system are efficiency and simplicity. Distributions can be made on a pro-rata basis pre-enforcement with respect to lending facilities and the potentially more difficult calculations can be deferred thereby enabling the restructuring agreement to be signed on an expedited basis, thereby giving the company breathing space and reducing costs. The other benefit is that none of the parties need to form immediate conclusions regarding the valuation of their security and the underlying assets: making calculations after the event (if at all) is always easier as there will be more time to do it. It is important to stress that many of the calculations that the institutions make in relation to the construction of such liquidation models rarely get tested as they are established for circumstances that may not in fact happen.

Concluding points on distributions pre and post insolvency

2.123 Even a cursory read of this section will reveal the difficulties of constructing a simple notional liquidation along the lines of the liquidation principles that have been articulated. This is not necessarily a futile venture that should be abandoned but rather the institutions involved should acknowledge the imperfections of an academic exercise and the reality that any convoluted structures to overcome them will have the same imperfections. Even if the structure did accurately reflect the assumptions that would be applied in a notional liquidation, the structure will inevitably completely ignore the impact of timing on asset values and actual realisations with consequences for the relative positions of each financier. As everyone who has been involved in the valuing of a business knows, its only true value is what someone will pay for it when those controlling it want to sell it.

2.124 Ultimately the structure for the sharing of the proceeds of the security must be as simple, fair and equitable and agreed upon as soon as possible. The construction of a well engineered security sharing system will not always necessarily facilitate a successful restructuring. Equally it needs to be recognised that a corporate customer is still trying to conduct its business against a backdrop of costly inter-creditor negotiations and experience has shown that the delays in reaching agreement on a mutually acceptable system may contribute to the restructuring failing.

2.125 The perspective of John Melbourne, the senior executive of NatWest, who masterminded many of the major corporate restructurings in the early 1990s remains as profound today as it was then. He described the process of determining the system of security sharing in the following terms: 'our present positions are like an uneven football pitch with bumps and troughs. What we are trying to do is raise the pitch by three feet thereby making us all much better off but in doing so in some ways we may benefit a bit vis-à-vis each other but in other areas we will have lost out a bit. What we must do is look at our improvement in the round and recognise that overall we are all much better off'.

Loss sharing and equalisation

Rationale

2.126 These concepts are agreed upon and adopted as fundamental restructuring principles pre-enforcement, but are applied only following enforcement and/or an insolvency. In a corporate restructuring where the capital structure includes a number of revolving (including contingent and hedging facilities) and/or overdraft facilities from different institutions, the Standstill agreement will need to provide for equalisation and loss sharing amongst those institutions in order to retain equality and parity between those institutions. A successful restructuring will be predicated on a continuation of these working capital facilities which must continue to be made available to the group (subject to new money treatment for headroom made available) on a fully revolving basis and which must be permitted to revolve.

2.127 *The restructuring process*

Equalisation (also known as 'tip-in' and 'tip-back')

2.127 The purpose of an equalisation arrangement (often seen as the corresponding compromise for the ceding of priority) is to reduce the effect on the exposure of an individual institution of the vagaries inherent in the timing of an insolvency or an enforcement. Equalisation simply requires an adjusting payment to be made to a central pot and applied between relevant institutions following an enforcement or an insolvency if on the relevant date of the enforcement or the insolvency one institution has experienced an increase or a decrease in its exposure relative to its Day 1 exposure because the company chose to utilise its facility rather than the facility of another institution or market movements (including currency) have distorted the relative position of hedging facilities. Equalisation is an integral component of the liquidation principles and it effectively procures that the exposures of each institution is the same, vis-à-vis the other institutions as it was as at Day 1.

Equalisation – inclusion of facilities and valuation issues

2.128 Historically certain financial creditors had a tendency to exclude certain contingent facilities such as performance bonds, swaps and foreign exchange facilities from the equalisation mechanism since it was not easy to determine the Day 1 level of exposure thereunder at the Standstill time. Quite often this meant that institutions providing such facilities could possibly see their exposure diminish because the restructuring would procure the completion of the underlying contract to which the bond related. By not equalising such a facility an institution could gain a windfall from the restructuring. More recently institutions have purported to value such instruments by applying an appropriate regulatory capital weighting to such a facility or alternatively have an independent expert value the relevant exposure (ie a 'call amount').

2.129 Ideally, equalisation calculations should take place shortly after the enforcement of the security by a security trustee or the date of an insolvency event and before any realisations from the security or the insolvency is distributed. In practice this rarely happens as the security trustee and lead bank are usually too occupied with the usual post insolvency/enforcement issues at such time.

Loss sharing

2.130 Loss sharing and equalisation are complementary concepts designed to address unequal pre-enforcement distributions once enforcement occurs, but it should be noted that they are invoked at different stages of the post-enforcement process with equalisation occurring first. Loss sharing merely requires a predetermination of the losses each institution has suffered on identified facilities and for the aggregate losses to be shared in proportion to each institution's original Day 1 exposure (after taking into account any priority new money and any entity priorities) following an insolvency or an enforcement against the group. A loss sharing provision will become operative once the full extent of the losses incurred by each institution have been determined. This means that the institutions will have to defer the loss sharing payments until all of the contingent facilities and particularly guarantees or hedging contracts have been cancelled, expired or called, and all of the realisations of all of the assets of each group company that has granted security have been received. Due to the fact that this can take a considerable amount of time, there may be some interim loss sharing adjustments made once a reasonable estimate can be made of the final outcome and after the bulk of the realisations from the security have been distributed. At the end of the process the institutions via the agents will make any final adjusting payments that are necessary.

2.131 Historically, the greatest source of error and potential opportunity for varying the relativity of the institutions' Day 1 positions could be found in the provisions relating to loss sharing or equalisation. These topics are increasingly given much more attention and they are intensively negotiated. Loss sharing and equalisation are complementary concepts, but they are not interdependent of one another. It is indeed possible to have one without the other even though they may produce the same mathematical consequences in some circumstances (ignoring changes in exposures due to currency fluctuations).

Listed below are a number simple equalisation and loss sharing examples.

SCENARIO 1 – EQUALISATION AND LOSS SHARING

2.132 Two banks, Berril and Coldman, are lending to a borrower Skint plc. Berril provides a revolving facility of £200m and Coldman provides a term loan of £200m.

At the Standstill date the revolver is fully drawn. Accordingly, the exposure of both banks is the same, ie £200m each.

The banks agree that they will equalise their lending upon enforcement of their security.

The turnaround does not succeed and Skint plc becomes insolvent with an administrator being appointed. On the date of appointment of the administrator, the Coldman term loan stands at £180m whereas through management of creditors, etc, the amount outstanding under Berril's revolver is only £120m.

The aggregate debt is therefore £300m, of which Coldman's share is £180m and Berril's share is only £120m. In order to equalise their lending so that each of them is owed half of the aggregate liability (ie £150m each), it is necessary for Berril to pay Coldman £30m.

2.132 *The restructuring process*

If the assets of Skint plc then go on to realise £150m, Berril and Coldman share such realisations equally and therefore get £75m each with both loss sharing proportionately to their Day 1 exposures ie losing £125m each.

SCENARIO 2 – SIMPLE LOSS SHARING (1)

2.133 Two banks, TBS and KSBC, are lending to a borrower Dodgy AG.

TBS provides lending facilities of £100m and a letter of credit facility of £100m (the call upon which is assumed to be 100%).

KSBC provides lending facilities of only (£100m).

TBS and KSBC agree that upon enforcement they will share any ultimate aggregate loss suffered by them proportionately two-thirds (TBS) and one-third (KSBC). In the meantime they agree that they will share reductions (pre-insolvency) and realisations (post-insolvency) in the same proportions, but applicable to the debt facilities only.

Dodgy AG becomes insolvent and at that point the total owed by Dodgy AG to KSBC is £100m ie the maximum exposure under its lending facilities.

However, because a number of the ancillary facilities provided by TBS did not crystallise (ie a standby letter of credit was never called because that part of Dodgy AG's business was hived off pre-enforcement) and a third party adopted the liability) the final liabilities of Dodgy AG to TBS are only £100m. Aggregate liabilities are therefore £200m.

The first step is for the banks to equalise their lending so that each is owed two-thirds and one-third of the aggregate exposure of £200m. This involves TBS making a payment of £33.334m to KSBC, such that the exposure of TBS is £133.334m and the exposure of KSBC is £66.666.

Total proceeds available in the insolvency of Dodgy AG are only £150m which are shared out proportionately so that TBS receives £100m and KSBC receives £50m.

There is, therefore, an aggregate loss of £150m.

TBS has suffered a loss of £33.33m, whilst B has suffered a loss of £16.666m.

TBS and KSBC have agreed that the loss of £150m should be shared proportionately and since these losses have already been shared proportionately no further payments are required.

2.134 Two banks, Alpha and Beta, are lending to a borrower in the construction sector, Cedric. Alpha provides a mixture of lending facilities (£100m) and ancillary facilities (£200m).

Beta provides lending facilities only (£200m).

Alpha and Beta agree that the ancillary facilities should be weighted at 100% and therefore the respective exposures of Alpha and Beta at the Standstill date are Alpha £300m and Beta £200m.

Alpha and Beta agree that upon an insolvency of Cedric they will share any ultimate aggregate loss suffered by them in proportion to their Standstill exposures (ie Alpha – 60%, Beta – 40%) and in the meantime will share repayments (pre-insolvency) and distributions (post-insolvency) in the same proportions. Beta is poorly advised and there are no equalisation arrangements.

At enforcement the total owed by Cedric to Beta is £200m (ie the maximum exposure under its lending facilities).

However, because a number of ancillary facilities provided by Alpha did not crystallise due to £140m of performance bonds never being called because Cedrics's business was hived off to a third party pre-enforcement who adopted the bond, the final liabilities of Cedric to Alpha are only £160m. Aggregate liabilities are therefore £360m.

Total proceeds available for distribution to the banks in the insolvency of Cedric are only £300m. Applying the agreed percentages (Alpha – 60% and Beta – 40%), A would be entitled to £180 and B would be entitled to £120m. However, Alpha's debt is only £160, therefore A gets £160m and B gets £140m. B has therefore suffered the whole of the loss of £60m.

Under the loss sharing arrangements, Alpha should have suffered 60% of the loss, ie £36m and Beta should only have suffered 40% of the loss ie £24m.

Accordingly, therefore, in order to share the losses as agreed Alpha must only pay Beta £36m, whereas had equalisation provisions been in place the payment would have been £56m because at the first stage of equalisation the £360m of exposure should have been equalised on the basis of 60% Alpha and 40% Beta ie £216m and £144m of exposure respectively. Due to the fact that Beta was holding £200m of exposure at enforcement he should have received a payment of £56m to equalise his exposure down to £144m and similarly because Alpha was holding £160m of exposure and not £216m he will have to make the payment of £56m. This is opposed to the payment of £36m which Alpha would have needed to make with simple loss sharing.

SCENARIO 4 – COMBINED EQUALISATION AND LOSS SHARING

2.135 Two banks, Starcap and Boyds, are lending to a borrower Potless.

Starcap provides a mixture of revolving credit facilities of £200m and ancillary facilities of £200m.

Boyds provides term lending facilities only of £200m.

Starcap and Boyds agree that applying an agreed 100% weighting to the ancillary facilities provided by Starcap the respective exposures at the Standstill date are Starcap £400m and Boyds £200m. The respective percentages of the exposure at the Standstill date are Starcap 66.667% and Boyds 33.333%.

Starcap and Boyds agree that upon the earlier of an insolvency of Potless or the date on which the security is enforced they will equalise their facilities. They will also share any aggregate loss suffered by them proportionately, and in the meantime will share repayments (pre-insolvency) and distributions (post-insolvency) proportionately.

Potless becomes insolvent and an administrator is appointed to Potless. On that date, Starcap's revolver is only drawn to £100m whereas Boyds's term loan remains at £200m.

The total amount outstanding under the lending facilities is £300m. The position under the ancillary facilities will not be known for some time. If at the interim stage the respective positions of the banks are to be equalised in order to correspond with their percentages of the exposure under the facilities at the Standstill date, Starcap should pay Boyds £100m so that they have an equalised exposure of Starcap £200m (66.667%) and Boyds £100m (33.333%) in the proportions of their lending exposure on the Standstill date.

Certain of Starcap's ancillary facilities do not crystallise and instead of having exposure under the ancillaries of £200m (Starcap's weighted exposure at the Standstill date) the actual exposure is only £150m.

As a consequence, Starcap's total exposure, including the £100m which it has paid to Boyds when the lending facilities were equalised is £350m and Boyds's total exposure is £100m.

In order to equalise the total aggregate exposure of £450m so that Starcap has 66.667% of the adjusted exposure (£300m) and Boyds has 33.334% (£150m) Boyds needs to pay £50m back to Starcap. At the second phase of equalisation Boyds's exposure is £150m (ie the £100m at phase 1 plus the £50m it has now paid to Starcap). Starcap's position is £300m (ie £200m at stage one plus £150m for the ancillary exposure less the £50m it recovers by way of a correcting equalisation payment from Boyds).

Realisations for the banks in the administration are relatively good and yield £400m. Of this two-thirds is distributed to Starcap (£266.668m) and one-third is distributed to Boyds (£133.332m). The net effect is that Starcap and Boyds having steadily equalised their exposure to retain the Day 1 status quo have now loss shared in the same proportions. Of the £50m loss suffered two-thirds (£33.332m) has been suffered by Starcap and one third (£16.668m) by Boyds.

SCENARIO 5 – A FURTHER DETAILED EXAMPLE

2.136 This example assumes:

— Three banks and one US Noteholder Group with a private placement.
— total lending facilities of £400m.
— existing security value of £95m.
— lending facilities utilisation on enforcement of £295m (£25m of existing security having been sold and the proceeds distributed to the relevant institutions).
— the new security realises £120m.

Banks	X	Y	Z	US Note-holders	Total
	£m	£m	£m	£m	
Facility utilisation at the relevant time	200	100	50	50	400
Consequential sharing percentage	50%	25%	12½%	12½%	100
Existing security value	70		25		95
Existing security realised pre-enforcement			25		25
Facility utilisation at enforcement	140	80	25	50	295
Notionally add back existing security realisations			25		
Notional utilisations (pre-equalisation)	140	80	50	50	320
Apply sharing percentages to 'equalise' utilisation ie 32 x sharing percentage	32 x 50% = 160	32 x 25% = 80	32 x 12½% = 40	32 x 12½% = 40	32 =32

Equalisations, payments and receipts	+ 20	-	(- 10)	(- 10)	
Post-equalisation utilisations	160	80	40	40	320
Final distributions realisations of 12m applied in sharing percentages	60	30	15	15	120
Therefore initial 'loss'	100	50	25	25	200
Subtract (on a notional basis) the existing security realisations retained			(25)		
Real interim 'loss' to each bank	100	50	nil	25	175
Disposals of other 'priority' assets subject to existing security	70				
Final loss to each bank	30	50	nil	25	105

Income equalisation

2.137 The concepts of loss sharing and equalisation effectively allocate risk post-enforcement but relative to Day 1 positions thus ensuring that no single creditor is better or worse off as a result of attempting the restructuring. Conversely, income equalisation deals with the allocation of reward and the distribution to institutions of the remuneration earned on the facilities during the restructuring period. Institutions that provide ancillary or revolving facilities may well request an income equalisation on the basis that a bank that is providing a fully drawn term loan which is not reduced during a restructuring will always receive full remuneration on the basis of a full utilisation and will also benefit from an equalisation payment if any other revolving lending facility is not fully drawn at the enforcement time. Conversely the ancillary and revolving facility providers who make such facilities available at a committed level will argue that they are comparatively disadvantaged since they will receive remuneration that will vary with the level of drawing and they will have to equalise their facilities.

2.138 Income equalisation provisions are quite complex to set up and monitor and their negotiation is likely to delay the execution of the restructuring agreement. In addition, the internal procedural difficulties for banks of not being able to book income to profit until the end of the restructuring when the income adjustment has been made, means that they are rarely included. Moreover, it is likely that the banks providing the ancillary and revolving facilities will also provide term facilities and so they are unlikely to pursue an income equalisation point. In any event the perceived inequality can always be tempered by uplifting the commitment fees that are payable on the revolving and ancillary facilities during the course of the restructuring.

Chapter 3

INFORMATION, DISCLOSURE AND YEAR END REPORTING

A INTRODUCTION

3.1 One of the most important prerequisites of a successful corporate restructuring is the availability of accurate information concerning the company and its trading and financial position. The availability of complete, up-to-date and accurate information will enable creditors to make an informed assessment of the company's position and determine (a) whether or not a corporate restructuring is viable, and (b) if it is, the most effective means to achieve it. Inevitably, the perceived cause of the company's difficulties will have a significant bearing on the level of business review that the lenders will require in order to enable them to determine an appropriate solution. This should not necessarily be perceived in a negative manner by the company because if the review is able to concur with the company's proposed capital improvements, operational turnaround and assessment of possible cost savings, the lenders may be persuaded to provide short and medium-term support in the form of interest and principal deferrals or equitisation of loans so as to create a competitive enterprise.

B ACCOUNTANT'S REPORT

3.2 As part of the assessment of a company and the viability of a restructuring it is common for investigating accountants to be engaged to investigate the company's financial position. The accountants are usually work-out specialists who are typically complemented by the relevant industry experts within their firm.

3.3   There is almost always a protracted debate between the company and its lenders as to whether the appointed firm of accountants should be the company's designated firm (usually its auditors) or whether a separate firm should be appointed by the lenders. The tension exists because the company will be reluctant to pay the costs of external accountants familiarising themselves with the situation and the group's operations. There is also a view that such external accountants, at least initially, consume a lot of management oxygen which might be better utilised addressing the causes of the company's distress and working on the solutions rather than educating outsiders. Conversely, the lenders will be seeking an independent review of the business that is not founded on management's perceptions of the business and their control and potential manipulation of their own accounting advisers. In cases where the financing only closed relatively recently or where there has been a fraud, a breakdown of information and reporting systems, a vacuum of information or the production of information by the company and its advisers that is questionable in terms of accuracy, then experience shows that the lenders will prevail and will usually succeed in having their own advisers appointed.

3.4   A potential compromise in these situations is for the company to suggest that its advisers will generate the information and liaise with the bank's advisers to distil the information, identify trends and patterns and formulate conclusions for the lenders. The company, on the basis of speed and efficiencies and cost usually justifies this. Inevitably the company and its accountants will have to agree the precise scope of work with the lenders and procure that its accountants extend an appropriate duty of care to the lenders. Alternatively, the lenders and the company may appoint accountants jointly so that the company will have a degree of input on the scope and role of the accountants. This will result in the accountants owing the company and the lenders a joint duty of care, which is a superior position for the company to be in.

3.5   The report will help identify the reasons why a company is in financial difficulties and make proposals for solving its problems. Whilst the accountant's fees will ordinarily be payable by the company the report is usually prepared for the benefit of all creditors, and will be relied upon by them. The company will be able to see the report although certain sections on management quality and capability and recommendations and conclusions may not be made available to the company.

C   CONFIDENTIALITY

3.6   Confidentiality is often the vital ingredient for a successful restructuring. As we will see in this Chapter, information relating to a listed company that is not public and which is 'inside' price sensitive information must be disclosed promptly through a Regulatory Information Service ('RIS'). However, where the information is commercially sensitive yet does not have the latter characteristics requiring prompt disclosure, a company's problems may increase if such commercially sensitive confidential information is made public prematurely or is otherwise disclosed to a third party. For example, customers and suppliers may impose harsher trading conditions or may stop dealing with the company altogether. For this reason the agreements or letters setting out the terms on which steering committees or restructuring co-ordinators are typically appointed contain detailed terms relating to the disclosure of information and confidentiality. Many corporates undergoing a restructuring usually request that these provisions are also extended to each of the lenders who will typically be required to countersign a letter appointing the steering committee or restructuring co-ordinator.

3.7 One of the main thrusts of these confidentiality provisions is to define 'confidential information'. Typically, confidential information means any information relating to the [Group], and any of its financings and facilities including, without limitation, information given orally and any document, electronic file or any other way of representing or recording information which contains or is derived or copied from such information including any records, contracts, books of account, budgets, reports, forecasts, projections or other information and also includes all notes, analyses, compilations, studies or other documents, whether prepared by the officers, or any member of the [Group] or by any of its, officers, directors, employees, representatives, agents or professional advisers.

3.8 Information that is or which becomes public knowledge other than as a direct or indirect result of any breach of confidentiality undertakings or is known to the finance parties before the date the information is disclosed to them, or which is lawfully obtained by the finance parties independently from the [Group] and which as far as the finance parties are aware, has not been obtained in violation of, and is not otherwise subject to, any obligation of confidentiality will be excluded from the scope of the confidentiality.

3.9 Such finance parties are invariably requested with respect to the information concerning the group and its affairs (which it receives in such capacity) to:

(a)   keep such information confidential and ensure that such relevant confidential information is protected with security measures and a degree of care that it would apply to its own confidential information;

(b)   not disclose to anyone the fact that such information has been made available to it;

(c)   in the case of a co-ordinator or steering committee member only, use such information for the purpose of performing its function as such an officer; and

(d)   use all reasonable endeavours to ensure that any person to whom it passes any such information (unless disclosed in accordance with an agreed permission) enters into and continues to be bound by a specific confidentiality agreement.

3.10 The agreed permissions by which information may be disclosed are listed below and include disclosures:

  (i) to professional advisers and to any such persons that have entered into and continue to be bound by a confidentiality agreement with the group;

 (ii) required by law or regulation or disclosure requested by any agency of state, a regulator or taxation authority with jurisdiction over any such an officer or their affiliates;

(iii) required by any court or any competent, judicial, governmental, supervisory or regulatory body;

(iv) which come into the public domain (other than as a result of a breach of a confidentiality undertaking); or

 (v) to auditors, professional advisers or rating agencies who are required in the course of their duties or role to receive such information.

3.11 Companies sometimes require that the relevant steering committee members or restructuring co-ordinator instruct the reporting accountants and their legal counsel to maintain the confidentiality of any information relating to the group that they receive, however most of the major accountancy firms will deal with confidentiality obligations specifically in their engagement letters and legal counsel will be obliged by their own professional rules of conduct to maintain confidentiality.

3.12 If there is already a Loan Market Association ('LMA') style facility agreement in place it may well be unnecessary for the various banks to execute a form of confidentiality undertaking since disclosure obligations will already be included in that facility agreement. Moreover, where the existing lender seeks to trade its debt and as a precursor disclose information to a potential transferee, the LMA facility will contain a form of confidentiality undertaking, or more likely will require the LMA standard form of confidentiality undertaking to be executed by any recipient of any confidential information. However, where there are creditors not subject to the terms of an existing confidentiality obligation or those provisions are felt to be inappropriate to deal with the complex flow of detailed information pursuant to a restructuring, it will be necessary for each recipient of information from a steering committee or restructuring co-ordinator to have initially signed up to a broadly equivalent form of LMA confidentiality undertaking in favour of the company.

D PUBLIC DISCLOSURE OF INFORMATION BY LISTED COMPANIES UNDERGOING A FINANCIAL RESTRUCTURING

Source and application of the Disclosure Rules

3.13 The general principles in relation to the public disclosure of information by listed companies are set out in the Disclosure Rules, which comprise three chapters of the Disclosure Rules and Transparency Rules sourcebook. The Listing, Prospectus, Disclosure and Transparency Rules sourcebook forms a specific section of the FSA Handbook[1]. The Disclosure Rules set out all the rules and guidance on disclosure made by the Financial Services Authority

('FSA') under the Financial Services and Markets Act 2000. The Disclosure Rules were introduced in order to implement key directives under the EU Financial Services Action Plan namely the Prospectus Directive[2], Market Abuse Directive[3] and Transparency Directive[4].

1   The FSA Handbook is periodically updated and this section is based on the February 2008 version of the Handbook.
2   Directive 2003/71/EC of 4 November 2003. The Directive sets out the initial disclosure obligations for issuers of securities that are offered to the public or admitted to trading on a regulated market in the EU.
3   Directive 2003/6/EC. This directive defines the behaviour considered to be insider dealing and market abuse and includes preventative measures aimed at making market abuse less likely to occur.
4   Directive 2004/109/EC of the European Parliament and of the Council of 15 December 2004 on the harmonisation of transparency requirements in relation to information about issuers whose securities are admitted to trading on a regulated market.

3.14 The disclosure obligations in Chapter 2 of the Disclosure Rules (DTR 2) apply to an issuer whose financial instruments are admitted to trading on a regulated market in the UK (such as the Official List of the London Stock Exchange)[1]. The Disclosure Rules are administered and enforced by the FSA which performs functions as the competent authority under Part VI of the Financial Services and Markets Act and, in that context, may use the name United Kingdom Listing Authority ('UKLA'). It should be noted that the rules do not extend to issuers who have securities quoted on the Alternative Investment Exchange and which do not have any other securities traded on the London Stock Exchange as a regulated market[2].

1   The definition of a 'regulated market' for these purposes under DTR 2 operates to exclude AIM listed companies from the DTRs. There is a separate disclosure regime for AIM listed companies that is considered in this section of the Chapter.
2   See AIM Rule 27.

3.15 The Disclosure Rules comprise three chapters of the Disclosure Rules and Transparency Rules sourcebook. DTR 1 and DTR 2 apply to an issuer whose financial instruments are admitted to trading on a regulated market in the UK or for which a request has been made for admission to trading on a regulated market in the UK, whereas DTR 3 applies to UK incorporated issuers of financial instruments[1] admitted to trading on a regulated market or for whose financial instruments a request has been made for admission to trading on a regulated market in the UK.

1   For these purposes the Disclosure Rules and Transparency Rules adopt the definition of 'financial instruments' used in the Markets in Financial Instruments Directive (MiFID) (2004/39/EC). MiFID revises the investment services directive and it had to be transposed into national law by 31 January 2007 and implemented by 1 November 2007.

3.16 DTR 1 sets out the application and purpose of the Disclosure Rules, the procedure to be adopted for modifications to or dispensation from the Disclosure Rules, penalties for breach, market abuse safe harbours and the issuer's obligation to take all reasonable care in notifying information to a RIS. DTR 2 in turn sets out the key obligation to announce inside information, the circumstances in which disclosure can be delayed or selective disclosures can be made, holding announcements, the obligation to compile and maintain insider lists and the publication of inside information on internet sites and the control of inside information.

3.17 The disclosure requirements in the Disclosure Rules run alongside the disclosure standards and continuing obligations of any Regulated Investment Exchange on which a company's shares are traded, for example, listed companies whose securities are traded on the London Stock Exchange must adhere to the Admission and Disclosure Standards[1].

---

[1] See the analysis of the Admission and Disclosure Standards at the end of this section.

The general principle

3.18 The fundamental tenet of the Disclosure Rules is that a listed company is obliged to disclose inside information[1] that directly concerns it as soon as possible via a RIS[2] unless disclosure of inside information is permitted[3]. The Disclosure Rules themselves contain rules and guidance in relation to the publication and control of inside information and the disclosure of transactions by persons discharging managerial responsibilities and their connected persons. The FSA have stated that the 'observance of the continuing [disclosure] obligations is essential to the maintenance of an orderly market in securities and of confidence in the financial system. The FSA therefore takes the most serious view of listed companies which fail to comply with these requirements'[4].

---

[1] As defined in the Financial Services and Markets Act 2000, s 118C.
[2] The RISs act as primary information providers by disseminating on behalf of listed companies the full text of regulatory announcements required by the Disclosure Rules to various news agencies such as Reuters.
[3] See DTR 2.5.1R and DTR 2.2.1R.
[4] See the FSA's 'Final Notice' to Marconi plc dated 11 March 2003 at www.fsa.gov.uk/pubs/final/marconi_11apr03.pdf.

Information gathering

3.19 The company and 'persons discharging managerial responsibilities' ('PDMRs')[1] or connected persons[2] must provide to the FSA as soon as possible following a request (i) any information that the FSA considers appropriate to protect investors or to ensure the smooth operation of the market, and (ii) any other information or explanation that the FSA may require to verify whether the Disclosure Rules are being and have been complied with. The guidance notes that the FSA may record calls and request responses to be made in writing.

---

[1] The so-called PDMRs are (i) the directors of the issuer, (ii) senior executives of the issuer who are not directors but who have regular access to inside information (relating directly or indirectly to the issuer and the power to make managerial decisions affecting the future development and business prospects of the issuer (see the Financial Services and Markets Act 2000, s 96B(1)).
[2] This includes spouses, relatives, associated body corporates, trustees of related trusts and partners of the PDMRs and a body corporate in which a PDMR within an issuer or any person connected with him by virtue of the above relationships is a director or other senior

executive who has the power to make management decisions affecting the future development and business prospects of that body corporate (see the Financial Services and Markets Act 2000, s 96B(1)).

Inside information

3.20 'Inside information'[1] is defined by reference to the Financial Services and Markets Act 2000, s 118C and in summary constitutes information that is precise, has not been made public or generally available, relates directly or indirectly to the listed company (and not to companies or financial instruments in general) and, if made public, would be likely to have a significant effect on the price of the listed company's financial instruments. It should be noted however that where the information is confidential and commercially sensitive but does not amount to 'inside information' the Disclosure Rules do not apply and the confidential nature of the information can be preserved.

[1]   Where the information does not amount to 'inside information' the Disclosure Rules do not apply.

3.21 Information is precise if it indicates circumstances that exist or may reasonably be expected to come into existence or an event that has occurred or may reasonably be expected to occur and is specific enough to enable a conclusion to be drawn as to the possible effect of those circumstances or that event on the price of qualifying investments[1].

[1]   See the Financial Services and Markets Act 2000, s 118C(5).

3.22 The Committee of European Securities Regulators ('CESR') has provided some guidance (albeit non-binding) on what constitutes 'precise' information in this context[1]. In determining whether a set of circumstances exist or an event has occurred, a key issue is whether there is firm and objective evidence, as opposed to rumours or speculation. When considering what may reasonably be expected to come into existence, the key issue is whether it is reasonable to draw this conclusion based on the ex ante information available at the time. Other than in exceptional circumstances or unless requested to comment by a competent regulator pursuant to art 6(7) of the Market Abuse Directive[2], issuers are under no obligation to respond to market rumours that are without substance.

[1]   See CESR's Level 3, second set of guidance on implementation of the Market Abuse Directive published in July 2007.
[2]   Directive 2003/6/EC.

3.23 Similarly, the CESR has expressed the view that if the information concerns a process which occurs in stages, such as a restructuring perhaps, each stage of the process as well as the overall process could be information of a precise nature. However, this would appear to be too conservative and companies must be able to conduct restructuring negotiations with a degree of privacy.

3.24 The CESR has also commented that it is not necessary for a piece of information to be comprehensive to be precise and a piece of information could be considered precise even if it refers to alternatives. For example, the fact that a company has a number of restructuring options such as a rights issue or a disposal programme, either of which will be necessary to implement a de-gearing strategy. However, unless either of these options is at an advanced stage of consideration and negotiation or there has been significant press speculation there will be no need to disclose if appropriate insider lists are maintained and the specific grounds for delaying disclosure of the information as specified in Article 3.1 of Directive 2003/124/EC (the Implementing Directive in respect of the Market Abuse Directive)[1] as reflected in Disclosure and Transparency Rule 2.5.3G apply[2].

[1] Commission Directive 2003/124/EC of 22 December 2003 Implementing the Market Abuse Directive (Directive 2003/6/EC of the European Parliament and of the Council) as regards the definition and public disclosure of inside information and the definition of market manipulation (Text with EEA relevance), Official Journal L339, 24.12.2003 pp 0070–0072.
[2] See the section of this Chapter entitled 'Specific grounds for delaying disclosure' for more detailed analysis and commentary on these provisions.

3.25 When assessing whether information has already been made public, companies should note that merely because it is possible for the information to be obtained by the public, it has not been 'publicly' disclosed for the purposes of the Disclosure Rules. However, if information can be obtained by research or analysis by users of the market it will tend to be construed as 'generally available'. Moreover, information can be publicly available even if it was not disclosed by the company in the manner required by the Disclosure Rules and the method of disclosure in itself constitutes a breach of the Disclosure Rules.

3.26 The Disclosure Rules contain guidance to assist listed companies in identifying inside information. The Disclosure Rules state that it is not possible to prescribe percentage changes in a listed company's share price, for example, that would trigger the disclosure obligation (by being interpreted as a 'significant effect' on the share price), as this will vary from company to company. It is clear from the FSA's perspective that they will not prescribe such parameters, and that it is the listed companies themselves and their advisers who are best placed to make an assessment of the potential price effect of information[1].

[1] DTR 2.2.4G(2).

3.27 In practice, companies should involve their advisers in difficult decisions[1], not only for their advice, but also to demonstrate sufficient measures and controls to assist it in identifying inside information, and therefore complying with the Disclosure Rules (in the event that the FSA investigates a particular decision to disclose, or not to disclose, certain information). The fact that information is commercially sensitive does not necessarily mean that it is inside information.

[1]   The FSA itself has expressed the view that the company should engage with its advisers to make an initial assessment of whether information is inside information.

3.28 Much of the FSA's guidance on identifying inside information relates to what is known as the 'reasonable investor test'. This test requires listed companies, when determining the likely price significance of information, to assess whether it would be likely to be used by a reasonable investor as part of the basis of his investment decisions and would therefore in turn be likely to have a significant effect on the price of the listed company's securities[1]. As a general rule, the more specific the information, the greater the risk of the information being inside information, for example, actual data relating to current like for like sales compared to an equivalent previous trading period which indicated a sharp decline in trading performance would be more likely to constitute inside information.

[1]   See DTR 2.2.4G(1).

3.29 The reasonable investor test requires an issuer to take account of the fact that the significance of information will vary widely between issuers and depend on a variety of factors such as the issuer's size and recent developments and market sentiment about the issuer and the sector in which it operates. The issuer is to assume that a reasonable investor will make investment decisions relating to the investment to maximise his economic self-interest[1]. It is however important to note that the reasonable investor test does not dislocate the need for the information to be inside information and for the information to be likely to have a significant price effect if it were made public. The reasonable investor test simply sets the context in which an issuer will need to make its assessment of the likely price significance of the information in question.

[1]   See DTR 2.2.5G.

3.30 The Disclosure Rules also set out certain categories of information which are likely to be considered relevant to a reasonable investor's investment decision, which include information which affects:

(i)   the assets and liabilities of the listed company;
(ii)   the performance, or the expectation of the performance, of the listed company's business;
(iii) the financial condition of the listed company;
(iv)   the course of the listed company's business;
(v)   major new developments in the business of the listed company; and
(vi)   information previously disclosed to the market[1].

[1]   See DTR 2.2.6G.

3.31 Information relevant to the commencement of a listed company's financial restructuring would almost certainly be relevant, since this information seems clearly to affect the company's financial condition, and may equally affect each of the other categories as well (its performance or the expectation of its performance, for example). This sometimes results in company's issuing a rather bland statement that they are in discussions with their bankers or that they have breached a financial covenant. However, the successive stages of restructuring negotiations should not ordinarily need to be disclosed as the guidance recognises that the decision on whether a piece of information is inside information may be finely balanced and that the listed company, with the help of its advisers, will need to exercise its judgment on each set of facts.

3.32 The CESR provides a non-exhaustive, indicative list of events that might constitute inside information and set out below are certain events specifically related to a restructuring that could potentially constitute inside information that might need to be disclosed by a distressed corporate:

(i) Changes in control and control agreements.
(ii) Changes in management and supervisory boards.
(iii) Changes in auditors or any other information related to the auditors' activity.
(iv) Decisions to increase or decrease share capital.
(v) Restructurings or reorganisations that have an effect on the issuer's assets and liabilities, financial position or profits and losses.
(vi) Filing of petitions in bankruptcy or the issuing of orders for bankruptcy proceedings.
(vii) Legal disputes.
(viii) Revocation or cancellation of credit lines by one or more banks.
(ix) Changes in asset value.
(x) Insolvency of relevant debtors.
(xi) Reduction of real properties' values.
(xii) Decrease or increase in value of financial instruments in portfolio.
(xiii) Decrease in value of patents or rights or intangible assets due to market innovation.
(xiv) Serious product liability or environmental damages cases.
(xv) Changes in expected earnings or losses.
(xvi) Relevant orders received from customers, their cancellation or important changes.
(xvii) Withdrawal from or entering into new core business areas.
(xviii) Relevant changes in the investment policy of the issuer.
(xix) Ex-dividend date, dividend payment date and amount of the dividend; changes in dividend policy payment.

Company processes – disclosure committees

3.33 The Disclosure Rules contain specific guidance for the company's directors to carefully and continuously monitor any changes in the company's circumstances that may mean that an announcement is required[1]. As a consequence many listed companies adopting best practice have established disclosure committees to ensure that the board can comply with the obligations imposed by the Disclosure Rules. The disclosure committee, which should be staffed with executive officers, will need to monitor performance and give consideration to whether there has been a change in the company's expectation as to its performance. They must draw any material change in expectation as soon as possible to the attention of the board for it to review and the disclosure committee will make a formal decision on any required announcement. Obviously, the disclosure committee should consult its financial advisers as early as possible if the company's circumstances are under consideration and its expectation as to its performance is expected to change.

1   See DTR 2.2.8G.

Insider lists

3.34 The Disclosure Rules oblige a listed company (and persons acting on its behalf, such as advisers) to maintain a list of those persons working for the company or the persons acting on its behalf who have access to inside information relating directly or indirectly to the issuer, whether such access is on a regular or occasional basis. This is known as an 'insider list', which must contain certain information in relation to the people on it, and be promptly updated when any facts or circumstances change (for example, to add additional people to, or to remove people from, it).

Timing of the disclosure and the ability to delay

3.35 The Disclosure Rules generally require information to be notified to a RIS 'as soon as possible' in order for it to be made public. The Listing Rules that preceded the Disclosure Rules required the disclosure of price sensitive material 'without delay'. Given that the FSA has indicated that in most cases the new disclosure regime under the Disclosure Rules should not be any different to that under the old Listing Rules[1], market precedents and FSA determinations under the old regime remain helpful and relevant. In this regard the FSA's 'Final Notice' to Marconi plc dated 11 March 2003[2] in relation to Marconi's breach of paragraph 9.2 of the old Listing Rules is particularly illuminating.

1   See the special edition of the UKLA newsletter 'List!', Issue No 9, June 2005.
2   www.fsa.gov.uk/pubs/final/marconi_11apr03.pdf.

3.36 The FSA in its public statement on Marconi declared that on the facts it was satisfied that on 2 July 2001 at around 14.00 Marconi changed its expectation as to its performance for the half year ending 30 September 2001 and the full year ending 31 March 2002. The FSA further concluded that such a change, if made public, was likely to lead to a substantial movement in the price of its listed securities and gave rise to an obligation to make a disclosure without delay[1].

1   See the FSA's 'Final Notice' to Marconi plc dated 11 March 2003 at para 2 'Decision' and para 39 'Conclusion' at www.fsa.gov.uk/pubs/final/marconi_11apr03.pdf.

3.37 The FSA effectively concluded that 'without delay' required a notification by, at the latest, the evening of 3 July 2001. By not actually making a disclosure until 18.41 on 4 July 2001, Marconi was in breach of its disclosure obligations because at 14.00 on 2 July 2001 management accounts had been reviewed by the CEO and the CFO and they changed their expectations as to Marconi's performance such that they knew that when that change was made public it was likely to lead to a substantial movement in the price of its listed securities[1]. As a consequence Marconi's obligation to inform the market arose at that time and the absence of the Deputy CEO on business was not a sufficient reason to delay such a notification[2]. Equally the FSA felt that Marconi placed too much importance on the repeated refinement of the figures and the language in the trading statement at the expense of its obligations to the market[3]. Indeed, the FSA suggest that planned board meetings should be brought forward in such a scenario, such that in the Marconi case this would have facilitated a prompt disclosure by the evening of 3 July 2001. However, the FSA has also indicated that it is unlikely to regard an inability to convene a full, physical board meeting as a justifiable reason for delaying an announcement.

[1] The 25-fold increase in the volume of securities traded after Marconi's listing was restored after a temporary suspension, as well as the 54% reduction in the share price are indicative of the price sensitivity of the information contained in the trading statement and the impact on the market of being prevented from trading for an entire day.
[2] See the FSA's 'Final Notice' to Marconi plc dated 11 March 2003 at para 39.
[3] See the FSA's 'Final Notice' to Marconi plc dated 11 March 2003 at para 40.

3.38 The Marconi case also provided the opportunity for the FSA to comment on the responsibilities of boards of listed companies and stipulated that the board of a public company cannot comply with its obligation to make a disclosure without delay 'unless its executive officers monitor performance and give continuous consideration as to whether there has been a change in the company's expectation as to performance. They must draw any material change in expectation without delay to the attention of the board for it to review and make a formal decision on any required announcement'[1]. Even if a board is acting in good faith in delaying a disclosure it will be irrelevant as a finding of bad faith is not a requirement in connection with the FSA determining that a breach of the disclosure regime has occurred.

[1] See the FSA's 'Final Notice' to Marconi plc dated 11 March 2003 at para 37.

3.39 In summary, the FSA have on a number of occasions declared that the period of time which it is reasonable for a listed company to take in making an announcement regarding a change in its expectations will depend upon all the circumstances relevant to the particular situation in which the company finds itself and in which the change occurs. The decision to delay will of course be judged by the FSA with the benefit of hindsight. As a consequence it is clear that a company that is to undergo a restructuring as a result of such a change, or which sees its prospects for implementing a particular restructuring change significantly[1], must prioritise its disclosure obligations accordingly. It will therefore be important for the company to be able to demonstrate that it reacted reasonably and expeditiously to the event in question, and made an appropriate decision to delay disclosure.

[1] As was the case with Marconi.

3.40 If a listed company is faced with an unexpected and significant event, a short delay may be acceptable if it is necessary to clarify the situation (so that a proper announcement may be made, if appropriate). A holding announcement should be used if the listed company believes there is a danger of inside information leaking before the facts and their impact can be confirmed[1].

> [1]   See Holding announcements, paragraph 2.2 of UKLA Newsletter List!, Issue No 9, June 2005 (www.practicallaw.com/3-200-9436) and Listing Principles 1 and 2.

Specific grounds for delaying disclosure

3.41 Although the general obligation imposed by the Disclosure Rules is to announce inside information as soon as possible, a listed company is entitled to delay disclosure in certain circumstances, such as where it is negotiating a transaction. Similarly, art 6.2 of the Market Abuse Directive[1] provides that an issuer may delay the disclosure of inside information so as to avoid prejudicing its legitimate interests, provided that such omission would not be likely to mislead the public and provided that the issuer is able to ensure the confidentiality of that information.

> [1]   Directive 2003/6/EC. This directive defines the behaviour considered to be insider dealing and market abuse and includes preventative measures aimed at making market abuse less likely to occur.

3.42 Article 3.1 of Directive 2003/124/EC (the Implementing Directive in respect of the Market Abuse Directive)[1] recognises two circumstances where legitimate interests justifying delaying public disclosure may exist:

(a)   negotiations in course, or related elements, where the outcome or normal pattern of those negotiations would be likely to be affected by public disclosure; and

(b)   decisions taken or contracts made by the management body of the issuer which need the approval of another body of the issuer to be effective.

> [1]   Commission Directive 2003/124/EC of 22 December 2003 Implementing the Market Abuse Directive (Directive 2003/6/EC of the European Parliament and of the Council) as regards the definition and public disclosure of inside information and the definition of market manipulation, OJ L339, 24.12.2003, pp 70–72.

3.43 Article 3, which has direct effect under English law, is extremely helpful in a restructuring context because it anticipates the disclosure dilemma faced by many listed companies of having to conform with its disclosure obligations whilst not prejudicing legitimate interests by conducting each stage of the restructuring in the full glare of the press. Article 3 should not be construed as a full exoneration from disclosure but it will permit restructuring negotiations to be concluded and for an announcement of the outcome of those negotiations to then be disclosed expeditiously to the market. Article 3 is therefore a well thought out provision that permits listed companies to delay disclosure where a sensitive and confidential restructuring is taking place if the fact of the restructuring or the nature of the company's financial and trading problems (to the extent that it constitutes precise price sensitive information) has already been disclosed.

3.44 Article 3 expressly provides that:

'For the purposes of applying Article 6(2) of Directive 2003/6/EC (the Market Abuse Directive), legitimate interests may, in particular, relate to the following non-exhaustive circumstances:

(a) negotiations in course, or related elements, where the outcome or normal pattern of those negotiations would be likely to be affected by public disclosure. In particular, in the event that the financial viability of the issuer is in grave and imminent danger, although not within the scope of the applicable insolvency law, public disclosure of information may be delayed for a limited period where such a public disclosure would seriously jeopardise the interest of existing and potential share-holders by undermining the conclusion of specific negotiations designed to ensure the long-term financial recovery of the issuer;'

3.45 Notwithstanding the wide construct given to the concept of 'inside information' referred to above, the CESR guidance in relation to art 3 is also helpful to companies undergoing a restructuring because it expressly states that the art 3.1 circumstances are non-exhaustive and that it is open to issuers to delay the disclosure of information in other situations, provided the conditions in art 6(2) of the Market Abuse Directive apply. CESR declined to provide further examples of other circumstances where there might be legitimate interests justifying a delay in public disclosure, but provides indicative examples of the two circumstances mentioned in the Implementing Directive.

3.46 The FSA also acknowledges that investors understand that some information must be kept confidential until developments are at a stage when an announcement can be made without prejudicing the legitimate interests of the listed company, and therefore a delay is permitted (under the listed company's own responsibility) 'such as not to prejudice its legitimate interests' and provided that:

(a) such omission would not be likely to mislead the public;
(b) any person receiving the information owes the listed company a duty of confidentiality (howsoever arising); and
(c) the listed company is able to ensure the confidentiality of that information[1].

[1] See DTR 2.5.1R.

3.47 As with art 3 of the Implementing Directive, DTR 2.5.1R similarly provides guidance as to circumstances which may indicate legitimate interests of the issuer (and so justify delay in public disclosure), including negotiations in course or related elements where the outcome or normal pattern of these negotiations would be likely to be affected by public disclosure. Whilst this does not allow a company undergoing a restructuring to delay public disclosure of the fact that it is in financial difficulty or its worsening financial condition and will be limited to the fact or substance of the negotiations to deal with such a situation[1], it does allow a company to avoid conducting its restructuring in the full glare of the business pages. The distressed company will initially make an assessment as to whether it has a legitimate interest which would be prejudiced by the disclosure of certain inside information and the exception will be available only where the issuer's financial viability is likely to be significantly prejudiced. Public disclosure of the information may be delayed for a limited time where it would seriously jeopardise the interests of the company and the company stakeholders (employees, a defined benefit scheme and its shareholders) by undermining the conclusion of specific negotiations focused on the company's continuation as a viable going concern.

[1]   See DTR 2.5.3G.

3.48 It is submitted that this exemption should be capable of being fully utilised in a restructuring scenario, where the negotiation of the restructuring in a public forum would impair the attitudes to the listed company of financial creditors, trade creditors, suppliers, employees, credit insurers and many other interested parties, thereby prejudicing its negotiating position and the success of the restructuring. However, it is important to note that, where a listed company is in financial difficulty or subject to a worsening financial condition, this ability to delay disclosure is restricted to the fact or substance of the negotiations to deal with the situation and does not permit a delay in announcing the underlying problem or indeed the worsening problem.

Communication with third parties

3.49 A listed company that is allowed to delay disclosure of inside information may selectively disclose the information to certain people (in the normal course of their profession, duties or employment) provided that such persons owe the company a duty of confidentiality. The people covered by this provision of the Disclosure Rules include advisers, negotiating counterparties, employee representatives, major shareholders, lenders and credit-rating agencies. It should be possible to apply this exemption to the parties involved in restructuring negotiations given that they will be constrained by a confidentiality undertaking or by legal or professional duties to preserve confidentiality.

3.50 This exemption will not however apply to disclosures made to journalists since DTR 2.2.10G of the Disclosure Rules provides that public disclosure should be conducted in accordance with the Disclosure Rules through a RIS. In addition, the press are hardly likely to owe the company a duty of confidentiality and so such a selective disclosure to the press (especially over the weekend as part of a PR campaign) would not qualify as a valid communication disclosure to a third party.

3.51 In these circumstances it is critical to note, however, that delaying disclosure is only permitted if the company is able to ensure the confidentiality of that information within the group of permitted recipients. It must therefore be prepared to record the basis or nature of a confidentiality undertaking owed to it by a third party and be ready to make an announcement as soon as possible if there is a breach of confidentiality (which would also be likely to jeopardise negotiations, and therefore impair the value of the listed company for all stakeholders).

3.52 As a practical matter, however, the provisions on delaying disclosure, and the ability to disclose selectively, do assist UK listed companies to maintain confidentiality until the major elements of a restructuring have been finalised, where premature release of the ongoing restructuring process would otherwise be prejudicial to legitimate interests and more misleading than informative.

Applications to the FSA to dispense with the Disclosure Rules

3.53 A distressed company may apply to the FSA in writing for modification or dispensation of any of the Disclosure Rules. At least five business days' notice of such an application must ordinarily be given to the FSA before the proposed modification or dispensation of the Disclosure Rules is to take effect. The application may be used by a company undergoing a restructuring process but it must contain all relevant information such as details of the restructuring, why the dispensation or modification is required, details of any special requirements requested by the distressed listed company and include copies of all documents relevant to the application[1].

[1] See DTR 1.2.

3.54 Consistent with the historic approach taken by the FSA under the similar procedure available under paragraph 9.8 of the preceding Listing Rules, this dispensation is likely to be granted only in exceptional circumstances such as when an announcement in the ordinary course might jeopardise the company's ability to continue to trade.

Market rumour and press speculation

3.55 Market rumour and press speculation can lead to a careful analysis of the Disclosure Rules, in order to assess whether an announcement obligation has arisen. For example, where such rumour or speculation is largely accurate, and the underlying information is inside information, then it will be likely that the listed company cannot delay disclosure since it cannot ensure the confidentiality of the inside information[1]. On the other hand, the knowledge that rumour and speculation is false is not likely to amount to inside information and, even if it does amount to inside information, the issuer will be likely to delay disclosure (perhaps indefinitely)[2].

[1] See DTR 2.7.1R and DTR 2.7.2R.
[2] See DTR 2.7.3R.

Misleading information

3.56 A company undergoing a restructuring process will be tempted to produce general disclosures which do not fully inform the market of all aspects of the restructuring. The objective of wanting to avoid 'washing dirty linen in public' is not particularly easy to achieve because the company is under a specific regulatory obligation to take all reasonable care to ensure that any information it provides to a RIS is not misleading, false or deceptive and does not omit anything likely to affect the import of the information[1].

[1]   See DTR 2.7.3G.

The Listing Principles

3.57 In addition, the FSA's Listing Principles apply in relation to listed companies' obligations under the Disclosure Rules (and the Listing Rules). Listing Principles 2 and 4 are of particular relevance in this regard.

3.58 In the context of the Disclosure Rules, Listing Principle 2 requires listed companies to have systems and controls in place to ensure that information is properly identified in a timely manner and that this information, and whether it should be disclosed, is properly considered by the company. Directors should carefully and continuously monitor whether changes in the circumstances of the listed company are such that an announcement obligation has arisen under the Disclosure Rules. Listed companies also need to establish effective arrangements to control access to inside information and deal with other procedural aspects of the Disclosure Rules (including establishing insider lists, as mentioned above).

3.59 Under Listing Principle 4, a listed company must communicate information to holders and potential holders of its listed securities in such a way as to avoid the creation or continuance of a false market – designed to ensure that the market is updated with accurate and timely information.

Interaction with the 'market abuse' regime

3.60 Listed companies, their directors, sponsors and advisers need to be aware that the disclosure obligations set out in the Disclosure Rules also overlap with the 'market abuse' regime set out in FSMA 2000, s 118 (which is discussed in further detail below). It is possible that the failure to make an effective disclosure could amount to market abuse, although certain 'safe harbours' in the FSA's Code of Market Conduct protect non-disclosure which is carried out in compliance with, for example, the Disclosure Rules. Therefore, a person complying with his obligations under the Disclosure Rules, the Listing Rules or other rules (such as the Companies Act) is unlikely to be affected by the market abuse regime in normal circumstances – although specific advice may need to be sought for specific situations.

Sanctions for breaching the Disclosure Rules

3.61 The FSA may impose a variety of sanctions for a breach of the Disclosure Rules. At one end of the enforcement spectrum the FSA may decide to give the issuer or relevant person a private warning. As an alternative the FSA may publicly censure the company in question and/or any person who was at the material time a director of the issuer, or a PDMR, or a person 'connected' to that director or PDMR and who was knowingly concerned in the contravention[1]. If the FSA does intend to take censure action against such persons, it must give them a warning notice.

[1]   See the Financial Services and Markets Act 2000, s 91(2) and (3).

3.62 A notable censure was made against Iceland plc (now The Big Food Group plc) on the basis that Iceland's financial trading performance in the period September 2000 to December 2000 had deteriorated significantly and that by 13 December 2000 an obligation had arisen under the (then applicable) Listing Rules to make an announcement about a change in the performance of Iceland's business. In addition, by January 2001, another obligation to make an announcement had arisen because of a deterioration in Iceland's financial performance over Christmas. These failures were not rectified until announcements were released on 22 and 31 January 2001. According to the FSA, Iceland also failed to take all reasonable care to ensure that an announcement issued on 13 December 2001 in connection with trading performance and merger benefits following the acquisition of Booker plc, was not misleading.

3.63 In addition, the FSA has the power to fine the issuer and/or a director or a PDMR or a person 'connected' to that director or PDMR who was knowingly concerned in the breach[1]. FSMA requires the FSA to have a policy to determine the amount of a penalty having regard to the seriousness of the contravention in question in relation to the nature of the requirement contravened, the extent to which that contravention was deliberate or reckless and whether the person on whom the penalty is to be imposed is an individual[2]. The FSA's policy on financial penalties for breach of the Disclosure Rules and Listing Rules is contained in the Enforcement Manual[3]. In its policy, the FSA states that it will consider all relevant circumstances of a contravention when it determines whether to impose a sanction. To ensure flexibility of approach there is no tariff of penalties for different kinds of contravention.

[1]   See the Financial Services and Markets Act 2000, s 91(1) and (1A).
[2]   This was the first time that the FSA exercised its statutory powers to fine a director of a listed company.
[3]   See paragraphs 21.6 to 21.10, FSA Enforcement Manual.

3.64 The breach of the Disclosure Rules by Sportsworld is a good example of the FSA's approach to enforcement. On 29 March 2004 the FSA released a public statement censuring Sportsworld Media Group plc for breaching clause 9.2 of the Listing Rules. Sportsworld's former CEO Geoffrey John

Brown was also fined for being knowingly concerned in the breach[1]. Sportsworld revised down its profit estimate of £16.1m for the forthcoming financial year in its 3 October announcement and repeated this in its preliminary results announcements on 29 November 2001. Subsequent management information that became available in the Christmas holiday period of 2001 indicated that the profit projections would not be met. Despite the situation becoming more apparent in the weeks following 24 December 2001, the board did not meet at any time until 25 January 2002. There was also clear evidence of a lack of board supervision and control of announcements as the board did not meet at any time between 17 September 2001, when the budget for the year ending 30 June 2002 was agreed, and 25 January 2002. The board eventually met on 25 January 2002 to discuss the changed circumstances and a trading statement. The company announced a reduced full year projected profit expectation of £9–10m on 28 January 2002. The FSA determined that if the information known within the company and to the CEO on 24 December 2001 concerning the changes in the performance of the company's business and/or the expectation as to its performance had been known to the market, it would have been likely to have led to a substantial movement in the price of the company's listed securities.

[1] This was the first time that the FSA exercised its statutory powers to fine a director of a listed company.

3.65 In its 'Final Notice' relating to breaches of the Disclosure Rules by Sportsworld, the FSA made it clear that a decision to disclose inside information involves both subjective and objective assessments: the assessment of the issuer's (subjective) expectation and the (objective) assessment of the likely market impact of any change in that expectation. The FSA specifically commented that in the absence of a change to the 'headline' full year profit expectation, a change in the phasing of that profit through the financial year could still, if made public, be likely to lead to a substantial movement in its share price. Indeed, it is not open to listed companies or their directors to refrain from informing the market of price sensitive information concerning the company's adverse performance on the basis of a belief that lost ground may be recovered in the remainder of the financial year. The market should be given the opportunity, via an announcement, to assess a company's optimism in those circumstances and the credibility of the company's increasingly ambitious expectations for the remainder of the year.

3.66 The FSA was able to conclude that the relevant information was inside information and that it should have been accelerated to board level and been made the subject of an announcement without delay. The failure to disclose until 28 January 2002 was a continuing breach of its obligations under Listing Rule 9.2. The FSA also stated that the CEO was required to be familiar with the requirements of the Disclosure Rules and, as he had knowledge of all the relevant facts, he was ultimately responsible for the company's failure to make a timely announcement. It was his duty to ensure that the full board was provided with the relevant information and to ask the board to consider the issue of an announcement without delay. In failing to do so he was knowingly concerned in the company's breach of its obligations to make a prompt disclosure. The breach was considered so serious in view of the length of the delay, the impact or potential impact on the market that a fine was considered appropriate.

3.67 Similarly, in May 2004, Universal Salvage plc, a vehicle salvage company, was subject to fines because it failed to disclose the loss of a major contract with Direct Line[1]. The company was informed of the loss of the contract on 18 March and whilst it may have been possible to delay an announcement for a short period in order to consult further with Direct Line and to assess the impact of the contract loss, the company did not make an announcement until 23 April. As a result of this serious and continuing breach[2], the company was fined £90,000 for breaching the previous version of the Listing Rules and its former CEO Martin Christopher Hynes was fined £10,000 for being knowingly concerned in the breach.

[1] See //www.fsa.gov.uk/pubs/final/universal_19may04.pdf.
[2] The share price of the company fell from 468p to 215p upon the announcement being made.

3.68 Fines are becoming progressively higher and in 2005 the FSA published a final notice and imposed a fine of £450,000 on Pace Micro Technology plc for failing to reveal in its interim results announcement on 8 January 2002 that its trade credit insurance in respect of one of its largest customers had been withdrawn. The largest fine imposed on a company was the £17m levied on Shell Transport and Trading Company, Royal Dutch Petroleum Company and the Royal Dutch/Shell Group of companies for the market abuse and breach of the Disclosure Rules as a result of substantial misstatements of its proved reserves.

3.69 Under DTR 1.4.1R, the FSA may suspend the relevant financial instruments from trading for such period as it may determine if there are reasonable grounds to suspect non-compliance with the Disclosure Rules. Notwithstanding the suspension, the obligations of the company, PDMRs and connected persons under the Disclosure Rules continue[1]. Inevitably, the FSA at its broad discretion can also impose specific conditions for the lifting of the relevant suspension where the company makes an application to lift a suspension under FSMA 2000, s 96C[2].

[1] See DTR 1.4.2R.
[2] See DTR 1.4.3R.

3.70 In its accompanying guidance the FSA provides specific examples of when the FSA may impose suspension for breach of the Disclosure Rules. These examples, which are not limited to the examples set forth in the guidance, include a scenario where the company fails to make an announcement to a RIS as required by the Disclosure Rules within the time limit or where there is a leak of inside information and the issuer is unable to issue an appropriate RIS announcement within a reasonable time.

3.71 The SFI Group plc censure in 2003 is a very good example of how the FSA applies the various enforcement weapons in its armoury. When SFI announced its preliminary financial results for the year ended 31 May 2002 on 30 July 2002, its net current assets had been overstated and the liabilities had been understated as a result of accounting errors and serious failures in managing cashflow and capital expenditure. The FSA found that SFI had failed to take reasonable care to ensure that the announcement was not misleading or false because its accounting systems and controls were inappropriate for its business and growth, did not determine the current or historical financial position reliably and were not robust enough to support internal forecasts and projections. In addition, during the relevant period SFI did not have a finance director for part of the time. It is however illuminating to analyse why the FSA merely censured SFI as opposed to imposing a fine. In this regard the FSA suggest in the censure that a fine was not imposed because of SFI's serious financial position and because there was no evidence of deliberate breach or disregard for the Listing Rules. The understatement of liabilities had been a consequence of poor systems and SFI notified the UKLA as soon as it became aware of the overstatement in its accounts, thereby facilitating immediate suspension of its shares. SFI also co-operated fully with the FSA and instituted a thorough review leading to a three-year recovery plan. New management and strategies were installed and the finance department's structure and processes were changed. It would appear that the co-operative attitude of SFI and its advisers and SFI's previous good record were also highly relevant to the decision of the FSA not to impose a fine.

Fraud Act 2006

3.72 The Fraud Act 2006, effective from 15 January 2007, creates a general offence of fraud which may be committed by failing to disclose information. The penalty for this general offence is up to 10 years' imprisonment and/or a fine. The general offence focuses on the offenders' intentions (rather than the outcome of their actions, such as the deception of the victim) and this may lead to it being used in preference to other pieces of specialist legislation. For example, the offence of fraud by failure to disclose information may be used alongside or in preference to legislation requiring directors to comply with a duty to disclose information (such as inside information) to the market or to provide complete and accurate accounting information.

The Admission and Disclosure Standards of the London Stock Exchange

3.73 The disclosure requirements in the Disclosure Rules run alongside the disclosure standards and continuing obligations imposed on listed companies whose securities are traded on the London Stock Exchange as set out in the Admission and Disclosure Standards and at the date of publication of this book the most up to date version is November 2007[1]. Given that the London Stock Exchange is a 'recognised investment exchange' it must ensure that all securities admitted to trading on its markets are conducted in accordance with the regulatory obligations set out in the FSA's sourcebook for recognised investment exchanges. The Admission and Disclosure Standards do not apply to the Alternative Investment Market operated by the London Stock Exchange as this is not a regulated market[2]. Separate disclosure rules apply to the Alternative Investment Market and these are considered in the next section.

[1] www.londonstockexchange.com/NR/rdonlyres/F3F9984E-3AB5–4923-BFF4-
    F3801C07211F/0 /LondonStockExchangeAdmissionandDisclosureStandards.pdf
[2] See AIM Rule 27.

3.74 The Admission and Disclosure Standards set out 'continuing obligations' that apply after admission which specify that the London Stock Exchange has 'a responsibility to ensure that it operates proper and orderly markets [and that] in order to achieve this it is essential that companies on our markets publish price sensitive information on a timely basis in accordance with the rules of their securities regulator, which impose a general obligation on companies whose securities are admitted to trading on a regulated market or prescribed market to release information of this type'. This provision of the Admission and Disclosure Standards effectively requires companies listed on the London Stock Exchange to observe disclosure obligations set out in the Listing, Prospectus, Disclosure and Transparency Rules sourcebook which forms a specific section of the FSA Handbook[1].

[1] The FSA Handbook is periodically updated and this section is based on the February 2008
    version of the Handbook.

3.75 Where a breach is detected the Admission and Disclosure Standards require action to be taken on a timely basis. As part of its own enforcement powers the London Stock Exchange can suspend trading in a company's securities and in extreme cases can cancel the right of a company's securities to be traded. The London Stock Exchange can also censure a company (publicly or privately) or issue a fine.

3.76 The requirements of the Listing Rules and the Disclosure and Transparency Rules reinforce FSMA 2000, s 397, which provides, in summary, that any person who knowingly or recklessly makes a statement, promise or forecast which is untrue, misleading or deceptive, or who dishonestly conceals material facts about a company, is guilty of an offence if such action is taken with the intention of inducing (or is taken recklessly as to whether it will induce) others to trade or refrain from trading in the company's securities. A person may be taken to be acting 'dishonestly' for these purposes by deliberately or recklessly not complying with market practice or market regulation. Accordingly, deliberate or reckless failure to comply with the disclosure requirements of the Listing Rules or the Disclosure and Transparency Rules might constitute evidence of dishonest concealment of material facts under s 397.

The Disclosure Rules of the Alternative Investment Market (now AIM)

3.77 AIM is regulated by The London Stock Exchange plc, but both the Admission and Disclosure Standards issued by the London Stock Exchange and the Disclosure and Transparency Rules sourcebook which forms a specific section of the FSA Handbook expressly state that their respective standards[1] and rules[2] do not apply to AIM listed companies. Therefore, with reference to the disclosure of information by AIM listed companies there is a separate regime set out in the 'AIM Rules for Companies'[3]. The general disclosure principles are set out in Rule 10 (Principles of disclosure) and Rule 11 (General disclosure of price sensitive information) which provide as follows:

'Rule 10:

The information which is required by these rules must be notified by the AIM company no later than it is published elsewhere. An AIM company must retain a Regulatory Information Service provider to ensure that information can be notified as and when required.

An AIM company must take reasonable care to ensure that any information it notifies is not misleading, false or deceptive and does not omit anything likely to affect the import of such information.

It will be presumed that information notified to a Regulatory Information Service is required by these rules or other legal or regulatory requirement, unless otherwise designated.

Rule 11:

An AIM company must issue notification without delay of any developments which are not public knowledge concerning a change in its financial condition, its sphere of activity, the performance of its business or the expectation of its performance, which, if made public, would be likely to lead to a substantial movement in the price of its AIM securities'.

[1] See 'Purpose and Scope' of the Admission and Disclosure Standards where it is expressly stated that the 'Standards apply to all securities admitted to trading on the Exchange's markets other than AIM' – see p 10 of the Admission and Disclosure Standards.

[2] AIM companies are not 'admitted to trading on a regulated market' for the purposes of the FSA Handbook and so are not subject to the Disclosure and Transparency Rules sourcebook.

[3] The AIM Rules for Companies are periodically updated and this section is based on the February 2007 version of the Rules.

3.78 Rule 17 (Disclosure of miscellaneous information) also lists a number of events or circumstances that with respect to which an AIM company must issue a notification without delay. With respect to restructurings the salient circumstances are 'any material change between its actual trading performance or financial condition and any profit forecast, estimate or projection ... made public on its behalf'. Due to the need to disclose trading updates half yearly, this will oblige a company experiencing a deterioration in performance or an inability to deliver against its published forecasts to make an announcement.

3.79 There may, on first analysis, appear to be an inconsistency between Rule 10 and Rule 11. Whilst Rule 11 states that information must be disclosed 'without delay', Rule 10 provides that information 'which is required by these rules must be notified by the AIM company no later than it is published elsewhere'. However, Rule 11 applies to price sensitive information (as referred to in the header to Rule 11 and as more precisely defined in Rule 11 itself), whilst Rule 10 applies to all other information. The Guidance Notes in Part Two of the AIM Rules for Companies reinforce this: Guidance Note (a) to Rule 11 provides that the Rule 11 requirements are 'in addition to any requirements regarding notification contained elsewhere in the rules'.

3.80 The requirements of the AIM Rules for Companies reinforce FSMA 2000, s 397, which is described above. Accordingly, deliberate or reckless failure to comply with the disclosure requirements of the AIM Rules for Companies might constitute evidence of dishonest concealment of material facts under s 397.

3.81 An AIM listed company must appoint a nominated adviser (or NOMAD) and a broker and Rule 31 requires a company to seek advice from its NOMAD regarding its compliance with the AIM Rules for Companies 'whenever appropriate and take that advice into account'. In practice, AIM listed companies keep in close contact with their NOMADs on disclosure issues.

3.82 Where there is a breach of the disclosure rules (or any of the other AIM Rules for Companies) or the Exchange considers that the protection of investors so requires, the Exchange may suspend the trading of AIM securities by issuing a dealing notice through a RIS[1]. In addition the Exchange has a similar array of enforcement measures that it can apply where it considers that an AIM company has contravened the AIM Rules for Companies, including the issue of a warning notice, a fine, a public censure and ultimately a cancellation of the admission of the AIM securities[2]. If the Exchange does propose to take any of the latter steps it must follow the procedures set out in the Disciplinary Procedures and Appeals Handbook[3]. Appeals are also conducted in accordance with the Disciplinary Procedures and Appeals Handbook[4].

[1] See Rule 40 'Precautionary Suspension' of the AIM Rules for Companies.
[2] See Rule 42 'Disciplinary action against an AIM Company' of the AIM Rules for Companies.
[3] See Rule 44 'Disciplinary Process' of the AIM Rules for Companies.
[4] See Rule 45 'Appeals' of the AIM Rules for Companies.

3.83 It is also submitted that as a practical matter the 'effect' test under the AIM Rules for Companies and the Disclosure and Transparency Rules is the same and should be applied in the same way by practitioners. Under the AIM Rules for Companies, if made public the information must be likely to lead to a substantial movement in the price of its AIM securities and under the Disclosure and Transparency Rules the information must be likely to have a significant effect on the price of the listed company's financial instruments. The result therefore is that the guidance and rule commentary on the price effect stated in the Disclosure and Transparency Rules will be equally relevant to AIM companies.

3.84 Notwithstanding the stated objective of AIM of creating a less rigorous regulatory and disclosure regime, in practice the disclosure regime in relation to price sensitive information operates in almost an identical manner for AIM listed companies as for companies listed on the Official List. This is certainly the assumption under which most advisers and practitioners and AIM companies themselves, have been operating.

E INFORMATION, DISCLOSURE AND APPROVAL REQUIREMENTS IN RELATION TO DISPOSALS BY DISTRESSED UK LISTED COMPANIES – CLASSIFICATION OF TRANSACTIONS

3.85 The company's financing banks may require, as part of a renegotiated debt package, that at least some of its existing debt is repaid immediately. A company in financial difficulty will be unlikely to have the necessary liquidity to achieve this, and so it may seek to realise cash from a disposal of assets (as well as, perhaps, raising cash by other means, such as a rescue rights issue, which is discussed in Chapter 10 *'Rescue rights issues'*.

3.86 When negotiating sale and purchase documentation with a potential buyer of assets, the company will also need to consider whether the transaction is sufficiently large that it will require shareholder approval. Chapter 10 of the Listing Rules sets out the framework for companies which undertake 'transactions' (which is broadly defined) and, importantly, a series of tests (known as 'class tests') which should be undertaken in order to classify a particular transaction. Certain types of transaction will require shareholder approval; others merely require a brief announcement to be made. It should be noted that, pursuant to LR 10.1.3, however, a 'transaction to raise finance' which does not involve the acquisition or disposal of a fixed asset, does not fall within the definition of 'transaction' for these purposes.

3.87 There are four class tests, being (i) the gross assets test; (ii) the profits test; (iii) the consideration test; and (iv) the gross capital test. The rules relating to the class tests are set out in full at the end of Chapter 10 of the Listing Rules but, broadly, they are concerned with the size of the proposed transaction (or elements associated with the assets which are the subject of that transaction) relative to the size of the company. So, for example:

- the gross assets test is calculated by dividing the gross assets the subject of the transaction by the gross assets of the company;
- the profits tests seeks to compare the profits attributable to the assets the subject of the transaction with the profits of the company;
- the consideration test takes the consideration for the transaction as a percentage of the market capital of the company's ordinary shares; and
- the gross capital test is concerned, on an acquisition, with the gross capital of the business or company being acquired relative to the gross capital of the company.

3.88 The detailed provisions of the class tests provide rules and guidance to companies which are using them in the context of a particular transaction (or transactions – since Chapter 10 also includes certain aggregation principles).

3.89 When considering a transaction, a company should calculate the percentage ratios which arise from each class test. If all percentage ratios are less than 5%, the transaction is a Class 3 transaction. Class 2 transactions arise when any percentage ratio is 5% or more, but all are lower than 25% and, if any percentage rate is 25% or more, this will be a Class 1 transaction. Very large transactions – or, indeed, transactions which appear disproportionately large because of the financial situation of the company (a company undergoing a restructuring may have a relatively low market capitalisation, for example) – where any percentage ratio is 100% or more will be classified as reverse takeovers. A reverse takeover also arises where there is a fundamental change in the business or change in board or voting control; this could conceivably be the case where a bank's equity in a company following a debt for equity conversion dilutes the existing shareholders to such an extent that there is a change of control[1]. However, there are likely to be significant consequences, of course, if a bank group obtains voting control of a listed company such as mandatory bid considerations, financial consolidation and change of control trigger events. If the shareholdings are widely dispersed following the debt to equity conversion, these potential consequences may not be insurmountable[2].

[1] See LR 10.2.2R(4).
[2] See Chapter 6 *'Restructuring exits'* and Section B 'Debt for equity swaps' in this regard.

3.90 Depending upon the classification of the transaction being undertaken, different requirements apply. For example, a brief announcement (specifying key details such as subject matter, parties and consideration) will suffice for a Class 3 transaction; a more detailed announcement is required for a Class 2 transaction. Both Class 1 transactions and reverse takeovers, on the other hand, require shareholder approval in general meeting, and any agreement entered into in relation to such a transaction must be conditional on that shareholder approval being obtained. For a reverse takeover, the company's listing will also generally be cancelled, and the company will be required to reapply, as a new applicant, for the listing of its shares. A company's articles of association, or other contractually binding document, should also always be checked to ensure that no other restrictions or requirements apply to its ability to enter into transactions.

3.91 A potential relaxation of the requirement to obtain shareholder approval for a disposal which constitutes a Class 1 transaction is set out in paragraph 10.8 of the Listing Rules, and is applicable to a company in 'severe financial difficulty'. Under the paragraph, a discretion exists for the FSA to dispense with the requirement to prepare a circular and seek shareholder approval where certain conditions are fulfilled, and in the context that the company, being in severe financial difficulty, 'may find itself with no alternative but to dispose of a substantial part of its business within a short time frame to meet its ongoing working capital requirements or to reduce its liabilities. Due to time constraints it may not be able to prepare a circular and convene an extraordinary general meeting to obtain prior shareholder approval' (LR 10.8.1G). There is, therefore, a real emphasis on the time it would take the company to seek shareholder approval (including preparation of all documents, convening the necessary general meeting and waiting the required notice period), the passage of such time threatening the survival of the company.

3.92 The company will, in order to persuade the FSA to modify the Class 1 requirement to seek shareholder approval, need to demonstrate to the FSA that:

- it is in severe financial difficulty; and
- it could not reasonably have entered into negotiations earlier to enable shareholder approval to be sought.

3.93 In addition, the company will need to provide documents showing that:

- all other avenues of funding have been exhausted;
- negotiation does not allow time for shareholder approval;
- the directors are acting in the best interests of the shareholders and company; and
- unless the disposal is completed quickly administrators, receivers or liquidators are likely to be appointed.

3.94 Paragraph 10.8.3 of the Listing Rules also requires:

- confirmation from the company's sponsor that it is in severe financial difficulty and that, on the basis of the information available, it would not be in a position to meet its obligations as they fall due unless the disposal takes place according to the proposed timetable; and
- confirmation from the persons providing finance that further finance or facilities will not be made available and that, unless the disposal is effected immediately, current facilities will be withdrawn.

3.95 There is, therefore, a high threshold to reach in order for the FSA to be persuaded to exercise its discretion under these provisions of the Listing Rules. There are relatively few examples of such discretion being exercised (Marconi in 2003 and Smartlogik in 2002 provide two such examples), and there is very little guidance from the FSA on when it may be minded to exercise such discretion. Recent experience has shown that it might be difficult for companies to avail themselves of this exemption and the FSA have been reluctant to apply it as it effectively disenfranchises shareholders.

3.96 It is clear however, that any financing banks will have a crucial role to play in procuring that this exemption is available given the requirement for a confirmation from the company's finance providers as to the imminent withdrawal of current facilities. The directors of the company will also need to be mindful of potential challenge from the shareholders themselves if they seek such a waiver from the requirement to obtain shareholder approval for a Class 1 disposal.

3.97 The company must however make a full announcement of any disposal that is subject to the exemption from obtaining shareholder approval, and for details of the disclosure contents, reference should be made to paragraph 2.3 of Guidance Note 5 of Appendix 4 to the UKLA Guidance Manual. The confirmations of a withdrawal of facilities referred to above must be reviewed and approved by the UKLA before any variation will be granted and the announcement being made.

3.98 During this process, paragraph 2.2 of the Disclosure Rules ('General obligation of disclosure for companies') will continue to apply. The market must be kept informed at all times of 'inside information' which directly concerns the issuer.

3.99 The directors may also need to consider whether the company's financial position is such that they should request the suspension of the company's listing pending publication of an announcement. Reference should be made to section F of this Chapter dealing with the suspension of shares.

3.100 Where the turnaround plan and the restructuring strategy of a listed company is dependent on a disposal programme and the disposal will involve the asset representing more than 25% of its gross assets this will constitute a Class 1 transaction and will therefore create the need for a working capital statement to be included in the circular to the company's shareholders. This in turn creates an important issue for the financial institutions supporting the company through a restructuring process. Indeed, where those lending institutions as a condition of their additional support require such a disposal to be executed, the company as a prerequisite to that disposal will in turn need its supporting lending institutions to confirm that their facilities will be available for at least the next 12 months. In practice, almost all auditors supporting a working capital statement will want to make their assessment of the sufficiency of the group's working capital for a period in excess of 12 months and typically market practice is for an 18-month working capital review to be conducted.

3.101 Inevitably, this will require that the institutions each need to obtain a credit approval to support such a working capital confirmation which may well delay the disposal process. Equally the institutions will incur additional fees for such a long dated credit approval. Historically, lending institutions have sought to limit the scope of their comfort regarding the continuation of such facilities and it was not uncommon to see carefully worded statements such as 'it is our present intention on the basis of the financial information provided to us and in the absence of unforeseen circumstances to extend our facilities to the group for a period of 12 months'. Obviously the auditors preparing the working capital statement resist such diluted and caveated expressions of support, and whilst working capital statements have been issued historically on the back of such declarations of support, this is now a rare occurrence. As a result the various stakeholders now negotiate the restructuring and the extension of facilities in advance on an accelerated basis so that the continuing facilities are properly defined and committed prior to the launch of the disposal. If a term sheet is to be used with respect to the future terms of the facilities, this will need to be detailed and it will be necessary for the term sheet to be accompanied by a detailed commitment letter which gives limited scope for the commitment in relation to the provision of facilities to be removed. As a consequence it is not uncommon for full facility documentation to be agreed and for the company's legal advisers to produce a report to the auditors on the terms of the facilities and their availability, in order to satisfy the auditors that there is certainty of funding over the relevant working capital period of 18 months.

F SUSPENSION OF SHARES WITH RESPECT TO DISTRESSED PUBLIC COMPANIES

3.102 This section sets out the situations when the suspension of listing or trading of shares of a UK public listed company may be ordered by the FSA (the UKLA for these purposes) or requested by the issuer in the context of a distressed restructuring. Chapter 5 of the Listing Rules principally sets out the basis upon which shares can be suspended, but for completeness this section also refers to suspension of trading under Chapter 1 of the Disclosure Rules and Transparency Rules.

Suspension of listing under the Listing Rules

3.103 Under the Listing Rules, shares in a public listed company may be suspended by the FSA if:

'(a)   the smooth operation of the market is, or may be, temporarily jeopardised; or
(b)   it is necessary to protect investors.'

3.104 The FSA may suspend the listing of shares if either it finds that the circumstances above exist or by a request from the issuer to suspend the listing of its shares on this basis[1]. The Listing Rules also provide a list of examples of circumstances where the FSA will suspend the listing of shares on these grounds[2]. Those that are mostly relevant in the case of a restructuring context are:

(a)   the issuer is unable to assess accurately its financial position and inform the market accordingly;
(b)   there is insufficient information in the market about a proposed transaction;
(c)   the issuer has appointed administrators or receivers, or is an investment trust and is winding up;
(d)   the issuer has failed to meet its continuing obligations for listing;
(e)   the issuer has failed to publish financial information in accordance with the listing rules;
(f)   the issuer's securities have been suspended elsewhere;

(g)   for a securitised derivative that relates to a single underlying instrument, the underlying instrument is suspended; or

(h)   for a securitised derivative that relates to a basket of underlying instruments, one or more underlying instruments of the basket are suspended.

1   See LR 5.1.1R(1) and 5.1.4G.
2   See LR 5.1.2G.

3.105 Even in a restructuring scenario, circumstance (a) is relatively uncommon given the need for public companies to issue a going concern statement for a 12-month period. As such public companies should be able to assess their financial position accurately. In rare cases, significant instability in a company's markets, a major breakdown of systems or serious unforeseen events may occur which will trigger such a suspension. Such a suspension occurred following a major fraud in the case of Versailles plc.

3.106 Prolonged restructurings which make it extremely difficult for the company to assess its financial position have on occasions prompted a suspension of shares. In June 2007 Inter Link Foods plc requested that the London Stock Exchange suspend trading in the company's shares on the basis of criteria (a) and (b) pending clarification of the company's financial position whilst bidders for the distressed company submitted amended bid offers and the company's bankers considered a request for a compromise of their position.

3.107 Although the appointment of administrators or receivers to the issuer will result in a suspension under circumstance (c) the case indicates that shares in a listed issuer will be suspended if its key operating subsidiary is subject to an insolvency regime. On 8 October 2001 the listing of Railtrack Group plc was suspended at the request of the company following the Secretary of State for Transport's successful petition to appoint an administrator to its subsidiary Railtrack plc under the Railways Act 1993.

3.108 Distressed companies often experience problems finalising their annual accounts and this will be a ground for suspension under limbs (d) and (e) above if the deadlines for publishing Preliminary Statements and Financial Reports pursuant to Chapter 9 of the Listing Rules ('Continuing Obligations') are breached. If a listed company prepares a Preliminary Statement, then that statement must be published 'as soon as possible after it has been approved by the board'[1]. The use of 'as soon as possible' rather than 'as soon as practicable' indicates that no delay is permissible other than the delay occasioned by procuring publication immediately after the board meeting.

1   See LR 9.7A.1R(1).

3.109 A listed company may be authorised to omit to publish a Preliminary Statement if the FSA considers that the disclosure of the information contained in it would be contrary to the public interest or seriously detrimental to the listed company. However, this will only be the case if such an omission would not be likely to mislead the public with regard to facts and circumstances, knowledge of which is essential for the assessment of the shares in question[1].

[1] See LR 9.7A.3G.

3.110 If a listed company fails to publish a Preliminary Statement as soon as possible after it has been approved by the board, and it has not agreed with the FSA in accordance with LR 9.7A.3G that it may omit to publish the Preliminary Statement, then the company's listing may be suspended by the FSA under its power in LR 5.1.1R(1).

3.111 Annual reports are a requirement of the Disclosure and Transparency Rules[1], but the Listing Rules also separately provide that certain information must be included in annual reports, in addition to that which is required by the DTRs. Therefore the requirement to publish an annual report is not strictly a part of the Listing Rules. However, in view of the fact that annual reports and their prescribed contents are considered in some detail by the Listing Rules, it is prudent to view a failure to produce and publish an annual report within the required time as a failure to meet a listed company's continuing obligations for listing, or a failure to publish financial information in accordance with the Listing Rules. The time limit for the publication of a company's annual report is four months from the end of the company's financial year[2]. If an annual report were to be published late, that is more than four months after the end of the company's financial year, or withheld indefinitely, then the company's listing may be suspended by the FSA under its power in LR 5.1.1R.

[1] See DTR 4.1.
[2] See DTR 4.1.3R.

3.112 Cytomyx Holdings plc is an example of a company that had been experiencing significant financial difficulties and which had its shares suspended from trading in September 2007 on the basis that it had been unable to publish audited accounts for the financial year ending March 2007 in accordance with the relevant listing rules. Similarly, the Joint Board of Eurotunnel decided on 11 April 2006 not to approve the Group's accounts until after the mid point in restructurings negotiations planned for mid May of that year. This was done in the light of the evolving restructuring negotiations which made it very difficult to reach a decision regarding the approval of the accounts and to accurately assess its financial position and inform the market accordingly. As a result a short suspension of the shares was effected.

3.113 If the issuer makes a request for a suspension, the request must be in writing and must include all the details and documents listed in LR 5.3 including the reasons and timing for the requested suspension. A request for a suspension must be made as soon as practicable and if made for the opening of the market, it should allow sufficient time for the FSA to deal with the request before trading starts.

3.114 An issuer may also withdraw its request at any time before the suspension or cancellation takes effect. The withdrawal request should initially be made by telephone and then confirmed in writing as soon as possible, with an explanation of the reasons for the withdrawal.

3.115 Even if an issuer withdraws its request, the FSA may still suspend the listing of the securities if it considers it is necessary to do so. If an issuer has published either a statement or a circular that states that the issuer is, or intends, to seek a suspension or cancellation and the issuer no longer intends to do so, it should, as soon as possible, notify a RIS with a statement to that effect.

3.116 The FSA may restore the listing of any securities that have been suspended if it considers that the smooth operation of the market is no longer jeopardised or if the suspension is no longer required to protect investors. Similarly, the FSA may restore the listing even though the issuer does not request it, but LR 4 also provides a procedure for a restoration request by an issuer.

3.117 The FSA will not suspend the listing of a security to fix its price at a particular level[1]. An issuer that has the listing of any of its securities suspended must continue to comply with all listing rules applicable to it (LR 5.1.1R(2)). If the FSA suspends the listing of any securities, it may impose such conditions on the procedure for lifting the suspension as it considers appropriate[2].

[1]   See LR 5.1.3G.
[2]   See LR 5.1.1(3).

Additional grounds for a suspension of trading under the Disclosure and Transparency Rules

3.118 Under DTR 1.4 the FSA may also require the suspension of trading of shares if it has reasonable grounds to suspect non-compliance with the Disclosure Rules. DTR 1.4 provides two examples of situations where the FSA will require the suspension of trading:

(a)   if an issuer fails to make a RIS announcement as required by the Disclosure Rules within the applicable time limits which the FSA considers could affect the interests of investors or affect the smooth operation of the market; or

(b)   if there is or there may be a leak of inside information and the issuer is unwilling or unable to issue an appropriate RIS announcement within a reasonable period of time.

G DELISTING OR EASING THE DISCLOSURE BURDEN THROUGH AN AIM LISTING

3.119 In order to ease the disclosure burden and the continuing obligations relating to a listing on the UKLA's Official List, a distressed company undergoing a restructuring may well consider terminating its listing on the Official List or transferring its listing to AIM where it will need to comply with the less stringent AIM Rules for Companies. This will almost certainly be a consideration if the company is to undergo a disposal process and wishes to minimise the nature and complexity of the shareholder approvals associated with the disposal programme.

3.120 In order to initially terminate the listing on the Official List the company will need shareholder approval under Listing Rule 5.2.5 and the threshold is 75% of votes cast in person or by proxy. An FSA approved shareholder circular would be required and the delisting date must be at least 20 business days after the passing of the shareholder approval. Listing Rule 5.2.7 disapplies Listing Rule 5.2.5 if the financial position of the issuer is so precarious that, but for a necessary delisting/reconstruction proposal[1] there is no reasonable prospect that the issuer will avoid going into formal insolvency proceedings. Again, at least 20 business days' notice of delisting is required.

[1]   See LR 5.2.7(2) for more detail.

3.121 If the company opts to re-list on AIM, then in order to comply with an AIM listing the company must still be able comply with the AIM requirements, and deal with any shareholder or other stakeholder resistance to such a change by procuring the necessary shareholder resolution carried by 75% of votes cast in person or by proxy. Listing on AIM, for a company which has held a listing on the Official List for at least 18 months, is a relatively straightforward process and, therefore, is relatively quick and cheap to implement.

3.122 Such a company would be eligible to be admitted to AIM via the 'fast-track' admission procedure. The advantage of the fast track route is that the applicant does not, for the purposes of admission, have to produce an admission document (unless otherwise required to do so by the Prospectus Rules), which will lead to significant time and cost savings.

3.123 The applicant must, however, make a detailed pre-admission announcement at least 20 days prior to the date of its expected admission to AIM, which announcement must contain information in relation to, for example:

- the size of any capital raising in conjunction with the application for admission to AIM;
- confirmation that the company has adhered to the legal and regulatory requirements of the Official List;
- details of the business of the company and its intended strategy following admission;
- a description of significant changes in the financial or trading position of the company since the date to which the last audited accounts were prepared;

- a statement that the directors have no reason to believe that the company's working capital will be insufficient for at least 12 months from the date of its admission to AIM; and
- the address of a website containing the company's latest published annual report and accounts, which must have a financial year end not more than nine months prior to admission.

3.124 A company in financial difficulty may, therefore, find it difficult to comply with the requirements of the pre-admission announcement. For example, there may well have been a significant change in the financial or trading position of the company – precisely the reason that it is in negotiations with its banks and seeking the less strict regime of AIM – and, although the working capital statement is less robust than if the company were to follow the standard (rather than the fast track) route to AIM, the directors of a distressed company may not be able to provide this confirmation. In addition, the company's 'nominated adviser' will still be required to confirm the appropriateness of the company for listing on AIM, which it may not be able to do in the case of a company in financial difficulty.

3.125 The AIM Rules for Companies do, however, provide a more relaxed regime for the entry into (and approval of) significant transactions, such as those which would be classified as Class 1 transactions under the Listing Rules. The AIM Rules for Companies contain similar class tests to the Listing Rules, discussed above, and a percentage ratio in excess of 10% will classify a particular transaction, including a disposal of assets (but excluding a transaction to raise finance which does not involve a change in fixed assets), as a 'substantial transaction'. As soon as the terms of a substantial transaction are agreed, the company must make an announcement and disclose certain information in relation to the transaction – similar to the information required for the announcement of a Class 2 transaction under the Listing Rules. Importantly, there is no need for the company to seek shareholder approval of that substantial transaction.

H 'YEAR END REPORTING' AND THE IMPACT OF INTERNATIONAL ACCOUNTING STANDARDS ON RESTRUCTURINGS

The introduction and development of IAS

3.126 The financial reporting legislation passed by the EU in recent years has made a number of changes to EU accounting requirements for EU companies. These legislative changes have affected the timing and the manner in which financial information is disclosed in a company's accounts and as will be explained in this section this has had an impact on the timing and conduct of restructurings. The three key pieces of legislation are set out below:

1   Regulation (EC) No 1606/2002 of the European Parliament and of the Council of 19 July 2002 on the application of International Accounting Standards (the 'IAS Regulation');

2   Directive 2003/51/EC of the European Parliament and of the Council of 18 June 2003 amending Council Directives 78/660/EEC, 83/349/EEC, 86/635/EEC and 91/674/EEC on the annual and consolidated accounts of certain types of companies, banks and other financial institutions and insurance undertakings; and

3   Directive 2001/65/EC of the European Parliament and of the Council of 27 September 2001 amending Directives 78/660/EEC, 83/349/EEC and 86/635/EEC as regards the valuation rules for the annual and consolidated accounts of certain types of companies as well as of banks and other financial institutions.

3.127 These can be downloaded from the Official Journal section of the EC's website http://eur-lex.europa.eu/JOIndex.do?ihmlang=en.

3.128 Some of the changes made by this European legislation are minor, and are designed to clarify or bring EU accounting requirements into line with modern best practice. But others, in particular those contained in the IAS Regulation, are more fundamental and far-reaching and regulate the manner in which a breach of a company's financing agreements are to be reported and disclosed to the markets.

3.129 The Secretary of State for Trade and Industry enacted the Companies Act 1985 (International Accounting Standards and Other Accounting Amendments) Regulations 2004, SI 2004/2947, to implement these changes imposed by European law for British companies through amendments to the Companies Act 1985 as amended by the Companies Act 2006. These Regulations came into force on 12 November 2004 and have applied to financial years beginning on or after 1 January 2005. Additional Regulations were also made by the Secretary of State to extend the use of summary financial statements and make other minor amendments to accounting and reporting requirements.

3.130 The legislation that has had the biggest impact on the timing and conduct of restructurings is the IAS Regulation which introduced important changes that have directly affected the way in which certain companies across the EU need to prepare their financial statements and disclose key financial information such as the nature of their financing and whether this is current or long term and committed.

3.131 Under Article 4 of the IAS Regulation, companies governed by the law of a Member State, whose securities are admitted to trading on a regulated market in any Member State in the European Union ('publicly traded companies'), are required to prepare their consolidated accounts on the basis of accounting standards issued by the International Accounting Standards Board that are adopted by the EC. This has applied to all financial years that commenced on or after 1 January 2005. The list of regulated markets at 17 February 2004 is set out at Annex C to the IAS Regulation. Although AIM ceased to be a regulated market from 12 October 2004, the London Stock

Exchange has mandated the use of IAS by companies listed on AIM for financial periods beginning on or after 1 January 2007.

3.132 Under Article 5 of the IAS Regulation, Member States also have the option to extend use of adopted IAS on a permissive or mandatory basis. In Britain, the application of the IAS Regulation is to be extended so that:

(a) publicly traded companies are permitted to use IAS in their individual accounts; and

(b) non-publicly traded companies are permitted to use IAS in both their individual and consolidated accounts.

3.133 For the purposes of the extension to the application of the IAS Regulation to private companies under Article 5, and the implementation of Article 5 into English law, the Companies Act 1985 (International Accounting Standards and Other Accounting Amendments) Regulations 2004, SI 2004/2947, defined 'company' in this context to mean a company required to prepare accounts by the Companies Act 1985. If a company elects to use IAS (or is required to do so by the IAS Regulation), it must state in the notes to its accounts that they have been prepared in accordance with IAS.

3.134 As intimated, the IAS Regulation introduces important changes that will directly affect the way in which certain companies across the EU prepare their financial statements. There are an array of acronyms, bodies and standards relating to financial reporting and by way of clarification it is useful to set these out: the International Financial Reporting Standards ('IFRS') are standards and interpretations adopted by the International Accounting Standards Board ('IASB'). Many of the standards forming part of IFRS are known by the older name of International Accounting Standards ('IAS'). IASs were issued between 1973 and 2001 by the board of the International Accounting Standards Committee ('IASC'). In April 2001 the IASB adopted all IASs and continued their development, calling the new standards IFRS. In addition International Standards on Auditing ('ISAs') are issued by the International Auditing Practices Committee (the 'IAPC') which is a committee of the International Federation of Accountants ('IFAC') whose task is to prepare and publish international standards on auditing procedures.

Financial covenant testing in the light of IAS

The importance of financial covenant 'Test Dates'

3.135 Most financial covenants which banks impose on larger investment grade borrowers and listed corporates to monitor the quality of their underlying credit are usually tested in accordance with the provisions of typical 'Loan Market Association' documentation. This effectively provides that such financial covenants are tested half yearly and at the date of the company's financial year end (each for these purposes being referred to as a

'Test Date'). The financial covenants are tested by reference to the relevant audited financial statements of the Group or unaudited half yearly financial statements as applicable.

3.136 By way of example, and by reference to a distressed company on the verge of a financial covenant breach (and ultimately a restructuring), if the relevant Test Date for such a company which is under scrutiny is say 31 December 2009, the financial covenants on that Test Date will be tested by reference to the audited financial statements of the company[1]. The audited financial statements are typically delivered to the 'Facility Agent' by no later than 120 days from the financial year end, but the terms of loan documentation can and do vary. Accordingly, the company in question cannot automatically be in breach of these financial covenants on the Test Date because as a practical matter the relevant financial data pursuant to which the test is made will not be available on the Test Date and as a matter of contract the relevant financial information used to test the financial covenants is not required to be delivered until after the Test Date. Most companies will typically deliver their signed audited financial statements together with an appropriate compliance certificate on or about the date of their preliminary announcement which for a public company would normally be within 90 days of its financial year end. It is of course possible that the company in this example could opt to defer its announcement and indeed the delivery of its accounts, but the important point to note is that whilst the breach of the financial covenant is referenced to the Test Date, the financial covenant cannot actually be tested or be capable of breach as a matter of contract, until a later date when the audited accounts are delivered. If the financial statements are not delivered by the date required under the loan agreement this will place the company in breach of the terms of its loan documentation as to the timing of delivery of relevant information and a separate waiver from a majority of the banks (usually 66.667%) will be required with respect to such late delivery.

[1] The financial covenants for the previous Test Date will have been tested on 30 June by reference to the interim accounts which although unaudited will have had a high degree of input from the company's auditors. These are usually deliverable 60 days after the half year end and where financial covenant compliance is finely balanced it may only be on the date of the delivery of the interims that it will be definitively clear that the company has breached a financial covenant. This is because the covenants are driven off the interims in their final published form.

IAS 1 and IAS 10

3.137 Paragraph 65 of IAS 1 is relevant to this scenario and a breach of an undertaking under a 'long-term loan agreement'. It provides that if there is a breach of a covenant 'ON OR BEFORE' the balance sheet date (which could be the year end balance sheet date or the interim balance sheet date) then a subsequent waiver of that breach by the lenders after the balance sheet date is a non-adjusting post balance sheet event. Whether the loan is presented as current or non-current (under IAS 1) is dictated by the condition of the loan as at the balance sheet date and if there is a breach at that date it should be recorded as current and any subsequent waiver cannot alter this. It is therefore vital to note that if a waiver of a breach existing as at the balance sheet date is not granted prior to that date (and for a minimum period of 12 months) and upon testing against the relevant financial statements there is a breach, the liability under the loan will have to be shown as current. By recording the liability as current it may in turn mean that the financial statements can no longer be prepared on a going concern basis[1].

[1]   See the proceeding section on the importance of being able to issue a going concern statement.

3.138 Clearly, if there is a breach of the undertaking on the relevant balance sheet Test Date then paragraph 65 of IAS 1 will not permit a subsequent waiver to have a retrospective effect. The impact of a breach of another borrowing covenant (including the same financial covenant the testing of which may have been deferred by consent until after the year end) which occurs after the balance sheet date is not expressly covered by paragraph 65 of IAS 1, but where such a breach occurs after the balance sheet date, but before the issue of the relevant accounts for the financial year end in question, the prevailing view is that the liability would still be shown as non-current. This may be of only token consolation to the company because if such a post balance sheet breach remains unremedied and unwaived and the facility in question can be put on demand, this may in turn also mean that the financial statements can no longer be prepared on a going concern basis[1].

[1]   See the proceeding section on the importance of being able to issue a going concern statement.

3.139 In any event, it should be noted that if at the balance sheet date an exiting facility is repayable within 12 months, then irrespective of any paragraph 65, IAS 1 analysis, the existing facility will still need to be classified as 'current' on the balance sheet of the company in question for the purposes of paragraph 63 of IAS 1. Notwithstanding the requirement to classify the loan as current (given its repayment date), the company (to the extent that it negotiates new facilities after the balance sheet date, but before the delivery of its audited accounts) will be able to make a positive disclosure against this item in the balance sheet under IAS 10.

3.140 As intimated, IAS 10 is relevant to this scenario because it provides that:

> 'If non-adjusting events after the balance sheet date are material, non-disclosure could influence the economic decisions of users taken on the basis of the financial statements. Accordingly, an entity shall disclose the following for each material category of non-adjusting event after the balance sheet date:
> (a)   the nature of the event; and
> (b)   an estimate of its financial effect, or a statement that such an estimate cannot be made.'

3.141 The renegotiation/restructuring of the loan will be a material non-adjusting event that occurs after the balance sheet date, which the company will want to disclose in its accounts. The disclosure will be made in the notes to the line item on the balance sheet where the existing facility is classified as current. In this scenario a company would of course want to make a detailed disclosure in connection with the renegotiation of the facilities, as this would constitute a positive post balance sheet date development. A detailed disclosure is also within the spirit of IAS 10. This will not however detract from the fact that the facilities need to be stated as current at the balance sheet date and the negative impact that this might have, despite the IAS 10 disclosure.

The key questions for IAS companies undertaking a restructuring

3.142 The overriding and fundamental questions under IAS 1 are (1) has there actually been a breach of a financial covenant, and (2) if so when did this occur, was it before or after the balance sheet date. In addressing these questions the International Manual of Accounting Practice clearly stipulates that 'the standard's approach to breaches of borrowing covenants focuses on the legal rights of the entity rather than on the intentions of either of the parties to the loan'. On a strict analysis of paragraph 65 of IAS 1 in the context of the fact pattern presented above, the correct view is that the covenant is breached and that the breach will have occurred on the balance sheet date but only when the financial information for the year end Test Date is presented.

Solutions

3.143 There are only three possible solutions for a company in this scenario, although the third option outlined below may be more difficult to achieve and may not constitute a solution as such because it does require the auditors to take a practical and sensible approach which, for reasons that will be explained, might not be possible if paragraph 65 of IAS 1 is applied rigorously.

3.144

(1)   The most obvious is to procure a contractual waiver of the breach (for a minimum period of 12 months) or an amendment of the covenant to perhaps give additional headroom so that there is no financial covenant breach at all 'ON OR BEFORE' the balance sheet date. This type of covenant re-set may not be feasible the closer that a company gets to the Test Date and in any event it is likely that the relevant lenders will seek to impose material terms and conditions as a condition of such waiver. Conditional waivers that are within the control of the relevant company, but the delivery of which has not yet been discharged, will usually satisfy the auditors. By way of examples such conditions may include inter alia an independent business review, the initiation of a disposal programme and the payment of a fee. Where the condition is outside the control of the company, such as the outcome of litigation or a regulatory review, the auditors would probably not be inclined to perceive this as an effective waiver and may well require the company to still report its debt as a current obligation.

3.145

(2)   The second option that could be adopted before the balance sheet date would be to remove the operative provisions of the relevant financial covenant on the 31 December Test Date with the effect that it would not be possible to construe as a matter of contract law that a breach had occurred at the Test Date. By removing the provision itself there is not technically a waiver of a breach and sheer weight of logic and legal analysis dictates that there cannot be a breach of a financial covenant at the relevant time when that covenant is determined to be no longer operative under the contract. In these circumstances where the covenant is removed, the lenders will typically substitute the financial covenant that was to be tested at the 31 December Test Date with an alternative test. This alternative test may well be a debt reduction obligation such that the group has to de-lever within 2–3 months after the 31 December balance sheet date perhaps through a rights issue or a material disposal. Equally, the lender could substitute the rolling 12-month financial covenant test which was to be tested at the 31 December Test Date with a rolling 15-month financial covenant test which would not be tested at the balance sheet date of 31 December but on 31 March in the next calendar year. Under both of the above scenarios there is no breach at the balance sheet date because the financial covenant that was to be tested on that date has been removed and replaced with something else.

3.146

In the fact pattern outlined above, this analysis enables the lenders to defer the present question of whether to waive a prospective breach of a financial covenant (without adversely affecting the accounting position of the company) until a time after 31 December 2009, but before the delivery of the audited financial statements, so as to maximise their negotiating position in connection with a strategic review of the company. If the company breaches the deferred debt reduction covenant or the amended 15-month financial covenant as described above before the audit is completed, it would be unable to issue a going concern statement and this would place the company in a precarious position with its lenders and the market. This second option therefore removes the IAS 65 pressure at the year end, but keeps the company's feet firmly dangled over the fire.

3.147

(3)   In light of the scenario outlined above, a potential third option would be the negotiation of a new replacement facility (which would completely discharge the existing facility) after 31 December 2009, but before the publication of the 2009 accounts in March 2010. This would enable the company's auditors to make the consequential positive disclosure under IAS 10 and approve the accounts on a going concern basis. It is anticipated that the company would make a disclosure under IAS 10 in this regard, to the extent that new facilities have been negotiated. Somewhat illogically this would not eradicate the breach at

the year end Test Date for the purposes of IAS 65 and on a purely technical level the debt at the company's year end would still need to be recorded as current because the existing facility would still exist at the Test Date. This is a somewhat bizarre result because the facility would no longer exist and would have been discharged by a completely new facility that would not be in breach and which would be committed for a sufficient period. It is incongruous to suggest that liabilities should still be current when they have been discharged pursuant to a refinancing and there is not even an obligation to test the covenants under a loan agreement that is extinct and now consigned to history at the time when the data is finally delivered. Ironically, the banks that were due to receive the annual accounts and compliance certificate and test the covenants may well not even receive the financial data that shows the breach.

3.148 The alternative and more pragmatic approach which has been adopted in the past with auditors would be to not deliver the information to the legacy banks in order to avoid the testing of the covenants. If the compliance certificate is in fact never delivered to the legacy banks there cannot be a breach since the covenant is not actually tested in accordance with the terms of the contract. As such the debt will not be recorded as current and the accountants will simply include a detailed positive non-adjusting event after the balance sheet date showing that the historic debt was refinanced. This should also have the positive consequence of enabling the company's auditors on or before March 2010 to approve the accounts on a going concern basis.

3.149 For a company with any concerns about its financial covenant compliance on the next Test Date or even successive Test Dates out in the future, the best advice is to plan ahead and to seek a covenant re-set 6–18 months ahead of the Test Date that is causing anxiety. This may result in the payment of a minimal re-set fee as opposed to a more substantial waiver fee once the problematic Test Date is approaching.

3.150 In the absence of a well planned covenant re-set, the next best option is a waiver or a deferral of the Test Date which are obviously the most favoured options in terms of navigating IAS 1 or IAS 10. This is certainly more advantageous than a substitute test that will preserve the lender's negotiating position and the negotiation of a new facility that discharges the existing facility containing the troublesome covenant. The problem with such a new facility that removes covenant pressure is that it is likely to be expensive.

3.151 As an overriding point however, it is vital to note that the difficulty posed by these accounting standards for a company seeking to negotiate new replacement facilities is that they place considerable pressure on the company to effectively achieve a successful restructuring and to negotiate new facilities after the balance sheet date but before the date for publication of the accounts, so as to enable the company to make a positive disclosure under IAS 10 and to procure a going concern statement. This is likely to improve the lender's negotiating position in connection with the refinancing and strategic review of the company.

I 'YEAR END REPORTING' AND THE IMPORTANCE OF GOING CONCERN STATEMENTS

Introduction

3.152 The previous section made reference to the considerable importance of listed companies being able to issue a 'going concern statement'. The going concern concept is perhaps the fundamental tenet of financial accounting for listed companies. IAS 1 (Presentation of Financial Statements), paragraph 23 expressly provides that 'when preparing financial statements, management shall make an assessment of an entity's ability to continue as a going concern. Financial statements shall be prepared on a going concern basis unless either management either intends to liquidate the entity or to cease trading, or has no realistic alternative but to do so'.

3.153 In addition, paragraph 24 of IAS 1 states that 'in assessing whether the going concern assumption is appropriate, management takes into account all available information about the future, which is at least, but is not limited to, twelve months from the balance sheet date'.

3.154 Independently, but consistent with IAS 1, the Listing Rules impose the same 'going concern' requirement as IAS. By stating that there is a reasonable expectation that the group has adequate resources to continue in operational existence for the foreseeable future, the directors are effectively stating that the balance sheet of the 'Group' must reflect the value of that Group as if it were to remain in existence for and beyond the foreseeable future. Conversely, the opposite of being able to issue a going concern statement, is to say that the company will be insolvent within the foreseeable period after the balance sheet date. Effectively, this means insolvency within one year because the Group will need to issue a further going concern statement one year later.

3.155 By issuing an unqualified going concern statement a group will be able to promote financier, employee, shareholder customer and supplier confidence and will therefore be creating a stable platform in which it can undertake a financial and/or operational turnaround. In particular, if the company, with the backing and support of its auditors, is able to state that there is a reasonable expectation that the group has adequate resources and liquidity to continue in operational existence for the foreseeable future it will be able to attract trade credit on favourable terms and will be able to maintain the confidence of credit insurers thereby effectively reducing the size of and dependency on its working capital facilities. As intimated the support of the company's auditors is pivotal in procuring a clean going concern statement and a clean audit sign-off. Given that a clean going concern statement evolves out of the audit process and given the importance of the auditors in this process it is worth initially considering the audit process by way of an insight into how such a clean audit sign-off might be obtained.

ISA 200 'Overall Objective of the Independent Auditor, and the Conduct of an Audit in Accordance with International Standards on Auditing'

General principles on the scope, conduct and objectives of an audit

3.156 ISA 200 should be read in the context of the Auditing Practices Board's Statement 'the Auditing Practices Board – Scope and Authority of Pronouncements (Revised)' which sets out the application and authority of International Standards on Auditing (UK and Ireland)) ('ISAs') and the conduct of an audit in the UK and Ireland (the 'Auditing Practices Board's Statement').

3.157 According to paragraph 6 of the Auditing Practices Board's Statement, engagement standards (which include ISAs (UK and Ireland)) contain basic principles and essential procedures and guidance in the form of other material including appendices. Principles and essential procedures are identified by bold type lettering and the level of authority of the text within the paragraphs is identified by the use of the expression 'the auditor should'. In some explanatory and other material the expression 'the auditor would' is used.

3.158 The objective of an audit of financial statements is to enable the auditor to express an opinion whether the financial statements are prepared, in all material respects, in accordance with an applicable financial reporting framework. The 'applicable financial reporting framework' comprises those requirements of accounting standards, law and regulations applicable to the entity that determine the form and content of its financial statements (paragraph 2). Although the auditor's opinion enhances the credibility of the financial statements, the user cannot assume that the audit opinion is an assurance as to the future viability of the entity nor the efficiency or effectiveness with which management has conducted the affairs of the entity.

3.159 The auditor should comply with the following principles when carrying out an audit:

(a)   the auditor should comply with the Code of Ethics for Professional Accountants issued by the International Federation of Accountants. The principles governing the auditor's professional responsibilities are independence, integrity, objectivity, professional competence and due care, confidentiality, professional behaviour and technical standards (paragraph 4);

(b)   in the UK and Ireland the relevant ethical pronouncements with which the auditor should comply are the APB's Ethical Standards and the ethical pronouncements relating to the work of auditors issued by the auditor's relevant professional body;

(c)   the auditor should conduct an audit in accordance with ISAs (UK and Ireland) (paragraph 5);

(d)   the auditor should plan and perform an audit with an attitude of professional scepticism recognizing that circumstances may exist that cause the financial statements to be materially misstated. The auditor makes a critical assessment, with a questioning mind, of the validity of audit evidence obtained and should be alert to audit evidence that contradicts or brings into question the reliability of documents or management representations. Such scepticism reduces the risk of over-looking suspicious circumstances, over generalizing and using faulty assumptions (paragraph 6);

(e)   the auditor should neither assume that management is dishonest or unquestionably honest. Representations from management are not a substitute for obtaining sufficient appropriate audit evidence (paragraph 6);

(f)   the audit procedures required to conduct an audit in accordance with ISAs (UK and Ireland) should be determined by the auditor having regard to the requirements of ISAs (UK and Ireland), relevant professional bodies, legislation, regulations and, where appropriate, the terms of the audit engagement and reporting requirements. The auditor of a public service body often has wider objectives and additional duties and statutory responsibilities, laid down in legislation, directives or codes of practice (paragraph 7); and

(g)   in exceptional circumstances, the auditor may judge it necessary to depart from a basic principle or an essential procedure that is relevant in the circumstances of the audit, in order to achieve the objective of the audit. In such a case, the auditor is not precluded from representing compliance with ISAs (UK and Ireland), provided the departure is appropriately documented as required by ISA (UK and Ireland) 230 (paragraph 7(a)).

The concept of reasonable assurance

3.160 An audit in accordance with ISAs (UK and Ireland) is designed to provide reasonable assurance that the financial statements taken as a whole are free from material misstatement. Reasonable assurance relates to the whole audit process as there are inherent limitations in an audit such that an absolute assurance cannot be given (paragraphs 8 and 9).

3.161 It should also be noted that the work undertaken by the auditor to form an audit opinion is permeated by judgment, in particular regarding the gathering of audit evidence (for example, in deciding the nature, timing, and extent of audit procedures) and the drawing of conclusions based on the audit evidence gathered (for example, assessing the reasonableness of the estimates made by management) (paragraph 10).

Audit risk – the importance of planning the audit

3.162 The auditor should plan and perform the audit to reduce the audit risk to an acceptably low level that is consistent with the objective of an audit. The 'audit risk' is the risk that the financial statements are materially misstated and an inappropriate audit opinion is given. The auditor reduces audit risk by designing and performing audit procedures to obtain sufficient appropriate audit evidence to be able to draw reasonable conclusions on which to base an audit opinion. Reasonable assurance is obtained when the auditor has reduced audit risk to an acceptably low level (paragraphs 13–16).

3.163 The audit process involves the exercise of professional judgment in designing the audit approach, through focusing on what can go wrong (ie, what are the potential misstatements that may arise) at the assertion level (see ISA (UK and Ireland) 500, 'Audit Evidence') and performing audit procedures in response to the assessed risks in order to obtain sufficient appropriate audit evidence.

3.164 The auditor is only concerned with misstatements the effect of which are, both individually and in the aggregate, material to the financial statements taken as a whole. The auditor considers the risk of material misstatement at two levels:

(a)   the overall financial statement level; and
(b)   in relation to classes of transactions, account balances, and disclosures and the related assertions.

3.165 Risks at the financial statement level refers to risks of material misstatement that relate pervasively to the financial statements as a whole and potentially affect many assertions. Risks of this nature often relate to the entity's control environment and are not necessarily risks identifiable with specific assertions. The auditor's response to the assessed risk of material misstatement at the overall financial statement level includes consideration of the knowledge, skill, and ability of personnel assigned significant engagement responsibilities, including whether to involve experts; the appropriate levels of supervision; and whether there are events or conditions that may cast significant doubt on the entity's ability to continue as a going concern.

3.166 To avoid risks in relation to classes of transactions, account balances, and disclosures and the related assertions the auditor seeks to obtain sufficient appropriate audit evidence as to the class of transactions, account balance, and disclosure level in such a way that enables the auditor at the completion of the audit, to express an opinion on the financial statements taken as a whole at an acceptably low level of audit risk.

Components of audit risk

3.167 The risk of material misstatement at the assertion level consists of two components as follows:

(a)   'inherent risk' is the susceptibility of an assertion to a misstatement that could be material, either individually or when aggregated with other

103

misstatements, assuming that there are no related controls. The risk of such misstatement is greater for some assertions and related classes of transactions, account balances, and disclosures than for others. For example, complex calculations are more likely to be misstated than simple calculations. Accounts consisting of amounts derived from accounting estimates that are subject to significant measurement uncertainty pose greater risks than do accounts consisting of relatively routine, factual data. External circumstances giving rise to business risks may also influence inherent risk. For example, technological developments might make a particular product obsolete, thereby causing inventory to be more susceptible to overstatement. In addition to those circumstances that are peculiar to a specific assertion, factors in the entity and its environment that relate to several or all of the classes of transactions, account balances, or disclosures may influence the inherent risk related to a specific assertion. These latter factors include, for example, a lack of sufficient working capital to continue operations or a declining industry characterized by a large number of business failures; and

(b) 'control risk' is the risk that a misstatement that could occur in an assertion and that could be material, either individually or when aggregated with other misstatements, will not be prevented, or detected and corrected, on a timely basis by the entity's internal control. That risk is a function of the effectiveness of the design and operation of internal control in achieving the entity's objectives relevant to preparation of the entity's financial statements. Some control risk will always exist because of the inherent limitations of internal control.

3.168 The assessment of the risk of material misstatement may be expressed in quantitative terms, such as in percentages, or in non-quantitative terms. In any case, the need for the auditor to make appropriate risk assessments is more important than the different approaches by which they may be made.

Detection risk

3.169 Risk that the auditor will not detect a misstatement that exists is a possibility that cannot be reduced to zero because the auditor usually does not examine all of a class of transactions, account balances, or disclosure and because of other factors including the selection of inappropriate auditor audit procedure, misapplication of appropriate audit procedure, or misinterpretation of the audit results. These other factors can ordinarily be addressed through adequate planning, proper assignment of personnel to the engagement team, the application of professional scepticism, and supervision and review of the audit work performed.

3.170 The greater the risk of material misstatement the auditor believes exists, the less the detection risk that can be accepted. Conversely, the less risk of material misstatement the auditor believes exists, the greater the detection risk that can be accepted.

Responsibility for the financial statements

3.171 While the auditor is responsible for forming and expressing an opinion on the financial statements, the responsibility for preparing and presenting the financial statements in accordance with the applicable financial reporting framework is that of the management of the entity, with oversight from those charged with governance. The audit of the financial statements does not relieve management or those charged with governance of their responsibilities.

Going concern and the audit process

3.172 Whilst the general principles of an audit have been explored to establish how an audit is conducted, particularly from a risk perspective, the fundamental objective for a company undertaking a restructuring is to procure a clean going concern statement. IAS 1 expressly requires that 'financial statements should be prepared on a going concern basis'. Independently, but consistent with IAS 1, the Listing Rules in LR 9.8.6R(3) impose the same 'going concern' requirement as IAS requiring the directors to confirm the going concern status of the business. In the case of a listed company incorporated in the UK, the annual financial report must include:

> 'a statement made by the directors that the business is a *going concern*, together with supporting assumptions or qualifications as necessary, that has been prepared in accordance with 'Going Concern and Financial Reporting: Guidance for Directors of listed companies registered in the United Kingdom', published in November 1994 (the 'ICAEW Guidance');'

¹   LR 9.8.6R(3).

3.173 This statement must be reviewed by the auditors before the annual report is published[1]. Therefore, there are two major parties involved in the assessment of a company as a going concern: the company's management and its auditors.

¹   LR 9.8.10R.

3.174 It is incumbent that the directors make an assessment of the going concern status of the company at the appropriate balance sheet date. The ICAEW Guidance referred to in LR 9.8.6R(3) effectively provides that in making their assessment, directors can arrive at one of three conclusions:

1   They have a reasonable expectation that the company will continue in operational existence for the foreseeable future and have therefore used the going concern basis in preparing the financial statements.
2   They have identified factors that cast doubt on the ability of the company to continue in operational existence for the foreseeable future, but they consider that it is appropriate to use the going concern basis in preparing the financial statements.
3   They consider that the company is unlikely to continue in operational existence for the foreseeable future and therefore the going concern basis is not an appropriate one on which to draw up the financial statements.

3.175 The ICAEW Guidance includes example wording for the first two situations and this is usually adopted by listed companies almost verbatim. The going concern statement issued by Trinity Mirror plc in its 2006 accounts is an example of this:

'After making enquiries, the directors have formed a judgement, at the time of approving the financial statements, that there is a reasonable expectation that the Group has adequate resources to continue in operational existence for the foreseeable future.

For this reason, the directors continue to adopt the going concern basis in preparing the financial statements'

3.176 The reference to the 'Group' in such statements is necessary because the ICAEW Guidance states that directors of the parent company should make their statement regarding going concern in respect of both the parent company and the group as a whole. This does not mean that each subsidiary within the group is a going concern, on the contrary, the group concept enables the director to take a view on the solvency or viability of a subsidiary if they can still conclude that the 'Group' is a going concern for the foreseeable future.

3.177 Where the directors have identified factors that cast doubt on the appropriateness of the going concern assumption, the directors should explain the circumstances so as to identify the factors that give rise to the problem (including any external factors outside their control which may affect the outcome) and an explanation of how they intend to deal with the problem.

3.178 Interestingly, the ICAEW Guidance does not specify the factors to be considered or the precise disclosures to be made. In order to identify what might be relevant factors for disclosure reference is inevitably made by directors to the auditing standard on going concern (ISA 570). This is relevant because this states that the auditors do not normally regard disclosures on going concern in financial statements as adequate unless they include certain key pieces of information[1]:

(a)   a statement that the financial statements have been prepared on the going concern basis;
(b)   a statement of the pertinent facts;
(c)   the nature of the concern;
(d)   a statement of the assumptions adopted by those charged with governance (including the executive and non-executive directors and members of an audit committee) which should be clearly distinguishable from the pertinent facts;
(e)   (where appropriate and practical) a statement regarding the plans of those charged with governance for resolving the matters giving rise to the concern; and
(f)   details of any relevant actions by those charged with governance.

[1]   The inference here is that if the consideration of and disclosure of certain information and factors by the directors at least satisfies the information and factors that the auditors would consider, then the relevant threshold will be met.

3.179 An example of a qualified going concern statement based on the ICAEW Guidance, is set out below:

'The company is in breach of certain loan covenants at its balance sheet date and so the company's bankers could recall their loans at any time. The directors continue to be involved in negotiations with the company's bankers and as yet no demands for repayments have been received. The negotiations are at an early stage and, although the directors are optimistic about the outcome, it is as yet too early to make predictions with any certainty.

In the light of the actions described elsewhere in the [Operating and Financial Review] on page [NUMBER], the directors have formed a judgement, at the time of approving the financial statements, that it is appropriate to adopt the going concern basis in preparing the financial statements.

While doubts about the ability of a company to remain as a going concern do not necessarily mean that the company is or is likely to become insolvent, directors are rightly concerned that disclosure of such doubts may have an adverse effect on the public's perception of the company's position which in turn, might exacerbate the company's problems. However, directors have a responsibility to make a reasonable judgment based on all available information at the time the financial statements are approved by them and report accordingly.'

3.180 Where the directors perceive that the company is no longer a going concern at all, they should no longer prepare the financial statements using the going concern assumption and an alternative basis must be used. The fact that the company is not a going concern does not necessarily mean that the company is insolvent, but the directors must still consider whether the company may be or become insolvent. If the directors know or ought to have concluded that there is no reasonable prospect that the company would avoid going into insolvent liquidation they risk the possibility of an action for wrongful trading.

The responsibility of the directors

3.181 Paragraph 23 of IAS 1, 'Presentation of Financial Statements', sets out management's responsibility for assessing going concern as follows:

'When preparing financial statements, management should make an assessment of an enterprise's ability to continue as a going concern. Financial statements should be prepared on a going concern basis unless management either intends to liquidate the enterprise or to cease trading, or has no realistic alternative but to do so. When management is aware … of material uncertainties … which may cast significant doubt upon the enterprise's ability to continue as a going concern, those uncertainties should be disclosed. When the financial statements are not prepared on a going concern basis, that fact should be disclosed, together with the basis on which the financial statements are prepared and the reason why the enterprise is not considered to be a going concern.

In assessing whether the going concern assumption is appropriate, management takes into account all available information for the foreseeable future, which should be at least, but is not limited to, twelve months from the balance sheet date.'

3.182 Management's assessment of the going concern assumption involves making a judgment, at a particular point in time, about the future outcome of events or conditions which are inherently uncertain. The following factors are therefore relevant:

(a)   The degree of uncertainty associated with the outcome of an event or condition increases significantly the further into the future a judgment is being made.

(b)   Any judgment about the future is based on information available at the time at which the judgment is made. Subsequent events can overturn a judgment which was reasonable at the time it was made.

(c)   The size and complexity of the entity, the nature and condition of its business and the degree to which it is affected by external factors all affect the judgment regarding the outcome of events or conditions.

3.183 Material uncertainties related to the types of events or conditions set out in paragraph 9 of this ISA may cast significant doubt upon the going concern assumption.

Assessing going concern

3.184 A company is regarded as a going concern if it 'will continue in operational existence for the foreseeable future'. The term 'foreseeable future' is not defined in the Companies Act, accounting standards or in the ICAEW Guidance for directors. The ICAEW Guidance for directors justifies not providing a definition by noting that it will vary for different industries and companies. What the ICAEW Guidance does say, however, is that directors should take account of all information of which they are aware at the time.

3.185 Where the period considered by the directors has been limited to a period of less than one year, the directors should determine whether the financial statements require any additional disclosure to explain adequately the assumptions that underlie the adoption of the going concern basis.

3.186 When making their assessment of going concern, directors should take into account the following factors and information:

(i)   forecasts and budgets;
(ii)   borrowing requirements;
(iii)   liability management;
(iv)   contingent liabilities;
(v)   products and markets;
(vi)   financial risk management;
(vii)   financial adaptability;
(viii) substantial operational losses incurred in the current year;
(ix)   the continuous availability of trade credit;
(x)   potential litigation;
(xi)   possible loss of major customers;
(xii)   headroom against loan agreement financial covenant limits;

(xiii)   the quantum of facilities; and
(xiv)   the accountant's duty to consider and action the ongoing concern principle.

3.187 The ICAEW Guidance sets out a list of detailed procedures which may be helpful to directors, particularly of smaller listed companies, in determining the appropriateness of the going concern basis in drawing up financial statements.

Interim reporting

3.188 There is arguably a lack of clarity on the nature of going concern reporting at the publication of the interim accounts. The ICAEW Guidance includes only one paragraph on interim reporting and states that the directors are only required to review the work performed at the previous year end to determine whether any of the significant factors which they had identified at that time have changed to such an extent as to affect the appropriateness of the going concern presumption. The lack of clarity arises because the ICAEW Guidance does not expand upon the nature and detail of any review to be undertaken as part of interim reporting. The safest course if the directors have genuine concerns about the going concern status of the group would be to increase the level of diligence at the half year and to make reference to the same factors listed above in terms of making the year end going concern assessment. They should also consider including wording on the appropriateness of the going concern basis in the statement explaining the group's future prospects in the context of the trading environment at the year end.

Liability for directors where the going concern basis is not met

3.189 In addition to the liabilities relating to internal financial control under the Companies Act 2006, the directors may also have liabilities under the Insolvency Act 1986, including liability under ss 213 and 214 where the company is wound up.

Going concern: guidance for auditors

3.190 LR 9.8.10R(1) requires the listed company to ensure that the auditor reviews the directors' going concern statement in order to meet the review requirements of this rule. As noted above, the Auditing Practices Board's Statement requires that the auditor:

(a)   assesses the consistency of the going concern statement with the knowledge obtained in the course of the audit of the financial statements. (This knowledge will primarily be obtained in meeting the requirements of ISA 570 referred to above);

(b)   assesses whether the directors' statement meets the disclosure requirements of the ICAEW Guidance; and

(c)   does not express an opinion on the ability of the company to continue in operational existence.

3.191 The Auditing Practices Board's Statement also states that it is important that the going concern statement is not inconsistent with any disclosures regarding going concern in the financial statements or the auditors' report. Where going concern matters are discussed in financial statements, the directors' going concern statement could cross refer to the relevant note in the financial statements for consistency.

ISA 570 'Going concern'

3.192 Since 15 December 2004, ISA 570 'Going concern' has applied to listed companies. Paragraph 9 of ISA 570 provides that it is the auditor's responsibility to consider the appropriateness of the management's use of the going concern assumption in the preparation of the financial statements and to consider whether there are any material uncertainties about the entity's ability to continue as a going concern that need to be disclosed in the financial statements[1]. The auditor is to consider the appropriateness of the management's use of the going concern assumption and whether there are adequate disclosures regarding the going concern basis in the financial statements in order that they give a true and fair view.

[1]   'Management' in this context comprises those persons who perform senior managerial functions.

3.193 If the use of the going concern assumption is appropriate, but a material uncertainty exists, the auditor is required by paragraph 9 of ISA 570 to consider whether the financial statements adequately describe the principal events or conditions[1]. In this situation, if the adequate disclosure is still made in the financial statements, the auditor should express an unqualified opinion but modify the auditor's report by adding an emphasis of matter paragraph[2]. If however, adequate disclosure is not made in the financial statements, the auditor should express a qualified or adverse opinion, as appropriate[3].

[1]   See paragraph 32 of ISA 570.
[2]   See paragraph 33 of ISA 570. ISA 570 'Going concern' should also be read in conjunction with ISA 706 'Emphasis of Matter Paragraphs and Other Matters Paragraphs in the Independent Auditor's Report'. For more detailed analysis of 'emphasis of matter' paragraphs see the proceeding section.
[3]   See paragraph 34 of ISA 570.

3.194 Although the primary purpose of ISA 570 is to provide guidance for auditors, it will affect the disclosures that directors are likely to make in annual reports and accounts. In particular, ISA 570 points out that FRS 18 requires that 'where the foreseeable future considered by the directors has been limited to a period of less than one year from the date of approval of the financial statements' that fact should be disclosed in the financial statements. However, paragraph 24 of IAS 1 on 'Presentation of Financial Statements' states that 'in assessing whether the going concern assumption is appropriate, management takes into account all available information about the future, which is at least, but not limited to, 12 months from the balance sheet date'. The practical effect of this is that pressure is put on directors to consider a period of at least one year from the date that the financial statements are approved when considering the going concern basis.

Emphasis of Matter paragraphs and Other Matters paragraphs in the independent auditor's report

3.195 ISA 570 'Going concern' should also be read in conjunction with ISA 706 'Emphasis of Matter Paragraphs and Other Matters Paragraphs in the Independent Auditor's Report'. ISA 706 is relevant where the auditor may consider a matter disclosed in the financial statements to be of such importance that it is fundamental to users' understanding of the financial statements as a whole and that it would be appropriate to draw their attention to it through an Emphasis of Matter paragraph in the auditor's report. The auditor is required to include an Emphasis of Matter paragraph in the auditor's report on financial statements to highlight the existence of a material uncertainty regarding an entity's ability to continue as a going concern.

3.196 Although paragraph 6 of ISA 706 suggests that a widespread use of Emphasis of Matter paragraphs diminishes the effectiveness of the auditor's communication of such matters, there has been a tendency since August 2007 and the onset of more difficult credit conditions for auditors to display much greater caution in the audit process and to seek to include Emphasis of Matter paragraphs far more readily.

3.197 The auditor is required, prior to determining that it is appropriate to insert an Emphasis of Matter paragraph, to ensure that he has obtained sufficient appropriate audit evidence that the matter is not materially misstated in the financial statements[1]. Conversely and quite often perversely there have been recent examples of auditors taking extraordinary steps to seek confirmations from third parties in order to avoid imposing an Emphasis of Matter paragraph. This has included auditors seeking confirmations and 'comfort' from a company's regulators such as the FSA and quite bizarre comfort letters from lenders where their facilities are not in breach and the company has demonstrated to its own audit committee's satisfaction and the satisfaction of its own lawyers that it has adequate committed facilities and funding for the forthcoming 15-month period.

[1]   ISA 706, para 7.

3.198 Although an Emphasis of Matter paragraph in the auditor's report is unhelpful and will be construed negatively by any number of stakeholders such as suppliers, credit insurers and prospective financiers, IAS 706 somewhat dubiously states that the inclusion of an Emphasis of Matter paragraph in the auditor's report does not affect the auditor's opinion. It also notes that an emphasis of matter is not a substitute for either (a) the auditor expressing a qualified opinion or an adverse opinion, or disclaiming an opinion, when required by the circumstances of a specific audit engagement, or (b) disclosures in the financial statements that the applicable financial reporting framework requires management to make[1].

¹ ISA 706, para 8.

3.199 ISA 706 can indeed be legitimately described as somewhat dubious in this regard because ISA 570, 'Going Concern,' requires the auditor to include an Emphasis of Matter paragraph in the auditor's report on financial statements to highlight the existence of a material uncertainty regarding an entity's ability to continue as a going concern[1].

¹ ISA 706, para 9.

3.200 When the auditor includes an Emphasis of Matter paragraph in the auditor's report, the auditor should include it immediately after the opinion paragraph in the auditor's report and use the heading 'Emphasis of Matter'. It should clearly highlight the matter being emphasized and indicate where relevant disclosures that fully describe the matter can be found in the financial statements. The Emphasis of Matter paragraph should also indicate that the auditor's opinion is not modified in respect of the matter emphasized[1]. The auditor does not make disclosures in the Emphasis of Matter paragraph beyond those included in the financial statements because doing so may imply that the matter has not been appropriately disclosed or that there is a disagreement with management[2].

¹ ISA 706, para 11.
² ISA 706, para 12.

3.201 If the auditor considers it necessary to communicate matter(s) other than those that are presented and disclosed in the financial statements and this is not prohibited by law or regulation, the auditor should do so in a separate paragraph in the auditor's report with the subheading 'Other Matter(s)', placed after the auditor's opinion and any Emphasis of Matter paragraph[1].

¹ ISA 706, para 14.

3.202 When the auditor expects to include an Emphasis of Matter or an Other Matter(s) paragraph in the auditor's report, the auditor should communicate with those charged with governance regarding this expectation, and the proposed wording of this paragraph[1].

¹ ISA 706, para 19.

3.203 In March 2007, the International Auditing and Assurance Standards Board (IAASB) published an exposure draft, ISA 570 (Redrafted). The exposure draft has been redrafted in the style designed to enhance the clarity of IAASB pronouncements and there has not been a wholesale revision of ISA 570. It is envisaged that the revised ISA 570 will be effective for audits of financial statements for periods beginning on or after 15 December 2008.

Status of ISAs

3.204 According to the Preface to the International Standards on quality, control, auditing, review, other assurances and related services (the Preface) paragraph 3, IAASB's pronouncements govern audit, review, other assurance and related services engagements that are conducted in accordance with International Standards. They do not override the local laws or regulations that govern the audit of historical financial statements or assurance engagements on other information in a particular country required to be followed in accordance with that country's national standards. In the event that local laws or regulations differ from, or conflict with, the IAASB's Standards on a particular subject, an engagement conducted in accordance with local laws or regulations will not automatically comply with the IAASB's Standards. A professional accountant should not represent compliance with the IAASB's Standards unless the professional accountant has complied fully with all of those relevant to the engagement. For these purposes ISAs and in particular ISA 700 is an IAASB Engagement Standard. According to paragraph 4 of the Preface, ISAs are to be applied in the audit of historical financial information.

3.205 Paragraphs 10–13 of the Preface confirm that the IAASB's Standards contain basic principles and essential procedures together with related guidance in the form of explanatory and other material, including appendices. The basic principles and essential procedures are to be understood and applied in the context of the explanatory and other material that provide guidance for their application.

3.206 The nature of the IAASB's Standards requires professional accountants to exercise professional judgment in applying them. In exceptional circumstances, a professional accountant may judge it necessary to depart from a basic principle or essential procedure of an Engagement Standard to achieve the objective of the engagement. When such a situation arises, the professional accountant should be prepared to justify the departure.

3.207 ISAs are also applicable to engagements in the public sector. When additional guidance is appropriate for the public sector, such guidance is included within the body of an International Standard.

The position adopted by the International Federation of Accountants regarding going concern statements

3.208 The IAASB which approves IASs is an independent standard setting body within the International Federation of Accountants (the 'IFAC') and therefore the comments of the IFAC on going concern statements are extremely relevant. Whilst recognising the key role auditors have to play and the obligations imposed on auditors pursuant to the Listing Rules and the Companies Act 2006 the IFAC correctly notes that auditors are not forensic detectives who should review every single aspect of a company's business in order to establish whether the going concern statement is valid or not.

3.209 The auditor's responsibility is to consider whether there is material uncertainty related to events or conditions which may cast significant doubt upon the entity's ability to continue as a going concern based on the auditor's knowledge of relevant events or conditions at the time of conducting the audit. The auditor's consideration of the going concern assumption applies irrespective of the accounting framework that has been used in the preparation of the financial statements, even if the going concern assumption is not specifically mentioned within that framework. The auditor cannot predict future events or conditions that may cause an entity to cease to continue as a going concern. Accordingly, the absence of any reference to going concern uncertainty or emphasis of matter in an auditor's report cannot be viewed as a guarantee as to the entity's ability to continue as a going concern. Management's assessment of the entity's ability to continue as a going concern is a key part of the auditor's consideration of the going concern assumption.

3.210 The auditor considers the going concern assumption for the same period for which management assumes responsibility, a period which should be at least, but is not limited to, 12 months from the balance sheet date.

3.211 Although the auditors are not required to take a forensic approach, the IFAC does recognise that in discussing and developing the audit plan, the auditor should provide input and anticipate going concern problems.

3.212 In terms of providing guidance as to when to question the going concern prospects of a company, the key issues that IFAC sets out (on a non-exhaustive basis) as events that the auditor ought to consider in the context of going concern statements are financial, adverse key financial ratios, operating and other factors.

3.213 With specific relevance to restructurings, the IFAC discuss the position in which fixed-term borrowings are approaching maturity, but the company may have no realistic prospects of renewal or repayment. This should of course affect the ability of the auditor to make a going concern statement. In addition, there could be evidence of over trading and an excessive reliance on short-term borrowings to finance long-term assets which should be considered relevant. In terms of IFAC advice, it is recommended that the auditor must also look for indications of withdrawal of financial support (in all its forms) and negative cashflows as shown either by the historical accounting records and/or by cash budgets or projections.

3.214 Clearly, misleading or difficult financial ratios that are potentially susceptible to breach are areas that should concern the auditors. Reference to the state of the economy in which the company is operating and the nature of the sector in which the company is operating is also highly relevant.

3.215 The IFAC also recommend that auditors discuss the impact of substantial operating losses, the significant deterioration in the value of assets used to generate cashflows as well as arrears or a discontinuance of dividends that are no longer being declared along with the possibility that the latest declared dividends have yet to be paid, well after their due date.

3.216 A persistent rescheduling of creditors' payments and maybe the shift from buying on account to buying for cash would ordinarily be cause for concern. The need to reschedule formal loans would also be a cause for raised eyebrows in the context of the going concern principle. Companies that find that they are unable to secure financing for essential new product development or other essential investments must clearly have pause for thought at least as to the view of others of their long-term viability.

3.217 Of course, whilst each of these issues, either singly or collectively, could be considered serious for any company, taken in isolation, the IFAC tacitly recognises that it could be possible to take a mistaken view of the situation. For example, even though a company might have to reschedule its creditor and debt repayments, management could be taking steps to reorganise its affairs in such a way that it resolves its financing situation within the forthcoming financial year.

Working Capital Statements

3.218 A 'Working Capital Statement' is a statement made by the directors of a company listed on the on the Official List of the London Stock Exchange (a 'listed company')[1] to the effect that in their opinion the working capital available to the company and its subsidiaries is sufficient for at least the next 12 months or, if it is not, how it is proposed that the company will procure the additional working capital that they think is necessary. The UK Listing Rules generally adopt the definition of a 'Working Capital Statement'[2], used in paragraph 3.1 (Working Capital Statement) of the Prospectus Regulation[3] as a 'statement by the issuer that in its opinion, the working capital is sufficient for the issuer's present requirements or, if not how it proposes to provide the additional working capital needed'.

[1]   For AIM listed companies see the analysis below.
[2]   See LR 13.4.1(2)R which in turn refers to LR 13 Annex 1R R and Annex 3 Item 1 'Working Capital' which refers back to the Prospectus Regulation definition of 'Working Capital Statement'.
[3]   Commission Regulation (EC) No 809/2004 – implementing the Prospectus Directive (Directive 2003/71/EC).

The need for a Working Capital Statement

3.219 Boards of directors of listed companies are required to give Working Capital Statements before entering certain transactions. In the context of restructuring, situations in which a company will typically require a Working Capital Statement to be issued are where the company is undergoing a reconstruction or refinancing, seeking to make a significant disposal, or where the company intends to make a rescue rights issue.

3.220 Of particular relevance to restructurings, the Listing Rules provide that if a listed company produces a circular containing proposals to be put to shareholders in a general meeting relating to a reconstruction or a refinancing, the circular must be produced in accordance with LR 13.3 and must include a Working Capital Statement.

3.221 Similarly, if a listed company seeks to undertake a rescue rights issue then it will need to have new shares admitted to the Official List. A listed company seeking admission of new shares to the Official List must satisfy the FSA that it and its subsidiary undertakings (if any) have sufficient working capital available for the group's requirements for at least the next 12 months[1]. This will be done by the directors making a Working Capital Statement.

[1]   LR 6.1.16R.

3.222 With reference to a listing of shares, the FSA has the option to waive the requirement that a company give a Working Capital Statement. However, such a waiver can only be on the basis that either:

(a)   the company already has shares listed and the FSA is satisfied that the prospectus/listing particulars contain satisfactory proposals for providing the additional working capital that the company thinks is necessary[1]; or

(b)   the company is a financial services provider, regulated by the FSA or another regulatory body, and is meeting its solvency and capital adequacy requirements and is expected to do so for the next 12 months without having to raise further capital[2].

[1]   LR 6.1.17G.
[2]   LR 6.1.18G.

3.223 The directors of a company which intends to make a rescue rights issue and which does not satisfy (a) or (b) above will have to give a Working Capital Statement.

3.224 A listed company in financial difficulty may decide to dispose of assets to raise money. A disposal may, if it is of an asset of significant value in relation to the overall value of the company, amount to a Class 1 transaction as determined in accordance with LR 10.2.2R(3)[1]. If the company is entering into a Class 1 transaction then it must obtain shareholder approval prior to making the disposal and produce a Class 1 circular[2] which in turn must include inter alia the information required by LR 13 Annex 1R R[3], which includes a Working Capital Statement[4].

[1]   For the circumstances where a company need not issue an explanatory circular see the section above 'Information, disclosure and approval requirements in relation to disposals by distressed UK listed companies – classification of transaction'.
[2]   LR 13.4.1R.
[3]   LR 13.4.1(2)R.
[4]   See Annex 3 Item 1 'Working Capital'.

3.225 Sponsors[1] are also constrained by the need to ensure that issuers entering into certain transactions have sufficient working capital. Listing Rule 8.4.12 provides that a sponsor must not submit to the FSA, on behalf of a listed company, an application for approval of a circular regarding a transaction set out in LR 8.4.11R[2], unless the sponsor has come to a reasonable opinion, after having made due and careful enquiry, that '... (3) the directors of the listed company have a reasonable basis on which to make the working capital statement required by LR 9.5.12R[3], LR 13.4.1R[4] or LR 13.7.1R[5]'.

[1] These are corporate finance advisers, investment banks and brokers. FSMA 2000, s 88(2) defines 'Sponsor' as a person approved by the competent authority for the purposes of the Listing Rules. Sponsors, and persons applying to become Sponsors, must comply with the requirements of Chapter 8 of the Listing Rules. The FSA maintains a list of sponsors (pursuant to FSMA 2000, s 88(3)(a)), and this is available on the FSA website: www.fsa.gov.uk/pubs/ukla/sp_register.pdf.
[2] This in turn inter alia refers to Class 1 transactions and circulars relating to reconstructions and refinancings that are not Class 1 transactions.
[3] Circulars relating to reconstructions and refinancings that are not Class 1 transactions.
[4] Circulars relating to Class 1 transactions.
[5] Circulars relating to the purchase of the listed company's own shares.

3.226 A company which is seeking to have its shares listed on AIM, including new shares issued as part of a rights issue, must produce an 'admission document'[1] which includes a statement about working capital that is substantially identical to a Working Capital Statement, save that it must be stated as having been made 'after due and careful enquiry'[2].

[1] Rule 3 of the AIM Rules for Companies.
[2] Paragraph c of Schedule 2 to the AIM Rules for Companies.

Documentary support for the Working Capital Statement

3.227 The company will produce a document (called a 'Working Capital Memorandum') which supports and provides the basis for the Working Capital Statement. Although the memorandum is prepared by the company, the company's accountants provide the directors of the company and (if relevant) the company's sponsor with the necessary work product and comfort on it.

3.228 There are no legislative requirements that dictate the level of work to be undertaken by reporting accountants in relation to working capital statements and the production of the Working Capital Memorandum. Best practice in the market is for the sponsor to request a comfort letter addressed to the sponsor and the board confirming the accountant's views on the working capital position of the company. The procedures of the reporting accountants in relation to working capital statements are performed in accordance with the Standards for Investment Reporting 1000 ('SIR 1000')[1], which are applicable to 'all engagements in connection with an Investment Circular'. SIR 1000 requires the reporting accountants to plan the engagement carefully and to consider all material matters[2]. The accountants are encouraged to identify and report concealment of information and to obtain representations from the directors on the information that has been provided to them by the directors. They are also required to obtain sufficient appropriate evidence on which to base their opinion and in this regard 'professional scepticism' is actively encouraged[3].

1   SIR 1000 was issued in July 2005 and is produced by the Auditing Practices Board which produces standards and guidance for auditing in the UK.
2   Paragraphs 28–30 of SIR 1000.
3   Paragraph 36 of SIR 1000.

3.229 Due to the fact that certain of the reports prepared in connection with investment circulars are public-reporting engagements, additional basic principles and essential procedures are typically followed and this will result in a more detailed analysis being conducted under a working capital review than would otherwise be the case in connection with a working capital assessment[1]. Therefore, in addition to the procedures addressed in going concern statements, the reporting accountants will consider more carefully the strategy and plans of the business and the risks of implementing that strategy, the impact of contemplated transactions such as a rights issue, disposal or loss of a contract. The reporting accountants will also want to base their review on an 18-month period of 'outlook', but can base their opinion on the working capital position on an assumption that the transaction subject to the shareholders approval and for which the working capital is required, has been executed.

1   Paragraphs 53–55 of SIR 1000.

3.230 Due to the fact that an 'emphasis of matter' cannot be attached to a working capital statement, the reporting accountants will tend to look much more closely at liquidity and when the Group may become very tight in relation to its cash requirements and indeed the availability of that cash. It is not uncommon therefore to see the requirements of the reporting accountants dictate more headroom on financial covenants and facilities of a larger size. The reporting accountants will invariably seek legal memoranda confirming covenant calculations and the interpretation of key provisions particularly an analysis of possible draw-stops under the groups banking agreements.

3.231 The reporting accountants will inevitably want to conduct additional sensitivity analysis on how the cashflow position of the company will look if certain unforeseen circumstances happen, if certain profit assumptions do not materialise or maintenance or growth capex is not spent during the period of the working capital outlook. This type of contingency analysis is becoming increasingly common and the level of work undertaken by reporting accountants and the level of supporting evidence that they require is increasing.

3.232 Base on the above taken by the reporting accountants, the Working Capital Memorandum will usually cover a period of between 12 and 18 months from its date, and will:

(a)   review the company's (and, if appropriate, its subsidiaries') other facilities;

(b)   take account of the estimated net proceeds of the transaction in question;

(c)   make assumptions about profit and cashflows over the coming 12 or 18-month period, which are based on information provided by the company; and

(d)   conclude whether or not the company (or, if appropriate, its subsidiaries) has sufficient working capital for its present requirements.

3.233 The need to produce a Working Capital Memorandum so that the directors can 'show their working-out' applies equally to AIM companies.

Making the statement

3.234 The Working Capital Statement itself is a short, simple statement. An example of a 'clean' statement is:

> 'Having regard to [*insert details of loan facilities, overdrafts and other finance*] and the proceeds of the [rights issue *or* contemplated disposal], the directors are of the opinion that the company has sufficient working capital for its present requirements, that is, for at least twelve months from the date of this statement'.

3.235 What is done with that statement depends on the context. If there is to be a rights issue then it will be included in the prospectus/listing particulars which precede(s) the issue. If there is to be a disposal of assets, and the company must make an RIS announcement pursuant to LR 10.8.4G(8), then the statement is a part of that announcement and will also from part of the explanatory circular.

3.236 If an issuer does not have sufficient working capital or cannot persuade the reporting accountants that it does, it can issue a 'qualified' working capital statement which should specifically explain how it proposes to provide the additional working capital needed. For example a company could make a declaration of an intention to raise capital through a rights issue or to improve its working capital position through a restructuring such as a debt for equity conversion. SIR 1000 anticipates that qualified opinions on a company's working capital position can be delivered by the reporting accountants and when giving a qualified opinion the opinion should be expressed 'except for' the matters to which the opinion relates[1]. It is obviously unsatisfactory for a company to issue such a working capital statement given the possible reaction of key stakeholders such as customers, regulators, employees and suppliers.

[1]   Paragraphs 62–63 of SIR 1000.

3.237 For AIM companies, the statement is included in the company's admission document, but is also included in a comfort letter given to the company's nominated adviser. This is necessary because it will give the nominated adviser comfort in confirming to the London Stock Exchange that the company complies with the AIM Rules for Companies.

The use of 'going concern statements' and 'working capital statements'

3.238 In many restructuring cases there is likely to be significant corporate activity at the time that a public company is delivering its accounts and making its going concern statement. Indeed, it is not unusual for a distressed company to undertake such corporate activity such as a disposal that will have a de-leveraging effect, in order to procure a provision of facilities by its lenders that will in turn facilitate the issue of the requisite going concern statement. If the company is also issuing a circular to its shareholders in connection with such corporate activity and is seeking a shareholder approval it will also have to procure the delivery of a working capital statement even though it is going through the process of satisfying its auditors that the accounts should be presented on an unqualified going concern basis. Indeed even where the approval is being sought at the time of the delivery of its annual accounts and preliminary announcement, the going concern statement will not operate as a substitute for a working capital statement. An example might be a Class 1 disposal or a rights issue that is to be approved by shareholders around the time of the preliminary announcement. However, there is a degree of administrative convenience in that the reporting accountants will use much of the same data and their presence within the company and access to senior management and the company's audit committee should ensure that the circular and the approvals sought are also synchronised with the delivery of the accounts containing the necessary going concern statement.

3.239 The difficulty for a company in this position is that it will not have obtained the requisite shareholder approval at the time that it has made its announcement which in all probability will be a condition precedent to the availability of the facilities that are in turn needed to ensure a clean and unqualified going concern statement. This circularity of needing the shareholder approval to procure facilities, but at the same time needing a working capital statement in order to issue the circular and obtain the all important approval is problematic, but experienced practitioners have navigated around this by making it clear in the circular that the unqualified working capital statement is wholly conditional upon the resolutions being passed which in turn are expressed to be conditions precedent under the relevant banking facilities.

3.240 Equally, the financial statements and the going concern caption will not need to include any adjustments to the accounts that would be necessary as a result of a failure to satisfy these conditions and the resulting failure to obtain the funding that the company requires. It will not therefore be necessary to provide an alternative qualified going concern statement or to re-model the accounts to show what they would look like without a bank financing, but a shareholder reading the circular will be in no doubt that the delivery of the accounts and an unqualified going concern statement will be conditional on the shareholder approval being granted. The circular will therefore provide a very clear and stark message that without the resolutions being carried there will be no going concern statement and that the auditors would have to go back and do further work and make further adjustments to their report which would take time and which could result in a delay in delivering the accounts, a possible suspension of the company's shares and quite possibly an eventual audit qualification. Conversely, the circular will clearly refer to the committed facility being provided by the company's lenders and will expressly confirm that if the resolutions are approved this would unlock the financing and in turn the working capital statement and the going concern statement.

3.241 Due to the potential uncertainty surrounding the going concern statement, the financial statements that are delivered with the circular are likely to include an 'emphasis of matter' caption to draw investor attention to this material uncertainty pending the approval of the resolutions.

Chapter 4

OFFICERS, FEES
AND REMUNERATION

A Role of the co-ordinator, steering committee, distribution agent and security trustee in a restructuring

B Fees and remuneration

A ROLE OF THE CO-ORDINATOR, STEERING COMMITTEE, DISTRIBUTION AGENT AND SECURITY TRUSTEE IN A RESTRUCTURING

Co-ordinator

4.1 The co-ordinator is appointed by the lenders and the company, and adopts the role of lead bank both during an initial Standstill period (if there is one) and the main restructuring process. It is not unusual for there to be two co-ordinators on larger cases where there are two banks with similar exposures and/or one of those banks is the company's clearing bank. Care should be taken in relation to defining the role of the co-ordinator and well advised companies may seek to define the co-ordinators role as a representative of the lenders in connection with a refinancing or other continuation or renewal of facilities. Use of the word 'restructuring' may well cause an unwanted breach of another financing agreement or an important commercial agreement. More recently, companies that request the appointment of a co-ordinator and which agree to discharge its fees and reasonable costs and expenses and indemnify it for its liabilities will wish to be more prescriptive about its role and will want to ensure that they are receiving value for money. It is not therefore uncommon to see the role of the co-ordinator include 'reasonable efforts to procure or provide' the following:

(a) feedback to the group on any proposals or presentations the group may make or wish to make to the lenders;

(b) act as the principal point of contact between the group, any facility agents and any bilateral lenders or other facility providers in respect of any proposed drawings under, changes or improvements to, or waivers under, the terms of the existing financing arrangements between the group and the relevant lender or the position of the relevant lender thereunder;

(c) discussions with the group in relation to future funding requirements and the position of the existing bank financing and other indebtedness or facilities of the group;

(d) liaison generally with the lenders and advisers in relation to the group's proposals for a future refinancing/restructuring of the group;

(e) collation of all financial and other information relating to the group received by the co-ordinators (in their capacity as such) either directly from the group or on its behalf from any of its advisers or from the advisers to the lenders or from any other source;

(f) assimilation of all information and the summation of it if considered necessary or appropriate to do so;

(g) the periodic dissemination to the lenders of relevant information in whatever format the co-ordinator reasonably considers appropriate. This may be subject to a minimum obligation to disseminate to the lenders in any event, the final form of all formal written reports of legal counsel, reporting accountants or other advisers retained by the co-ordinators; and

(h) responses to inquiries raised by the lenders or the group.

4.2 The company will usually be required to make one or more presentations to its banks outlining its financial position or proposed strategy, on which the co-ordinator will provide feedback from the perspective of the lenders. The co-ordinator therefore acts as the point of contact and conduit between the company and the lenders, making itself available to discuss future bank funding requirements and the default, continuation or renewal of the existing financings and other indebtedness or facilities. This may de facto constitute the co-ordination of a 'restructuring' (even though this word may not have been used in the formal letter appointing the co-ordinator) or a refinancing of the group's facilities.

4.3 The co-ordinator can typically appoint such professional advisers as it thinks necessary, usually following consultation with the company. However, it is not uncommon for the company to seek its consent to the appointment of such advisers or its pre-agreement to the level of fees of such adviser that it will be liable for.

4.4 As part of the agreed terms of the co-ordination and subject to any minimum dissemination obligations as referred to above, the co-ordinator will be able to disclose such information as it thinks relevant to the advisers and the lenders. Each lender and the co-ordinator may well sign into confidentiality undertakings in the formal co-ordinator appointment letter even if the bilateral or syndicated loans that the company has entered into contain confidentiality obligations. This is because the confidentiality undertakings may be different for each lender and may well not cover the circumstances of a complex restructuring.

4.5 The co-ordinator will receive the company's financial reports and other information, and has a wide discretion to act in its own best interests as a lender, creditor or counterparty, and in the best interests of the lenders as a whole. The co-ordinator has no obligation to agree to or support any proposal which the company may suggest, and all dealings are done on an informal 'without prejudice' basis. The co-ordinator will not take on any duties of care or trust or indeed any fiduciary duty to any person.

4.6 The fees of the co-ordinator are negotiated with the corporate and are typically subject to a confidentiality restriction. The fees will cover management time and may well include a 'success' element which will be driven by the specific objectives of the company and its financing needs. This all depends on the circumstances that the company finds itself in and may include the co-ordinator procuring a refinancing, a continuation of facilities, a covenant waiver, ongoing support facilitating a clean audit sign off or the lender's agreement to the company's long-term restructuring plan. Like the co-ordinator's work fee the success fee is also confidential.

4.7 The co-ordinator is expressed to have no duties except those for where express provision is made in the agreement. In addition, market practice has developed so that the co-ordinators can exclude their liability for a multitude of actions, omissions and potential liabilities. Typically this will include the following exclusions or clarifications of the co-ordinator's role:

(a) the co-ordinators shall only convey to the company the views of the lenders to the extent that they can be discerned, but shall not (and shall not be taken to) have any authority to act on behalf of or commit any of the lenders;

(b) the co-ordinators shall not be responsible for the adequacy, accuracy and/or completeness of any information supplied by any member of the group or by any other person in connection with the transactions contemplated by the restructuring;

(c) the co-ordinators shall not be responsible for the legality, validity, effectiveness, adequacy or enforceability of any agreement, arrangement or document entered into, made or executed in anticipation of, pursuant to or in connection with any of the transactions contemplated by the restructuring;

(d) the co-ordinator(s) shall not be responsible for the adequacy, accuracy and/or completeness of any advice obtained by the co-ordinators in connection with the transactions contemplated by the restructuring;

(e) the co-ordinator(s) may each (in their respective capacities as lenders) continue to deal with the group for its own benefit and on its own account; and

(f) the co-ordinator(s) shall have no general duties or duty of care to members of the group, the lenders, or any other person whatsoever.

4.8 It is also market practice for the company and the other lenders and financial constituents to indemnify the co-ordinator for any liabilities including any unpaid professional fees (not paid by the company) that it incurs in performing its duties as a co-ordinator. Such indemnity from the other lenders is not joint and several and is only several. The indemnity is typically provided by the lenders (including the co-ordinator in its capacity as a lender) rateably in the proportion that the sum of the commitments of each lender under its respective facility agreements bears to the total commitments of all of the lenders under all of the facility agreements in each case at the date of the co-ordination letter. In any event the co-ordinator is not to be held liable for any acts or omissions with the usual carve-outs for fraud, gross negligence and wilful default.

4.9 As an indemnified party, the co-ordinator will usually require that it shall be entitled to defend, compromise, settle or deal with any claims or proceedings to which the indemnity applies as it sees fit (acting reasonably and perhaps after consultation with the company and possibly the other lenders).

4.10 The group and the lenders further agree that the co-ordinator shall not have any liability (whether direct or indirect, in contract, tort or otherwise) to any member of the group or any of their shareholders or creditors or to the lenders for or in connection with the restructuring transactions, except to the extent such liability is found, in a final, non-appealable judgment, to have resulted from the co-ordinator's gross negligence, fraud or wilful misconduct.

4.11 While the co-ordinator must convey to the company the views of the lenders, it does not have any authority to represent or act on behalf of any lender, and there will typically be a non-reliance representation from the lenders and the company in favour of the co-ordinator.

Steering committees

4.12 Where there are a great many lenders to a group and in order to retain a consensus amongst such a large group it might be necessary to have either two co-ordinators or to form a steering committee of lenders to lead and co-ordinate the restructuring. In the past certain defined groups of lenders perhaps drawn together by language or their recourse to a specific entity or group of entities have put forward a representative onto a steering committee. By way of example, in the first Gate Gourmet restructuring Danske Bank representing the European banks and Deutsche Bank representing lending interests in the Americas also worked effectively with representatives of an Asian syndicated loan on an informal steering committee.

4.13 Equally where there are a number of dominant institutions having the majority of the exposure in a large syndicate (such as in the Telewest and NTL restructurings of 2002) it is not uncommon for those banks to form a group which will usually be labelled a steering committee rather than joint co-ordinators. In this respect the difference between a co-ordinator and a steering committee will be minimal and the label is typically one of mere description as opposed to one of any notable substance. Indeed it is even possible that the restructuring would still require a co-ordinator and steering committee with the co-ordinator being the focal point of the steering committee. The large Polestar restructuring for example was managed by a steering committee of three key banks and one hedge fund (effectively representing a number of hedge funds who had bought into the Polestar debt in the secondary market) who operated in an identical fashion to joint co-ordinators. As such the terms of the steering committee appointment will incorporate the same type of terms on which co-ordinators are appointed and which have been examined in detail in the preceding section. The only difference will be that there will be additional provisions relating to steering committee voting and the removal of steering committee members.

4.14 In the modern era of multi-tiered financings incorporating separate classes of debt such as inter alia senior loans, privately placed notes, publicly traded bonds, commercial paper, swing-line or liquidity facilities and equipment lessors as mere examples, or where there are facilities made available to the group with different features such as asset-based facilities or project finance debt or perhaps where there is subordinated debt or a diverse array of financings and financial accommodation made available to a group such as derivatives, it is likely that a single co-ordinator or joint co-ordinators representing all constituencies will be unworkable. Co-ordination of these numerous constituencies will however be imperative in order to ensure an efficient restructuring process and to achieve this a steering committee might be formed with a representative of each financial constituency represented on it. The restructuring of Scottish Media Group in 2001 operated in this manner with the working capital bank (which was under constant pressure to provide liquidity) co-operating through a committee with the agents of a senior and mezzanine facility and a representative of the US$ privately placed notes.

Distribution agent/account bank

4.15 The distribution agent or account bank will be appointed by the lenders to act as their paying agent under and in connection with the finance documents pursuant to the restructuring. The distribution agent or account bank will usually be the existing agent and will liaise closely with the co-ordinator/agent or the security trustee/agent in terms of making distributions to the institutions both prior to and following an insolvency event. The distribution agent/account bank will calculate the respective lenders' entitlements under the finance documents in line with their commitments and exposures, will receive all payments and fees in connection with the original facilities, and allocate the amounts recovered to the original lenders. The distribution agent may also need to calculate equalisation payments and loss sharing under the original facilities. Unlike the co-ordinator who can act in its own capacity, the distribution agent acts for and on the instructions of the lenders. The distribution agent's fees and expenses are paid by the company and like other administrative parties (such as co-ordinators/steering committee member agents and security trustees) such fees will be usually discharged out of the first tier of priority that is negotiated under the restructuring or other similar agreement.

Security trustee/agent

4.16 A security trustee will be appointed where there is a security take-up as part of the restructuring. Where the security is granted in overseas jurisdictions (particularly civil law jurisdictions) where the concept of a trustee and a trust is not recognised the role will be one of security agent.

4.17 A raft of security trustee/agent protections and indemnities are included in the restructuring agreement and it is probable that the security trustee/agent will charge a separate fee. The security trustee/agent will be entitled to appoint professional advisers and to be reimbursed for their costs out of the first tier of priority that is negotiated under the restructuring or other similar agreement.

Conflict of interest

4.18 On occasion the various interests of one or more lead banks in connection with a corporate rescue may conflict. For instance, it may act as financial adviser to the company or be a lender to the company in a capacity which differs from that of some or all of the other lenders, with the result that its interests potentially conflict with those of other lenders. A lead bank is not (at least in its capacity as a banker) subject to express regulation in this respect. The obligations of a lead bank in relation to conflict of interest are derived from general law and in particular the law of agency. The general rule is that an agent, in accordance with his fiduciary obligations, should not allow himself to remain in a position in which his personal interests and his duty to his principal conflict, without full disclosure. As an extension of this he should not enter into any transaction in which his personal interest might conflict with his duty to his principal, unless the principal, with full knowledge of all the material circumstances and of the exact nature and extent of the agent's interest, consents.

4.19 The presence of a conflict of interest will not necessarily mean a particular lender should not act as lead bank or steering committee member. Whether or not it does so is a matter for the bank concerned and the lenders on behalf of whom it is acting and any other party involved in the restructuring, for instance the company, following disclosure of the conflict issue. If all of the affected parties are in agreement that a lender should act as a lead bank notwithstanding a conflict of interest, it may do so. In assessing its position the lead bank should identify its various capacities and roles in the restructuring or as a result of its existing relationship with the company and determine whether it is prevented from discharging any of them by reason of having to discharge any other functions in the restructuring or any obligations outside of the restructuring to another person. Once its various roles and obligations have been identified, full disclosure should be made to the affected parties and the appropriate consents, if the parties are agreeable, obtained.

4.20 The conflict provisions are carefully drafted and will provide that the group acknowledge that the co-ordinators or one or more of its respective affiliates may be providing financing or other services to third parties whose interests may conflict with those of the group and that by signing the co-ordination letter the group is consenting to financing or other services being provided to such third parties. However, against this consent it is still provided that neither the co-ordinators nor any of its respective affiliates will furnish confidential information obtained from the group to any of their other customers. Equally, the group will acknowledge that neither the co-ordinators nor any of their respective affiliates will make available to the group confidential information that they have obtained or may obtain from any other customer.

4.21 Due to the fact that co-ordinators, lead banks and steering committee members receive information ahead of the general body of lenders, it is not unusual for the company and other financial constituents to press for an undertaking from those involved in the leadership of the restructuring that they will not trade in the company's debt (either as a seller or a purchaser) during intervals where key information has not been disseminated to the various lenders.

B FEES AND REMUNERATION

Fees

4.22 The range and the structure of fees payable on a restructuring are only really limited by the imagination of the various constituencies and their respective advisers. In almost all restructurings those leading the restructuring effort whether as a sole co-ordinator, joint co-ordinator or steering committee member will legitimately seek to charge a 'work fee' for the enormous amount of management time and specialist restructuring and turnaround knowledge that is invested in managing the process and ensuring that the restructuring is conducted in an efficient and orderly manner. In order to manage complex situations effectively the larger banks that specialise in this arena need to be adequately resourced with professional restructuring bankers of the highest quality and it is inevitable that as the costs of establishing and preserving these teams has increased, 'work' fees have similarly increased.

4.23 In many cases the company in question will be or is likely to be in breach of certain of its covenants and undertakings or an event or circumstance may have occurred which operates to 'draw-stop' a facility thereby affecting the company's liquidity. Inevitably those lenders or constituencies who are required to agree to a variation to their existing relationship with the company may legitimately seek to charge a 'waiver' fee in return for their agreement to waive their contractual rights. Similarly, if a mere waiver will not suffice and a company requires a permanent amendment of its facilities or financial covenants such that they require an actual amendment to the contract, then it is not unreasonable for those agreeing to reset the agreement to charge an amendment or arrangement fee. Typically the quantum of an amendment fee might well be higher than a waiver fee, but in both scenarios the fee will be shaped by the magnitude of the waivers or amendment, the duration and frequency of it, the life of the current facility, the quantum of the current margin and the concern that an amendment is necessary so soon after the facility was implemented and of course the change in the underlying credit risk and the reason for and basis and nature of the amendment or waiver. A waiver of a payment default might cause much greater concern than a waiver of a disposal restriction which is being sought in order to de-leverage. Equally a wholesale amendment and restatement of an existing facility will legitimise a much higher amendment fee and likely change to lending margins.

4.24 If lenders are being asked to extend their facilities, for example in order to ensure that a company's auditors are able to issue an unqualified going concern statement (see Chapter 3 *'Information, disclosure and year end reporting'* in this regard) or would otherwise be unable to issue a Class 1 circular and associated working capital statement in relation to a planned disposal as part of the restructuring, then it is not unusual for lenders to charge an 'extension or renewal' fee. Inevitably, the reason for such an extension, its duration and the credit outlook for the company and the associated refinancing risks will drive the fee.

4.25 In many restructuring scenarios there will inevitably be a liquidity or funding crisis of some description requiring a new money injection. New money is typically afforded priority status, but the very need for new money and its dilutive effect as a result of its priority inevitably triggers a detailed assessment of the corporate's underlying credit quality not only for those providing it but those ranking behind it (see Chapter 2 for a full analysis of the new money process). Even with its priority status there are a number of cases in recent years where new money has not been repaid in full and therefore those providing it will wish to ensure that it is priced appropriately both in terms of margin, but also in terms of a 'new money arrangement or underwriting fees'.

4.26 Most restructurings usually culminate in a refinancing of some description, quite often on amended terms and for an extended maturity. Such a refinancing provides stability and because it replaces existing commitments and requires a new facility to be put in place, such a facility will almost certainly include an arrangement and underwriting fee as a condition precedent.

4.27 In many cases the distressed company will formulate a restructuring plan or strategy in conjunction with its advisers. Such a plan will obviously seek to maximise returns for the company side stakeholders which will include existing shareholders, new investors, pension funds and directors and employees. It would be rare for any plan not to require significant support from a number of financial creditors not merely in terms of running an efficient restructuring process which justifies a 'work fee' for those involved in managing the process, but also in terms of persuading and 'delivering' those constituencies and getting them credit approved and over the line. Depending on the nature of the request of lenders, the extent of the support required from them and the difficulty of achieving this, those co-ordinating the process and achieving a successful outcome for the company side stakeholders will seek to recover a success-based fee. This will typically be a cash-based fee and may well be linked to the recovery in the share price and the enhanced shareholder return through some form of synthetic warrant or equity derivative. The success fee may well be back-ended and may be payable if the company has not repaid the facilities by a specified period or the shareholders have not injected any equity capital. As such it can operate as an incentive to a refinancing or a rights issue.

Warrants, options or equity-based fees

4.28 Creditors who are required to agree to a variation to their existing relationship with the company may extract a price in return for its agreement to the rescue. A fee as outlined in the preceding section could be payable, but on occasions and quite often in addition to a fee, more sophisticated incentives will be negotiated in the form of warrants. A warrant is, essentially, a right to subscribe for share capital at a given point in time and at a given price. Warrants are typically requested in circumstances where there is insufficient liquidity to pay an adequate cash fee or where the level of support provided by lenders is so important to the survival of the business as a going concern or to the preservation of shareholder value that it is legitimate for a more substantive reward to be allocated to the lenders which is linked to the incremental shareholder value arising from the restructuring. There will inevitably be more pressure for an equity-based fee if existing equity investors are not contributing to the restructuring by injecting new equity capital and a dilution to that value is appropriate. The dilutive effect of giving an equity interest to lenders is obviously an emotive issue for shareholders and directors alike, but where the level and quality of credit risk has deteriorated to a demonstrable level, for example because the earnings of the company compared to its level of indebtedness has spiralled to unacceptable multiples, then lenders may well argue that they are taking 'equity risk' and should be rewarded accordingly. Lenders may be persuaded not to take warrants where the shareholders are injecting new money through the grant of subordinated shareholder loans or through a rights issue, but there are many cases where this has still been deemed insufficient by lenders to de-leverage a company and remove the significant risks for lenders, such that warrants have still been granted contemporaneously with a rights issue. This proved to be the case on the John Laing restructuring of 2002 and the AEA technology restructuring of 2005.

4.29 As intimated a warrant is, essentially, a right to subscribe for share capital at a given point in time and at a given price, possibly at 'par' value or at a price below market value. As well as approving and entering into the warrant instrument itself, thereby granting the warrants to the lenders for a specific consideration (typically set at a de minimis level), certain legal considerations need to be undertaken by the company, as set out below. Although the company should also consider the commercial and public impact of issuing warrants, especially as this will dilute existing shareholders, in the context of a restructuring, this may be a necessary element of the transaction and the company's survival.

4.30 The company's authorised share capital must be sufficient to cover the number of shares over which subscription rights will arise upon exercise of the warrants. Such authorised share capital must be kept available (and otherwise uncommitted) whilst any warrants remain unexercised after being granted. If the company has insufficient authorised share capital at the time that the warrants are granted, an ordinary resolution of the company's shareholders will be required to make the necessary increase, pursuant to the Companies Act 1985, s 121[1].

[1] The Companies Act 1985, s 121(1) is to be replaced (with some changes) by the Companies Act 2006, s 617(1). The Companies Act 1985, s 121(2) is to be replaced (with some changes) by the Companies Act 2006, ss 617(2), (3), 618(1) and 620(1). The Companies Act 1985, s 121(3) is to be replaced by the Companies Act 2006, s 618(2). The Companies Act 1985, s 121(4) is to be replaced (with some changes) by the Companies Act 2006, ss 618(3) and 620(2). These Companies Act 2006 provisions are not yet in force although it is anticipated that they will be brought into force on 1 October 2009.

4.31 In order to allot 'relevant securities' the directors of the company must have appropriate authority to do so pursuant to the Companies Act 1985, s 80[1]. 'Relevant securities' include any right to subscribe for shares (such as a warrant), and an allotment of relevant securities includes, therefore, the grant of warrants. Therefore, and pursuant to the Companies Act 1985, s 80[2], the relevant authority which is to be granted to the directors must cover the maximum amount of shares which may be allotted pursuant to the warrants and, provided that this is the case, no further authorities will be required at the time the warrants are exercised and the underlying shares are allotted.

[1] The Companies Act 1985, s 80(1) is to be replaced by the Companies Act 2006, ss 549(1) and 551(1). The Companies Act 1985, s 80(2) is to be replaced by the Companies Act 2006, ss 549(1)–(3), 551(1) and 559. The Companies Act 1985, s 80(3)–(8) is to be replaced by the Companies Act 2006, s 551(2)–(8). The Companies Act 1985, s 80(9) and (10) is to be replaced (with some changes) by the Companies Act 2006, s 549(4)–(6). These Companies Act 2006 provisions are not yet in force although it is anticipated that they will be brought into force on 1 October 2009.
[2] See footnote 1.

4.32 If the directors have insufficient authority to allot relevant securities at the time that the warrants are granted, then an ordinary resolution of the company's shareholders will be required. The Association of British Insurers ('ABI') has published guidelines on directors' authority to allot shares for the purposes of granting warrants and in the case of a listed company these guidelines provide that such an authority is not to exceed the authorised unissued share capital and one third of the company's issued share capital, whichever is lower. These guidelines will need to be taken into account if seeking shareholder approval, and any proposed derogation should be considered with shareholders and shareholder bodies or representatives as early as possible. These guidelines do not prevent a distressed company from seeking an ordinary resolution permitting its directors to allot relevant securities in excess of the ABI's recommended level if this is necessary in order to meet the commercial requirements of its lenders, but the dilutive effect of granting a significant number of warrants to third parties will obviously be considered carefully by shareholders and shareholder bodies or their representatives.

4.33 Where a company proposes to allot 'equity securities' wholly or partly for cash, the Companies Act 1985, s 89[1] requires that it may not do so unless a pre-emptive offer is made, on a pro rata basis, to the current holders of 'relevant shares' (or 'relevant employee shares', being shares which would be 'relevant' but for the fact that they are held in an employee's share scheme). Warrants will fall within the definition of 'equity securities', being a right to subscribe for relevant shares (since relevant shares are shares other than those which carry only a limited right to income and capital) and, therefore, if the subscription price for the allotment of shares upon exercise of the warrants is to be paid up in cash, the pre-emption provisions of the Companies Act 1985, s 89[2] will be relevant.

[1]   The Companies Act 1985, s 89(1) is to be replaced by the Companies Act 2006, s 561(1). The Companies Act 1985, s 89(2) and (3) is to be replaced by the Companies Act 2006, s 568(1) and (2). The Companies Act 1985, s 89(4) is to be replaced by the Companies Act 2006, ss 561(2) and 565. The Companies Act 1985, s 89(5) is to be replaced by the Companies Act 2006, s 566. These Companies Act 2006 provisions are not yet in force although it is anticipated that they will be brought into force on 1 October 2009.

[2]   See footnote 1.

4.34   To the extent that the company wishes to avoid making a pre-emptive offer – which will be the case where a third party lender is seeking to take an equity interest as part of a debt restructuring deal – it will need to take advantage of the disapplication provisions of the Companies Act 1985, s 95[1]. Listed companies typically have approval in place each year which allows a certain amount (usually 5%) of the company's share capital to be allotted for cash on a non-pre-emptive basis but, depending upon the dilution which would result from the grant and exercise of the Warrants, this may not be sufficient.

[1]   The Companies Act 1985, s 95(1) is to be replaced by the Companies Act 2006, ss 570(1) and (2) and 573(2), (3) and (5). The Companies Act 1985, s 95(2) is to be replaced by the Companies Act 2006, ss 571(1) and (2) and 573(4). The Companies Act 1985, s 95(2A) is to be replaced by the Companies Act 2006, s 573(1)–(5). The Companies Act 1985, s 95(3) is to be replaced by the Companies Act 2006, ss 570(3) and 571(3). The Companies Act 1985, s 95(4) is to be replaced by the Companies Act 2006, ss 570(4), 571(4) and 573(3) and (5). The Companies Act 1985, s 95(5) is to be replaced (with some changes) by the Companies Act 2006, ss 571(5)–(7) and 573(5). The Companies Act 1985, s 95(6) is to be replaced by the Companies Act 2006, s 572(1)–(3). These Companies Act 2006 provisions are not yet in force although it is anticipated that they will be brought into force on 1 October 2009.

4.35   Shareholder approval, by special resolution, is required to disapply the statutory pre-emption rights discussed above. In addition, listed companies need to consider the Statement of Principles issued by the 'Pre-Emption Group', which principles apply to companies on the Official List, and with which companies listed on AIM are also encouraged to comply. The key feature of the Statement of Principles is that any routine or annual disapplication should, generally, be limited to 5% of the relevant share capital in any one year, with a cumulative limit of 7.5% of relevant share capital in any rolling three-year period. The maximum discount at which shares should be issued on a non-pre-emptive basis is expected to be 5% to the market price. If the company is considering exceeding these parameters, it should raise the issue of such a non-routine request with shareholders and shareholder bodies or representatives at the earliest opportunity.

4.36   If it is key for the company to avoid seeking a special resolution from its shareholders (such as to disapply statutory pre-emption rights), the company could consider receiving payment for the shares which will be allotted upon exercise of the warrants in non-cash consideration. This has two main consequences. Firstly, appropriate non-cash consideration will need to be paid by the bank, as holder of the warrants, upon their exercise. It should be noted, however, that the release of a liability of the company for a liquidated sum (such as the waiver of a debt) will be treated as cash for the purposes of the Companies Acts. Given that this type of mechanic may well be under consideration by the parties (effectively, a 'debt for warrant' swap), a section 89 disapplication will still be required in these circumstances.

4.37 Secondly, the Companies Act 1985, s 103[1] requires that where a public company allots shares as fully or partly paid up otherwise than in cash, it must obtain an independent valuation of such non-cash consideration, which must have been prepared in the six months immediately preceding such allotment. This valuation requirement does not apply to a preliminary issue of rights to subscribe for shares (such as the granting of warrants), but will apply at the time when the shares are eventually allotted to the warrantholder.

[1] The Companies Act 1985, s 103(1) and (2) is to be replaced by the Companies Act 2006, s 593(1) and (2). The Companies Act 1985, s 103(3) and (4) is to be replaced by the Companies Act 2006, s 594(1)–(5). The Companies Act 1985, s 103(5) is to be replaced by the Companies Act 2006, s 595(1) and (2). The Companies Act 1985, s 103(6) is to be replaced by the Companies Act 2006, s 593(3). The Companies Act 1985, s 103(7) is to be replaced by the Companies Act 2006, ss 594(6) and 595(3). These Companies Act 2006 provisions are not yet in force although it is anticipated that they will be brought into force on 1 October 2009.

4.38 At the time that any warrants are granted (perhaps for nominal consideration), the underlying shares are not being allotted – this occurs when a person acquires the unconditional right to be included in the company's register of members. It is, therefore, only upon exercise of the warrants, and payment up of the subscription price for the underlying shares, that such shares will be allotted. If, at this stage, the allotment is for non-cash consideration, an appropriate independent valuation, prepared by the company's auditor, will need to have been prepared.

4.39 In all circumstances where the underlying shares are allotted upon exercise of the warrants, such shares must not (pursuant to the Companies Act 1985, s 100[1]) be allotted at a discount to their nominal value. For public companies, such shares must also be paid up as to at least 25% of their nominal value, plus any premium, at the time of allotment.

[1] The Companies Act 1985, s 100 is to be replaced by the Companies Act 2006, s 580, which is not yet in force although it is anticipated that it will be brought into force on 1 October 2009.

4.40 If the approval of the company's shareholders in general meeting is required for the grant of the warrants, perhaps to increase the authorised share capital, grant authority to allot shares or disapply pre-emption rights, then the listed company must send out a notice of general meeting to its shareholders, accompanied by an explanatory circular.

4.41 The explanatory circular must comply with the contents requirements of chapter 13 of UKLA's Listing Rules, and may need to be approved by the FSA prior to publication. Although the Listing Rules set out circumstances in which the FSA's prior approval is not required, it will always be prudent for the company to have an open dialogue with the FSA (particularly if it is in difficulty), and to give the FSA the opportunity to comment on its public documents.

4.42 Although a nominal consideration may only be payable at the time the warrants are issued, the company issuing the warrants will seek to negotiate a 'strike-price' at which the warrantholder can subsequently exercise the warrants when the underlying shares are allotted. The strike price is therefore the subscription price for the underlying shares that is subsequently payable when such warrant shares are allotted to the holder. Such shares must not (pursuant to the Companies Act 1985, s 100[1]) be allotted at a discount to their nominal value and so the negotiated strike price is therefore within a range from the nominal value of the shares to a discount on the current share price. Listed companies are often quite reluctant to give the lenders a complete windfall by fixing the share price at the nominal value of the shares, especially in less distressed situations where there is likely to be a significant recovery of the share price and so quite often the agreed position is a strike price based on the average share price of the company during the period commencing on or just after the first all-lender meeting and ending on the date that the restructuring is completed or an agreed period thereafter.

[1]   See para 4.39, footnote 1.

4.43 One of the key points for negotiation with respect to the grant of warrants or options as part of a restructuring is the size of the equity stake to be issued to the lenders upon exercise. Most listed companies typically have approval in place each year which allows a certain amount (usually 5%) of the company's share capital to be allotted for cash on a non-pre-emptive basis but, depending upon the dilution which would result from the grant and exercise of the warrants, this may not be sufficient and a shareholder approval to increase the amount of the company's share capital that can be allotted on a non-pre-emptive basis may be required. This will require a circular and a shareholder approval and so it is not unusual for a public company to resist a request for an increase on this basis.

4.44 In cases of significant distress, it is not uncommon for lenders to seek a significant amount of warrants that can give rise to a sizeable equity stake. There are however limits on the size of the equity stake that can be subject to the warrants. Indeed under (Rule 9) of the Takeover Code, when a person acquires or persons acting in concert acquire:

(a)   shares which carry 30% or more of the voting rights of a company; or
(b)   (if such person or persons already hold between 30% and 50% of the voting rights of a company) an interest which increases the percentage of voting rights held by it or them,

a general offer to all other shareholders to acquire their shares must be made on the same terms. Rule 9 will capture shareholdings that are created as a result of the exercise of warrants and options and so it does impose a 30% ceiling on the amount of warrants that can be issued.

4.45 In addition, under Listing Rule 6.1.22(1), the total of all issued warrants to subscribe for equity shares or options to subscribe for equity shares must not exceed 20% of the company's issued equity share capital (excluding treasury shares) as at the time of the issue of the warrants or options. Rights under employees' share schemes are not included for the purpose of this 20% limit.

4.46 Prospectus Rule 1.2 and the Financial Services and Markets Act 2000, ss 85 and 86 provide that before an offer to the public of transferable securities can be made, a prospectus approved by the FSA will be required. It is unlikely that an issue to the banks of warrants or of the underlying shares would constitute an offer to the public for these purposes, but a prospectus would be required before a request were made to admit transferable securities to trading on a regulated market (including the main market of the London Stock Exchange). This would not apply to the issue of unlisted warrants and there is an exemption to this requirement[1] where shares representing, over a period of 12 months, less than 10% of the number of shares of the same class are already admitted to trading on the same regulated market. This exemption would apply in respect of the issue of shares underlying the warrants until such time as a request for admission were made which would take the number of shares issued over a period of 12 months above the 10% threshold. As such there is a de-facto limit on the number of shares that can be subject to a warrant without the need to publish a prospectus with the effect that the amount of underlying shares should not be more than 10% of the number of shares of the same class already admitted to trading on the same regulated market.

[1]   Set forth in Prospectus Rule 1.2.3(1).

4.47 One solution to the 10% limit imposed by the Prospectus Rules might be to convert the listing from the Official List to AIM because a prospectus would not be required in connection with the issue of warrants or the underlying shares if the company were AIM listed, even if the 10% threshold were exceeded, since AIM is not a 'regulated market'[1]. The conversion to AIM will however require an approval of 75% of the shareholders[2] and will not permit warrants in excess of 30% of the underlying shares in the company to be granted without breaching Rule 9 of the Takeover Code.

[1]   AIM Rule 27.
[2]   See Chapter 3 '*Information, disclosure and year end reporting*', Section G 'Easing the disclosure burden through an AIM Listing'.

4.48 In order to retain lender support and commitment to the restructuring, listed corporates that issue warrants to lenders as part of a restructuring process may seek to provide that the warrants are 'stapled' to the debt, such that if a lender sells or otherwise transfers its lending commitments and loan interests then the warrants issued to that lender cease to be exercisable. Many lenders resist this fetter on their liquidity and the transferability of their debt and so insist that the warrants are detachable and can be sold and transferred independently and irrespective of whether the lender is still a holder of the original underlying debt. It might also be possible to stagger the issue of warrants into two separate series so that, for example, further warrants are issued to a lender if they have not transferred their debt by a given date or if they participate in a refinancing.

4.49 In order to enable lenders holding warrants to extract value from the warrants efficiently, it is common for well advised lenders to seek a 'broker assistance' clause in the warrant instrument. This type of clause typically provides that if the warrantholder serves a notice of exercise electing to exercise its warrants pursuant to the specific 'broker assistance' provision then the company shall within a specified number of business days instruct its brokers to use their reasonable endeavours to procure subscribers for the warrant shares at the best cash price available in the market on the business day following receipt of such instructions from the company. The brokers will then notify the company and the relevant warrantholder of whether or not it has found subscribers for the warrant shares in the market and, if it has, of the market price to be payable by the subscriber. If the relevant warrantholder accepts such market price by notice in writing to the company, the company then instructs the brokers to arrange for such subscription to take place as soon as reasonably practicable and the company shall, within a specified period of such subscription, instruct the brokers to pay to the relevant warrantholder the amount by which the market price (after deduction of reasonable broker's commission and other reasonable expenses associated with the procurement of such subscribers) is greater than the agreed strike price in the warrant instrument. This is a neat mechanism that gives lenders access to the market for their shares without becoming a registered shareholder and physically paying the strike price.

4.50 In order to protect the warrantholder a professionally drafted warrant instrument will contain a number of warrantholder protections. These protections will inevitably include provisions providing that the warrant shares issued shall be credited as fully paid, shall have the same rights set out in the articles relating to ordinary shares and shall rank pari passu in all respects with ordinary shares then in issue. More specifically the protections will provide that warrant shares issued shall rank for any dividend or other distribution which has been previously announced or declared if the date by which the holder of shares must be registered to participate in such dividend or other distribution is after the date in which the warrantholder validly served a notice exercising its warrants.

4.51 The most obvious mechanism for eroding the value of warrants granted to a warrantholder is for the company to dilute the warrant shares by issuing more shares or conducting other forms of equity raising. It is therefore common for professionally drafted warrant instruments to include extensive anti-dilution provisions. This type of provision usually provides that the number of warrant shares in respect of each outstanding warrant shall be subject to adjustment from time to time upon the occurrence of any of the following:

(a) any cancellation or reduction of any of the company's share capital or its share premium account or capital redemption reserve;

(b) any purchase or redemption by the company of any of its share capital;

(c) any allotment, issue or grant of any right to subscribe for, or to convert securities into, share capital of any member of the group (other than pursuant to the issue of any warrant shares or any existing employee share scheme);

(d) any subdivision, consolidation or reclassification of any of the company's shares;

(e) any distribution of income, capital, profits or reserves in cash whether of cash, assets or other property, and whenever paid or made and however described (and for these purposes a distribution of assets includes without limitation an issue of shares or other securities credited as fully or partly paid up).

4.52 If any of the above events occur then the company will be obliged to adjust the number of warrant shares a warrantholder is entitled to on exercise of its warrant in a manner certified in writing by the auditors who typically act as an independent arbiter in the case of any such event occurring.

4.53 Whilst much of this analysis has focused on public company restructurings the issue of warrants for lenders undertaking a restructuring of a private company in the leveraged loans market is also common. Given the private company status of the entity certain of the constraints articulated above, such as the ABI guidelines, will not apply. However, the underlying financial sponsor or private equity firm might well have significant relationships with the lenders in question (unless the debt has traded) and will seek to ensure that any equity participation proposed by the lenders is not opportunistic or disproportionate.

Funding bonds

4.54 Shares issued by a company in satisfaction of its obligations to pay interest on debt will be funding bonds for the purposes of the Income and Corporation Taxes Act 1988 ('ICTA 1988'), s 582. ICTA 1988, s 582 applies to debt incurred by a body corporate and 'funding bond' includes any bonds, stocks, shares, securities or certificates of indebtedness. The issue of funding bonds is treated as the payment of interest for all purposes of ICTA 1988, with the effect that a company which is obliged to deduct an amount in respect of lower or basic rate tax from payments of interest will be obliged to deduct a similar amount represented by the issue of funding bonds. The company may be released from its obligations to deduct funding bonds on account of tax if the Revenue is persuaded that such a deduction is impractical. This is conditional on the company providing the Revenue with details of the person to whom the bonds are issued so that assessments under Case VI, Schedule D can be made on these recipients.

4.55 If the company is not obliged to deduct an amount in respect of tax from interest payable by it, for instance because the interest is paid in the UK on an advance from a bank (within the meaning of ICTA 1988, s 840A), and, at the time when the interest is paid, the person beneficially entitled to the interest (either the original lender or an assignee of the loan) is within the charge to corporation tax as respects that interest, the company will not be obliged to make a deduction from funding bonds issued in satisfaction of interest. A lender, which receives funding bonds in satisfaction of a company's obligations to pay it interest, must treat the funding bonds as a payment of interest, and will be required to account for the funding bonds in determining its liability to tax.

Chapter 5

THE IMPORTANCE OF VALUATIONS IN THE RESTRUCTURING PROCESS

A   General introduction
B   Liquidation analysis
C   Going concern valuations
D   Valuations based on bid interest
E   Valuation tensions

A GENERAL INTRODUCTION

5.1 For those stakeholders interested in a company and its undertaking and how its estate might be distributed either through an insolvent liquidation or a consensual restructuring, it is essential that a valuation of its business and assets be conducted under both scenarios based upon the current view of value.

5.2 Invariably the isolation of the point in the capital structure where value breaks can be determinative of the whole restructuring process and the negotiation of it. Inevitably where the value of the business is less than the quantum of the total debt one will peer into the capital structure to see which debt is impaired. Despite the plethora of leveraged finance transactions in the period from 2002, and the steady increase in senior leveraged multiples, one would still expect that the most senior debt with the lowest coupon will be performing and so senior lenders who are potentially unimpaired may be less likely to be the driving force in the restructuring. These senior lenders will often monitor the restructuring process to ensure that their value is maintained and not hampered by any actions taken by other stakeholders in the restructuring process. Conversely, those creditors whose debt is most likely to be impaired will perceive the equity value to be negligible and will often seek to negotiate either a total or partial ownership interest as part of the restructuring process. Of course where the value of the business exceeds the value of the debt current shareholders will seek to retain ownership of the troubled corporate. In a restructuring it is therefore obvious why valuation is an issue of such magnitude.

5.3 Impending financial distress compounds the difficulties of reaching an agreed valuation and this is true irrespective of whether the restructuring is executed through a formal court process or consensually through a contractual process. Of course the potentially dilutive effect of a court process (due to the resulting adverse publicity, inevitable delays, inherent uncertainty and professional costs) would be one additional factor that would need to be taken into account in making a determination as to value.

5.4 Another factor that complicates any valuation process is the tension between valuing the whole of a business on a wholly consolidated basis or the sum of its constituent parts. This is particularly relevant with respect to corporates that are highly divisionalised or which operate a number of different businesses. Both approaches (single enterprise or sum of the parts) would appear feasible, but where there is a centralised head-office function or internal trading subsidies between group companies, those expenses need to be correctly accounted for in reaching a valuation. Valuing a business by its constituent parts is often instructive and facilitates a broader strategic review because it will highlight the viability of each constituent business and enables those businesses to be identified as consumers or generators of value.

5.5 Typically valuations of financially impaired corporates in a restructuring process are conducted under two bases: as either a going concern or on the basis of a liquidation analysis. However, as we will see, in restructuring scenarios where a specific creditor constituency is on the evidence 'out of the money', the English courts have thus far declined to allocate value to such a constituency by adopting more hypothetical valuations based on the projected future value of the entity.

B LIQUIDATION ANALYSIS

5.6 If a corporate is not economically viable[1] because the value of its business as a going concern is worth less than the break-up value of its assets then any prolonged operation of the business will compound the losses of the stake-holders and it is logical in such circumstances that assets would be sold piecemeal on an expedited basis ahead of a liquidation and ideally in an efficient market for a price equating to their market value.

[1]   A business will not be considered economically viable if it cannot earn a sustainable economic return on capital, where capital is defined by reference to the liquidation value of the assets.

5.7 In order to achieve market value it will be necessary to have an efficient sale process, involving market testing, adequate marketing, competitive tension, opportunities for adequate due diligence and time to negotiate a sale, to maximise price. Often existing lenders agree a standstill or short-term support to defer a possible insolvent liquidation in order to create such a favourable environment so as to maximise value for stakeholders and ensure that appropriate contingency planning is undertaken. Equally, circumstances may dictate a more accelerated and less conventional sale process. In an insolvent liquidation, for example, the aspiration of a liquidator is to maximise net realisations as soon as possible, which often takes the form of a quick sale. Quite often a liquidator or other insolvency office holder will conduct a sale on an expedited basis to protect against the negative impact of 'cash-burn' and the resulting erosion of value.

5.8 Liquidation analysis is inevitably more sophisticated than a more simpli-fied desktop calculation of the fire sale value of the assets. Most specialist insolvency advisers engaged by creditors will spend time establishing the aggregate accounting and liquidation value of all assets before embarking on a calculation of enforcement returns for secured and unsecured creditors after taking into account enforcement costs. It should be noted that whilst this mode of valuation is referred to as a *'liquidation analysis'*, in both the UK and other jurisdictions, the precise process of effecting realisations through an enforcement process can be varied and may include diverse processes such as administrative receivership for pre-Enterprise Act 2002 security, fixed charge receivership, sale by public auction in certain European and civil court jurisdictions or administration or similar processes including liquidation itself. The point here is that liquidation analysis is a generic term denoting some form of enforcement process to realise value either through a private or contractual means or via a legislative or court process.

5.9 Any valuation on a liquidation basis will require an assessment of the value of each asset class on a balance sheet and will take into account a raft of factors such as asset type, liquidity, condition, encumbrances, degree and purpose of annexation in the case of fixtures and the level of marketing required. There is inevitably a degree of due diligence and verification conducted by the insolvency office holder and prospective purchasers as to ownership, existence and location of the relevant assets, taxation and base costs of the asset, the range of prospective purchasers and the degree of competitive tension and the impact of insolvency laws and procedures.

5.10 For more specialised or intangible assets such as brands, trade marks and intellectual property and fixed assets such as real estate, fixtures and plant the assistance of surveyors and other professional valuers is required. The spectrum will typically range from nominal value on fire sale to market value or possibly even premium value in the case of vital intellectual property or key component tools or parts. In the automotive sector, for example, where tooling is often owned by a key supplier (as opposed to the customer) and a cessation of 'just-in-time' supply by that insolvent supplier could terminate a whole production line, premiums have been levied[1].

---

[1]   See *Re TransTec Automotive (Campsie) Ltd* [2001] BCC 403.

5.11 Where the prospects for sale or recoverability are uncertain, such as with inventory, much will depend on the nature of the asset, including its condition and perishability, whether it is bespoke or generic and the extent of supplier's claims under 'retention of title' arrangements. Invariably inventory is discounted, sometimes by almost its entire book value.

5.12 Receivables are a similar case in point, current receivables with credit-worthy counterparties may be valued at close to 100% after applying a minor discount for collection costs, whereas aged receivables may be valued at a figure as low as zero depending on the level of dispute relating to the debt, the credit worthiness of the counterparty and the opportunities for counterclaims and set-off. The nature of the business is the biggest potential factor here – a receivable owed to a simple wholesaler of goods will typically see high levels of recoveries whereas receivables owed to a contractor will quite often see very low recovery levels.

C GOING CONCERN VALUATIONS

5.13 Valuation and value realisation becomes much more blurred and far more debated by the stakeholders when the company is in the middle ground: where it is neither a basket-case that is cashflow insolvent and beyond economic redemption nor a stable entity with good fundamentals merely requiring support in order to maximise value via a managed disposal process or a stand-alone restructuring. The middle ground is occupied by corporates that are financially distressed yet economically viable and which require turnaround operationally and/or restructuring financially – Eurotunnel is a classic example of such a business. It may have a wholly inappropriate balance sheet and may be over-leveraged with illiquid assets and unable to meet its liabilities as they fall due but it is still generating EBITDA (earnings before interest, taxes, depreciation and amortisation) and the business is worth preserving as a going concern since returns are arguably higher than in a liquidation or other enforcement process. Such a business is said to be a going concern and it will be possible to attribute to it an *'enterprise value'*.

5.14 In the context of a restructuring, an entity with negative cashflow may be regarded more negatively than an entity with positive cashflow that can't meet its liabilities as they fall due[1]. In the first scenario the entity is said to be economically distressed (not merely financially distressed) and liquidation is likely to produce the best return to creditors. In the second scenario the company may be perceived as a good company with a bad balance sheet, but because it is generating positive cashflows it will be perceived to be worth preserving as a going concern and will be judged to have an enterprise value.

[1] There are exceptions of course – biotechnology and internet businesses may have negative cashflow but as growth opportunities they may well be perceived positively by investors and financiers.

5.15 As Jay Westbrook[1] has stated 'Going concern value may be much greater than market value (and therefore much, much greater than liquidation value) because a living business with established customers, knowledgeable employees and so forth may well bring a higher price as a unit than would the sale of each asset separately, even in the unlikely event that those separate sales would obtain market value for each asset'.

[1] Jay Westbrook, 'The control of wealth in bankruptcy' (2004) 82(4) Texas LR 795, 811.

5.16 Realising the enterprise value of a company which is financially distressed is akin to navigating a stormy sea. Initiating a sale process by an investment bank or conducting an auction of a company (especially with a strong sector focus where that sector itself is depressed) might not prove fruitful, because in the absence of financial buyers the potential trade buyers may themselves be financially constrained and may well have little desire or ability to use limited cash resources taking out the competition, thereby making a realisation of enterprise value more difficult. Anybody attempting to sell a printing business in the period from 2004–2007 would corroborate this and would also confirm that the plethora of printing businesses on the market has driven values downwards. There is also a sense of 'mission impossible' that pervades amongst buyers with the effect that they are pessimistic that a distressed company in a distressed sector will be capable of returning to profitability. This pessimism is compounded where the entity has had good management and professional attention and has already undergone a phase of restructuring. Buyers are inclined to conclude that the business is beyond redemption and as a result the only potential buyers tend to be those with opportunistic characteristics offering very low bids referenced to liquidation value.

5.17 This is not to say that companies which are financially distressed cannot be valued and the valuation of a company on a going concern basis usually takes into account four cases: the *base case* which is aligned to the core business plan used by the debtor to formulate the restructuring plan; the *downside case* which incorporates the adverse effect of certain business risks so that the business can still survive without another round of restructuring; and a *best case* which purports to estimate an optimum outcome applying certain upside opportunities. A *sensitised case* may also be produced which is a combination of both the downside case and the base case.

5.18 Whilst the four *cases* will be relevant in terms of reaching a valuation, valuation techniques will also need to be applied rigorously. There are three key techniques: (1) comparable multiples, (2) a discounted cashflow method, and (3) market testing valuations based on bid interest and potential supply and demand.

5.19 If a company is listed and has access to the capital markets there may also be a so-called 'liquidity premium' and for valuation purposes this will distinguish a listed company from an unlisted company operating in the same sector.

Comparable multiples – sector analysis and precedent transactions

5.20 Business value: This method arrives at a value for a business by comparing it to its peers in the same sector and geographical location by reference to comparable variables such as EBITDA, gross revenues or net income or some other industry specific barometer such as tonnes mined or even subscribers to a business news service. Comparables can be arrived at by reference to publicly available information for competing public companies or exit values achieved by comparable private companies in the same sector through information made available through information sites such as Mergermarket, the press and other reporting services.

5.21 Multiples of business earnings and revenues are a common form of value comparison, but quite often they will only serve to highlight the potential of a business operating in the same geography as a competitor with a high multiple. A company with a high multiple will serve to highlight what may be achieved through strong branding and marketing, operational efficiencies and cost reductions all of which will result in upper quartile performance. As such this methodology is most relevant where the companies are of a very similar industry type, operate in the same geography and account is taken of the barriers to entry. In addition, the method of data collection and the relevant accounting periods for which the figures for the supposedly comparable business relate may well be different.

5.22 In the 2006 restructuring of Uniq plc a high multiple was ascribed to its continental branded foods business because many of the key comparable variables that were facilitating high earnings within their peer groups were evident in the business. Such a high valuation was critical to demonstrating that there was still considerable 'equity value' notwithstanding a degree of financial uncertainty caused principally by a substantial pensions deficit.

5.23 Using this methodology total enterprise value will be impacted by the specific capital structure of the company. In the current world of high leverage, high interest costs and more sophisticated tax structuring these variables will have a key impact on an equity valuation as will contingent liabilities such as pension, tax and litigation liabilities. The net effect of the tax and capital structure is important because it has an accumulative effect on the net income of a corporate during successive fiscal periods.

5.24 An example of such an equity multiple is the price earnings multiple which for public companies divides the market price of a single share by the net income per share. A market to book value multiple operates differently by comparing the market capitalisation of a company (market price x the total shares in issue) with the accounting equity value of the company.

Discounted cashflow valuations

5.25 Discounted cashflow ('DCF') methodology derives a going concern valuation by calculating the net present value of all future cashflows over an initial period of say 5–10 years. These cashflows are then discounted back to a present value using a 'weighted average cost of capital' formulae. A 'terminal value' of the business into perpetuity at the end of the initial period is then established by applying a perpetual growth rate to the final year of cashflows. The last step is to discount this terminal value back to a present value using the weighted average cost of capital formulae and this amount is added to the present value of the projected near term cashflows to obtain the company's DCF enterprise value.

5.26 A detailed business plan (incorporating relevant assumptions and sensitivities) is initially needed to establish the forecast cashflows. Having forecast what are perceived to be sustainable standardised free cashflows before financing costs (ie EBITDA less capital expenditure with an adjustment for improved or deteriorating working capital and disregarding any interest deducibility stemming from tax structuring) for the business during this projected period it is then possible to discount those cashflows back to a present value before establishing the important terminal value of the business into perpetuity by applying a perpetual growth rate to the final year of cashflows.

5.27 Having calculated the projected free cashflows over the relevant period, these cashflows are discounted back to a net present value. This is achieved by applying an appropriate discount rate equal to the opportunity cost of the investor's funds: or to put it another way the return an investor could expect to earn on an alternative investment that has a similar risk profile to the one currently being appraised by the investor. Establishing the appropriate opportunity cost for a distressed company is of course not straightforward and, as indicated above, one will typically use either a 'weighted average cost of capital' formulae or an 'adjusted present value' formulation.

5.28 A 'weighted cost of capital formulae' is perhaps the most common method of establishing the requisite discount rate. In simple terms the weighted cost of capital represents the composite return that typical debt and equity investors seek from an investment in the company. The weighted cost of capital approach takes into account the cost of debt and the cost of equity each weighted respectively by the proportion of debt and equity on the balance sheet of the distressed corporate subject to the valuation. One anomaly that should be noted however is that in a restructuring the weighted cost of capital goes down as equity value is eroded and leverage goes up, therefore potentially resulting in a higher valuation that can be misleading.

5.29 The assumed cost of debt is adjusted to take into account savings arising from the tax deductibility of certain interest expenses. The cost of equity is determined by applying the 'Capital Asset Pricing Model' that effectively applies a cost of equity based on the rate of return an investor would seek from investing in a business with comparable risk (the 'equity beta'). The starting point is to work out the rate of return on a risk-free investment (ie an investment with no perceived default risk such as a Gilt or a US Treasury Bond) then add a risk premium for investing in a certain stock (a 7% market risk premium is not uncommon) before adjusting this further by comparing the risk of the specific shares with other shares – a process known as establishing the equity beta.

5.30 As intimated, an alternative to the 'weighted cost of capital' approach for determining the discounted cashflows of a distressed company is the application of an 'adjusted present value' formulation. This approach is very rarely used and values a company as the aggregate value of the company on a debt-free basis plus the value of certain variables associated with the company's financing namely the deductibility of its interest expenses as a result of its tax structuring. The value of the projected tax saving arising from the deductibility of interest is derived by discounting the savings by the weighted average cost of debt of the company.

5.31 The adjusted present value is determined by again calculating for a specific business the standardised free cashflows (ie EBITDA less capital expenditure with an adjustment for improved or deteriorating working capital and disregarding any interest deducibility stemming from tax structuring) during the projected period and then discounting such free cashflows by the unlevered cost of equity. This method of valuation does of course pre-suppose that the company is funded only with equity and that such equity was contributed without any form of funding associated to it.

5.32 This method of valuation enables a comparison to be made of companies in the same sector but with very different capital structures whilst also incorporating the impact of tax deductibility on interest as a means of isolating further value and the impact that leverage can have on business value.

D VALUATIONS BASED ON BID INTEREST

5.33 The most reliable indicator of value is arguably the existence of historical bids, especially if these were recent and they were supported by an investment banking adviser that had conducted thorough market testing and invited interest from trade buyers, financial investors and potential private equity acquirers and such interested parties had been able to conduct detailed due diligence through a properly organised process.

5.34 Inevitably the advice and recommendations of the investment bank may not be available to creditors without the consent of the company and the execution by creditors of the requisite confidentiality undertakings and hold-harmless letters.

5.35 If the true nature of a company's distress had not been evident during a due diligence process, it is possible that such bids may initially value the company on the high side and this may well result in lower revised bids as the bid process develops. Certain stakeholders depending on their motivation and negotiating stance may of course contest the valuation being ascribed to the business via indicative bids and may argue that they are opportunistic and ill-informed. Interestingly, in one major restructuring of a print company the absence of any meaningful bids was perceived to be indicative of the distressed and impaired nature of the business which supported a valuation at the lower end of the range proposed by investment banking advisers that had been applying both liquidation and DCF valuations to the company.

E VALUATION TENSIONS

5.36 Whichever valuation approach is used experience shows that in any restructuring scenario there is a great deal of valuation tension. This tension arises principally because creditors in different parts of the company's capital structure have an incentive to reach valuations that correlate with their motivations. Senior creditors invariably reach conservative valuations whereas junior creditors and the 'equity' quite often overvalue the company, to the extent that in certain cases this becomes a self-fulfilling prophecy such that they buy the senior claims or procure a refinancing of them. In the Meridian restructuring for example, the junior creditors exercised pre-emption rights in the inter-creditor agreement and purchased the senior debt claims to avoid an enforcement by the senior creditors that would potentially have impaired their claims. An operational restructuring and a subsequent sale process was then conducted which substantially improved the value of junior debt holders.

5.37 In cases where a sale process is not feasible because exposing it to the market could (for the reasons articulated above) result in its undervaluation then other value enhancing solutions will need to be considered. Subject to tax analysis, the solution to avoid an insolvency could be a joint venture or merger with a competitor, a rescue rights issue (albeit on a highly dilutive basis), debt forgiveness or a debt for equity swap whereby the business of the distressed company is transferred to a new corporate vehicle owned by the creditors of the distressed entity[1].

[1]   For a detailed analysis of the rationale for debt for equity swaps see Chapter 6.

5.38 In this scenario the valuation tension will be fully played out by the senior and junior creditors and in certain cases the equity. Each stakeholder will argue that the value (based on the *four cases* and the valuation methodologies outlined above) breaks within their constituency, such that they should procure the equity ownership in the newco if there is a necessary conversion of their impaired debt as part of a balance sheet restructuring. Certain out of the money creditors may even suggest that a net present value calculation be made as part of a discounted cashflow valuation, as this provides a more flexible valuation methodology.

5.39 In most consensual restructurings the valuation that is eventually prescribed and the allocation of equity in a newco will be the product of intense negotiation and each stakeholder is likely to engage professional accounting, valuation and investment banking advice to substantiate its position. Such creditors will invariably resort to a combination of these valuation techniques to support its case.

5.40 In restructuring cases involving a court process such as a scheme of arrangement or an administration where there is to be a pre-packaged sale, a court will face the same uncertainties in a valuation and may well need to take into account the depressed nature of the company's sector and the future strategy of prospective buyers. A court will therefore have to analyse and appraise the valuation evidence proffered by each interested party. In doing so the court will need to be cognisant of the strategic incentives to overvalue or undervalue the company's business.

5.41 In the US and the context of Chapter 11, the courts have displayed a readiness to construe a company as a going concern when it is subject to a sale out of bankruptcy and to value it accordingly. In the case of *Lippe v Bairnco Corpn*[1], for example, the court excluded the testimony of a business valuation expert on the basis that 'by failing to use the DCF method and relying solely on the comparable companies method, the expert did not have the ability to do a "check" on his determinations'. Certainly US jurisprudence in this area indicates an expansive approach whereby several methodologies are applied as a safety net. In almost all cases a DCF analysis will be applied to at least ensure that a valuation is derived from the historic performance of the company itself and its future earnings potential[2].

---

[1]   288 BR 678, 701 (SDNY 2003).
[2]   See e g *Re Med Diversified Inc* 334 BR 89 (Bankr EDNY 2005). The following recent cases provide examples of the combined use of the DCF and comparable transaction methods: *Re Bush Indus Inc* 315 BR 292, 299–302 (Bankr WDNY 2004); *Re Exide Techs* 303 BR 48, 65 (Bankr D Del 2003); *Re Cellular Info Sys Inc* 171 BR 926, 930 (Bankr SDNY 1994); *Re Pullman Constr Indus Inc* 107 BR 909 (Bankr ND III 1989). For recent examples of the comparable companies and DCF combination, see *Andaloro v PFPC Worldwide, Inc* (19 August 2005, unreported) (Del Ch); *Taylor v American Speciality Retailing Group Inc* 29 Del J Corp I 208 (2003).

5.42 When conducting any valuation under any of the *four cases* and the valuation methodologies outlined above it should be noted that the quality of the forecasting and the ability of the management to deliver against the business plan will be extremely important in terms of delivering value. If the data and basis for the projections is flawed or the management team are incapable or inexperienced then this will be highly determinative of value and the valuation will be misleading.

5.43 In the case of *Re MyTravel Group plc*[1], the English courts had the opportunity to assess the basis upon which a distressed company should be valued. MyTravel was an international travel business and tour operator selling travel services and holidays. It was financed by an extremely complex capital structure including multi-currency credit facilities, privately placed loan notes, bonding facilities provided by banks and sureties, leasing arrangements for hotels and aircraft and various other credit facilities. Significantly, it had also issued convertible notes with a 7% coupon. The bonds were expressed to be fully subordinated in the event of a liquidation such that at that time they had the characteristics of an equity claim having been subject to a deemed conversion on the day immediately preceding the date of the winding up. The group had suffered adverse trading conditions between 2002–2004 leading to significant trading losses and a substantial excess of £672m of balance sheet liabilities over assets.

---

[1]   [2004] EWHC 2741 (Ch), [2005] 1 WLR 2365; the Court of Appeal transcript is to be found under a different case name *Fidelity Investments International plc v MyTravel Group plc* [2004] EWCA Civ 1734, [2005] 2 BCLC 123.

5.44 Attempts at a consensual restructuring based on a notional liquidation model had become prolonged and the Civil Aviation Authority ('CAA'), the regulator of the UK travel sector, was considering terminating the company's Air Travel Organiser's Licences ('ATOLs') on the basis of the financially imperilled state of the company and its failure to restructure its balance sheet and that for it to continue trading it would soon enter a period whereby it would need to take on additional financial risk. The company and the various lender constituencies had formed the view that the CAA would not permit this. The loss of the ATOLs would have constituted the final death knell for the company.

5.45 As a consequence the company embarked on the process of instituting a scheme of arrangement under the Companies Act 1985, s 425[1] (in an attempt to 'cram-down' recalcitrant convertible bondholders). The business would be transferred to a newco under the scheme pursuant to the Companies Act 1985, s 427[2] and the existing shareholders would be allocated 4% of the equity in the newco. The main creditor constituencies would be allotted 94% of the equity in newco following a conversion of their debt claims and the remaining 2% would be allotted to the convertible bondholders, but their debt claims would remain in the old MyTravel. General creditors, customers and the Inland Revenue would have their claims transferred to newco. New working capital facilities and bonding lines would be made available to newco outside of the scheme.

1 This principle was made clear by Buckley J in *Re South African Supply and Cold Storage Co* [1904] 2 Ch 268 (which was approved by Mann J) where he held that a reconstruction means a continuation of the undertaking in some altered form but, 'in such a manner that the persons now carrying it on will substantially carry it on. It involves I think that substantially the same business shall be carried on and substantially the same persons shall carry it on'. The authors would suggest that this construction is too limited and does not take account of the modern rescue culture where reconstructions result in more diverse ownership.

2 It should be noted that in addition to the invocation of s 425, the scheme required the application of s 427 to transfer assets and liabilities.

5.46 The bondholders had previously been offered 8% of the equity in newco on the basis of agreeing to the consensual restructuring on an expedited basis. The resulting litigation focused on MyTravel's contention that the convertible bondholders were effectively disenfranchised from voting on and participating in the scheme on the basis that 'the bondholders had no economic interest in the company and that the only alternative to the scheme was a liquidation and in a liquidation their subordinated status and the deficiency of assets meant that they had no prospect at all of recovering any of the sums due under the bonds'[1].

1 [2005] 1 WLR 2365 at 2382.

5.47 In some ways it is regrettable that Mann J in the first instance judgment did not need to decide on this economic interest issue since he separately held that the scheme as prescribed to court failed under another limb, namely that the proposed scheme could not commence under the Companies Act 1985, s 427[1] since it is essential to the concept of a reconstruction under s 427 that the shareholders in the new company should be the same, or substantially the same as in the old company[2]. Since the existing MyTravel shareholders would only own 4% of newco this substantial shareholder requirement would not be met.

[1] The Companies Act 1985, s 427 is to be replaced by the Companies Act 2006, s 900 on 6 April 2008 (SI 2007/3495). For transitional provisions and savings, see SI 2007/3495, arts 6, 9, 12, Schs 1, 4.

[2] [2004] EWHC 2741 (Ch), [2005] 1 WLR 2365; the Court of Appeal transcript is to be found under a different case name *Fidelity Investments International plc v MyTravel Group plc* [2004] EWCA Civ 1734, [2005] 2 BCLC 123.

5.48 Due to the fact that Mann J did not have to consider the 'economic interest' argument his judgment is only obiter dicta, but he did accept that the only viable option for MyTravel in the absence of the consensual restructuring was an administration that would result in an eventual insolvent winding up. In this regard it is important to point out that because the CAA would revoke the licence upon a default, the company would not survive an administration.

5.49 Under the proposed scheme, no compromise or arrangement was proposed with the bondholders. As intimated, their debt was simply to be left in the company without any assets to satisfy it. The company had made the correct decision in Mann J's view that a consultation with the bondholders was unnecessary because they had no economic interest in the company; the only alternative to the scheme was a liquidation and in a liquidation their subordinated status and the deficiency of assets meant that they had no prospect at all of recovering any of the sums due under the bonds.

5.50 It is clear from the case that an assertion of 'no economic interest' will require the company to present clear and incontrovertible evidence to that effect[1]. Mann J also made it absolutely clear that class-related issues such as determinations as to who would participate in the scheme and be bound by it by reference to the 'no economic interest' argument could be dealt with at the practice directions stage when the company was seeking to convene meetings of shareholders and creditors for the purposes of approving the scheme. However, it is clear from his judgment that if the company is to raise the argument of 'no economic interest' it would need to expressly raise the issue in its application. This would enable those contesting the submissions to deal with the point at the directions hearing and for the judge to deal with such a dispute in his directions. In the instant case he was completely satisfied that the company had raised the issue adequately in its application and that the bondholders having had the opportunity to prepare for the 'no economic interest' submission should have prepared for and dealt with it.

[1] In the hearing before Mann J this evidence was constituted by a detailed witness statement from Miss Margaret Mills, a partner at Ernst & Young, who made detailed reference to a complex liquidation model and a witness statement from Mr Peter McHugh, the CEO of MyTravel.

5.51 Since the company needed to know whether it was obliged to consult the bondholders on the footing (if true) that they had an economic interest in the company, then whilst this might not actually be described as a true class issue, Mann J correctly stated that it is nevertheless the sort of issue which it is appropriate to determine at the directions stage.

5.52 Referring to the *Re Tea Corpn Ltd*[1] authority, Mann J confidentially held that in a scheme of arrangement, as a matter of principle, it is not necessary to consult any class of shareholders who have no economic interest in the company. The votes of those who have no interest can and should be disregarded. Mann J then referred to the judgment of Vaughan Williams LJ in *Re Tea Corpn Ltd* where he stated that:

> '... if you have the assent to the scheme of all those classes who have an interest in the matter, you ought not to consider the votes of those classes who have no interest at all. It would be very unfortunate if a different view had to be taken, for if there were ordinary shareholders who really had no interest in the company's assets, and a scheme had been approved by the creditors, and all those who were really interested in the assets, the ordinary shareholders would be able to say that it should not be carried into effect until some terms were made with them'[2].

[1] [1904] 1 Ch 12, CA.
[2] [1904] 1 Ch 12 at 23, CA.

5.53 Mann J also relied on the judgment of David Richards J in the case of *Re Telewest Communications plc, Re Telewest Finance (Jersey) Ltd*[1] where he stated that:

> 'There is no dispute that in the circumstances of a case like the present, the relevant rights of creditors to be compared against the terms of the scheme are those which arise in an insolvent liquidation. Strictly speaking, because the company is not in liquidation, the legal rights of the bondholders are defined by the terms attached to the bonds. However, the reality is that they will not be able to enforce those rights and that in the absence of the scheme or other arrangement their rights against the company will be those arising in an insolvent liquidation'[2].

[1] [2004] EWHC 924 (Ch), [2005] 1 BCLC 752.
[2] [2004] EWHC 924 (Ch), [2005] 1 BCLC 752 at [29].

5.54 Mr Michael Crystal QC who represented the bondholders in MyTravel did not challenge the clearly established principles in *Re Tea Corpn Ltd* and the successive line of cases, but purported to distinguish the MyTravel case on the facts on the basis that in *Re Tea Corpn Ltd* the company was already in liquidation and the insufficiency of the assets was clearly established such that the claimants in that case had no possibility of getting a dividend. In *MyTravel*, Mr Michael Crystal QC argued that the assets were not agreed and could not at that stage be seen to be so insufficient to allow no return to the bondholders. He relied on statements by Vinelott J in his judgment in the case of *Re British and Commonwealth Holdings plc (No 3)*[1] where it was suggested that he would not proceed on the basis of assumptions of no economic interest and that clear concessions may need to be made by creditors that there is an insufficiency of assets that lead to them having no economic interest. Mann J was rightly unimpressed with these arguments given that

Vinelott J was still able on the evidence to reach the conclusion that the assets of the company were insufficient to meet the claims of certain creditors who as a result had no economic interest.

[1]   [1992] 1 WLR 672 at 679.

5.55   Mann J did however emphasise that a finding of no economic interest was a serious one and he expressly stated that '... I certainly accept that the court has to be careful in relation to these matters and not embark on a casual or glib exercise in a complex situation'[1]. However, he ultimately rejected the bondholder's submission that the *Re Tea Corpn Ltd* principle can only be applied in circumstances of a concession by a creditor as to insufficiency of assets or absolute clarity as to no economic interest arising out of simple mathematical calculations. The question in every case will be decided on the factual evidence and what it shows on the correct standard of proof. On this basis, fanciful or theoretical possibilities of sufficiency of assets should be excluded.

[1]   [2005] 1 WLR 2365, 2388–2392.

5.56   The other major question raised in the *MyTravel* case was the context in which it has to be calculated and hence decided that an impaired creditor like the bondholders have no economic interest. In *MyTravel* the company was of course asserting that the context should be a winding up because without the scheme the expert evidence set out in Margaret Mills's witness statement was that the company would be insolvent and that the only alternative would be an insolvent liquidation where the bondholders would have no economic value in their claims.

5.57   Mr Michael Crystal QC in his case submissions (and in a subsequent article written with Rizwaan Jameel Mokal[1]), contested that the company's approach was to treat the bondholders as subordinated when they were not, they were only subordinated on a winding up and until then their claims ranked pari passu. In Mr Crystal's view, the company's interpretation was tantamount to a rewriting of the contract.

[1]   The Valuation of Distressed Companies: A conceptual Framework Part II – International Corporate Reserve, Volume 3, Issue 3 2006, pp 123–131 at p 126.

5.58   In response to this submission Mann J correctly stated that the question should be whether the bondholders have any *real* economic interest and this must 'involve looking at reality. Economic interests for these purposes are real and not theoretical'[1]. Mann J legitimately described Mr Crystal's submission as a fallacy because there was absolutely no possibility that the claims of the bondholders totalling £216m could be recovered from a company as insolvent as MyTravel. Moreover, the claims of the bondholders were limited to the 'plc' and on an insolvency of the group where other creditors had direct claims against a number of operating subsidiaries their entity priority claims would ensure that there would be no recovery from an insolvent liquidation. This was abundantly clear on the evidence contained in Margaret Mills's witness statement which in turn referred to a detailed liquidation model that had been verified by Ernst & Young. The bondholders were also unable to identify any additional assets of substance that would enable the court to reach a different view. As such the bondholders could therefore be legitimately excluded from having a vote approving the scheme[2].

1   [2005] 1 WLR 2365, 2388–2392.
2   [2005] 1 WLR 2365, 2388–2392.

5.59 It was also critical in Mann J's view that the liabilities on the bonds could not be enforced and that the bonds could not be repaid either on a current basis outside of a winding up or on a winding up. He therefore held that the '... conceptual debate as to whether or not they are subordinated now or rank pari passu now was a sterile one. Where there is evidence to show that the only solution to a consensual scheme is insolvent liquidation, the return on liquidation will determine the economic value of the interests of the relevant creditor'[1].

1   [2005] 1 WLR 2365, 2388–2392.

5.60 The final argument of the bondholders raised by Mr Michael Crystal QC (which is repeated in his article with Rizwaan Jameel Mokal[1]) is that it must be perceived that there is value in the company if certain creditors perceive this by being prepared to convert their debt claims into equity. In essence Mr Crystal and Rizwaan Jameel Mokal are presenting an argument that a successful restructuring could yield value which should be reflected in the value of the currently insolvent company. On the facts, however, where the company was hopelessly insolvent and a value deficit of some £435m would have to be bridged in order to return value to the bondholders this was an unrealistic premise on which to accord the bondholders any value in MyTravel. Mann J therefore effectively held that impaired creditors whose claims have some value in a liquidation are entitled to weigh up the potential realisations in a liquidation. If such creditors conclude that a restructuring and a continuation of the business as a going concern is a better way of them recovering more value for their debts at some point in the future, then they are clearly entitled to pursue such a restructuring. Mann J concluded on this point by stating that for the bondholders (on the facts of *MyTravel*) to perceive the restructuring efforts of others as proof that 'the <u>present</u> company <u>presently</u> has a value which exceeds the amount of the unsubordinated debt is an enormous leap. [He asked] Where is that value to come from? The hopes of the other creditors as to the future prospects for another company (newco) do not generate extra value in the present company'[2].

1   The Valuation of Distressed Companies: A conceptual Framework Part II – International Corporate Reserve, Volume 3, Issue 3 2006, pp 123–131 at p 127.
2   [2005] 1 WLR 2365, 2388–2392.

5.61 In this regard the decision of Mann J (although only obiter dicta) can be seen as a victory for common sense and where a creditor constituency is so clearly out of the money, a scheme or other pre-packaged restructuring process (such as a sale by an administrator or receiver) should be able to proceed in a manner that disregards those with no economic interest. However, where the value breaks more closely between two constituencies of creditors and there is a possibility that a competing constituency might have a real prospect of a return in a liquidation, the application of liquidation principles will be more difficult to justify since liquidation in such a scenario incorrectly assumes that there is no going concern surplus or at any rate a value higher than a fire sale value which should give one party the right to determine the company's destiny. There is more substance to the views of Mr Crystal and Rizwaan Jameel Mokal in this scenario where it might indeed be more appropriate to establish the current value of the company's assets and to determine whether there is value above and beyond that which might be achieved through a liquidation sale. The pertinent question therefore is what is the value of the company and even more importantly where does it break with respect to each creditor constituency so as to establish which stakeholder has a real economic interest. A disgruntled creditor who is positioned on the cusp of the value break will be much more able to perceive that there is value in the company for it (and hence a seat at the restructuring table especially on a scheme or pre-packed sale) if certain competing creditors are prepared to convert their debt claims into equity and to see value return through a restructuring process.

5.62 Despite the compelling logic of Mann J's judgment, the committee of convertible bondholders still appealed to the Court of Appeal on the economic interest point. Chadwick LJ gave the leading judgment and he held that the only point for the Court of Appeal to decide was whether the scheme was properly constituted in terms of the classes of creditors. He went on to confirm that the bondholders by virtue of their subordinated nature were clearly a distinguishable class of creditor with a materially different interest to the main body of creditors. This in turn meant that the class of general creditors properly excluded the bondholders and that the general class of creditors would be able to carry the scheme as between themselves and the company. As such the Court of Appeal was able to rule that it was unnecessary for it to consider Mann J's analysis of the 'no economic interest' point. It is regrettable that the Court of Appeal expressed no view on Mann J's finding of fact regarding the bondholders having no economic interest in the company. However, it is submitted that the arguments Mann J proposed are so logically compelling that it would have been extremely difficult for the Court of Appeal to reverse his obiter dictum or his finding of fact.

5.63 Immediately following Mann J's judgment, MyTravel, for pragmatic and commercial reasons, resolved that it would not challenge the judge's decision that there was no jurisdiction to make an order under the Companies Act 1985, s 427. It chose instead to amend the proposal so as to remove reference to a transfer of the undertaking pursuant to that section. Instead the amended scheme provided that upon approval of the meetings of:

'Shareholders and creditors – and the sanction of the court to the arrangements binding those classes – and with the consent of the converting creditors, the company would enter into an asset transfer agreement pursuant to which it would transfer to Holdings [newco] all its assets (other than those excluded under the scheme) in consideration for the assumption by Holdings of all of the company's liabilities (other than the excluded liabilities). Amongst the excluded liabilities, of course, were the liabilities of the company to the subordinated bondholders'.

5.64 The important distinction under the amended scheme was that the undertaking of the company would not now be vested in the newco by an order of the court under the Companies Act 1985, s 427. Under the scheme as amended the necessary transfer would be effected by the company and the scheme would not of course bind the bondholders. In essence the company had opted to proceed on this basis and would contest any proceedings from the bondholders relating to the transfer of assets to newco on the basis that the bondholders did not have any economic interest in the company. In any event before the Court of Appeal hearing, the bondholders quickly accepted the original 8% of the equity in newco previously offered pursuant to the consensual restructuring negotiations (which treated the bondholders as a pari passu creditor despite their subordinated nature).

5.65 In some ways the valuation perspective of Mann J which assumes an insolvent company in appropriate circumstances, has been enshrined in the recent Banking (Special Provisions) Act 2008. This Act was the precursor to the nationalisation of Northern Rock and the purposes of the Act is described in the preamble which states that it is 'An Act to make provision to enable the Treasury in certain circumstances to make an order relating to the transfer of securities issued by, or of property, rights or liabilities belonging to, an authorised deposit taker ...'.

5.66 The Banking (Special Provisions) Act 2008, s 5(4) provides that '[i]n determining the amount of any compensation payable ... it must be assumed (a) that all financial assistance provided by the Bank of England or the Treasury to the deposit-taker in question has been withdrawn ... and (b) that no financial assistance would in future be provided by the Bank of England or the Treasury to the deposit-taker in question (apart from ordinary market assistance offered by the Bank of England subject to its usual terms)'. The shares in Northern Rock were transferred to the Treasury under the Northern Rock plc Transfer Order 2008[1] and the compensation arrangements for shareholders are set out in the Northern Rock plc Compensation Scheme Order 2008[2].

[1] SI 2008/432.
[2] SI 2008/718.

5.67 Northern Rock plc Compensation Scheme Order 2008, article 6 (Valuation Assumptions) provides that '[i]n determining the amount of any compensation payable ... it must be assumed (in addition to the assumptions required to be made by section 5(4) of the Act ...) that Northern Rock (a) is unable to continue as a going concern; and (b) is in administration'. In essence, the legislation is establishing as a matter of principle that in the case of an insolvent deposit-taking institution that is surviving as a going concern due to government support, it must be assumed that this support has been withdrawn and that the company is in administration.

5.68   Although article 7 (Appointment of Independent Valuer) of the Northern Rock plc Compensation Scheme Order 2008 appoints an independent valuer to assess the compensation payable to former shareholders, the valuation will be made on the basis of the assumptions in article 6 (including s 5(4)) together with such rules as to the procedure in relation to the assessment of any compensation as the valuer considers appropriate[1]. The final determination of the independent valuer has not yet been made, but it will be interesting to see how this process plays out.

1   SI 2008/718, art 10 (Procedure).

Chapter 6

RESTRUCTURING EXITS

A   Debt trading
B   Debt for equity swaps
C   Tax issues arising on restructurings
D   Management tax issues

A DEBT TRADING

Introduction

6.1 Certain investors buy distressed debt securities (typically high yield or corporate bonds) or loans that are in or near default. For years a relatively small band of specialist investors made fantastic returns – and occasionally fantastic losses – by buying up the bank loans and debt securities of companies in financial difficulties in what was perceived as effectively a gamble on recovery. In the past few years the distressed debt market (the 'Market') has gone mainstream with intensive activity in the trading of highly structured and multi-tiered loans and high yield bonds in the leverage buyout market. The supply of distressed investment opportunities is at an all time high. In 2004 for example the top 100 leveraged buyouts were funded by €40bn of debt. Given the leveraged nature of these transactions a substantial proportion have inevitably experienced an impairment of one or more of the debt obligations in their capital structure and in many cases this has resulted in intensive debt trading both before and during the restructuring. Investors in the Market pursuing these assets now include institutional investors and pension funds as well as a raft of 'vulture funds' and more recently hedge funds and what has been phrased 'opportunity funds' who typically are private equity funds making strategic investments in the acquisition of a corporate debt as a precursor to a distressed M&A transaction or some form of debt for equity conversion as part of a 'cram down' of the position of other creditors in the capital structure most usually through a scheme of arrangement. Investors exert influence by taking a majority or blocking position in either bonds or bank debt in order to influence either the board, the main financial creditor constituencies or even the insolvency practitioner. Companies whose distressed debt is being traded are naturally concerned by the possible motives of these investors.

The market in distressed debt and the participants

6.2 There are three main types of distressed debt investor. The first are the long-term, buy-and-hold funds, which get heavily involved in the restructuring process. The second are the more trading-oriented managers, who look to exploit inefficient markets and mispricing opportunities. These tend to be hedge funds with a more short-term investment strategy. The third are the opportunity funds that buy senior debt solely on the basis that it will be converted, hopefully as part of a wider capital reorganisation or corporate merger and acquisition transaction.

6.3   Although the market has been fuelled by the large number of hedge funds that have been set up to specialise in distressed debt, the other major source of capital that has been attracted to this Market more recently is private equity. For the private equity funds, distressed debt offers attractive opportunities to gain control of a company by buying up their bank loans or bonds, taking the driving seat in restructuring and ending up with control. The distressed loans and market securities are seen as a cheap and effective way of buying companies. Private equity funds will often have the corporate survival of the company in mind on a restructuring.

6.4   Commercial banks are offloading loans because regulators under the capital and equity framework imposed by Basel II are effectively forcing them to clean up their portfolios. In addition, where one member of a loan syndicate sells its exposure, losses being concealed by other lenders cease to be a secret and more intensive trading activity usually follows. These banks may lose out on the high returns eventually made by distressed debt traders, but the creation of a liquid market in bad loans has made it possible for banks to extract a return from assets that previously would have been stuck on their books. Creditors now have greater flexibility as to how they can handle problem situations. From a reputational perspective, banks are under pressure not to push companies into insolvency and are taking the view that it is better to take a provision, sell the debt to distressed investors and redeploy their capital into a fully performing asset.

6.5   Distressed debt has also satisfied investor demand for a return from alternative investments. Many of the underlying corporate entities have been well-known names, such as Xerox and MyTravel whose credit quality has plummeted and amid the recent abundance of buyers and sellers of distressed debt it seems that the real winners have been the investment banks who act as the middlemen of the investors in the market. Deutsche Bank, Credit Suisse First Boston, Morgan Stanley, Goldman Sachs and JP Morgan are believed to be the most active players, they not only make returns on the loan portfolios they acquire, but also make attractive commission revenue. Spreads on distressed debt transactions can stretch to 4% (see the *Joy of Distress*, Euromoney 2003).

Disruptive vultures or catalysts for change?

6.6   Investors in the distressed debt market are variously painted as vultures interfering with the restructuring process or alternatively positive catalysts for change who bring forward the point in time at which management come to terms with the need to implement a restructuring. It has become increasingly clear however that distressed investors can and do promote M&A solutions with compatible businesses. Whatever their motive, the presence of US investors in particular has certainly been felt in the European market in recent years.

6.7 Certain investors are extraordinarily active in the Market and are prepared to pay a premium on a debt trade in order to be involved in the restructuring process at an early stage and so have an opportunity to influence the turnaround. Indeed, it is arguable that distressed players do provide vital impetus to the process of recovery. Most of the funds either thrive on liquidity and favour an early exit or have a long-term invest and hold strategy. As a consequence the funds of all types can be supportive of an accelerated turnaround process and the fact that they may well have invested at a substantial discount to par will mean that they can be more flexible in evaluating an acceptable exit return.

6.8 Distressed investors can however interfere with the workout process by trying to force early solutions to a turnaround process. In addition, corporates tend to be concerned that as distressed debt is sub-participated down to a number of hedge concerns the economic interest will not be set at the restructuring table. Distressed debt trading which gives negative control to a debt trader via a blocking minority can also be extremely disruptive to the restructuring process. Indeed, distressed players with an 'equity play' may wish to starve the company of new money in the interim to facilitate their long-term aspirations for a debt for equity swap.

6.9 Confidentiality can also be a major concern for stakeholders retaining their position and the corporate itself since debt trading like any other form of trading feeds off the disclosure of information to the Market.

The economic dynamics

6.10 As we have seen, the profusion of complex capital tiers in highly structured LBO transactions which has been accomplished by a diverse array of new investors has broadened the scope of the stakeholders and increased liquidity in debt instruments. Whilst the sensible principles constituting the London Approach continue to be adhered to in many restructurings at least in part, the structural changes in the debt markets have created increasingly sophisticated intercreditor agreements where the rights, claims and recourse of the relevant holders of the tiered debt such as senior, second lien, mezzanine, high-yield noteholders and PIK noteholders have become increasingly regulated at outset.

6.11 Given that the senior pieces in such deals would not ordinarily be expected to be impaired and would expect to be covered on any insolvency model by the relevant security or by reason of the contractual or structural subordination that is a feature of such deals, the holders of senior debt are as a result ambivalent as to the restructuring of any distressed LBO credit and it is the interplay of the various holders of debt lower down the capital structure that has become far more interesting. As the credit crunch hits, it will be interesting to see whether or not this remains the case and whether value starts to break in the senior facilities.

6.12 Increased complexity and risk invites and creates new opportunity and it is in these scenarios that the involvement of sophisticated distressed investors and opportunity funds has become more pronounced. By focusing on the debt that is impaired and the holders thereof that are facing losses this debt can potentially be purchased at a significant discount and opportunities are presented by which creditors who rank behind the impaired debt can be squeezed. If this results in a substantive capital restructuring the holders of the most immediately impaired debt can (subject to sufficient credit being available in the debt markets) refinance the unimpaired senior tranches of debt above them and recapitalise the remainder of the debt by converting their own impaired debt into equity either on a consensual basis or as part of a scheme of arrangement if a consensus cannot be procured.

Recent examples of the economic dynamics in operation

6.13 *NTL:* A good example of these processes in operation is the cable company NTL, which faced £18bn in debts in 2002. In April of that year, after months of negotiation with creditors, the company announced its planned recapitalisation. Under this recapitalisation, bondholders, including a number of specialist US distressed players such as Oaktree Capital Management, Franklin Resources, Appaloosa Partners and Angelo Gordon, ended up with about 95% of the equity. The unimpaired senior debt was refinanced. It was questionable at that time whether NTL would survive, even in its new form, but it does seem clear that such a recapitalisation could not have been formulated if the distressed players had not taken such an active role.

6.14 *Vantico A.G:* Where there is a majority bank requirement decisions taken by a syndicate must be backed by the specified majority. In these situations a smaller share of the debt may provide a blocking position which lends enormous influence to the distressed debt investor. In 2003 US private equity firm Apollo Management acquired a 35% share of the senior debt of distressed chemicals company Vantico. The high yield bonds in Vantico had been acquired by distressed investor Matlin Patterson who planned a debt for equity swap of those bonds and a new high yield issue that would enable a recapitalisation of Vantico. Apollo effectively blocked a recapitalisation with its 35% dissenting holding by objecting to the terms upon which the senior debt in which they had invested would be rolled into a merger of Vantico into a Matlin Patterson portfolio entity Huntsman. Apollo's strategic investment in the impaired senior debt resulted in it arbitraging a discounted position to a par position on the basis that Matlin could not refinance the senior debt on a negotiated discount. They were required to effectively pay the par price because Apollo could have refused to take a 'haircut' due to its negative control.

6.15 *Cablecom A.G:* Once the bondholders or committee has taken a position in bond or bank debts there are various tactics that may be employed to increase the 'leverage' of the bondholders. Funds may form a consortium to push for a deal of their own. An example of this was the contractual consortium between three opportunity funds in the Cablecom restructuring. In November 2003 three US investors, Apollo Management, Soros Private Equity Partners and Goldman Sachs Capital Partners took control of Swiss cable TV company Cablecom A.G. During 2003 Cablecom worked with a group of 38 banks to restructure its bank debt. In February 2003 a deal was struck whereby some of the existing debt would be written down and each bank would get a proportion of Cablecom's equity.

6.16 Apollo, Soros and Goldman, investors in Cablecom's sub-par debt, thought that Cablecom would have trouble servicing its remaining debts. The three investors formed a contractual consortium and started to push for a deal of their own. The consortium eventually procured a debt reduction of 60% in return for which the debt holders would get over 95% of Cablecom's equity. Cablecom's capital structure was overhauled with its bank facility repackaged into three tranches: a tranche of senior debt, a second tranche of slightly junior debt and a separate layer of equity. Despite holding less than 50% of Cablecom's debt, the consortium took control of Cablecom by receiving a disproportionately high allocation of the equity and the second tranche of debt and a lower proportion of the senior debt (see *The team approach to distressed debt* Euromoney, January 2004). The consortium demonstrated the leverage that secondary investors can have over a bank syndicate in a restructuring.

6.17 *TMD Friction*: In this case the value was perceived to break in the mezzanine facilities and as a result of concerted purchasing of the mezzanine loans at a sufficient discount the secondary debt investors were able to negotiate a significant conversion of their debt into equity thereby reducing the holding of the exiting private equity sponsor to a nominal amount. Interim new money was made available by the secondary debt investors as a prelude for the debt for equity conversion which was in turn accompanied by a simultaneous refinancing of the senior debt, albeit on less favourable terms. The case was interesting in that the senior lenders created a deadline for their indebtedness to be refinanced, at which point they retained their discretion to accelerate the senior indebtedness and to effectively implement their own restructuring.

6.18 *Colt Telecom*: Where bondholders are structurally and/or contractually subordinated to senior and/or mezzanine lenders the tactics may involve an attempt to overcome or mitigate the effects of either structural or contractual subordination and to create leverage via legal proceedings. An example of such an attempt, albeit unsuccessful, is the Colt Telecom litigation.

6.19 Traditionally structural subordination in the European finance markets, whereby higher margin debt is made available at a level of the corporate structure that sits above the main operating companies, is designed to give bondholders almost no influence in any workout scenario and to mitigate the impact of them enforcing or litigating at what would effectively be the holding company level.

6.20 The English courts have shown themselves willing to police efforts by distressed investors to provoke formal insolvency prematurely in the Colt Telecom litigation. In the case of *Highberry Ltd v Colt Telecom Group plc*[1], Highberry, an affiliate of US hedge fund Elliot Associates, attempted to place Colt in administration. Colt's debt finance had principally been raised through the capital markets via a series of note issues. Highberry acquired £75m worth of notes and were applying for an administration order in respect of Colt on the grounds that, having regard to the dramatic fall in its price since the year 2000, and its substantial operating losses and negative cashflows, Colt was, or was likely to become, insolvent both in respect of its cashflow and balance sheet and would be unable to meet the loan notes when they fell due.

[1] [2002] EWHC 2503 (Ch), [2003] 1 BCLC 290.

6.21 As a precursor to the hearing of its administration petition, Highberry applied for disclosure of documents, the provision of information and examinations of Colt's expert witnesses and chief executive officer on the basis that it would be necessary to test the evidence put forward by Colt to resolve the dispute as to the solvency of Colt on the eventual hearing of the administration petition. Highberry maintained that the hearing of the petition would be a trial with the consequence that disclosure of documents and information would be necessary and the general rule that there should be oral cross-examination on witness statements under CPR 32.5 should apply unless the court ordered otherwise. This argument clearly put the burden on Colt to satisfy the court that cross-examination was not appropriate.

6.22 Conversely, Colt submitted that it had paid interest on the notes and had discharged its other obligations as they had fallen due, that the administration petition was part of a wider strategy to make a speculative profit from the distressed debt trading in the notes and that the hearing of an administration petition was not a trial with the effect that normal disclosure rules and the normal trial process incorporating detailed cross-examination did not apply.

6.23 In reaching his decision Lawrence Collins J confirmed that insolvency proceedings were governed by the Insolvency Rules 1986 ('IR 1986') and the practice and procedure of the High Court under the Civil Procedure Rules ('CPR') as applied, with any necessary modifications by CPR 7.51(i)[1]. The effect of IR 1986 was that insolvency proceedings including administration petitions were normally conducted on the basis of written evidence subject to the court's discretion to order disclosure of documents and information and order cross-examination under IR 1986, rr 7.7(1) and 7.60 on the application of any person to the insolvency proceedings.

[1] This reference is in the case, but the reference should actually be to IR 1986, r 7.51(1).

6.24 Given the nature and purpose of an administration order, the nature of the enquiry by the court and the usual urgency of the application, Lawrence Collins J confirmed that only very exceptional circumstances justified an order for disclosure or cross-examination in proceedings for an administration order.

6.25 Moreover, the judge held that because IR 1986 made express provision for disclosure or cross-examination, the equivalent CPR provisions are not incorporated by reference through IR 1986, r 7.51(1), as that rule provided that the CPR and the practice and procedure of the High Court applied to insolvency proceedings 'except so far as inconsistent with the 1986 Rules'. Since IR 1986 covered the point on disclosure and Highberry had not shown any exceptional circumstances justifying an order for disclosure or cross-examination, the judge dismissed Highberry's application. In the most telling passage of his judgment (paragraph 47), Lawrence Collins J stated that 'if [Highberry] need the documents to respond to Colt's position, then I consider that they are simply 'fishing' for information or documents to bolster their position, and that this is not a legitimate use of the exceptional power to make an order for disclosure of information'.

6.26 The case clearly demonstrates that where a distressed noteholder is striving to push a company into an administration process so as to make a speculative profit from the acquisition of the debt by transferring value from shareholders to noteholders as part of the administration process, the court will not assist those seeking to wreck a company by permitting them to ransack its documents.

6.27 In the subsequent hearing of the administration petition almost one month later, Highberry, armed with less evidence and information than it had otherwise hoped for, failed in its application for an administration of Colt Telecom Group plc[1].

[1] See *Re Colt Telecom Group plc* [2002] EWHC 2815 (Ch), [2003] BPIR 324.

6.28 In its application Highberry argued that Colt was or was likely to become insolvent notwithstanding its favourable net asset position of £977m and the fact that there had been no default on the notes which were not due for repayment until the period 2005–2009. Highberry were relying on Colt's negative cashflows and its substantial operating losses since 2000.

6.29 In reaching his decision to dismiss the administration petition Jacob J resolved that it is not enough merely to show a 'real prospect' of insolvency as opposed to insolvency being more likely than not. He clearly articulated that Parliament could not have intended that companies should be exposed to a hostile administration petition where it was more likely than not that the company was not insolvent. In any event the court was of the view that insolvency was not even proved on the real prospect test. The court effectively refused to speculate that a company was insolvent since anything might arguably happen to the company and its business, but this did not amount to a real prospect of insolvency which required something more definite and tangible.

6.30 The court also considered the traditional 'no action' clause in the terms of the notes which prohibits a noteholder 'pursuing any remedy' under the notes save as specified in the notes. In terms of non-performance the noteholders would have to show a continuing event of default in order to take enforcement action which under the terms of the note Indenture could not be established. As such Colt argued that the administration petition breached the 'no action' provision. Jacob J agreed by stating at paragraph 55 of his judgment that being able to petition for an administration when the financial condition of the company was not so serious as to constitute an event of default made no sense. He articulated the point by declaring that the 'suggestion that the [no action] clause did not apply to pre-Event of Default situations produces an illogicality – freedom for all to act at a time when the situation is not so serious as a default'. He went on to say that he could see 'no rational purpose in limiting the [no action] bar to contractual claims. If it were so limited then individuals could undermine the [no action clause] by applying for a receiver or pursuing the sort of action taken in this case'.

6.31 The suggestion by Highberry's counsel that English public policy over-rode the 'no action' clause was similarly met with short shrift by the judge when he stated at paragraph 60 that 'if the suggestion was right, the effect is startling. It would mean that English companies could readily issue bonds with 'no action' clauses – whatever the terms of the bond, and whether pre or post-default, they would be exposed to the potentiality of a single bondholder bringing an administration petition. Certainly such bonds are regarded as enforceable under New York law with no harm to public policy. Nor is there any evidence of harm to the public by the enforceability of these clauses so far as this country or any other country is concerned'.

6.32 Having considered the expert evidence in detail Jacob J was unable to be satisfied that on the balance of probabilities Colt was likely to become 'unable to pay its debts' within the meaning of the Insolvency Act 1986, s 123, variously describing the evidence as flimsy and at one point declaring at paragraph 87 that 'such a shaky, tentative and speculative peering into the middle distance is no basis for forcing a company into administration'.

6.33 As such Jacob J had no jurisdiction to put Colt into administration. One of the most interesting parts of his judgment however is the obiter statement that even if he had jurisdiction he would not have exercised it so as to avoid Colt falling into an administration. His reasons for this which are articulated at paragraph 109 of the judgment are highly illuminating particularly for those vulture funds considering a distressed debt play as a precursor to the hostile filing of an administration petition. On the facts of this case he declared that:

'(a) The making of an administration order would be an event of default under the terms of the Indenture – that would mean all the debt was repayable now. That would well destroy the entire business rather than serve the statutory purpose of the survival of the company and the whole or part of its undertaking.

(b) The petition has very little support – no bondholder other than Highberry (holding just 7% of the notes) supports it. Mr Brisby [for Highberry] suggested that there might be silent supporters. I reject that – I can see no reason why a supporter, if there were one, could not have written a letter of support.

(c) It is premature – there is not even a suggestion of urgency given that it is conceded that creditors will be paid until at least 2006.

(d) There is no indication that an administrator with no knowledge of the telecoms business could improve the current specialised management – it would almost certainly stop the business in its tracks. Normal corporate governance would be suspended for no clear or useful purpose.

(e) An administration order would simply add to the company's costs (if its business survived).'

6.34 In addition to the legal shortcomings of its case, the court was unimpressed with Highberry's style of bondholder activism. The court essentially endorsed the principle that 'administration is a rescue procedure and that it must be shown that the rescue is properly needed before asking for a rescue team'.

Legal mechanics of the transfer

6.35 With respect to publicly traded bonds that have become distressed, purchasers acquire those bonds in the market in the normal way albeit at a discount to par. The purchase of distressed bank debt is more interesting and although the mechanics of transferring distressed debt are the same as for the transfer of performing debt, the fact that the debt is 'distressed' exposes the purchaser to far greater risk than would be the case with the purchase of a performing loan.

6.36 As a result, the documentation for the sale and purchase of distressed debt has to deal with many more issues than an agreement for the sale of performing debt. In particular the documentation effectively defines the allocation of risk between the seller and the purchaser.

6.37 The three main methods of transfer are novation, assignment and participation and the differences between these various methods are set out below.

6.38 *Novation:* With a novation, the existing agreement between the bank selling and borrower is cancelled and replaced with a new contract (on exactly the same terms and conditions as the initial one) between the bank, borrower and new purchaser. Under the novation agreement, the selling bank is relieved of its obligations vis-à-vis the borrower and the new purchaser assumes the same obligations vis-à-vis the borrower, thus creating a direct legal relationship between the borrower and the new purchaser.

6.39 In order to overcome the practical difficulties inherent in the novation procedure, most syndicated loan agreements provide for transfer by way of 'transfer certificates'. These effectively provide a method of transferring a lender's loans and commitments by obtaining the borrower's consent in advance to the transfer providing that the purchasing institution satisfies the criteria in the credit agreement.

6.40 *Assignment:* Assignments may be either legal or equitable. A legal assignment complies with the conditions of the Law of Property Act 1925, s 136 whilst an equitable assignment does not. The main distinction is that in a legal assignment the assignee is entitled to sue the borrower directly without assistance from the assignor. The equitable assignee also has the right but must join the assignor as a matter of procedure.

6.41 The important distinction between an assignment and a novation is that the assignment only operates to transfer rights and benefits and not obligations, whilst both the benefits and obligations are transferred by novation. This distinction is clearly important in debt sales as the original seller does not want to remain obligated to advance further funds. It is for this reason that the novation procedure using an agreed form of transfer certificate is the preferred route.

6.42 *Participation/Sub-participation:* If the participation is 'funded', the participant will usually place funds with the original bank on terms that the bank will repay those funds only to the extent that it receives payment from the borrower. If the participation is 'unfunded' the purchaser will effectively be indemnifying the seller for any losses on the transferred portion of the loan and so the seller is effectively taking a credit risk on the purchaser. In both cases the fees and interest will be passed through to the participating purchaser.

6.43 A participation may be useful where there are excessive restrictions on transfers of loans because the legal relationship between the borrower and the lender are unchanged under a participation and the selling lender will remain the lender of record.

The Loan Market Association

6.44 In order to make trading in distressed loans more efficient, the Loan Market Association (LMA) was opened for membership in December 1996 with the objective of fostering an environment in the Euromarkets that would facilitate the constructive development of a secondary market for loans. The LMA was established as a response to market conditions and as part of a perceived willingness on the part of the banking community to bring greater clarity, efficiency and liquidity to the relatively under-developed secondary market that existed at the time.

6.45 Since December 1996, the LMA website can be found at www.loan-market-assoc.com and on its home page it articulates its five aims in connection with loan trading:

- standardise and simplify the sale of loan assets;
- establish a market standard for settlement procedures;
- establish codes of conduct for market activity;
- establish a loan valuation mechanism; and
- persuade borrowers, banks and other market participants of the merits of a more structured and liquid market.

6.46 Since December 1996, the LMA has had a productive output of standard form documents and guidelines and the relevant items in relation to loan trading as at 31 March 2008 are listed below:

(a) LMA Termination and Transfer Agreement (Novation) (distressed);
(b) Users Guide to LMA Distressed Debt documentation;
(c) Memo explaining latest revisions to documentation;
(d) LMA Trade Confirmation (distressed/bank debt);
(e) LMA Trade Confirmation (distressed/claims);
(f) LMA Standard Terms and Conditions (bank debt/claims);
(g) Standard Representations and Warranties (bank debt/original lender of record);
(h) Standard Representations and Warranties (bank debt/secondary lender);
(i) LMA Standard Representations and Warranties (claims/original holder);
(j) LMA Standard Representations and Warranties for Distressed Debt Trade Transactions (claims/secondary holder);
(k) LMA Funded Participation (distressed);
(l) LMA Assignment (distressed/bank debt);
(m) LMA Assignment (distressed claims); and
(n) LMA Transfer Agreement (distressed).

6.47 The trade confirmation enables the principals to set out the economic terms of the trade and it includes a clear identification of the loan obligations being transferred, the standard form closing documentation to be used, the price paid, the settlement and trade dates and whether interest is for the account of the seller or purchaser from the settlement date. It is usually accompanied by a separate pricing letter and a transfer certificate in the form set out in the underlying credit documentation.

6.48 The LMA standard form representations and warranties avoid pro-longed negotiations in relation to statements about the quality of the loan assets and essentially confirm the seller's title, the credit documentation that is in existence, the currencies and amount transferred, whether the seller is or has been connected with the borrower for the purpose of the Insolvency Act 1986, whether the seller has engaged in any conduct to impair the loan assets, that there have been no governmental claims against the seller in relation to the loan assets and that the seller is not obliged to advance loans in excess of its commitment.

6.49 The standard terms and conditions are also an extremely useful document which provide contractual certainty as to the point when the contract was made which is typically on the consummation of the trade date. They also confirm the nature and status of the trade confirmation, the procedure for the satisfaction of any further conditions, the impact of the due diligence and the delivery of the credit documents. Settlement and payment, expenses and interest are also regulated by the standard terms and conditions and clarity and definition is given to the commercial terms set out in the standard form trade confirmation.

6.50 For those conducting trades in distressed debt in the secondary markets the LMA have produced an invaluable 'Users Guide to LMA Distressed Debt documentation' which provides an extremely helpful introduction to the trading of distressed debt. It also includes an anatomy of a trade by reference to a timeline and highlights the important issues of confidentiality and how this can be navigated by the use of confidentiality letters. The User Guide also explains the use of trade confirmations and standard terms and conditions and the operation of the LMA standard representations and warranties. Specimen pricing letters and sample trade confirmation are also included as schedules.

Insider dealing

The offences

6.51 The prohibition on insider dealing is dealt with under Part V of the Criminal Justice Act 1993 ('CJA 1993'). There are three separate offences (applicable to individuals only and not, therefore, companies) which are, broadly, that:

(a)   a person in possession of inside information deals in price-affected securities (CJA 1993, s 52(1));

(b)   a person in possession of inside information encourages another to deal in price-affected securities (CJA 1993, s 52(2)(a)); and

(c)   a person discloses inside information (CJA 1993, s 52(2)(b)).

6.52 The circumstances in which dealing is prohibited are either that the acquisition or disposal of securities in question (which may take place as principal or agent) occurs on a regulated market, or that the person dealing relies on a professional intermediary or is himself acting as a professional intermediary (whether he has the inside information himself or has been encouraged to deal by an insider).

6.53 It should be noted that both the encouraging and disclosing offences can be committed even if no-one in fact deals in price-affected securities.

6.54 Inside information is information which:

(a)   relates to particular securities, or to a particular issuer or issuers, and not to securities or issuers generally;
(b)   is specific or precise;
(c)   has not been made public; and
(d)   if it were made public, would be likely to have a significant effect on the price of such securities (with such securities being 'price-affected' securities).

6.55 The provisions of the CJA 1993 apply to a wide range of securities. The relevant securities, defined in the CJA 1993, s 54 and Sch 2, are shares, debt securities, warrants to subscribe for shares, options over debt securities, depositary receipts, options over other securities, securities futures contracts and certain securities or index-related contracts for differences, provided that they satisfy certain conditions relating to (broadly) the securities being listed or traded on a regulated market, or that if they are warrants, depositary receipts, options, futures or contracts for differences, that the underlying shares or debt securities are to be so listed or traded.

6.56 Interestingly this definition means that trading in distressed (listed) bonds is regulated by the CJA 1993, whereas the secondary market in distressed loans is not. The impact of the CJA 1993 can therefore often be felt on a restructuring where a company has bonds in issue which are traded on a regulated market. Typically, because of their position as creditors of a distressed company (and assuming that there is some value in the debt represented by those bonds), bondholders will form an ad hoc committee upon the restructuring of the issuer of such bonds, that committee will have certain responsibilities in relation to the negotiation of the restructuring with the company and its other financial creditors. Bondholders (and the committees which represent them) have had quite an aggressive reputation in the past, and are frequently parties which drive forward the restructuring and seek to negotiate favourable outcomes for themselves.

6.57 In the meantime, whilst negotiation on the restructuring is ongoing, the members of the committee will in all likelihood be restricted from trading in their bonds because of the provisions of the CJA 1993 – they may well be in possession of inside information as a direct consequence of their involvement in and negotiation of the restructuring. This obviously affects the liquidity of the listed bonds in the hands of such committee members, and so they will seek to maintain an extensive flow of information from the company into the market, so that the inside information is 'made public'. This will purge the committee members of their restricted status, and allow them to trade freely again – but may also have an impact upon the price of the bonds, depending upon the nature of the information so disclosed.

6.58 This can create a real tension between the company and its other stakeholders, and often results in the negotiation of detailed provisions relating to the dissemination of information. It should be noted, however, that the frequent existence of bondholders with a restricted status can lead to selected 'leaks' to the financial press and to news services (such as Debtwire), so that the restricted holders are able to trade freely once the relevant information is public.

6.59 Under the CJA 1993, s 57, a person with information is an insider if:

(a)   the information is, and he knows that it is, inside information; and
(b)   he has the information, and knows that he has it, from an inside source.

6.60 A person has information from an inside source if he has it through being a director, employee or shareholder of an issuer of securities, or he has access to it by virtue of his employment, office or profession, or has the information, directly or indirectly, from a person in either category. Consequently, a bondholder, director, key employee or professional adviser may be an insider for the purposes of the CJA 1993 offences.

Defences

6.61 Defences may be available if the defendant can show that, for any of the three insider dealing offences, the insider did not expect the dealing to result in a profit (or the avoidance of a loss) attributable to the fact that the information was price-sensitive. (Price-sensitive information, in relation to securities, is defined as information which would, if made public, be likely to have a 'significant effect' on the price of the securities).

6.62 There are further defences to the dealing and encouragement offences where an insider can show that:

(a)   he reasonably believed that the information had been (or, in the case of encouragement, would be) sufficiently widely disclosed to ensure that no-one taking part in the dealing would be prejudiced by not having the information; or
(b)   he would have done what he did even if he had not had the information.

6.63 The second defence above is likely to be difficult to establish in cases other than where an agent's dealing is attributed to a principal who has inside information, or where a trustee acts on the basis of independent professional advice in a situation where he has inside information.

6.64 It is a further defence to the disclosure offence for the insider to show that he did not expect the disclosure to result in a dealing.

6.65 There are three further special defences to the dealing and encouragement offences, as follows:

(a)   where a market maker is acting in good faith in the course of his, or his employer's, approved market making business;

(b)   where the inside information is 'market information' (broadly, information about the actual or proposed acquisition or disposal of securities, and including the fact that an acquisition or disposal is not to take place) and the insider can show:
  (i)   it was reasonable for someone in his position to act as he did despite having the information as an insider; or
  (ii) that he was acting in connection with, and with a view to facilitating, a particular acquisition or disposal and his information arose out of his involvement with that acquisition or disposal; and

(c)   where the dealing or encouragement takes place in connection with stabilisation activities, being conducted in accordance with the Financial Services Authority's ('FSA's') rules.

6.66 Directors should take advice before relying on these defences as breach of the CJA 1993 is a criminal offence, punishable by imprisonment or a fine (or both). Having said that, successful prosecutions are rare, due to, amongst other things, the difficulties of establishing evidence to satisfy the required burden of proof, the ability to deal offshore from unregulated offshore jurisdictions, impenetrable banking secrecy laws and a combination of other factors such as the costs and difficulties of obtaining evidence and mounting prosecutions.

Market abuse

6.67 When analysing whether a person in possession of inside information can deal, encourage another to deal, or disclose the information, insider dealing issues should be considered alongside the 'market abuse' provisions of the Financial Services and Markets Act 2000 ('FSMA 2000'), s 118 and the FSA's Code of Market Conduct ('CoMC'). The prohibition on market abuse, in FSMA 2000, s 118, defines seven market abuse offences, the three most relevant of which are (in summary):

(a)   dealing, or attempting to deal, on the basis of inside information – market abuse (insider dealing);

(b)   engaging in behaviour, based on information which is not generally available but which is likely to be regarded as relevant information by a regular user of the market, and the behaviour is likely to be regarded by the regulator as a failure to observe the standard of behaviour reasonably expected – market abuse (misuse of information); and

(c)   disclosure of inside information other than in the proper course of an insider's employment, profession or duties – market abuse (improper disclosure).

6.68 There are clear overlaps with the offences set out under the CJA 1993, and indeed the definitions of 'inside information' in the CJA 1993 and in the FSMA 2000 are very similar. However, the provisions on market abuse in the FSMA 2000 cover behaviour in relation to a wide range of 'qualifying investments' that are admitted to trading on a domestic market or an EU regulated market, or in respect of which a request for admission has been made. They therefore apply to a wider range of markets, and at an earlier stage, than the equivalent provisions of the CJA 1993.

6.69 In the CoMC, the FSA provides guidance on these three offences, and contains a number of defences (or 'safe harbours') which are similar to the CJA 1993 defences discussed above. If any of the safe harbours apply, it is conclusive that the behaviour does not amount to market abuse. Of particular relevance may be the 'bid facilitation' safe harbour, which provides that behaviour (based on inside information) relating to another company in the context of a public takeover bid or merger for the purpose of gaining control of that company does not amount to market abuse. In addition, behaviour in accordance with certain other specified rules will not constitute market abuse – such as price stabilising rules, rules relating to Chinese Walls, certain of the Listing Rules and rules of the Code.

Other constraints on insider dealing

6.70 Other constraints on insider dealing, alongside the CJA 1993 and the FSMA 2000, are:

(a)   in the context of directors of, and 'persons discharging managerial responsibilities' in relation to, a listed company, the Model Code (set out in the Listing Rules) provides a set of rules restricting the ability of such persons to deal in the listed company's shares;

(b)   certain General Principles and Rules of the Code (such as Rule 4, which prohibits dealings by anyone other than the offeror, and restricts the dealings of the offeror and its concert parties);

(c)   the guidance of certain professional bodies (including the FSA's Conduct of Business sourcebook); and

(d)   certain common law rules in relation to the making of secret profits (pursuant to the case of *Regal (Hastings) Ltd v Gulliver*[1]).

---

[1]   [1967] 2 AC 134n, [1942] 1 All ER 378, HL.

6.71 In analysing whether an individual may commit an insider dealing offence in certain circumstances, it is therefore useful to have a checklist, and to seek specific advice, in order to minimise the risk of an offence being committed. For example:

- Does the potential insider have information which is 'inside information'?
- If so, does he know that information to be inside information, and did he knowingly obtain it from an inside source?
- For a proposed dealing, are the securities in question of a kind regulated by the CJA 1993, and are they 'price-affected securities'?
- Is the insider proposing to deal, proposing to encourage someone else to deal, or proposing to disclose the information otherwise than in the proper performance of his office, employment or profession?
- Does a defence apply?

Conclusion: vultures or samaritans?

6.72 In many recent restructurings of distressed companies, particularly Telewest, MyTravel and Marconi, bondholders and other creditors have consistently transferred any value from the existing shareholders to themselves. Why does this happen? The simple answer is that bank creditors and bondholders are higher up the insolvency pecking order than equity shareholders when a company is insolvent.

6.73 The power of the creditor is not always bad news for the long-term survival of a company. Marconi and MyTravel were saved from formal insolvency only by banks and bondholders agreeing a debt for equity swap that virtually eradicated the value of the shares. This underlines the importance for a company in distress of dealing with creditors with whom they have a relationship and with whom negotiation is possible. Had the creditors involved in the Marconi restructuring been distressed debt investors with no interest in maintaining a relationship with the company then its chances of surviving restructuring might have been severely diminished. In the Marconi restructuring, the banks who were involved in the debt for equity swap were rewarded recently when Marconi announced that it had paid off £750m of its remaining debt ahead of schedule as well as recreating some shareholder value as the price had doubled since the restructuring.

6.74 Often, the survival of the company is in the interest of the investor. The preferred strategy of many distressed investors is to assume control of the debtor by buying up discounted debt which is then swapped into new equity on a restructuring. The distressed investment gains in value as old equity is recapitalised and/or debt is paid off.

6.75 Restructuring negotiations are often complex, costly and volatile. The greatest enemy of progress is delay. Problems can be compounded if a distressed investor with a blocking stake halts the restructuring plans of the rest of the bank syndicate members. However, the intervention of such investors need not be negative. As noted throughout this section, in a typical restructuring the senior debt may be adequately collateralised and so it is at the more junior debt levels that the intervention of distressed investors can be a positive catalyst for corralling stakeholders into committees capable of making and implementing restructuring decisions.

B DEBT FOR EQUITY SWAPS

Introduction

6.76 A debt for equity swap describes a transaction whereby one or more financial creditors discharge indebtedness owed to it by a borrower company, in exchange for one or more classes of that company's share capital. Alternatively, the indebtedness could be discharged in exchange for another equity instrument, such as a warrant or an option to subscribe for shares of one or more classes of shares in that company. This discharge of debt in exchange for share capital is frequently referred to as a 'debt for equity swap' or 'debt for equity conversion' (a 'DES').

Rationale for a consensual DES

For the company as a whole

6.77 A DES is likely to form a key part of the restructuring strategy for a heavily distressed company. It has the benefit for the company of reducing gearing and leverage, which will ease cashflow concerns thereby enhancing liquidity. Creditor pressure will be relieved and the company's circumstances should be such that a turnaround is thereby facilitated.

6.78 In addition, the conversion of debt to equity will improve the strength of the company's balance sheet considerably, which may, alongside enhancing liquidity, be a vital factor in stabilising the company. In particular, creditors and suppliers will see that the company has both a reduced financial burden in terms of interest costs and a stronger capital base, with less gearing, which should therefore temper their concerns about continuing to supply the company with goods, services and improved credit terms in order to provide liquidity. Following the DES there may even be scope for receiving such goods and services on extended or preferential credit terms and persuading credit insurers that had previously reduced or cancelled their limits to reopen them.

6.79 The completion of a DES is also of fundamental importance to customers and other stakeholders of the company. There are many cases where a DES and the resulting balance sheet improvements have been a precursor to the participation in a transaction with other sponsors, or investors or the continuation of an existing contract, or the award of a new contract.

6.80 A DES will also improve the company's solvency, which will be important for the directors who may have concerns about wrongful trading (and other related risks, such as giving preferences). It is fair to say that whilst a restructuring is being planned and implemented, the directors ought to keep a close eye on the solvency (and anticipated future solvency) of the company in order that the risks of issues such as wrongful trading are carefully evaluated, and one would expect them to receive separate advice in this regard.

6.81 For listed companies, and in extreme cases where there has been a suspension of listed shares from trading as a consequence of an intensive restructuring or such a suspension is threatened, the completion of a DES and the resulting positive effect on its balance sheet may procure a restoration of the listing or may avoid such a suspension in the first place (which would inevitably be harmful to the company). The risk of such suspension may arise, for example, because the company has been unable, during the restructuring process, to assess accurately its financial situation and inform the market accordingly, or because the company is unwilling or unable to make a holding announcement when faced with an unexpected and significant event, and there is a risk of inside information leaking into the market before the facts and their impact can be confirmed.

6.82 Where shares have been so suspended, the FSA may restore the listing of the shares upon completion of a DES on the basis that there is a more certain and stable financial situation for the company. In either case, avoiding suspension or restoring listing will be important to preserve liquidity in the listed shares for the benefit of the shareholders.

For the lenders

6.83 For the lenders, a DES crystallises their positions in relation to the company – their debt position does not fluctuate (since, for example, interest no longer accrues) and their shareholding in the company is established.

6.84 Being shareholders, in the (anticipated) event of a recovery, subsequent sale or flotation of the company (or any part of its business), the lenders will participate in any equity value that has been created as a result of their own efforts and actions. This equity upside may ultimately enable the lenders to not only release any provision that was previously made, but to also record a profit on an ultimate sale of their shares. The restructuring of British Energy in 2004 and the ensuing recovery in wholesale electricity prices in the UK resulted in a dramatic increase in the share price of that company in a relatively short space of time thereby facilitating not only a release of provisions by a number of institutions but a significant profit.

Development of DESs

6.85 Historically, a DES was considered as a component of a restructuring as a last resort only where other mechanisms were not possible (or had failed) or where the returns on a formal insolvency process were wholly unattractive, or did not represent the best means of realising value from a business. Whereas, formerly, opportunity investors would buy into bond and bank debt in the secondary market in order to arbitrage prices and take advantage of market inefficiencies in pricing debt (and particularly bank debt), more recently they have proactively acquired such debt with the principal objective of converting that debt position into a strategic equity position (a 'loan to own' strategy) with potentially unlimited upside value. As significant participants in the debt, they acquire a pivotal seat at the restructuring table, and quite often they have a strong negotiating position in relation to the structuring and implementation of the restructuring.

6.86 As more particularly analysed in Chapter 5 (*'The importance of valuations in the restructuring process'*), value in a company can be identified at various levels in a company's capital structure whether this be in the senior debt, the second lien or other form of subordinated debt including without limitation, mezzanine, PIK or high yield. If applying sophisticated valuation methodology and techniques and it is concluded that only part of the indebtedness of a particular layer of the capital structure can be repaid on a going concern or insolvency basis (or quite often a combination of both) the value is said to 'break' in that layer of the capital structure. Those institutions holding debt at the level where the value breaks will, as previously mentioned, inevitably drive any DES process that it is felt is necessary to stabilise the company and improve its balance sheet.

6.87 Typically strategic opportunity loan-to-own investors will determine where the value breaks as part of their purchasing due diligence and will skilfully acquire debt at this level of the capital structure for the maximum discount possible with the specific intention of converting that debt into equity and ideally (possibly in conjunction with other similar investors and counterparties) an eventual controlling stake in the company. Quite often such investors will adopt a private equity style approach to the management, turnaround and transformation of the company that will result in a significant return for their own investment funds. In effect strategic investors rather than acquiring the equity of good (albeit over-leveraged) companies with solid EBITDA, acquire the debt of poorly performing businesses at a discount, and then force through a restructuring that results in a recapitalisation whereby the acquired debt is converted into a controlling equity stake prior to a return to profitability that is facilitated in part from the de-gearing achieved pursuant to a DES. This has led to what many commentators identify as a new era of 'distressed M&A'.

6.88 Historically, such loan-to-own investors had primarily focused on acquiring the company without focusing too much on tax efficiencies and the maximisation of the tax position. Recently, there has been much more focus on tax issues in large restructurings not only to circumvent potential secondary tax liabilities, but also to reduce stamp duty, preserve embedded tax losses and to maximise the tax deductibility of interest going forward on debt that is being preserved or recapitalised[1].

---

[1]   These issues are discussed in more detail in the section of this chapter entitled 'Tax issues arising on restructurings'.

Executing a DES

6.89 The difficulties and indeed the complexities of executing a DES have been exacerbated by the ever increasingly complicated terms of the intercreditor arrangements that are entered into between the myriad of lenders to companies at the various layers of their capital structures. To regulate their rights and claims against companies and the rights of other capital providers, institutional lenders, and most typically senior lenders who are keen to preserve their senior priority claims and security interests, will require other capital providers, such as second lien lenders, mezzanine lenders, noteholders, bondholders, PIK holders, preference shareholders or any other imaginable providers of debt, equity or hybrid instruments, to sign into an intercreditor agreement.

6.90 With the explosion of private equity since 2000 and as companies have become increasingly leveraged and adopt layered capital structures incorporating many of the facets of indebtedness listed in the preceding paragraph, it is inevitable that intercreditor agreements have quite often become ever more complicated and sophisticated in order to regulate a multitude of competing claims often with respect to capital providers and members of groups that are resident or domiciled in a diverse number of jurisdictions.

6.91 In many cases the intercreditor marks the new battleground between competing creditors and will inevitably regulate the prospects and even the feasibility of implementing a DES.

6.92 A consensual DES will generally be the preferred route, over the more expensive, more time consuming and more complex procedures relating to a scheme of arrangement (under the Companies Act 1985, s 425[1] (a 'Scheme')). A Scheme may ultimately involve a 'mandatory' DES, but it also involves shareholder votes, the involvement and sanction of the court, and therefore a fairly inflexible process and timetable[2].

---

[1] The Companies Act 1985, s 425(1) is to be replaced by the Companies Act 2006, ss 895(1), 896(1) and (2). The Companies Act 1985, s 425(2) is to be replaced by the Companies Act 2006, ss 899(1), (3), 907(1) and 922(1). The Companies Act 1985, s 425(3) is to be replaced (with some changes) by the Companies Act 2006, ss 899(4), 901(3) and (4). The Companies Act 1985, s 425(4) is to be replaced by the Companies Act 2006, s 901(5) and (6). The Companies Act 1985, s 425(6) is to be replaced by the Companies Act 2006, s 895(2). The Companies Act 2006, ss 895–935 are to come into force on 6 April 2008 (SI 2007/3495). For transitional provisions and savings, see SI 2007/3495, arts 6, 9, 12, Schs 1, 4.

[2] See Chapter 7 '*Schemes of arrangement as a restructuring tool*' in this regard.

6.93 A company voluntary arrangement ('CVA') may also be less favourable, because whilst such an arrangement can be used to execute a DES it cannot of itself restructure a company's share capital. Shareholder meetings must be convened to approve the arrangement and they can therefore effectively challenge the CVA. However, if the creditors approve the CVA then it will take effect regardless of the shareholder decision unless the shareholders apply to court to have the arrangement overturned[1].

[1] See the Insolvency Act 1986, s 4A(3).

6.94 A consensual DES, where lenders (as a matter of contract) discharge their debt in exchange for an issue or transfer of shares, is generally more attractive than a mere subordination of the existing senior institutional debt behind new money. This all of course depends on the viability of the business and its debt capacity. The introduction of new, senior ranking, money does not necessarily address issues of gearing, even where the subordination of existing debt is structured so that the lenders are issued with warrants, options or other instruments to subscribe for (or otherwise acquire) equity. Whilst such instruments will enable the lenders to participate in any increase in the equity value of the company, they (and this structure) will not necessarily address any balance sheet deficit, liquidity and creditor pressure issues from which the company may suffer.

6.95 In the UK, in order to execute a DES outside of a formal court-controlled insolvency process such as administration, it is often necessary to adopt one of the following three structures:

(1)   a consensual conversion of debt for a controlling equity stake;

(2)   the sale of a relevant group holding company or intermediate holding company initiated on behalf of the relevant shareholders to a new company owned by the relevant institutional creditors. This will require the appropriate institutional creditor consents and the release of security; or

(3)   via an enforcement process under the various facility documents and security documents which will result in a security trustee or security agent appointing a fixed charge receiver or administrative receiver (where there exists pre Enterprise Act 2002 security) under the relevant intercreditor arrangements to transfer the shares to a new company typically owned by those debt holders who are prepared to convert their impaired debt into equity and procure a refinancing of the priority unimpaired debt. This is colloquially known as a 'pre pack' or 'pre-packaged arrangement'.

6.96 It should be noted however that the flexibility of adopting any one of these three structured options will depend on a whole multitude of factors such as the nature of the impaired and non-impaired indebtedness, the terms of the intercreditor position, the nature of the consent required (and the existence of hold-out creditors), the attitude of the directors, the existence, position and nature of any unsecured claims or pensions liabilities and the overall tax position as determined from detailed tax due diligence and planning (for which there is no substitute). In addition, accounting rules will dictate the level of ownership by a single lender and type of equity taken. For example, a lender may well only take a 49% stake in the ordinary shares of a company with the balance constituted by non-voting preference shares in order to avoid the company being restructured constituting a subsidiary of that lender[1]. As a consequence variations, adjustments and supplements to these three structural themes will inevitably be required.

[1] See the section of this chapter entitled 'International Accounting Standards and their impact on a DES'.

A consensual conversion of debt for a controlling equity stake

6.97 This is the simplest means by which a DES can be executed. In the example set out in Diagram 1, it should be assumed that Holdings has charged its shareholding in the Borrower to the Lenders. As part of the restructuring transaction the existing 'equity' agrees to a comprehensive dilution in their position (from 100% ownership to say 5%) in a holding company (for convenience hereinafter referred to as 'Holdings') to avoid a total loss of their equity on an insolvency, an enforcement or a sale of the Borrower executed by the directors of Holdings. Equally, the banks have had to convert 50% of their debt in return for 95% of the equity. Obviously the degree of conversion and the level of ownership in Holdings will depend on the valuation of Holdings relative to the entire indebtedness and the need to de-lever the group so that it is competitive and has an appropriate level of 'gearing' (the ratio of its total indebtedness to earnings) and liquidity.

6.98 It should be noted that this type of structure is only likely to be feasible if there is no other institutional debt existing at the Holdings level[1]. This is because this structure would result in the lenders eventually owning Holdings with other impaired financial indebtedness not being discharged, left behind or otherwise dealt with. If other institutional financial debt did exist at the Holdings level this indebtedness could be converted as part of the overall transaction, but in the form of a subordinated or deferred equity instrument or at a higher conversion rate or on a pro-rated basis so that the holders of such debt would receive a smaller equity stake. Failing this, it would be necessary to effect a sale to a lender-sponsored vehicle of the Borrower by the directors or by enforcing a change over its shares granted by Holdings. Reference should be made to Diagrams 2 and 3 in this regard.

[1] In many DESs of this type, the converting lenders will typically keep trade creditors whole and will tolerate this type of indebtedness in Holdings.

6.99 Typically, Holdings will have given a guarantee of the facilities or may have direct indebtedness residing in it. In any event a portion of the debt will be moved around the group in the most tax efficient manner so that it ultimately resides in Holdings in readiness for the DES. This may be achieved by way of a novation of part of the facility from the Borrower to Holdings or a claim might be made under the guarantee granted by Holdings which will crystallise indebtedness in Holdings. This debt held by the institutions will then be used to subscribe for new shares in Holdings, which will create a majority shareholding in Holdings in favour of the institutions. This type of structure is reflected diagrammatically in Diagram 1.

6.100 *Restructuring exits*

6.100 If there was any subordinated debt that was impaired and subject to the DES it may well be this indebtedness, or a proportion thereof, that would be moved around the group into Holdings and then converted. In this scenario the senior non-impaired debt and any balance of the subordinated debt would be likely to be simultaneously refinanced.

Diagram 1
Current Structure of the Group

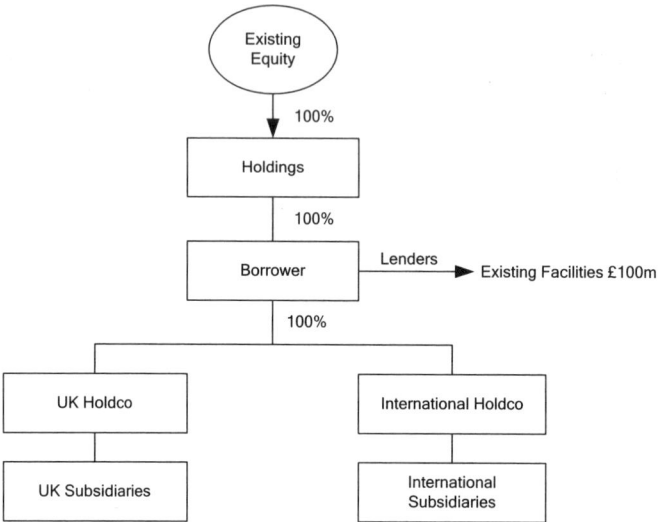

```
            ┌──────────────┐
            │   Existing   │
            │    Equity    │
            └──────────────┘
                   │ 100%
                   ▼
            ┌──────────────┐
            │   Holdings   │
            └──────────────┘
                   │ 100%
            ┌──────────────┐  Lenders
            │   Borrower   │ ─────────►  Existing Facilities £100m
            └──────────────┘
                   │ 100%
        ┌──────────┴────────────────────┐
┌──────────────┐            ┌────────────────────────┐
│  UK Holdco   │            │  International Holdco   │
└──────────────┘            └────────────────────────┘
┌──────────────┐            ┌────────────────────────┐
│UK Subsidiaries│           │     International       │
│              │            │     Subsidiaries        │
└──────────────┘            └────────────────────────┘
```

Structure of the Group after the Proposed Reorganisation

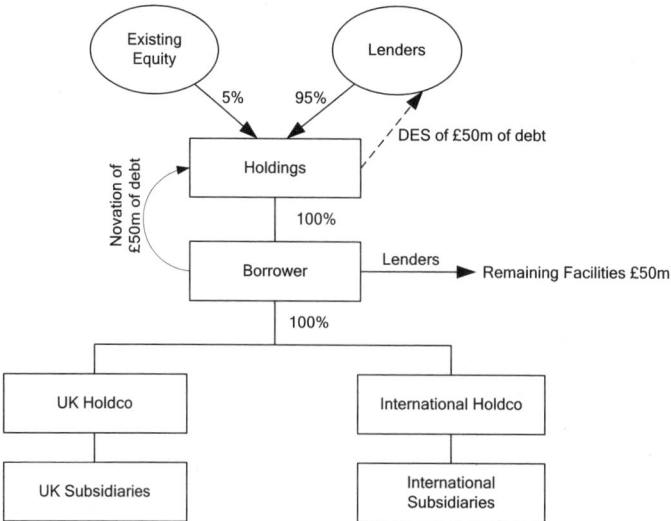

```
   ┌──────────┐              ┌──────────┐
   │ Existing │              │ Lenders  │
   │  Equity  │              │          │
   └──────────┘              └──────────┘
         \  5%          95% /
          \                /        DES of £50m of debt
           ▼              ▼     ↗
        ┌──────────────────┐ ┄┄
  │     │    Holdings      │
  │     └──────────────────┘
  │            │ 100%
  │     ┌──────────────┐  Lenders
  │     │   Borrower   │ ─────────►  Remaining Facilities £50m
  │     └──────────────┘
Novation of     │ 100%
£50m of debt
        ┌───────┴────────────────────┐
┌──────────────┐            ┌────────────────────────┐
│  UK Holdco   │            │  International Holdco   │
└──────────────┘            └────────────────────────┘
┌──────────────┐            ┌────────────────────────┐
│UK Subsidiaries│           │     International       │
│              │            │     Subsidiaries        │
└──────────────┘            └────────────────────────┘
```

182

Sale by directors and a resulting DES

6.101 Achieving ownership of the group via a sale by existing management using a 'Newco' structure (as set out in Diagram 2) is possible without a formal insolvency appointment. This would require the directors of the selling company, typically a holding company (for convenience hereinafter referred to as 'Holdings'), to agree to sell the assets of that company (ie shares) in an operating company or intermediate holding company below Holdings as the selling company, to a new company ('Newco') in consideration for a release by the institutional creditors of their debt in Holdings or a guarantee claim that they have against Holdings. Care will need to be taken by the directors of Holdings where other third party creditors have claims against Holdings. If institutional lenders have priority secured claims (which is typically the norm) such a sale by management of Holdings:

(i) where there has been a legitimate application of pressure by those institutional creditors on management; and

(ii) which occurs outside of insolvency and which will yield a superior realisation for the benefit of those institutional creditors,

will almost certainly be in the best interests of those creditors and will be unlikely to constitute a preference under the Insolvency Act 1986, s 239. This conclusion is even more likely if the directors of Holdings have received detailed valuations from professional advisers.

6.102 In these types of transaction it is assumed that the selling entity would be Holdings as the ultimate holding company, but the same issues would arise at other levels within the group where there is a sale of companies sitting below an intermediate selling company.

6.103 The directors of Holdings can only be advised to sell if to do so is in the best interests of Holdings. The interests to whom directors must have regard are, in times of prosperity, the company's shareholders. However, as the prospect of insolvency looms the interests of creditors intrude so as to become overwhelming from the time at which the company becomes insolvent[1]. On the basis that Holdings' liabilities exceed its asset value, the directors must now have exclusive regard to the interests of the other creditors. As intimated earlier it will be important for the directors to know:

(a) that the relevant constituency of creditors under the group's financing documents have consented to such a sale and that they will instruct the security trustee to release any guarantees granted by companies lower down the corporate structure or any security over the shares to be transferred;

(b) where the asset value 'breaks' within the overall capital structure in order to be sufficiently comfortable to effect a sale which returns no value to unsecured creditors; and

(c) that unimpaired debt held by creditors will be refinanced or otherwise preserved in the Newco structure so as to maintain the position of those unimpaired creditors.

[1] *West Mercia Safetyware Ltd v Dodd* [1988] BCLC 250.

6.104 The directors will inevitably be advised of the risk of criticism and potential action from certain unsecured creditors of Holdings (if any) or more likely unsecured and structurally/contractually subordinated creditors in the capital structure such as PIK holders, loan noteholders or possibly high yield bondholders, with claims against Holdings or companies sitting above Holdings, that the sale was at an undervalue and that the duties owed to those creditors were not met. Such contractually subordinated debt as depicted in Diagram 2 is usually 'overreached' pursuant to the terms of the intercreditor agreement which will require subordinated security, intercompany claims, guarantees and all other claims including subrogation claims of group companies to be released as part of a contractual sale process consented to by the majority senior lenders. If such overreaching provisions are not sufficiently expansive and do not allow primary subordinated claims to be extinguished (which is the case with certain intercreditor agreements used in the LBO Market) then this may cause a potential problem, especially if subordinated debt is made available at the 'Tradeco' level in Diagram 2. This would mean that the subordinated debt would 'travel' across with Tradeco into the SPV corporate group as it could not be discharged or overreached. Such inadequate intercreditor agreements may well be an impediment to a restructuring where the value breaks in the senior debt or dissentient mezzanine refuse to have their debt disenfranchised or converted into equity.

6.105 The fact that criticism of the directors may be without merit is no guarantee that criticisms will not be made. It may be of little comfort to the directors that these are the same criticisms that an administrator or receiver of Holdings might face if he were to effect a sale of any shareholdings held by Holdings. Indeed, whereas an administrator or receiver has recourse to the assets under his control (and possibly an indemnity) and is a professional insolvency practitioner familiar with the risks, the directors risk personal liability and will be unfamiliar with the territory of a distressed sale. In the absence of clear and unambiguous legal advice and a detailed valuation they will in all likelihood be reticent to proceed.

6.106 Compared with a sale by an administrator or receiver, a sale by Holdings as a company in distress will attract greater scrutiny in any on-sale, particularly when the on-sale is conducted within two years of the original DES transaction if the first purchaser is 'connected' with Holdings. For these purposes connectivity will exist if the Newco and Holdings have common directors, which will usually be the case. In the absence of such a connection, the period of scrutiny will only be six months.

6.107 Conversely, a sale by an administrator or receiver appointed by the institutional creditors pursuant to their contractual rights following an event of default would be less likely to attract scrutiny. As with an administrator or receiver, the directors will, as indicated above, need to be satisfied that the consideration represents a fair market value for the shares to be transferred by Holdings. Unlike administrators or receivers, the directors might be unwilling to conclude a sale without a full and fresh marketing exercise. Evidence of prior marketing may be unlikely to persuade lay directors that it is appropriate to sell and, as a consequence, senior institutional creditors tend to 'over-bid' their debt and convert more aggressively or release Holdings from its guarantee liabilities at a higher level in order to provide a 'knock-out' bid that trade or financial buyers could not reach. The directors will also need to be comfortable that the value has shifted to the appropriate level of the capital structure and they will typically engage their own advisers in order to be able for this to be demonstrated to their own satisfaction. Conversely, an administrator or receiver would be expected to take a more informed view of prior marketing efforts and of movements in value.

6.108 The directors' insistence on a fresh marketing exercise may cause delay and value erosion while the shares are marketed. A pre-packaged sale by an administrator or receiver could however be completed within hours and this will need to be taken into account when one is considering whether to invest the time and effort in a sale by management.

6.109 Where such a sale by management is to be implemented it is not uncommon for a 'Chief Restructuring Officer' ('CRO') to be appointed to the board to assist the other directors in understanding the issues they face. If the CRO concludes that a sale is the best way of discharging directors' duties in a difficult situation, this may influence other directors. The directors will of course be cognisant that a sale by them will preserve value for the key creditors who now have an economic interest in the company as well as other stakeholders such as unsecured creditors and employees who will be likely to fare much better in a consensual sale rather than in a more uncertain sale taken by the appointment of a receiver or an administrator which might result in a dilution of value for those lenders having the key economic interest.

6.110 If some or all of the directors of Holdings are also to be directors or otherwise involved in the management of the purchase going forward, their concerns as to their ability to sell are likely to become heightened. It is the duty of each director not to make a profit that is secret from the company he serves and to avoid conflicts. Although each such director could declare his interests, his proximity to both sides of the transaction, when added to the other factors, could further militate against their co-operation.

6.111 If the directors adopt a recalcitrant attitude, the institutional creditors could seek to persuade the directors to sell. This might be possible where there is a composite group guarantee structure in place by all companies from Holdings and below. The institutional creditors may well agree to refrain from calling on the guarantees (and thereby triggering the insolvency of the subsidiaries of Holdings) if the sale is completed promptly. It would be an appropriate exercise of those directors' duties owed to the creditors of the other subsidiary companies (especially where they are also directors of such subsidiary companies) to seek to minimise their loss by avoiding the guarantees being called.

6.112 Any action for breach of duty, transaction at an undervalue, etc can only be taken by a subsequently appointed liquidator. However, institutional creditors could further seek to persuade the directors to sell by confirming that it is the view of the secured creditor that the sale is in their best interests. Implicit (or expressly stated) within that comfort would be the threat that a failure to effect the sale would be perceived to constitute an increase in the institutional creditor's losses for which the directors would risk personal accountability.

6.113 Of course a number of consents will be required under the relevant finance documents for the directors to execute such a sale. Indeed, certain actions or decisions may require unanimity, or at least a large majority of two-thirds of creditors or more. There can therefore be significant ransom or hold-out value in a relatively small holding of debt, which again can present an attractive position for an opportunity investor seeking to influence or control a restructuring process and to prevent an efficient and expeditious sale by directors. Such lenders may of course wish to extract a fee or other concessions in the deal as a condition to granting its consent.

Diagram 2

Management Executed Sale and DES

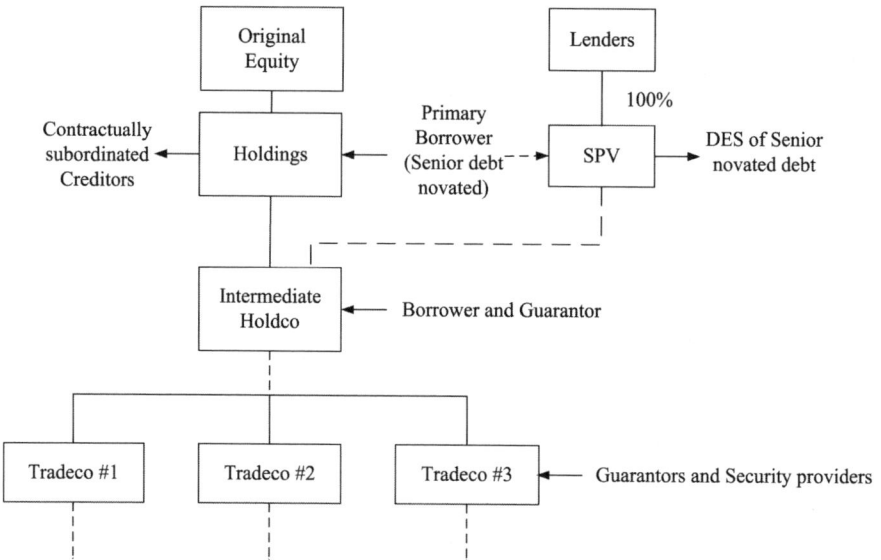

- Holdings is released from its obligations (either directly as a borrower or as a guarantor) to repay the bank debt.
- The contractually subordinated debt is 'overreached' via the intercreditor.
- SPV accepts liability for bank debt (by way of novation) and becomes a borrower.
- SPV is an entity owed by the Lenders.
- Sub-group continues to guarantee bank debt.
- Security for guarantees remains in place.
- SPV replaces Holdings as group parent.
- Debt for equity of the novated debt.

A DES via a sale undertaken pursuant to an enforcement process

6.114 Typically following an event of default and an instruction from a majority of the relevant constituency of institutional creditors to the security agent to commence an enforcement process, the security agent in the case of a secured financing will commence enforcement of the relevant security. Usually this will involve the enforcement of security over shares granted by a holding company or an intermediate holding company so that the lenders can effectively 'cut the group off at the neck' and dispose of an intermediate holding company that owns the main operating companies or each of the relevant operating companies in each case, under an appropriate security instrument. In certain jurisdictions such as the UK an instrument will entitle the institutional creditors to appoint a receiver of those shares. In continental jurisdictions the enforcement is less flexible and is likely to be more protracted and may involve a sale of the shares by a public auction following a court ruling or the security agent otherwise obtaining an executory title.

6.115 Diagram 3 shows how a sale might be achieved by a receiver. For these purposes a receiver refers not only to an administrative receiver appointed in accordance with Part III 'Receivership' of the Insolvency Act 1986, but also a fixed charge receiver appointed under a fixed charge over shares existing in a specific security document creating security over those shares or a full mortgage debenture which creates a number of fixed charges over certain assets such as shares as well as a floating charge over all of the chargor's assets and undertaking. Assuming that the security trustee can release and overreach the subordinated indebtedness and security as articulated above, the security trustee will be able take possession of the relevant securities pursuant to the terms of the intercreditor agreement and on the basis that they constitute 'financial collateral' and the secured obligations constitute a 'security financial collateral arrangement' (in each case as defined in and for the purposes of the Financial Collateral Arrangements (No 2) Regulations 2003, SI 2003/3226) the security trustee shall have the right to appropriate all or any part of such financial collateral in or towards discharge of the secured obligations.

6.116 It is possible for the receiver to accept a 'credit bid' for the shares in an amount that corresponds to the value of the relevant shareholding, but it is important to note that in order to release the relevant shares from the underlying security the receiver will require the assistance of the security agent to effect such a release typically in accordance with the provisions of an intercreditor agreement or the underlying security agreement.

6.117 Under English law it is clear that a receiver can accept a credit bid or a release of indebtedness as consideration for the sale of the shares over which he is the receiver. The powers of an administrative receiver as specified in the Insolvency Act 1986, Sch 1 provide that an administrative receiver has a power to 'sell or otherwise dispose of the property of [the] company' and as such clearly envisages such a transaction whereby property can be disposed under this power for a consideration other than cash. This is entirely logical because the company to which the receiver has been appointed derives real value as a result of a significant portion of its indebtedness being discharged as a result of such a sale. Moreover, case law including authorities such as *Thurlow v Mackeson*[1] and *Belton v Bass, Ratcliffe and Gretton Ltd*[2], supports such a transaction. Most professionally drafted charges over shares will incorporate as a matter of contract the powers of an administrative receiver as set out in the Insolvency Act 1986, Sch 1 into the security document, thereby giving a fixed charge receiver of shares the same power to accept a credit bid (in lieu of cash) in consideration for the sale of the shares.

[1] (1868) LR 4 QB 97.
[2] [1922] 2 Ch 449.

6.118 The disadvantage of accepting a credit bid as consideration for the sale of the shares is that the consideration subject to stamp duty will be deemed to be the full amount of the credit bid. As a consequence it may well be preferable for the receiver having regard to any competing bids for the shareholding to simply transfer the assets in the form of the shares to a Newco for a nominal price, but subject to all of the existing guarantees and indebtedness in the corporate group. If the share asset is sold on an encumbered basis the price will logically and legitimately be much lower thereby resulting in a much lower payment of stamp duty. The DES would then take place at a later and separate stage as depicted in Stage 2 in Diagram 3.

6.119 It is likely that a significant proportion of the debt in Holdings will continue to reside in that company and will not be transferred into the new acquiring group. This is so that the lenders will continue to be the major priority secured creditors in Holdings and so will be able to control its destiny and any challenge to the transaction via its controlling position as the majority priority secured creditor. In any event this retention of a significant proportion of debt in Holdings that is non-performing and which will ultimately be written off in a liquidation of Holdings is a clear indicator that the value did break in the relevant senior debt and that this was not a transaction at an undervalue designated to benefit the senior lenders. Given that senior impaired debt has been left behind and will also be subject to a further conversion in the typically offshore acquiring group, it would be extremely difficult to contest that this was a transaction designed to transfer all value to the senior lenders at the expense of subordinated and unsecured creditors. Due to its favourable tax regime, flexible corporate laws and sophisticated and reliable legal system, the Cayman Islands is typically the offshore jurisdiction of choice[1]. These are important issues that have to be considered and reconciled in every case in the context of where the value is breaking. Assessing the risks of a challenge from creditors that are perceived to be impaired and out of the money is a key aspect of the structuring and execution of these types of DES transactions. As intimated the security agent and the senior lenders will eventually give Holdings an appropriate 'burial' via an insolvent liquidation.

[1]   In the TMD Friction restructuring of 2006 and the Polestar restructuring of 2007, the new
       Holding companies formed as part of the DES were incorporated in the Cayman Islands.

6.120 As part of the general tax planning (which is covered at the end of this chapter[1]) and as already intimated, it is likely that the lender vehicle making such an acquisition is incorporated in a low tax jurisdiction such as the Cayman Islands or Jersey. On an eventual exit from the deal, Cayman Topco in this example, could sell Cayman Holdco to reduce capital gains tax liabilities and to avoid stamp duty as shares in an English company are not being sold which would otherwise attract stamp duty. Holdco as the 'new' borrower would typically be a UK tax resident in order to achieve normal deductibility on the new refinancing facilities and the new money facility.

[1]   These issues are discussed in more detail in the section of this chapter entitled 'Tax issues
       arising on restructurings'.

6.121 One of the key difficulties in a DES is 'pushing' the debt up to the relevant level of the new corporate structure in order to execute the conversion. In this third scenario it can be seen that this is to be achieved by making a demand under the guarantee at the appropriate operating company level so as to crystallise a debt. This debt can then be dealt with flexibly to move it up the corporate structure in readiness for the conversion. In this example the guarantee debt is to be formalised and refinanced via a new on-demand interim facility which 'set-off' the amounts to be otherwise advanced under that facility by a deemed repayment and discharge of the guarantee debt. The new interim facility is established on terms that make it capable of novation to another member of the group and this is all depicted at steps 3, 4 and 5 of Stage 2.

6.122 Part of the novated debt is then converted at the appropriate rate depending on the ongoing level of leverage in the Topco Group. In addition new money and working capital is also likely to be raised in Cayman Holdco. Typically the remaining debt will be rolled into a new facility on amended terms containing appropriate financial covenants to reflect the new capital structure.

6.123 The shares in Cayman Holdco are initially issued to the original lenders or their nominee. Those Cayman Holdco shares are then in turn exchanged by the lender or its nominee for shares in Cayman Topco. The

189

shares are allocated to the lenders pro rata to their original debt holdings and exchanged by the lenders or their nominee for shares in Cayman Topco.

6.124 One of the potential problems with Scenario 3 is that it may (depending on the exact intercreditor provisions) require 100% consent of the majority senior creditors, perhaps by reason of the need for a unanimous consent to the disposal, the release of security or guarantees or the incurrence of further new money in the Topco Group or the eventual compulsory conversion of the debt that has been novated up through the corporate structure, in this case to Cayman Holdco. A conversion of debt cannot be made without the consent of the holder of that debt. In order to procure the necessary certainty that such unanimity exists it is usual to arrange for the relevant constituency to sign into a lock-up agreement whereby all lenders agree to and consent to all relevant steps within such a DES restructuring plan.

6.125 If unanimity cannot be obtained it may well be possible to create an alternative structure for a sale by a receiver to a 'Newco'. This would be conditional upon the execution of a lock-up agreement by 75% or more of the senior lender constituency so as to demonstrate that if a scheme of arrangement needed to be implemented to achieve such a restructuring plan there was at least demonstrable support for this which would cause those exercising a 'hold-out' to reconsider their position.

6.126 A possible alternative structure would involve:

(a) Newco issuing a divisible secured note (the 'Note') to the receivers as consideration for a transfer to it of the relevant shares.

(b) The Note being distributed to the security trustee in toto, who would then divide it and distribute it pro rata to all the senior lenders in discharge of their senior debt claims.

(c) A proportion of the value of the Note automatically converting into equity in Newco and the balance of the Note being converted into an appropriate debt instrument within a new capital structure of Newco which depending on the circumstances could rank either parri passu with or in priority to the balance of the Note.

6.127 As already intimated, the receivers are under a duty to carry out such acts as are reasonably practicable that allow them to obtain the best price for the relevant shares as may be reasonably obtainable. In this regard it may be that a better price would be obtained for the shares if there were a sale asset-by-asset rather than a sale pursuant to such a Note. Such a sale would require the consent of the security trustee to the release of the security and encumbrances over the shares and ahead of deciding to effect such a sale of the shares the receivers would need to consider the practicability and likely recovery from an asset-by-asset sale, and may need to approach the security trustee for consent to such a sale. Exits implemented on an asset by asset basis typically yield a lower level of return and realisation and the security trustee may view such a sale structure negatively. Refusal by the security trustee of such consent may help to demonstrate that a sale asset-by-asset was not the preferred option and support a case that a sale of the shares should in fact be implemented by the receivers and should take place pursuant to the terms of the Note.

6.128 As already noted, receivers do have the power to accept non-cash consideration for a disposition of property constituted by shares given that under the Insolvency Act 1986, Sch 1, they have a power to 'sell or otherwise dispose of' property, and it is clear that property may be transferred under this power for a consideration other than cash. Moreover, a power of sale includes a power to transfer property for a deferred consideration with the consideration secured on the property transferred (a proposition supported by *Belton v Bass, Ratcliffe and Gretton Ltd*[1]). On this basis such a Note may be regarded as deferred consideration.

[1] [1922] 2 Ch 449.

6.129 In order to reach a decision regarding the legitimacy of such a note a receiver would need to be able to ascribe a value to it. This may mean that the receivers would have to be satisfied that Newco had reasonable prospects of being able to discharge the relevant indebtedness under the Note. Equally, in order to be confident that the Note was an instrument of value, the receivers may well need to consider whether there is likely to be a secondary market for the Note and the price at which the Note would trade on such a market. These considerations are slightly interrelated given that any potential lack of liquidity would likely make it extremely hard to value the Note in a reliable manner. Some form of market testing with the lenders and other participants in the secondary loans market may help in this regard.

6.130 As between the receivers and the beneficiaries of the security held by their appointor, such a Note does attract a number of concerns. Potentially, the acceptance of a Note such as this could constitute a breach of fiduciary duty especially if the sale could be construed as one at an undervalue. There is a potential risk that a dissenting minority may argue that the receivers are in breach of a fiduciary duty by accepting the Note as consideration for the transfer of the shares on the basis that cash consideration would have provided more value for the senior lenders. If it transpires that the Note is not, in fact, as valuable as was originally believed by the receivers then such a dissenting minority could have a strong case especially if they are able to obtain a generous *ex post facto* valuation of the shares or the underlying assets of the companies that would be transferred pursuant to such a sale. Given the uncertainties in valuing such a Note, any valuation of it obtained by the receivers would have to come out at a level materially above the amount of cash that would be distributed on a cash sale and in order to demonstrate this the receivers may be inclined to conduct a high degree of market testing ahead of a pre-packaged sale in order to establish that the Note is indeed the best deal in town.

6.131 Another related concern on the part of the receivers might be 'unfair discrimination'. The receivers are not permitted to do something that unfairly discriminates against the dissenting minority and so whilst the dissenting minority would have to prove an alternative transaction would have generated more in money or money's worth, they could seek to set aside the transfer in the event of unfair discrimination.

6.132 With a view to mitigating the risk of the receivers attracting liability it might well be prudent to offer a fair alternative to the Note route to the dissenting minority. Such an alternative might take the form of a cash offer to the dissenting minority at a level representative of the valuations of the assets and business of Holdings as received or arrived at by the receivers. If the cash that is offered represents the highest of the valuations prepared, this would be of further assistance in mitigating the risk described. However, in many cases where there is no substantial interest in the shares and any market testing has previously resulted in no valuable offers being made for the shares or assets and the debt is significantly impaired it will probably be the case that the receivers can demonstrate that the Note is indeed the most favourable route and that a sale via a Note represents the best prospects of recovery for the beneficiaries of the security held by their appointor. Obviously, the receivers will be inclined to rely on independent valuations in reaching such a conclusion.

6.133 If a sale cannot plausibly be executed using the above note structure due for example to dissent from creditors who refuse to have their debt converted at the appropriate rate, one alternative option would be to implement a scheme of arrangement of the indebtedness that has been novated to Cayman Holdco. Lawrence Collins J in *Re Drax Holdings Ltd*[1] considered the principles which guide a court in determining its jurisdiction, and exercising its discretion, to sanction a scheme involving an unregistered overseas company. He held that there must be a sufficient connection with England which may, but need not necessarily, consist of assets within the jurisdiction. In the *Drax Holdings* case, Lawrence Collins J was able to find a sufficient connection with England on the facts: Drax Holdings was incorporated to raise finance to acquire a power station in Yorkshire; key finance documents were governed by English law and contained submissions to the jurisdiction of the English courts; assets charged under the finance documents included the power station in Yorkshire and shares in English companies[2].

---

[1] [2003] EWHC 2743 (Ch), [2004] 1 All ER 903, [2004] 1 WLR 1049, [2004] BCC 334, followed in *Re La Mutuelles du Mans Assurances IARD* [2006] BCC 11; and *Re DAP Holding NV* [2006] BCC 48.
[2] [2004] BCC 334 at [32].

Diagram 3
DES Via an enforcement process
Group Structure Pre-restructuring

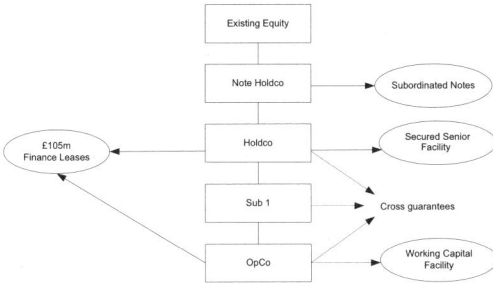

```
                    ┌─────────────────┐
                    │ Existing Equity │
                    └────────┬────────┘
                             │
                    ┌────────┴────────┐        ┌──────────────────┐
                    │   Note Holdco   │───────▶│ Subordinated Notes│
                    └────────┬────────┘        └──────────────────┘
                             │
   ┌──────────────┐  ┌────────┴────────┐        ┌──────────────────┐
   │   £105m      │◀─│     Holdco      │───────▶│  Secured Senior  │
   │Finance Leases│  └────────┬────────┘        │    Facility      │
   └──────────────┘           │                 └──────────────────┘
                    ┌────────┴────────┐
                    │      Sub 1      │────────▶ Cross guarantees
                    └────────┬────────┘
                             │                  ┌──────────────────┐
                    ┌────────┴────────┐          │ Working Capital  │
                    │      OpCo       │─────────▶│    Facility      │
                    └─────────────────┘          └──────────────────┘
```

Stage 1 - Appointment of Receiver

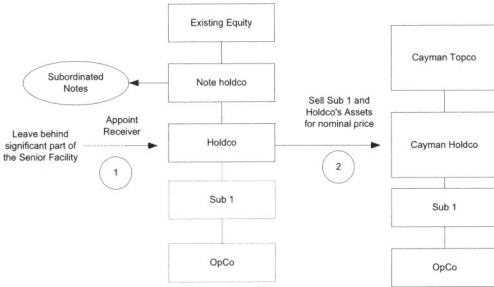

```
                                    ┌─────────────────┐
                                    │ Existing Equity │
                                    └────────┬────────┘
                                             │
   ┌──────────────┐           ┌────────┴────────┐              ┌─────────────────┐
   │ Subordinated │◀──────────│   Note holdco   │              │  Cayman Topco   │
   │    Notes     │           └────────┬────────┘              └────────┬────────┘
   └──────────────┘     Appoint        │                                │
                        Receiver  ┌────┴───────┐  Sell Sub 1 and  ┌─────┴──────────┐
   Leave behind       ··········▶│   Holdco   │  Holdco's Assets │ Cayman Holdco  │
   significant part of           └────┬───────┘  for nominal price└────────┬───────┘
   the Senior Facility    (1)         │              (2)                   │
                               ┌──────┴─────┐                      ┌──────┴──────┐
                               │   Sub 1    │                      │   Sub 1     │
                               └──────┬─────┘                      └──────┬──────┘
                               ┌──────┴─────┐                      ┌──────┴──────┐
                               │    OpCo    │                      │    OpCo     │
                               └────────────┘                      └─────────────┘
```

Stage 2 (Reorganisation)

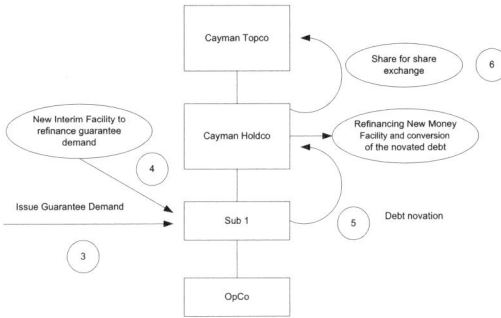

```
                              ┌─────────────────┐
                              │  Cayman Topco   │◀──  Share for share    (6)
                              └────────┬────────┘       exchange
                                       │
   New Interim Facility to   ┌────────┴────────┐    Refinancing New Money
   refinance guarantee       │  Cayman Holdco  │───▶ Facility and conversion
   demand                    └────────┬────────┘◀──  of the novated debt
              (4)                      │
   Issue Guarantee Demand    ┌────────┴────────┐
   ──────────────────────▶   │     Sub 1       │     (5)   Debt novation
              (3)            └────────┬────────┘
                             ┌────────┴────────┐
                             │     OpCo        │
                             └─────────────────┘
```

Stage 3 (Group post DES)

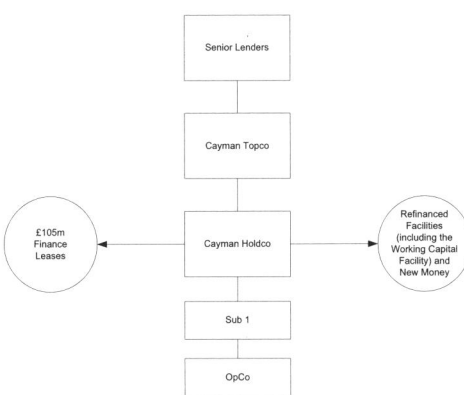

```
                             ┌─────────────────┐
                             │ Senior Lenders  │
                             └────────┬────────┘
                                      │
                             ┌────────┴────────┐
                             │  Cayman Topco   │
                             └────────┬────────┘
                                      │
   ┌──────────────┐          ┌────────┴────────┐      ┌──────────────────┐
   │   £105m      │◀─────────│  Cayman Holdco  │─────▶│   Refinanced     │
   │  Finance     │          └────────┬────────┘      │   Facilities     │
   │   Leases     │                   │               │ (including the   │
   └──────────────┘          ┌────────┴────────┐      │ Working Capital  │
                             │     Sub 1       │      │ Facility) and    │
                             └────────┬────────┘      │   New Money      │
                             ┌────────┴────────┐      └──────────────────┘
                             │     OpCo        │
                             └─────────────────┘
```

Differing interests in a DES

6.134 Clearly, in order for a DES to be an attractive play for any investor – whether a legacy lender or an acquirer of debt in the secondary market – the underlying business of the company, when de-geared, must be viable and have a reasonable prospect of a turnaround and thus increase in value. It needs to be recognised however that lenders may hope to achieve different results from the DES, illustrating their potentially diverse underlying economic interests; some may be looking to salvage value, without having to write off an entire investment, whilst others may be looking to a longer-term equity investment, with potential upside coming from future value creation in a revitalised business. There may of course be lenders occupying the middle ground who have acquired debt at below its par value, and who will be looking to trade out of the equity in a relatively short period of time – having made a profit in the interim because of the improved fortunes of the company in question.

6.135 The lenders to a company may therefore have diverse interests as between themselves. Frequently, in order to represent the interests of the lenders in a DES, the steering or other committee that will have typically been established to oversee and negotiate the restructuring transaction will specifically hold discussions as to the conversion amount and the ultimate equity structure with the company and its advisers, and other parties interested in the DES process, such as other debt and equity stakeholders, accountants, and their respective advisers. The financial advisers to the company are likely to have an important role in positioning the company, particularly as regards value, with its stakeholders, as well as exploring other value enhancing opportunities that may exist outside of solely a restructuring context. The aim of this will be to drive the best deal through for the company and its management and other stakeholders in terms of the ongoing structure of debt and equity that remains in the company.

Management and other stakeholders

6.136 Clearly, the company and its advisers, together with any separate advisers retained by management and existing shareholders, will seek to negotiate the best deal for their constituency under the DES. This often constitutes the primary focus of the negotiations between the lenders, the company management and the existing shareholders of the company. Quite often these negotiations are protracted and tense as they effectively result in a transfer of economic ownership and control from the existing equity to other stakeholders. In rare cases where there is a perceived need to preserve some members of existing management due to their unique knowledge and understanding of the business or their personal relationships with key customers those members of the management team who may well have presided over the decline of the company into its current difficulties will seek to negotiate their own equity stake.

6.137 Existing shareholders will, of course, be keen to ensure that they retain some stake in the company – either because the valuation dictates such, or because there is some other holdout value attached to their stake. For example, a shareholder may own a key piece of intellectual property such as a trademark or a patent. A shareholder may also hold a significant amount of shareholder debt, for example, or provide a key piece of plant or machinery or real estate relating to the business.

6.138 Conversely, whilst the management team may not always have been successful, if they are retained, they will be at pains to point out that a fundamentally sound business may have been hindered by an inflexible and expensive capital structure. In addition, lenders need knowledgeable management that understand the business and who have the key relationships with important customers and suppliers. Whilst they can bring in external management this may take time and may prove to be expensive. In the interim the lenders are likely not to have management or sector expertise to run the business on an ongoing basis, nor the resources necessary to see a company through a restructuring. This all improves the negotiating position of the incumbent management who quite often seek remuneration and equity packages that resemble those of management teams in a private equity context.

6.139 Where the value break is in the external debt, and therefore the equity is of little or zero value, it will therefore be a purely commercial negotiation between the lenders and the management (and other stakeholders) as to how the equity – or other method of incentivisation – is shared. When the equity is worth nothing, it is of course easier for lenders to 'give some of it up', creating hope value and therefore a means of incentivisation. Typically, this will be coupled with mechanisms such as ratchets, performance targets and vesting, in order to keep management incentivised even if their stake becomes valuable on paper. Taking place alongside negotiations regarding management's potential participation in the capital structure will be discussions on management's contractual arrangements – salary, bonus and other employment terms (such as notice periods and restrictive covenants). Lenders must therefore be alive to, and be prepared to negotiate, the whole package with people that can have a considerably strong negotiating position, despite the sub-optimal state of affairs of the company.

Commercial negotiation

6.140 Having taken a decision to implement a consensual DES, the key negotiations between the company, its shareholders, other stakeholders (such as subordinated lenders, finance lessors and unsecured creditors) and the senior lenders will likely focus on:

(a) the proportion, and type, of debt to be converted to share capital;

(b) the proportion of the total share capital that such converted debt amount represents (and therefore the proportion of such share capital that the lenders receive relative to any other stakeholder, particularly management and existing shareholders);

(c) the class of share that should be issued to the lenders, as opposed to the class that should be issued to anyone else (such as management), and the rights attaching to each class of share;

(d) the restrictions if any on the ability of the shareholders to transfer their shares;

(e) the minority protections that are afforded to shareholders (such as mandatory offer obligations, 'tag along' and 'drag along' rights);

(f) the ongoing governance arrangements of the corporate;

(g) any uplifted return for the lenders in circumstances where they do not hold a majority of the shares (perhaps for International Accounting Standard reasons and the need to consolidate shareholdings on to their own balance sheet);

(h) exit arrangements; and

(i) the comfort that will be given to the lenders in relation to certain corporate and business matters.

Proportion of debt to be converted

6.141 Clearly, the amount of debt to be converted to share capital will be a key consideration for all parties concerned, taking into account factors such as the amount of debt which is unimpaired (in other words, above the value break) compared to that which is impaired, and the resultant capital structure of the company in question. As suggested the company and its directors will typically want to de-gear as much as possible by converting as much debt as possible into equity.

Proportion of equity represented by converted debt

6.142 Even where the existing equity has no residual value, because the value break sits in the lenders' debt, there will be a negotiation around the proportion that the 'lenders' equity' represents of the whole. This may be because of management participation, or other stakeholders' ability to negotiate an allocation of equity for themselves because of their individual situation – former shareholders. In private companies for example, those persons with a historic interest in the company could have some value to add to the new proposition justifying an equity stake. In public companies however, existing shareholders will be required to vote in favour of a consensual transaction unless there is a scheme of arrangement, which is a transfer scheme that effectively transfer all of the assets of the company to a Newco.

6.143 Increasingly, directors of certain corporates undergoing a DES are scrutinising the correlation between the amount and economic value of the debt converted and the proportion of the shares allocated to a converting lender. In particular, there is a concern (on the part of the directors) that, where the debt is unsecured, the conversion of a financial creditor's debt which potentially gives it an enhanced position in relation to other creditors might constitute an unlawful preference, especially where the institutional creditor may not have had such a return on a liquidation.

Class of share capital

6.144 In creating the new equity capital structure, the lenders may adopt a 'private equity' approach to the relevant shareholdings – giving themselves the 'institutional' share capital (and, of course, holding debt), and other stake-holders taking the 'management' share capital. This may require the shares held by those other than the lenders to be non-voting, non-participating (except on a capital distribution, and so without rights to dividends, for example) and non-transferable depending on whether the corporate entity is a private or public company. Particularly where management are concerned, lenders will be keen that any equity stake they have is a genuine incentivisation tool, and so early realisation of this stake (by way of sale, for example) is unlikely to be acceptable.

Transfer restrictions

6.145 In terms of transfers, whilst lenders will be keen to ensure management are 'locked in', they may themselves wish to have a degree of flexibility around the transfer of their own shareholdings. In a private context, when a lender comes from a context of being able to trade debt relatively freely – obviously there is a very active secondary market in corporate debt – it is sometimes tricky to convince them that equity should in certain situations be less transferable. Whilst contractual sub-participation, nominee or other arrangements could be entered into, it will likely be more appealing for lenders if they have a fair amount of freedom to transfer the share capital resulting from a DES. This would likely be negotiated as part of the company's new constitutional documents.

6.146 There can be a sensitive line here since, in a private company context at least, the shares will not be 'traded' in the traditional sense, and there will be no regulated or formal market. Indeed, there could be legal issues with offering shares to the 'public', and so appropriate advice and undertakings will need to be sought.

6.147 The company, or indeed the lenders, may also insist upon being granted a pre-emptive right in the event of a proposed transfer of shares, so that the non-transferring shareholders have a right of first refusal to acquire those shares (usually provided that the original offer price is matched). This is a matter for negotiation, and of course relies upon the appetite of shareholders to take up the shares being offered, but provides a useful form of protection against 'unknown' third party transferees becoming shareholders.

6.148 When the company being restructured is a public company, with listed shares, the shares themselves must be freely transferable. Any transfer restrictions can be negotiated (as before), but are only able to be implemented at an underlying contractual level, with formal 'Standstill' or 'lock-up' agreements. This will not only promote a stable shareholder base, but also (particularly in the context of a new issue of listed shares) assist in maintaining an orderly market for those shares. However, where there is more than one lender accepting such a restriction on the transfer of its shares, this might give rise to a 'section 204 agreement' Concert party Free Float maintained (25% freely transferable) with the related disclosure obligations (see later).

Minority protections

6.149 Again, principally in a private company context, shareholders may expect to see certain minority protections in place to prevent transactions being done by some shareholders to the exclusion of others (on a 'sweetheart' basis, for example), or to prevent undesired third parties from becoming significant shareholders. In the public arena, such protections will be afforded by regulations such as The City Code on Takeovers and Mergers and the Listing Rules.

Governance

6.150 The ongoing governance of the company is likely to be of critical importance to lenders coming into the equity, as they will not want to see an erosion of value, or a recovery being jeopardised, immediately after a DES, because of poor management or a return to old habits. They will therefore want a specific and strong right to exert influence over the direction of the restructured company, perhaps through board appointment rights (or, for a lesser degree of control and influence, rights to appoint observers to the board). Even where the lenders have no right to be represented on the board of the company, and are therefore detached from its management, it would also be common for the lenders, in their capacity as shareholders, to have veto rights over certain key corporate and commercial decisions. This will typically be achieved by preventing (on a contractual basis) the company from taking any decision or action without specific shareholder consent – a concept which can (and is) applied equally to the lender representative, if any, on the board of the company, where perhaps the matter in question is more operational in nature, and therefore not of sufficient importance to secure a shareholder vote.

6.151 The most appropriate place to document the governance arrangements of the company, and the accompanying contractual protections for the lenders, would be in a shareholders' agreement (although certain more procedural provisions, such as the method of appointing directors and passing certain resolutions, would be set out in the company's articles of association). On occasion, the relevant provisions would be in both a shareholders' agreement and the articles, thereby putting third parties on notice of the specific provisions – although, for the same reason, parties may prefer to keep such provisions in the shareholders' agreement alone, which (unlike the articles) is not a public document in the UK. It would not be unusual for key commercial matters (such as business plans and budgets, acquisitions and disposals and material contractual arrangements), as well as corporate matters in relation to capital structure and distributions, to be subject to some form of lender consultation or consent, and frequently consent at the shareholder level.

6.152 Broadly, and in a little more detail, there are seven key protections that lenders might seek:

(1)   restrictions on the operation of the business, so that the company undertakes to confine its activities to the business as described in either the articles or its annual financial budget and business plan (which may themselves be subject to the approval of the lenders);

(2)   restrictions to protect the lenders from prejudicial dilutive capital operations, such as a new share issue on a non pre-emptive basis. Where lenders hold warrants, options or convertible shares, mechanisms to protect dilution upon similar events will be included by way of appropriate adjustments to the relevant conversion rate;

(3)   restrictions to protect dividend and redemption rights are also common, particularly to ensure that the company's distributable profits are not adversely affected by capital operations such as bonus share issues, and to ensure that there is no dividend leakage;

(4)   restrictions to prevent the company from creating shares ranking in priority to, or pari passu with, the lenders' shares (whether ordinary, preference or otherwise);

(5)   the inclusion of tag-along rights so that, upon the proposed sale of a certain percentage of the company's share capital, the purchaser must make an offer on the same terms to acquire the entire share capital;

(6)   the inclusion of drag-along rights on the proposed sale of a certain percentage of the company's share capital (which will usually be higher than the trigger for tag-along rights), which will entitle those proposing a sale of the relevant percentage to force other shareholders to sell on the same terms (so that a purchaser can be sure it will acquire the entire share capital);

(7)   financial controls on directors' remuneration, debt and capital raising, material contracts, acquisitions and disposals and capital expenditure.

6.153 In addition, approving and implementing an exit transaction will also be a subject area where lenders will expect to have at least negative control. In cases where the converting lenders could not take a majority of the shares due to IAS consolidation concerns, the alternative would be for a shareholders' agreement with a modified voting process to be put in place, whereby on specific exit proposals the lenders could approve that exit.

Exit

6.154 In keeping with the theme of typical financial investors, lenders will likely have one eye on an exit strategy for their investment. Attitudes to exit will reflect the differing interests of the investors – some longer term than others – and will need to be reconciled by them and their advisers. Whilst some may be more concerned with transferability of shares, so that they can 'trade out' quite quickly, some may be looking to create a valuable long-term enterprise with a view to a sale, merger, takeover or IPO in the future.

Contractual protection and due diligence

6.155 With a normal M&A transaction, a purchaser will seek a great deal of contractual comfort from a seller in relation to the historical, as well as the current, status of the company and the business, typically through representations and warranties. In many ways, concluding a DES is like concluding an acquisition, albeit that the consideration for the acquisition is the debt itself – discharged in exchange for equity. However, a lender taking equity as a result of a DES is very unlikely to receive the same contractual comfort from the former shareholders in relation to the condition of the business of which it finds itself the owner.

6.156 Management may be prepared to give some comfort, possibly as part of the deal for their own ongoing shareholding, but lenders will not draw any financial comfort from these statements since the management's financial exposure will be limited. It therefore falls to the lenders' due diligence to demonstrate that they, as shareholders, will not be exposed to greater liability than anticipated, and this in itself can be an exercise which is difficult to gauge.

6.157 For example, a typical due diligence process can take a significant amount of time, and incur significant costs. Where the lenders are faced with a choice of a DES, or some other (less desirable) restructuring procedure, they may take the view that diligence is worthless since they will end up taking equity anyway. However, diligence can form an important part of the overall decision-making regarding the restructuring, since, at the very least, lenders will want to know that contingent liabilities for them, or the company, are not triggered by the transaction – such as secondary tax liabilities, pensions liabilities and environmental liabilities. It will also be important to know that the company's key contractual arrangements, with suppliers and customers, perhaps, are not jeopardised by any 'change of control' that may take place as a result of a DES.

Equity composition

6.158 One of the main questions is whether the lenders will be issued with ordinary shares in the company, or a more bespoke form of equity such as a preference share, possibly convertible into ordinary shares or attracting a fixed and/or cumulative dividend. A brief summary of the types of share capital that may be considered is set out below. However, critical to any analysis of the share capital to arise on a DES is the possible tax impact, on both the company and the lender, of taking certain types of shares. Some of the tax issues arising on restructurings are discussed in more detail below.

Preference shares

6.159 By issuing a properly constructed preference share, the lenders will acquire share capital which is 'quasi debt'. The preference shares will typically attract a coupon (structured as a dividend) – possibly fixed – which may well also be cumulative. They will also rank in priority (as to income and capital return) to other classes of share capital, but behind all debt. The coupon and the priority ranking is essentially the lenders' reward for taking equity, and subordinating themselves to other creditors.

6.160 In certain circumstances, the dividend entitlement may increase (for example, upon a disposal of assets, or upon a default in payment of the dividend). Whilst this may encourage timely payment of the relevant amounts, the company's own cashflows may make these types of share very onerous in terms of equality – in which case, the issue of ordinary shares from the outset may be more appropriate.

6.161 Dividends may also be structured as 'participating' – that is, having a right to participate in the amount of profit made by the company in any given period, ahead of the ordinary equity. Preference shares with such dividends attached to them are a useful restructuring tool which enable the institutions to participate in the success of the rescue without necessarily holding and disposing of ordinary shares.

6.162 However, the dividend can only be paid out of distributable profits – a different test to mere cashflow or profit – and so the financial projections of cashflow must indicate that servicing such a preference is practicable and lawful. Clearly, the smaller the proportion of equity represented by the preference share, the greater the chance that its dividend will be able to be serviced. If it is unlikely that the company will be able to service the dividend on this special class of share, because of its projected cashflows (including interest payments) and distributable profits position, it would usually be preferable for the lenders to be issued with ordinary shares immediately. If the company is listed, this will provide the immediate benefits of a listing and (subject to selling restrictions) a ready market for the ordinary shares.

6.163 Preference shares are often drafted to be redeemable, either on scheduled redemption dates, or at the option of the company (or, possibly, the holder). The schedule of dividend payments, particularly where such dividends are cumulative or participating (and the participation is relatively high), may encourage discipline for the company, and also encourage it to achieve redemption in order to remove the pressure on its cashflow. However, redemption, like dividend payments, generally needs to be made out of distributable profits, and so the concerns about cashflow and profit projections are equally relevant to redemption as to dividends.

6.164 *Restructuring exits*

Convertible preference shares

6.164 A preference share issued on a DES may also be convertible, in certain circumstances and at a certain ratio, into ordinary shares. This right of conversion would provide the lenders with their 'reward' and potential equity upside.

6.165 There could be significant disadvantages with making the equity convertible, however, relating to whether a lender becomes 'connected' with a company and therefore jeopardises its own ability to claim bad debt relief. This may also be the case where a preference share, with a fixed rate dividend, is contemplated to provide the lenders' equity participation[1].

[1] These issues are discussed in more detail in the section of this chapter entitled 'Tax issues arising on restructurings'.

6.166 In addition, and in the context of a listed company, there will be limits upon the amount of convertible equity that the company can issue without either seeking additional shareholder approval, or contravening certain investor body guidelines.

Voting rights in relation to preference shares

6.167 It is conventional – for tax and other reasons – for preference shares to be non-voting, save in limited circumstances such as:

(a)   where there is a resolution for the winding up of the company;
(b)   where the preference dividends are in arrears;
(c)   where the fixed redemption dates have not been complied with; and/or
(d)   where the preference share class rights are to be modified, varied or abrogated.

6.168 Preference shares with limited voting rights of this kind are generally treated as non-voting shares. Possible advantages should be balanced with any desire of the lenders to exert control over the company's affairs through their shareholdings, as discussed above in relation to governance. If, on balance, ordinary voting shares (granting a majority of the votes in general meetings, or granting veto rights on certain matters) are required, the debt should be converted into ordinary shares and the transaction should be structured carefully to address the tax risks.

Shareholding levels

6.169 As discussed above, a key commercial issue is the proportion that the lenders' shares bear to the total share capital of the company. Separate tensions exist here:

(a)   existing shareholders will need to accept a substantial dilution of their shareholdings, whilst the lenders will be seeking control of the equity – which may, of course, be part of the intention of the DES; and

(b)   there will be different consequences (both regulatory and non-regulatory) depending upon the size of the lenders' shareholdings and whether the shares are in a private or public company.

6.170 The following levels of shareholding (by reference to voting shares – that is, following conversion of any convertible shares) may be relevant. The first table illustrates the general effect of particular shareholding levels in any company, and the second table focuses on public companies.

All companies

6.171

Shareholding level (fully diluted)	Consequence
75%	Ability to pass special and extraordinary resolutions (including changing constitutional documents)
More than 50%	Ability to pass ordinary resolutions (including appointment of directors) Consolidation as a subsidiary
50%	Ability to block ordinary resolutions
More than 25%	Ability to block special resolutions (which may prevent a further restructuring)
10%	Ability to requisition a general meeting Ability to demand a poll in general meeting
5%	Ability to prevent a general meeting being held on short notice Ability to put forward a resolution to be considered in general meeting (and have related statements circulated)

Public companies

6.172

Shareholding level (fully diluted)	Consequence
30%	Application of City Code mandatory bid (Rule 9) requirements. Becoming a 'controlling shareholder' for the purposes of the Listing Rules (the company will be required to demonstrate itself capable of operating 'independently' of the 30% shareholder)
More than 25%	At least 25% of the company's share capital must be in the hands of the 'public' for its listing to be maintained – the so-called 'free-float' requirements
20%	Treated as an 'associated' company of the shareholder (which may impact on a lender's capital adequacy ratios)
10%	Shareholder will be treated as a 'related party' for the purposes of the Listing Rules
3%	Obligation of disclosure of shareholding level to the company (and onward disclosure by the company to the market, in the case of listed companies) (This disclosure obligation may be onerous where two or more lenders are treated as acting together for the purposes of the Companies Act 1985, s 204[1] as dealings by all the banks will need to be aggregated for disclosure purposes and a dealing in the company's shares by one lender will be deemed to be a dealing by each of the other lenders, requiring a separate disclosure by each lender)
1%	Disclosure of dealings if the company is in an 'offer period' (for the purposes of the City Code)

[1]   The Companies Act 1985, s 204 has been replaced by the Companies Act 2006, ss 824 and 988(4)–(7). The Companies Act 2006, s 824 came into force on 20 January 2007 (SI 2006/3428) and s 988 came into force on 6 April 2007 (SI 2007/1093).

6.173 Of course, shareholders of any shareholding level have certain rights, such as the right to:

(a)   dividends;
(b)   attend, speak at and vote at general meetings;
(c)   participate in the surplus assets of the company on a winding up;
(d)   apply to court under the Companies Act 1985, s 459[1] ('unfair prejudice');
(e)   apply to court in order to requisition a general meeting; and

(f)   apply to court for the winding up of a company where it is 'just and equitable'.

¹ Companies Act 1985, s 459 was replaced by the Companies Act 2006, s 994 on 1 October 2007 (SI 2007/2194).

Rule 9 of the City Code

6.174 Important provisions of the City Code may apply to a transaction involving a DES. As referred to in the table above, Rule 9 of the City Code provides that when a person acquires or persons acting in concert acquire:

(a)   shares which carry 30% or more of the voting rights of a company; or
(b)   (if such person or persons already hold between 30% and 50% of the voting rights of a company) an interest which increases the percentage of voting rights held by it or them,

a general offer to all other shareholders to acquire their shares must be made on the same terms. (It is similar to the tag-along provisions, in the context of private companies, described above.) It may therefore be necessary to pre-clear with the Panel that an acquisition of shares by way of a DES does not trigger the mandatory bid requirement. This is particularly important where two or more lenders are involved and, individually, the 30% threshold is not breached, but together the 30% threshold could be breached, if the lenders are treated by the Panel as 'acting in concert'.

6.175 If a mandatory offer under Rule 9 is required, it must be made to all shareholders (other than the offeror and its concert parties) in cash or a cash alternative at not less than the highest price paid by the offeror or its concert parties for shares in the preceding 12 months. Therefore, whilst a mandatory offer is generally undesirable, it will almost certainly be artificially onerous in the case of a DES, particularly if the company's financial position and share price has weakened in this period.

Rule 9 and convertible preference shares

6.176 Note 10 to Rule 9.1 of the City Code makes it clear that the acquisition of non-voting convertible securities (such as convertible preference shares) will not in itself give rise to an obligation under Rule 9 to make a general offer. However, the exercise of any rights of conversion into voting shares will be considered to be an acquisition of voting shares for the purposes of Rule 9.

The 'whitewash' procedure

6.177 Where the issue of voting shares, such as on a DES, would otherwise result in an obligation to make a general offer pursuant to the provisions of

Rule 9 of the City Code, the Panel will normally waive that obligation if there is an independent vote at a shareholders' meeting. This procedure is known as a 'whitewash'.

6.178 If a single lender acquires the relevant interest in voting shares on a DES, then a whitewash will be required to avoid the consequences of Rule 9. If several lenders acquire such an interest, then whether Rule 9 is triggered (and therefore whether a whitewash is required) will depend upon whether the lenders are 'acting in concert' with one another.

6.179 Persons 'acting in concert' comprise persons who, pursuant to an agreement or understanding (whether formal or informal), co-operate to obtain or consolidate control of a company. This is a notoriously difficult definition to interpret, and the Panel will doubtless be required to confirm the application of the definition to a given set of persons (particularly given the presumptions of concertedness which are set out in the City Code). For lenders acquiring shares in a DES, such confirmation will be vital.

6.180 In a straightforward rescue situation, it is unlikely that lenders would, in fact, be acting in concert. In order to reduce further any arguments as to the concertedness of lenders, it might be preferable for each lender to hold its shares (commensurate with the value of its debt conversion) separately, rather than appointing a security trustee to hold such shares collectively.

6.181 In an urgent rescue situation, where perhaps the time required to obtain an independent shareholder vote will jeopardise the survival of the company in question, lenders may be able to complete the DES and the restructuring, and seek a post-transaction whitewash.

6.182 The whitewash procedure would involve an ordinary resolution (on a poll vote) being put to the independent shareholders of the company, resolving to waive any obligation to make a mandatory bid arising as a result of the DES. If this procedure is adopted, the circular to shareholders setting out the resolution to be voted upon will need to contain an independent recommendation to vote in favour of the whitewash, as well as detailed information in relation to the lenders which would otherwise be caught by Rule 9 – which can be sensitive. In the case of rescues, the Panel may give a dispensation on the amount of information required in such a whitewash circular.

6.183 If lenders rely on any confirmation given by the Panel that there is no concert party, rather than a whitewash, that confirmation will only relate to the current DES. It is therefore crucial that lenders avoid any subsequent actions which might fall within concert party provisions (such as co-ordinated voting, stake-building or attempts to render the company 'bid-proof') or which would otherwise trigger an obligation to make a mandatory offer. Due to the onerous nature of the Rule 9 obligation, any lenders considering subsequent actions which may be interpreted as attempts to 'obtain or consolidate control' of the company should seek advice and, if necessary, Panel guidance.

6.184 Separation of a shareholder relationship and banking relationship with the company (as referred to in the paragraph below on insider dealing) should reduce the likelihood of concert party provisions applying, and many lenders' shares are held by nominee companies for this reason.

UKLA considerations

6.185 If the restructured company is listed, the UKLA is likely to examine the restructuring (and its results) closely to ensure that the company remains a suitable candidate for listing after the DES process. Particular issues to consider are:

(a) shares in public hands: as mentioned above, 25% of the company's listed share capital must remain in the hands of the 'public' (and lenders holding less than 5% will usually be treated as 'public');

(b) no conflicts: there must be no 'conflict of interest' between the interests of shareholders generally (and the interests of a shareholder holding 30% or more of the share capital);

(c) continuing management: there must be a degree of continuing management at board level, and the business of the company must not be substantially different, in order to avoid the company being treated as a 'new applicant' for listing after the restructuring;

(d) related parties: as well as 10% shareholders, lenders which provide finance to a company in financial trouble may be treated as 'related parties' by virtue of their influence at that time. This applies even before (and whether or not) the lenders become shareholders, and the Listing Rules contain specific provisions and restrictions in relation to related party transactions.

Timing issues

6.186 Ideally, no substitution of the lenders' debt into share capital should take place until all new money from other sources and DESs by other creditors have completed – though this will be subject to the conditions precedent in any new money facilities, and therefore the subject of negotiation. Much will also depend on the urgency by which the new money is required. In the TMD Friction restructuring for example, new money was made available to stabilise the position of the relevant company ahead of the DES.

6.187 In the case of an associated rights issue (which may be referred to as a 'rescue rights issue', since without the cash injection from the shareholders, the company's survival would be in doubt), payment for the shares so issued will not be due until approximately three weeks after that issue. This type of rights issue as part of a DES would be highly unusual other than as part of a mechanism involving a certain lender subscribing for the new equity by way of a conversion of a proportion of their debt. If the DES is to take place independently of the rights issue and the lenders are not converting part of their debt by way of a participation in the rights issue then the converting lenders should ideally ensure that the DES should only take place once the funds from the rescue rights issue are received by the company (or, at least, until any underwriting agreement in relation to that rights issue has become unconditional, so that the company is certain that the funds are forthcoming).

Creation and allotment of shares

6.188   In order to issue shares as part of a DES, the company in question must have sufficient authorised but unissued share capital. If this is not the case, the company must increase its authorised share capital (pursuant to the Companies Act 1985, s 121[1]) by ordinary resolution.

1   The Companies Act 1985, s 121(1) is to be replaced (with some changes) by the Companies Act 2006, s 617(1). The Companies Act 1985, s 121(2) is to be replaced (with some changes) by the Companies Act 2006, ss 617(2), (3), 618(1) and 620(1). The Companies Act 1985, s 121(3) is to be replaced by the Companies Act 2006, s 618(2). The Companies Act 1985, s 121(4) is to be replaced (with some changes) by the Companies Act 2006, ss 618(3) and 620(2). These Companies Act 2006 provisions are not yet in force although it is anticipated that they will be brought into force on 1 October 2009.

6.189   In addition, the directors of the company must have sufficient authority to allot the 'relevant securities' (which includes ordinary and preference share capital), which will take the form of either a general or specific authority from the shareholders. In the case of private companies, the relevant authority may well be contained in the company's articles of association, and will typically allow the directors to allot shares up to the authorised share capital figure. For public companies, there will likely be a general authority to allot shares in place up to the lesser of the authorised but unissued share capital, and one-third of the issued share capital (in accordance with institutional investor guidelines).

Pre-emptive offers

6.190   Since shares allotted in satisfaction of a liability of the company for a liquidated sum – such as pursuant to a DES – are deemed to be allotted and paid up for cash (the Companies Act 1985, s 738(2)[1]), the statutory pre-emption provisions of the Companies Act 1985, s 89[2] will apply. This section prohibits a company from allotting shares to any person for cash unless it has made an offer to its existing shareholders to have such shares allotted to them pro rata to their existing shareholdings.

1   The Companies Act 1985, s 738(2) is to be replaced by the Companies Act 2006, s 583(2)–(3)(d). This Companies Act 2006 provision is not yet in force although it is anticipated that it will be brought into force on 1 October 2009.
2   The Companies Act 1985, s 89(1) is to be replaced by the Companies Act 2006, s 561(1). The Companies Act 1985, s 89(2) and (3) is to be replaced by the Companies Act 2006, s 568(1) and (2). The Companies Act 1985, s 89(4) is to be replaced by the Companies

Act 2006, ss 561(2) and 565. The Companies Act 1985, s 89(5) is to be replaced by the Companies Act 2006, s 566. These Companies Act 2006 provisions are not yet in force although it is anticipated that they will be brought into force on 1 October 2009.

6.191 A private company may exclude, as a general matter (and pursuant to the Companies Act 1985, s 91[1]), such a restriction on the allotment of its shares by including relevant provisions in its memorandum or articles of association. In addition, both private and public companies may exclude the application of the restriction, either generally or specifically, by way of special resolution.

[1] The Companies Act 1985, s 91 is to be replaced by the Companies Act 2006, s 567. This Companies Act 2006 provision is not yet in force although it is anticipated that it will be brought into force on 1 October 2009.

6.192 Assuming that no disapplication of the pre-emption provisions is already in place – which could be the case for a private company, and is likely to be the case for a public company, albeit only for an issue of up to 5% of the existing share issued capital (again, in accordance with institutional investor guidelines) – such a disapplication will need to be approved if a pre-emptive offer is to be avoided. Since the incoming shareholders are unlikely to be the same persons as existing shareholders, this will frequently be desirable.

6.193 The bargaining power of the lenders and the reluctance of the existing shareholders to subscribe for new shares in a troubled company usually dictates that any resolution to disapply the statutory pre-emption provisions is passed.

Class rights

6.194 If a company proposing a DES has more than one class of shares, it may be necessary to obtain the consent of each class to the proposals, since the Companies Act 1985, s 125[1] provides that rights attaching to a class of shares may not be varied other than with the written consent of the holders of three-fourths in nominal value of the issued shares in that class, or the passing of an extraordinary resolution.

[1] The Companies Act 1985, s 125(1) and (2) is to be replaced (with some changes) by the Companies Act 2006, s 630(1)–(4). The Companies Act 1985, s 125(6) is to be replaced (with some changes) by the Companies Act 2006, s 334(1)–(4) and (6). The Companies Act 1985, s 125(7) is to be replaced by the Companies Act 2006, ss 334(7) and 630(5). The Companies Act 1985, s 125(8) is to be replaced by the Companies Act 2006, s 630(6). It is anticipated that these sections of the Companies Act 2006 will be brought into force on 1 October 2009.

6.195 It is arguable whether the issue of preference shares is a variation of the rights of an existing class of shares, of whatever nature. The issue of preference shares ranking pari passu with existing preference shares of the company will not constitute a variation of the rights attached to the existing preference shares (and the terms of the preference shares may be explicit on this point). The Companies Act 1985, s 125 has generally been strictly construed with the effect that for the section to apply the variation must be an actual variation of the rights attached to the class in question, rather than a separate matter which whilst having an effect on the shares in a class, does not result in a variation of the existing rights attached to them.

6.196 As a result, the creation and issue of preference shares having preferential rights over existing ordinary or deferred share capital should not, of itself, be a variation of the rights attaching to that other share capital. However, it is generally prudent to obtain the requisite consent of each class to the proposals, which should not be problematic on a consensual transaction. Consent of a class of shareholders will be required in any event if an existing class right requires the company to obtain the consent of a qualified majority of the holders of shares in that class, to any issue of shares in the capital of the company, which could well be the case in a private equity or other leveraged investment situation.

Other consent issues

Shareholders

6.197 As well as the consent of shareholders to any restructuring proposals, which may be required because of the need to create and allot shares, perhaps on a non pre-emptive basis, in the case of a listed company a restructuring transaction may be of sufficient magnitude that it requires the approval of shareholders by way of an ordinary resolution in general meeting, pursuant to Chapter 10 of the Listing Rules. That Chapter sets out certain 'class tests', which assess the size of the transaction based on various tests (related to, for example, gross assets, profits and consideration). To the extent that a transaction falls into the 'Class 1' category, shareholder approval will be required.

6.198 The restructuring of a listed company in 'severe financial difficulty' may involve the disposal of a substantial part of that company's business within a short time frame, in order to meet its ongoing working capital requirements. Where such disposal would ordinarily require shareholder approval as a Class 1 transaction, the FSA may waive the requirements for such shareholder approval in extreme circumstances. To persuade the FSA to modify the requirement for shareholder consent is a high burden, however, and involves the company, amongst other things:

(a) demonstrating that it has no alternative but to dispose of the assets in question;
(b) demonstrating that it could not reasonably have entered into negotiations earlier to enable shareholder approval to be obtained;
(c) confirming that all alternative methods of financing have been exhausted;
(d) its banks confirming that no further finance will be made available, and that existing facilities will be withdrawn in the absence of the disposal.

6.199 As discussed above, shareholders may have reserved to themselves certain consent rights in a shareholders' agreement (more common in a private company context), and these would typically require a certain level of shareholder consent where significant transactions (either capital transactions or commercial transactions) are proposed. An informal restructuring will likely fall within these categories of 'reserved matters', and therefore the relevant provisions will need to be followed in order to comply with the contractual restrictions on the company of entering into the proposed arrangements.

Lenders

6.200 Intercreditor arrangements between a company and its creditors will commonly require lender consent (or, at least, majority lender consent) to be obtained before significant transactions – such as a restructuring – are entered into, regardless of whether the financing facilities are prejudiced in any way. The same result may also occur where loan facilities contain restrictions on the company's freedom of action, for instance by way of a negative pledge. Of course, if the terms of a loan are to be varied, lender consent will be required – and this will almost always be the case where debt is being exchanged for equity, for example.

6.201 It is possible, although relatively unusual, that the terms of an agreement between a company and a syndicate of banks will provide that the matters required in relation to the rescue may be agreed to by a qualified majority of the banks, usually calculated by reference to lending exposure. However, such a requirement is unlikely to apply to all aspects of a restructuring and variations to payment obligations will almost certainly require unanimity. A requirement for unanimity causes obvious difficulties as it is necessary to obtain the agreement of various lenders with different exposures and possibly different lending cultures.

6.202 For this reason, advisers to a company will frequently have a 'plan B', which can be implemented if not all lenders agree to the proposals. Plan B may involve a similar restructuring being proposed, which achieves a similar ultimate result, but which can be implemented without unanimity from lenders. Obviously this will require detailed structuring in the context of a detailed review of all relevant finance documents, but typically a Plan B will involve a restructuring through an enforcement process, an insolvency process or a scheme or company voluntary arrangement. It would be usual for plan B to be more onerous, and for its implementation to be more complicated and perhaps more expensive. When the exposure of the banks is increased because of additional expense in the borrower company, or when the borrower company in which lenders are about to take shares pursuant to a DES becomes less valuable because of increased costs, lenders may be more ready to provide their consent to the proposals and implement them on a consensual basis.

Other creditors

6.203 A restructuring, or particular aspects of it, may require the consent of other categories of lender to the company, such as bondholders or noteholders and the holders of other types of interest in the capital of the company, such as warrants and options. For example, redemption dates may be extended, interest accruals may be capitalised, instruments may be diluted or discharged.

6.204 This will need to be reviewed and considered on a case by case basis, by reference to the terms on which such interests have been created and issued. In particular, it may be necessary to call meetings of the holders of the relevant instruments, and for their consent to the proposals to be obtained. It would not be unusual for such holders to provide their consent in exchange for value – effectively a price for consent. The cost of this to the company will need to be factored into any capital structure, cashflow and other relevant calculations, and may also require consent under intercreditor arrangements.

Suppliers

6.205 Depending upon the nature of a company's business, it may also be necessary to inform major suppliers of the restructuring process and, on occasion, consult with them as to its terms. Whilst a supplier will usually be an unsecured creditor, it is able to disrupt the company's trading by withholding supplies, or enforcing more strict credit terms (impacting cashflow), and consequently impede a restructuring.

6.206 In addition, a supplier may have protected its interests by including a retention of title provision in its conditions of sale. In such a case both the company and its lenders will be vulnerable to actions taken by suppliers irrespective of the security position, as goods subject to an effective title retention will never form part of the assets of the company and are therefore not subject to any fixed or floating security.

6.207 Supplier contracts may also contain termination rights, or renegotiation rights, upon both a change of control of the company (which could be triggered by a DES), and on a liquidation process or other restructuring being triggered. Careful due diligence will need to be undertaken to identify these risks, and to understand the implications of them – and careful negotiation with suppliers may also be necessary.

New banking facilities, borrowing powers and shareholder undertakings

6.208 Most DESs are likely to need approval at an extraordinary general meeting of the company – so that share capital can be increased, pre-emption rights can be disapplied and authority to allot new shares can be given to the directors, for example. If there is a delay between the restructuring documents being executed, and completion of the restructuring after the extraordinary general meeting, it may be necessary for new interim banking documents to be entered into for this period. This will be most relevant for public companies which have to call a general meeting on specific notice, rather than private companies who may be able to avail themselves of the short notice provisions of the Companies Act 2006 (and may be able to pass written resolutions if all shareholders are in agreement, and its articles permit).

6.209 If the lenders are making interim facilities available during this period (likely to be a minimum of three weeks, in order to comply with the notice requirements for general meetings where special resolutions are proposed), they can mitigate their risk that the proposals will not be approved at any relevant extraordinary general meeting by requiring the company to obtain from major shareholders:

(a)   undertakings to vote in favour of the resolutions at the extraordinary general meeting; and

(b)   undertakings to participate in any associated cash-raising exercise (such as agreeing to take up rights under a rights issue).

6.210 In each case it would be desirable for the lenders to consider at an early stage what minimum level of undertakings will be acceptable, and the directors will also be expected to recommend that shareholders vote in favour of the relevant resolutions. Again, this is more relevant to public rather than private companies.

6.211 Lenders who have lent additional funds to a company during this interim period, when such lending causes the company to breach the borrowing limits in its articles of association, will also be exposed to the extent that a shareholders' resolution ratifying such breach is not passed at the relevant general meeting. Of course, undertakings to vote in favour of the resolution will be of assistance, but problems may arise if a winding-up petition is presented prior to the resolutions being passed. The additional funds may be irrecoverable as a matter of law (since the company was effectively acting ultra vires) but, depending on the amount, the lenders may take a view given the significant degree of credit risk and the benefits of securing a restructuring rather than an insolvency.

6.212 It is normal for any further funding commitment to be given to the company prior to details of the restructuring being sent to the company's shareholders, not least so that the circular to shareholders can confirm the working capital position of the company (as required by the Listing Rules). This commitment will be conditional on the restructuring taking effect.

6.213 If new facilities are being put in place which are on less advantageous terms than the facilities being capitalised, and assuming that there is an acquisition of shares taking place (either by way of a DES, transfer of shares or otherwise), consideration needs to be given as to whether the transaction amounts to unlawful financial assistance (Companies Act 1985, s 151[1]). This may also be the case where existing loans are being refinanced upon completion of the restructuring, and the company incurs certain break or other costs in relation to the refinanced facilities, and so appropriate advice should be sought in these circumstances.

[1]   The Companies Act 1985, s 151(1) is to be replaced (with some changes) by the Companies Act 2006, ss 678(1) and 679(1). The Companies Act 1985, s 151(2) is to be replaced (with some changes) by the Companies Act 2006, ss 678(3) and 679(3). The Companies Act 1985, s 151(3) is to be replaced by the Companies Act 2006, s 680(1) and (2). It is anticipated that these sections of the Companies Act 2006 will be brought into force on 1 October 2009.

6.214 In the case of private companies, a financial assistance 'whitewash' could be considered if there are no appropriate exemptions which the company can take advantage of (for example, the company does not materially reduce its net assets in giving the financial assistance). It is also worth noting that the prohibition on providing financial assistance, for private companies at least, is to be abolished when the relevant parts of the Companies Act 2006 come into force – expected to be in October 2008.

Indebtedness of subsidiaries

6.215 Indebtedness to be substituted for shares will often be indebtedness of a subsidiary of the company in which the lenders ultimately wish to have their equity stake. In these circumstances, certain issues arise but, assuming that the company guarantees the indebtedness of the subsidiary (which would typically be the case), they can be dealt with relatively easily.

6.216 If the indebtedness of the subsidiary can be transferred to its parent company (in which the shares are to be issued), then the DES can take place at the correct level, with shares being issued by the parent company to the lenders in exchange for the discharge of the appropriate amount of debt. The transfer of debt is best achieved by novation – a tripartite agreement between the subsidiary, parent and lenders. Alternatively, the parent's guarantee may be called (subject to there being no cross-default problems).

6.217 Counsel has advised that neither of the above transactions would constitute unlawful financial assistance provided that the parent company guarantee is pre-existing.

6.218 Alternatively, lenders could effect a DES in the subsidiary company which holds the indebtedness, thereby acquiring shares in that company. If this is followed immediately by a pre-agreed 'share for share exchange' pursuant to which the lenders transfer the shares in the subsidiary to the parent company, in exchange for an issue of shares in the parent company, then the original aim, of providing the lenders with shares in the parent company, is achieved. Of course, there will have been an increase in the share capital of the subsidiary company equivalent to the amount of the debt discharged in the DES and, to the extent that there is more than one company between the indebted subsidiary and the parent company, there will need to be additional share for share exchanges to 'flip up' the shareholding arising from the DES into a shareholding in the parent company.

Regulatory implications

6.219 Certain lenders, particularly banks, insurance companies and investment firms, are subject to prudential financial regulation. A swap of debt for equity changes the nature of an asset held by a lender, from a loan asset to an equity asset. Such a change may have implications for its regulatory capital.

6.220 Banks are required to maintain a minimum level of capital calculated by reference to the value of their assets adjusted on a risk weighted basis. What comprises capital, and the principles for risk weighting assets, are set out in the FSA's Handbook of Rules and Guidance and, in particular, the General Prudential sourcebook (GENPRU) and the Prudential sourcebook for Banks, Building Societies and Investment firms (BIPRU). The rules give effect to the EU Capital Requirements Directive, which in fact comprises two separate Directives: the Banking Directive (2006/48/EC) and the Capital Adequacy Directive (2006/49/EC).

6.221 A loan to a non-bank private sector company will be adjusted for risk by a weighting which depends, under the 'standardised approach' on the rating of the company's debt by the credit rating agencies or, under the 'internal ratings based approaches', on more sophisticated calculations of credit risk based on the bank's own estimate of the probability of default and under the 'advanced approach', the loss that it will suffer if there is a default. Under the standardised approach, the risk weighting for a corporate can vary from 20% to 150%. On the other hand, a holding of shares in the capital of a similar company will be risk weighted under the standardised approach at least at 100%. Similarly, under the internal ratings based approach, different methodologies are applicable to equity and debt exposures respectively. Furthermore, if the resultant holding of equity amounts to 10% or more of the capital or voting rights of the company, then the full amount of the holding or a portion of it may be required to be deducted in determining the level of a lender's capital base. If the amount is so significant as to make the company in which the lender now holds shares an unconsolidated subsidiary or associate of the lender (investments in non-financial subsidiaries are not consolidated for this purpose), the amounts invested are deducted from capital. Consequently, a swap of debt for equity may have an effect on the capital required to be maintained by a lender.

6.222 Banks are permitted to include within their capital base (as Upper Tier 2 capital) reserves in respect of general provisions (GENPRU 2.2.187). General provisions are held against possible or latent losses which have not been identified. Specific provisions are not dealt with in the same manner. If a bank reduces its 'general provisions' as a result of a borrower's debt being swapped for shares, the capital base of the bank will consequently be reduced.

Capital adequacy implications of a DES

6.223 A DES may affect a lender's capital adequacy requirements in relation to 'banking book' transactions by virtue of the different methodologies applicable to calculating debt and equity exposures (see 'Regulatory implications' above).

6.224 Transactions that result in the acquisition of a significant proportion of the borrower's total share capital can have a particularly significant effect. Investments in subsidiary undertakings and participations of a bank are not treated as assets subject to risk asset weighting, but as deductions from the bank's capital. If a bank were to hold, as a result of the DES, a shareholding which resulted in the corporate becoming a subsidiary undertaking of the bank or which was regarded as a 'participation', the bank might suffer severe adverse consequences in relation to its capital adequacy requirements. A subsidiary undertaking for these purposes includes a corporate over which the bank has the right to exercise a 'dominant influence'. A participation is generally a direct or indirect ownership interest of 20% or more of the voting rights or capital of a corporate. As will be seen below a similar deduction may need to be made for qualifying holdings in non-financial companies.

6.225 If a subsidiary undertaking of a bank or a company in which a bank holds a participation carries on certain defined financial activities, it will generally need to be consolidated with the bank for reporting purposes. Most corporates will not be engaged in such activities and there is therefore a risk that if the bank acquires more than 20% of the voting rights or capital of the corporate, its 'investment' may give rise to disadvantageous pound for pound capital deductions (if the corporate was consolidated with the bank, these deductions would still be required in calculating the bank's own capital resources on a 'solo' basis, but not in calculating the group's consolidated capital requirements). Whilst this may not be of importance immediately, since the investment will usually be entered at only a nominal book value, it might become a concern in the future if the holding in the corporate later appreciates.

6.226 Furthermore, deductions may be required to be made from Tier 1 and Tier 2 capital for qualifying holding in non-financial companies. Qualifying holdings are holdings of 10% or more of the voting rights or capital of non credit or financial institutions. However, a deduction is only required to be made to the extent that qualifying holdings exceed (individually) 15% or (in aggregate) 60% of a bank's capital resources. With large clearers this threshold is unlikely to be exceeded.

6.227 It is therefore desirable to obtain clearance from the FSA at the outset to ensure that there is no question of the corporate being classified as a subsidiary undertaking of the bank, or of the bank's investment being regarded as a participation, for reporting purposes.

Competition

6.228 If a debt for equity swap will result in a lender, even one which is not a competitor of the company, acquiring a significant minority interest in the shares of the company, consideration should be given to the potential application of either:

(a) the EC Merger Regulation (Council Regulation (EEC) No 4064/89 of 21 December 1989 on the control of concentrations between undertakings) (the 'ECMR'); or

(b) Part V of the Fair Trading Act 1973 relating to mergers (the 'FTA 1973') or Part I (Chapter 1) of the Competition Act 1998; and

(c) the competition law provisions of any other jurisdiction which may be triggered by the acquisition.

6.229 The ECMR and FTA 1973 contain detailed rules to establish whether a minority share acquisition would constitute either a 'concentration' falling within the scope of the ECMR or a 'qualifying merger' for the purposes of the FTA 1973. If a share acquisition falls within the scope of the ECMR, notification to the European Commission, within a tight prescribed time period, is mandatory and national authorities may not apply their own competition laws to it, except in very limited circumstances. If a share acquisition falls within the ambit of the FTA 1973, pre-notification to the UK Office of Fair Trading is voluntary.

6.230 In either case, the relevant EC or UK regulatory authority has the power, *inter alia*, to prohibit the acquisition. However, although no formal exemption exists under either the ECMR or the FTA 1973 for corporate rescues which fall within their scope, as a general rule, transactions of this kind are viewed sympathetically by the regulatory authorities.

6.231 It should be noted that, as regards the FTA 1973, it seems that an acquisition of an interest falling short of an equity holding may also fall within the scope of the FTA 1973. The Report of the Monopolies and Mergers Commission on the transaction (Stora/Swedish Match/Gillette transaction [CM 1473 (1991)]) concluded that a minority participation deriving from contractual arrangements or from protective rights attaching to convertible securities or financial instruments could constitute a qualifying merger for the purposes of the FTA 1973.

6.232 The Competition Act 1998 will restrict anti-competitive agreements, decisions and concerted practices. It does not generally apply to mergers or share issues. In most cases where there is a domestic competition law issue, it will therefore be the FTA 1973 which applies. However, it is possible that the Competition Act 1998 could still apply in a case where the particular transaction falls outside the scope of the FTA 1973.

Consents

6.233 Depending upon the details of relevant loan agreements, the consent of lenders to a company will usually be required to a rescue involving a significant restructuring of existing obligations. The consent of lenders not directly affected by the proposals, and of shareholders, and other creditors, such as bondholders or noteholders, may also be required.

Lenders

6.234 The consent of a company's lenders will be required if the terms of a lender's loan are to be varied and the loan agreement will not allow the company to make the variation unilaterally. Even if a loan is not directly affected by the rescue, the terms of a loan agreement may restrict the company's freedom of action, for instance by way of a negative pledge. It is possible, although relatively unusual, that the terms of an agreement between a company and a syndicate of banks will provide that the matters required in relation to the rescue may be agreed to by a qualified majority of the banks, usually calculated by reference to lending exposure. However, such a requirement is unlikely to apply to all aspects of a restructuring and variations to payment obligations will almost certainly require unanimity. A requirement for unanimity causes obvious difficulties as it is necessary to obtain the agreement of various lenders with different exposures and possibly different lending cultures.

Shareholders

6.235 The consent of a shareholder may be required to an informal restructuring if particular veto rights have been reserved to shareholders, or specific categories of them, either in the articles of association of the company concerned or in a shareholders' agreement regulating the management of the company. Specific aspects of a restructuring, such as a debt for equity swap or the disposal of a significant asset, may also require shareholder consent because of the requirements of the Companies Act 1985 or, in the case of a company whose shares are traded on The London Stock Exchange, the Listing Rules.

6.236 The requirement to obtain shareholder consent can be waived if a company can demonstrate that it is in severe financial difficulties. There is no definition of 'severe financial difficulties'; the company, sponsor or lender (as the context requires) must submit prescribed documents to the FSA (as competent UK Listing Authority) which include confirmation that:

(a)   receivers, administrators or liquidators are likely to be appointed unless the disposal is completed;

(b)   all alternative methods of financing have been exhausted; and

(c)   unless the disposal is effected immediately, current facilities will be withdrawn.

6.237 A company applying for a waiver must be able to demonstrate that it could not reasonably have entered into negotiations earlier, to enable shareholder approval to be sought. Waivers will never be granted retrospectively.

6.238 Listing Rules Guidance Note No 05/2000 explains the modification, for companies in severe financial difficulties, of the usual rules relating to large disposals. The Guidance Note should be read in conjunction with the Listing Rules, which alone have binding effect.

6.239 The question of whether or not a shareholder is entitled to vote his shares in opposition to elements of a restructuring was considered by the court in relation to the restructuring of the Brent Walker Group plc[1]. The court granted an injunction restraining two substantial shareholders from voting against resolutions required to implement a restructuring. The court's decision was based upon its general jurisdiction, consistent with freezing order (Mareva) principles, to prevent the wilful dissipation of assets in certain circumstances. Whilst the court accepted that it should hesitate before making an order requiring someone to deal with his own property in a particular way, it held that it would do so where the result of dealing with the property in the manner intended was patently harmful. The evidence was that if the restructuring was not implemented, and the lenders would not implement the restructuring unless those aspects of the restructuring requiring shareholders' approval were approved, the company would fail. The court also cited another ground for its decision, which was that one result of the restructuring not being implemented would be a loss of value of security held by certain lenders by way of charges over shares. The court held that the lenders were entitled to seek an order which would protect their security from being deprived of any value. The court stressed that in only the most extreme case would it restrain a person from dealing with his property as he wished.

[1] *Standard Chartered Bank v Walker* [1992] 1 WLR 561, [1992] BCLC 603.

6.240 Whilst the decision in *Standard Chartered Bank v Walker* is based on freezing order (Mareva) principles and the jurisdiction of the court to prevent the wilful dissipation of assets, it is consistent with recent judicial policy of substituting the interests of the members of a company with those of its creditors in circumstances where the company is insolvent or near to it. In *Brady v Brady*[1], Nourse LJ regarded the interests of the company as synonymous with the interests of the creditors where the company was insolvent or 'doubtfully solvent'. In the analogous circumstances of a rescue implemented under the statutory predecessor of the Companies Act 1985, s 425[2], the court held that the interests of a particular class of shareholders may be ignored if the economic reality is that there are in any event no assets available for the benefit of the dissenting class (*Re Tea Corpn Ltd*[3]). The decision of the court in *Re British and Commonwealth Holdings plc (No 3)*[4], which also concerned a proposed section 425[5] scheme, confirms the validity of ignoring the interests of an affected party in circumstances where it has ceased to have an economic interest in the assets of the company. In that case, however, the relevant party did not admit that it had no economic interest, a view the judge described as fanciful, and the decision, which was that the party could be ignored in determining who would be required to approve the scheme, proceeded on the basis that because the claim of the party was subordinated to all other creditors it did not have an interest in the scheme at all.

1   [1988] BCLC 20.
2   The Companies Act 1985, s 425(1) is to be replaced by the Companies Act 2006, ss 895(1), 896(1) and (2). The Companies Act 1985, s 425(2) is to be replaced by the Companies Act 2006, ss 899(1), (3), 907(1) and 922(1). The Companies Act 1985, s 425(3) is to be replaced (with some changes) by the Companies Act 2006, ss 899(4), 901(3) and (4). The Companies Act 1985, s 425(4) is to be replaced by the Companies Act 2006, s 901(5) and (6). The Companies Act 1985, s 425(6) is to be replaced by the Companies Act 2006, s 895(2). The Companies Act 2006, ss 895–935 are to come into force on 6 April 2008 (SI 2007/3495). For transitional provisions and savings, see SI 2007/3495, arts 6, 9, 12, Schs 1, 4.
3   [1904] 1 Ch 12.
4   [1992] 1 WLR 672, [1992] BCLC 322.
5   See footnote 1.

Other creditors

6.241 A rescue, or particular aspects of it, may require the consent of other categories of lender to the company, such as bondholders or noteholders and the holders of other types of interest in the capital of the company, such as warrant holders and the beneficiaries of options including under an employee share option scheme. Whether or not it will be necessary to obtain the consent of any of these persons, and if so how such consent may be obtained, is determined by reference to the document governing the issue of the relevant instrument and in the case of a company whose debt securities are listed on The Stock Exchange, on the Listing Rules.

Bondholders

6.242 A rescue which requires the variation of terms under which an instrument has been issued, such as an extension of redemption dates in the case of a bond or note, or which involves a debt for equity swap, will almost certainly require the consent of a qualified majority or of all the holders of the notes and bonds in question. The document governing the issue of the instrument will usually set out the procedure for calling meetings of instrument holders and the passing of resolutions by them. In practice, it is often more difficult for a company to renegotiate the terms of bonds or notes than of bank debt, because of the wider distribution of capital market instruments and the anonymity of the investors.

6.243 A company whose debt securities are listed on The Stock Exchange is generally obliged to comply with the Listing Rules, although parts of the Rules are not applicable if the company has only listed debt securities. For instance, a company is obliged to notify the Company Announcements Office of any new issue of debt securities and of any proposed change to the company's capital structure.

Suppliers

6.244 Depending upon the nature of a company's business, it may also be necessary to inform major suppliers of the rescue process and on occasion consult with them as to its terms. Whilst a supplier will usually be an unsecured creditor, it is able to disrupt the company's trading and consequently impede a rescue. This is because suppliers usually extend credit terms to a company and a reduction in the credit period may adversely impact on the company's cashflow position. In addition, a supplier may have protected its interests by including a retention of title provision in its conditions of sale. In such a case both the company and its lenders will be vulnerable to actions taken by suppliers irrespective of the security position, as goods subject to an effective title retention will never form part of the assets of the company and are therefore not subject to any fixed or floating security.

International Accounting Standards and their impact on a DES

Introduction

6.245 This section sets out an initial analysis of certain of the key legal implications of International Accounting Standard 27 ('IAS 27') (defined and discussed in more detail below) with respect to a DES. It will be recognised and appreciated that IAS 27 is an accounting principle and as such the initial analysis contained in this section is subject always to any further analysis carried out from an accounting perspective.

6.246 As indicated above a typical restructuring may involve an acquisition by the bank of equity in the target asset (for example by way of debt for equity swap). In terms of the internal corporate structure in which those equity holdings are placed and held, it is typical for a corporate vehicle to be incorporated by an institution (or by one of its subsidiaries) ('Newco'). Ordinarily Newco will acquire and hold equity in the target.

6.247 Newco may either be a direct or indirect subsidiary of the bank/ financial institution holding the relevant shares in the intermediate holding company and therefore the group structure would appear as in the diagram on the following page.

6.248 The key objective in relation to IAS 27 is to avoid the requirement for the bank to consolidate the results of any target company held by the bank (via Newco).

Background and objectives of IAS 27

6.249 International Accounting Standards are issued by the International Accounting Standards Board ('IASB') and are designed to ensure greater certainty in, and comparability between, financial statements in EU Member

6.249 *Restructuring exits*

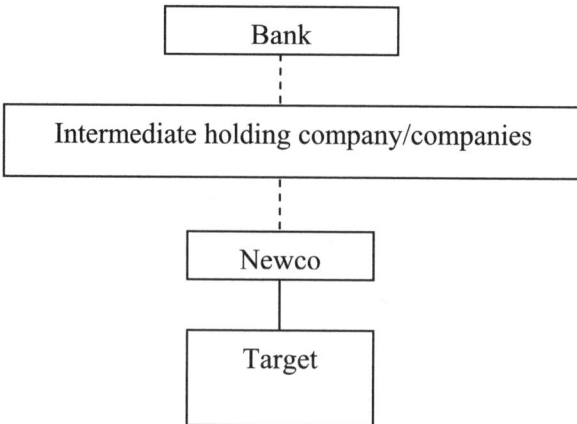

```
                    ┌──────────────────┐
                    │       Bank       │
                    └──────────────────┘
                             ┊
   ┌─────────────────────────────────────────────┐
   │  Intermediate holding company/companies      │
   └─────────────────────────────────────────────┘
                             ┊
                    ┌──────────────────┐
                    │      Newco       │
                    └──────────────────┘
                             │
                    ┌──────────────────┐
                    │      Target      │
                    │                  │
                    └──────────────────┘
```

States. Companies governed by the law of a Member State whose securities are listed to trading on a regulated market in a Member State are required to comply with these standards. IAS 27 'Consolidated and Separate Financial Statements' sets out the requirements for the consolidation of the financial statements of an entity into those of its parent.

6.250 The key objective of IAS 27 is to prescribe requirements for preparing and presenting consolidated financial statements for groups of enterprises (subsidiaries) under *control* of a parent entity. For these purposes a subsidiary is an entity that is *controlled* by another entity. *Control* is the power to govern the financial and operating policies of an entity so as to obtain benefits from its activities.

6.251 Control is presumed when the parent acquires more than half of the voting rights of the entity. This can be rebutted, but only in exceptional circumstances. Even when more than half of the voting rights are not acquired, control can be evidenced by the power:

(a)   to direct over more than half of the voting rights by virtue of an agreement with other investors;

(b)   to govern the entity's financial or operating policies of the entity by statute or agreement;

(c)   to appoint/remove a majority of the members of the board of directors; or

(d)   to cast a majority of votes at general meetings of the board of directors.

6.252 Most of the well advised restructuring teams in the leading financial institutions will adopt tick the box checklists which test control on the basis of the above tests.

Potential safeguards and solutions

6.253 As set out above, IAS 27 is an accounting principle and detailed analysis from both a legal and accounting perspective must be carried out before a final decision is made in relation to the shareholding to be taken under a DES. Set out below is an initial guide as to some of the potential protections and solutions to the risk of IAS 27 consolidation:

(a)   Restrict the bank voting power in Newco/target to 49% or less (this does not automatically remove evidence of power as articulated above but it is likely to create a rebuttable presumption as to power and control).

Whilst holders of debt may ensure that they acquire and control less than 50% of the ordinary shares, they may take 100% of the preference shares, which will typically carry significant rights (such as the right to determine when an 'exit' should occur via a disposal or a flotation and the right to a greater allocation of the disposal proceeds), but which do not carry the day-to-day rights that are implicit to the ordinary shares.

(b)   Convert a large proportion of debt to equity and vest such equity in the private equity investment division of the relevant institution. This should be accompanied by a restriction on voting rights to 49% (unless a sale or floatation take place or an event of default occurs in respect of certain matters, such as insolvency, in which case the bank would have the right, but not the obligation, to carry 100%).

(c)   Use a joint venture so as to split the bank's power/governance of Newco/target with a third party.

(d)   Use a shareholders' agreement to give the bank a degree of power (eg by using voting rights to block a special resolution requiring 75%) without triggering consolidation under IAS 27.

(e)   Create different categories of shares in Newco allowing the bank to hold certain shares with respect to certain reserved matters that would require the consent of shareholders of that type.

(f)   Use a convertible instrument or a warrant which would convert into ordinary shares upon certain events, such as exit or sale by the bank. As the conversion to ordinary shares would take place upon exit, there should be no consolidation problem under IAS 27.

(g)   Establish the requisite control over key issues such as acquisitions, disposals, capital expenditure, management change, debt incurrence and amendments to the constitutional documents via the covenants in the accompanying loan agreement.

(h)   Use of 'golden shares' which give a substantial economic return to the holder on a pre-defined exit.

C TAX ISSUES ARISING ON RESTRUCTURINGS

6.254 Tax considerations will generally be of fundamental importance on corporate restructurings. To effect a restructuring without seeking appropriate tax advice risks incurring otherwise avoidable tax liabilities. Furthermore, tax planning strategies may be employed to minimise tax costs arising on subsequent exits. The following discussion focuses primarily on the UK tax implications of DES, but also touches upon various other UK tax related issues that, in the authors' recent experience, fall to be considered in the context of corporate restructurings.

Tax implications of a DES

The borrower's position

6.255 From a borrower's perspective, the main objective will be to avoid any charge to corporation tax arising by reference to a release or waiver of the debt held by the lenders. By way of example, if indebtedness were simply to be released, a taxable profit of that amount could arise in the borrower. This could give rise to a significant cash tax liability, or at least an unnecessary use of tax losses. Such a tax liability would also be undesirable from the lenders' perspective, as the value of their holding (post DES) would be reduced.

6.256 The borrower will only be able to avoid a charge to tax on release of the debt to the extent that the debt is a 'loan relationship', and the release takes place in an accounting period for which an 'amortised cost basis of accounting' is used as respects that debt (Finance Act 1996, Sch 9, para 5(3)). Broadly speaking, a debt will be a loan relationship where it is a money debt arising from a transaction for the lending of money (Finance Act 1996, s 81). In the situations with which we are concerned, these requirements will typically be met.

6.257 In addition to these requirements, it will also be necessary, if the borrower is to avoid a tax liability on a release or waiver, that an additional condition is met. The condition that most obviously applies on a DES is that the transaction is structured as a subscription by the lenders for shares forming part of the ordinary share capital of the borrower, in consideration for the release (Finance Act 1996, Sch 9, para 5(8))[1]. No tax charge should arise in the borrower in this situation.

[1] Other important circumstances in which a tax liability may be avoided on a release or waiver include where the release is part of a statutory insolvency arrangement or, broadly, where the parties are not connected and the creditor is in insolvent liquidation.

6.258 In this context, 'ordinary share capital' means 'all of the issued share capital (by whatever name called) of the company other than capital the holders of which have a right to a dividend at a fixed rate but have no other right to share in the profits of the company' (Income and Corporation Taxes Act 1988 ('ICTA 1988'), s 832(1)). This therefore excludes some forms of share capital, such as certain fixed-rate preference shares and (probably) some convertible preference shares.

The lenders' position

6.259 Where the lenders are treated as 'connected' with the borrower for an accounting period, bad debt relief will not be available to them for any waiver of debt during this period (Finance Act 1996, Sch 9, para 6).

6.260 Parties will be connected for these purposes either where one controls the other or both are under common control (Finance Act 1996, s 87(3)). It should be noted that where parties are connected for any part of an accounting period, they will be treated as connected for the whole of that period (including for periods within that accounting period before the point in time at which they first became connected) (Finance Act 1996, s 87(3)).

6.261 Control for these purposes means the power of a person to secure, either by means of the holding of shares or the possession of voting power, or by virtue of any powers conferred by the articles of association or other document regulating the 'controlled' company's affairs, that the affairs of that company are conducted in accordance with the wishes of the 'controlling' company (Finance Act 1996, s 87A(1)). This condition will typically be satisfied where there is de facto control at board level[1].

[1] See generally *Irving (Inspector of Taxes) v Tesco Stores (Holdings) Ltd* [1982] STC 881 and dicta in *Steele (Inspector of Taxes) v EVC International* [1996] STC 785, CA.

6.262 Bad debt relief for the lender is not, however, excluded as between connected companies where the creditor company treats the debt as discharged by the issue to it of ordinary shares in the debtor company – ie in the DES circumstances discussed above. This rule is subject to the further proviso that the creditor and debtor must not have been connected before the issue of shares (ignoring the effect of the Finance Act 1996, s 87(3), discussed above, which deems a connection to have existed for the whole of an accounting period).

6.263 In the sort of case with which we are concerned, therefore, the lenders should be able to claim relief for any losses arising on the debt owed to them up to the time that they acquire their shares, such that they should be able to claim relief for any loss arising on the DES (Finance Act 1996, Sch 9, para 6(4) and (5)).

6.264 Another good reason for avoiding a connection prior to the debt conversion, at least where the debt in question is impaired, is that the Finance Act 1996, Sch 9, para 4A(4) may then apply to give a deemed release of the debt upon the creditor and debtor becoming connected, which may be taxable. Note that this rule may apply where there is a *partial* conversion to equity, such that the requisite connection between the parties is established, but impaired debt nonetheless remains outstanding.

Stamp duty

6.265 In a properly structured DES, shares will be issued in consideration for a release or discharge of the debt. Accordingly, no stamp duty or stamp duty reserve tax ('SDRT') should be payable, as neither stamp duty nor SDRT are ordinarily chargeable on an issue of shares[1]. Where a sale is being executed by an insolvency office holder, such as a receiver, and that office holder is accepting a credit bid as consideration for the transfer of the shares, the consideration subject to stamp duty will be deemed to be the full amount of the credit bid. In these circumstances stamp duty will be levied at 0.5% of the consideration given for the transfer.

[1] An exception to this general rule is where shares are issued into a depositary or clearance system, in which case there will be a 1.5% charge on issue (although subsequent transfers within the system should then be free of charge).

Tax on exit

6.266 As mentioned above, in the event of the recovery of a company following a restructuring involving a DES, one of the ways in which the lenders might look to participate in the upside is by means of a sale of the company, or the group of which it forms part.

6.267 As discussed above, the more flexible corporate laws of certain non-UK jurisdictions (such as the Cayman Islands or Jersey) may make it more attractive for lenders to hold their equity stake in the corporate through a non-UK incorporated holding company. This approach may also have tax benefits. Where, for instance, the ultimate holding company (below which the restructured group is sold out) is not UK resident, any capital gain arising to it on a sale should not fall within the charge to UK corporation tax (Taxation of Chargeable Gains Act 1992, s 2(1))[1].

[1] It is important to appreciate the distinction between a company's 'incorporation' and its 'residence'. The former looks to where a company is formed and registered, the latter to where it 'belongs' for tax purposes. Under UK law, whilst there is a presumption that a company will be resident in the jurisdiction in which it is incorporated, the issue will ultimately be determined by where the company is centrally managed and controlled. Different jurisdictions have different rules for determining tax residence.

6.268 Further, if a two-tier holding company structure is used, so that the ultimate holding company (non-UK incorporated and tax resident) sells out a subsidiary holding company (also non-UK incorporated), which is the direct parent of the corporate, then, on the basis that the shares transferring will not be shares in a UK company, a charge to stamp duty may also in practice be avoided.

Deemed release on impaired debt becoming held by a connected party

6.269 In practice, a restructuring may often involve impaired debt being transferred to a company that is connected with the borrower (Finance Act 1996, Sch 9, para 4A). Examples of where this may occur include in relation to 'pre-pack' sales, where existing groups (including their debts) are sold to newly formed holding companies, incorporated and owned by the enforcing lenders; and also where lenders holding impaired debt are paid out some proportion of the debt owed to them, in consideration of the transfer of the remaining debt to a company within the borrower group.

6.270 Where the Finance Act 1996, Sch 9, para 4A(2) is in point, there is deemed to be a release by the (new) creditor company of its rights under the loan relationship on the debt being transferred to it. Without care being taken over the structuring of any such transfer, this release may be taxable on the debtor company. (Note that an amendment to the Finance Act 1996, Sch 9, para 5(5) ensures that the debtor company is not entitled to rely upon the exemption ordinarily available in respect of releases of connected party debt.)

6.271 One method of avoiding this rule may be to *novate* the debt to the new creditor, as opposed to assigning it. This is on the basis that the Finance Act 1996, Sch 9, para 4A(2)(b) requires that the new creditor 'becomes party as creditor to *the* loan relationship' (emphasis added): a novation involves the creation of a *new* debt[1].

[1]   The Special Commissioners' decision in *Greene King No 1 Ltd v Adie (Inspector of Taxes)* [2005] STC (SCD) 398 is helpful here.

6.272 An alternative method of avoiding this rule is to rely upon a specific carve out in the Finance Act 1996, Sch 9, para 4A(3). This exception applies where:

(a)   the new creditor acquires its rights under the debt under an arm's-length transaction; and

(b)   there has been no connection between the new creditor and the debtor in the period:
    (i)   beginning four years before the date of the transfer of the debt; and
    (ii)   ending 12 months before that date.

6.273 The drafting of this provision therefore allows for the incorporation of a new company connected to the debtor company specifically for the purposes of acquiring the distressed debt. It is understood that the Revenue agree that this approach is effective to avoid the application of the Finance Act 1996, Sch 9, para 4A(2). However, it is possible that this could be affected by a future change in law.

Maintaining carried forward losses

6.274 An important point to bear in mind on restructurings will be the rules which can apply to restrict the use of carried forward trading losses and non-trading deficits (in the case of non-trading deficits, this will most often equate, in practice, to a restriction on the use of the company's historic deductions for its financing costs) (see ICTA 1988, s 768 ff). In order for these rules to bite, there must have been both a change in ownership of a company and one or more of:

(a)   a major change in the nature or conduct of the business carried on by the company within the period starting three years before the change of ownership and ending three years after that date; or

(b)   at any time before the change in ownership, the scale of the company's business activities has become small or negligible, and there has not been any considerable revival of the business.

6.275 A 'pre-pack' sale of the type discussed above will certainly involve the requisite change in ownership. There may also often be a change in ownership on a DES, to the extent that (broadly speaking) the new equity holders who have exchanged their debt for shares each hold at least 5% of, and between them hold more than half, the ordinary share capital of the company following the DES (ICTA 1988, s 769(1)).

6.276 In practice, it is very easy to trip over the tests described above, and it may be necessary to put strong control mechanisms in place to avoid triggering them. A particularly tricky rule is the one in ICTA 1988, s 768B, which applies where there is both a change in ownership and a significant increase in the amount of the company's capital: an increase of just £1m will be 'significant' for these purposes (ICTA 1988, Sch 28A, para 2). The 'company's capital' is widely defined, and will include not only its share capital, but also various common types of debt (see ICTA 1988, Sch 28A, para 5(1) and ICTA 1988, s 417(7)).

Capital gains tax

6.277 It is worth briefly mentioning the capital gains tax ('CGT') implications of a pre-pack sale. The basic rule is that the selling company will be taxed (or relieved) on any positive (or negative) difference between the sale price of the shares sold and its indexed base cost in those shares. Where certain conditions are satisfied, the sale may fall outside the charge to CGT (gains not taxable, losses not relievable) by virtue of the substantial shareholdings exemption applying. To the extent that there are losses available in the selling company, these may often be available to shelter any gains arising on the sale. It will also be necessary to consider the impact of degrouping charges, which may arise where assets have been transferred into the company or companies being disposed of from elsewhere in the group (on a tax-free 'no-gain, no-loss' basis) within the previous six years, but the original transferor is not leaving the selling company's group at the same time as the target. In appropriate circumstances, degrouping gains may be elected back into the selling company or its residual group, so that they will not pass with the target.

Secondary tax liabilities

6.278 A 'secondary tax liability' is a tax liability that is primarily the responsibility of one person, but which goes unpaid by that person, and as a result is visited on some other person. There are a number of provisions in the

UK tax code that seek to impose secondary tax liabilities – the two that are most relevant in the restructuring context are ICTA 1988, ss 767A and 767AA.

6.279 The conditions under which these provisions will apply are complex, and a full description is beyond the scope of this discussion. However, broadly speaking, both provisions require there to have been a change in ownership of a company, together with an amount of corporation tax going unpaid, either by the company whose ownership has changed (ICTA 1988, s 767A), or by an 'associated company' of that company (ICTA 1988, s 767AA). As discussed above in the section on 'Maintaining carried forward losses', a restructuring will often involve a change in ownership of a company. And, where a company is already in restructuring proceedings, it would not perhaps be surprising if it were unable to pay its tax liabilities as they fell due.

6.280 Where the secondary tax liability provisions apply, the range of companies on which the unpaid tax liability may be visited is wide, and includes not only any person who at any time in the three years before the change of ownership had control of the transferred company, but also any company of which that person has had control within the period of three years before that change (whether or not such other company has any other connection with the transferred company) (ICTA 1988, ss 767A(2) and 767AA(4)).

6.281 It is also worth noting the wide definition of 'control' for these purposes. The concept is not limited to direct or indirect control over a company's affairs, nor even to economic or voting control by means of holding shares, but also includes the right to receive the greater part of the assets of the company that would be available for distribution to participators on a winding up (ICTA 1988, s 416). Furthermore, for these purposes, where a group of persons have 'acted together' (itself a widely construed term) *collectively* to gain control of a company, then each of them *individually* will be treated as having control of the company (ICTA 1988, s 416(3), as amended by ICTA 1988, s 767B(6)). Given the scope and potential impact of these provisions, it will often be necessary on restructurings to seek specialist tax advice as to how best to avoid or mitigate the effect of secondary tax liabilities.

D MANAGEMENT TAX ISSUES

6.282 The impact of a DES on existing incentive arrangements and the design and implementation of equity participation arrangements for management are likely to be important considerations in corporate restructurings. As previously mentioned, the company and its advisers will want to negotiate the best deal for management and therefore the strength of management's negotiating position should not be underestimated.

The fundamental issues for management and the company

6.283 The two most commonly encountered forms of equity participation in the context of a DES are a subscription for shares in the company and the grant of share options (being a right to acquire shares in the company at a future date).

6.284 To protect the lender's interests, it would be common for the shares acquired by management (whether on subscription or on exercise of an option) to be subject to restrictions on transfer and/or disposal and provisions under which management are required to forfeit the shares in certain circumstances (for example, voluntary resignation) for an amount which is less than their market value. Where such restrictions depress the value of those shares, which is usually the result, those shares will be 'restricted shares'.

6.285 From managements' perspective, a subscription for restricted shares is unlikely to be attractive unless an income tax charge on acquisition of the shares can be avoided. The tax implications for management and for the company on the acquisition of restricted shares will be complex and there may be a charge to income tax on acquisition of the shares and on future events unless management are willing to pay the full market value for the shares (disregarding the impact of the restrictions) when they subscribe for them. If this is not the case, the alternative, being the grant of share options, will appear much more attractive given that the taxation of share options is straightforward. There will be no income tax charge on the grant of share options but a potential charge to income tax on exercise.

6.286 In negotiating the equity participation arrangements, the company's key objectives will be two-fold. First, to minimise the cost to the company of providing the management equity – effectively, this means reducing the company's liability to employer's National Insurance Contributions ('NICs') and avoiding the risk of an uncapped future employer's NICs cost. Second, to ensure that it bears no risk in respect of management's liability for any income tax and employee's NICs arising as a result of the arrangements. Provided that these objectives are satisfied, the company is unlikely to have particular concerns about the form which the equity participation takes.

6.287 As it will be in the best interests of both the company and management for there to be certainty as to the tax treatment of the equity participation arrangements, management might consider making a Code of Practice 10 application to HM Revenue and Customs ('HMRC') to seek confirmation of the tax treatment. Such an application can only be made after the participation arrangements are entered into.

6.288 Given that the tax consequences of the equity participation arrangements for both management and the company will be a key factor in determining the form which the arrangements take, the following discussion focuses on the tax considerations in relation to the acquisition of restricted shares and the grant of share options. For completeness, the discussion also touches on the key issues which might arise in relation to existing incentive arrangements.

Tax considerations for management and the company

Management

TAX CHARGES ON ACQUISITION/GRANT

6.289 No charge to income tax (or employee's NICs) should arise on acquisition of restricted shares if:

(i)   the amount subscribed for the shares is at least equal to their initial unrestricted market value ('UMV') (ie the market value of the shares valued disregarding the restrictions). In this case, any growth in value of the shares will fall to be taxed under the capital gains regime and, if maximum business assets taper relief applies, may be taxed at an effective rate of 10%;

(ii) an amount equal to the restricted market value of the shares (ie the market value of the shares valued on the basis of the restrictions) is paid on subscription for the shares; or

(iii) the shares are subject to a forfeiture provision which lifts within five years of the acquisition.

6.290 It is not unusual for a company to ask management to enter into protective tax elections when they acquire restricted shares for UMV (Income Tax (Earnings and Pensions) Act 2003 ('ITEPA 2003'), s 431). By entering into the election, management would be electing (a) to disregard the restrictions attaching to the shares, and (b) to pay income tax on acquisition of the shares by reference to their unrestricted market value. Of course, where the UMV of the shares has been paid (it is advisable to obtain an independent third party valuation for this purpose) no income tax charge would arise on acquisition whether or not a s 431 election is made. The company's argument in favour of making the election where this is the case is likely to be two-fold: (i) that if UMV has been paid, the manager is not at risk of any tax charge arising as a result of entering into the election, and (ii) if no s 431 election is entered into and HMRC determine that an amount less than UMV has been paid, the company is at risk of incurring an employer's NICs charge in future and it is unwilling to take this risk. From management's perspective, the question of valuation is therefore paramount.

6.291 Provided that management are both resident and ordinarily resident in the UK at the date of grant of options, no charge to income tax will arise on grant of the options (ITEPA 2003, Pt 7, Ch 5).

POST-ACQUISITION/GRANT TAX CHARGES

6.292 If management subscribe for restricted shares at UMV, no charge to income tax will subsequently arise. However, if restricted shares are acquired in the circumstances referred to at (ii) or (iii) above, a charge to income tax may arise on the earlier of the lifting of the restrictions which apply to the shares or sale of the shares.

6.293 A charge to income tax will arise on exercise of share options on the amount by which the market value of the shares at the date of exercise exceeds the exercise price (if any) of the option (ie the amount paid to acquire the shares).

THE INCOME TAX CHARGE

6.294 Whenever a charge to income tax arises in respect of restricted shares or options, income tax will be payable at a rate of 40% (assuming that the manager is a higher rate tax payer) and, if the shares are deemed to be 'readily convertible assets', they will also attract a charge to employee's NICs (at 1%) on the amount that is chargeable to income tax.

6.295 Shares in companies which are listed on the London or New York Stock Exchanges are 'readily convertible assets' as are shares in other companies for which 'trading arrangements' are in existence or are likely to come into existence under either arrangements or an understanding in existence at the time. For example, shares in a private company acquired on exercise of options shortly before a planned exit are likely to constitute 'readily convertible assets'. Also, shares which are not readily convertible assets will be deemed to be readily convertible assets if they are shares in a company in respect of which it is not possible to obtain a corporation tax deduction under the Finance Act 2003, Sch 23.

The company

PAYE

6.296 On each occasion on which a charge to income tax arises in relation to the shares acquired by management or options granted to management, the company will be required to withhold its best estimate of the amount of income tax and employee's NICs under the Pay as You Earn (PAYE) system and account to HMRC for these amounts.

6.297 Management will be required to reimburse the company in respect of the income tax liability within 90 days following the event giving rise to the tax charge and if management fail to do this, the amount of unpaid income tax will be deemed taxable income of the manager and chargeable to income tax and employee's NICs.

6.298 The company should ensure that the manager agrees to enter into any arrangement specified by the company to satisfy the tax liability which arises in connection with the restricted shares or options (including authorising the company to sell some of the shares acquired by the manager to satisfy the tax liability). The terms of the subscription and/or option grant should provide that shares will not be issued until arrangements for the funding of the tax liability have been entered into.

EMPLOYER'S NICS

6.299 The company also will be required to account to HMRC for employer's NICs (at a rate of 12.8%) on each occasion on which a charge to income tax arises (provided that the shares are readily convertible assets at that time – see the discussion above) on the amount which is subject to income tax. However, the amount of that liability should be a deductible expense for corporation tax purposes.

6.300 The company may, as a condition of issue of the shares to management or grant or exercise of the option, require each manager to fund the employer's NICs liability which arises in connection with the restricted shares or exercise of the option. This can be achieved in one of two ways:

(a)   the company may enter into a 'joint election' with each manager. Such an election legally transfers the employer's NICs liability to the manager so that the company is no longer legally liable for payment of the employer's NICs; or

(b)   the company may enter into an agreement with each manager in which the manager agrees to reimburse the company for the cost of the employer's NICs liability. The company remains legally liable for payment of the employer's NICs and has a right of reimbursement from the manager.

6.301 A joint election or an agreement to reimburse cannot be entered into if a s 431 election is entered into on the acquisition of restricted shares.

CORPORATION TAX RELIEF

6.302 The company should be able to claim relief from corporation tax in respect of the cost to the company of issuing the restricted shares and satisfying the exercise of options. The amount on which relief can be claimed is the amount by which the unrestricted market value at the date of acquisition of the shares exceeds the amount subscribed for the shares or paid on exercise of the option by management (Finance Act 2003, Sch 23, paras 8 and 15).

6.303 The relief would be available for the accounting period in which management acquire the shares (Finance Act 2003, Sch 23, paras 10 and 17).

Existing incentive arrangements

6.304 The impact of the DES on existing incentive arrangements should not be forgotten. It is possible that options or share awards could be outstanding under various employee share plans. The rules of the employee share plans (and any individual option or share award arrangements entered into by the company) should be reviewed as part of the due diligence process. For example, in the context of a DES involving a scheme (and the incorporation of a new holding company), it would be expected that outstanding options and share awards would be rolled-over into shares of the new holding company and would not become exercisable or vest. However, this is not always the case and failure to verify the position could lead to employees being inadvertently disadvantaged

Insider dealing and compliance issues

6.305 The prohibition on insider dealing contained in the CJA 1993, Part V should not give rise to concern on the DES itself since the Government in the shape of the Department of Trade and Industry has stated specifically in relation to DESs that advantage can be taken of the statutory defence 'that the information has been disclosed widely enough to ensure that none of those taking part in the dealing would be prejudiced by not having the information, particularly where the parties involved in the transaction (ie existing shareholders) possess the relevant information'.

6.306 Great care does however need to be taken in relation to any subsequent dealing in the shares acquired. To avoid the risk of inadvertent insider dealing following the DES, individuals making decisions on any dealing in the shares and the individuals managing the banking relationship within the company should be separate with 'Chinese Wall' procedures being put in place between them.

6.307 Institutions which are authorised to conduct investment business under the Financial Services Act 1986 will also need to comply with the rules created pursuant to that Act. These are the rules and the rules of the relevant self-regulating organisation which is currently The Securities Association. These rules are likely to be succeeded by new rules issued by the FSA.

6.308 Breach of these investment business rules may give rise to the possibility of civil proceedings. In addition, each institution should have its own compliance procedures governing dealings in the shares of a company whether it is a banking or other relationship. Dealings in such shares should be discussed with each institution's compliance officer as there may be additional internal compliance procedures within the institution that will need to be considered.

6.309 Debt, both capital and accrued interest, may be reduced by lenders agreeing to swap debt for an equity interest in the company. The equity interest will often be preference shares. The consideration for a subscription for shares can be the discharge of a specific amount of debt, although a debt for equity swap can also be achieved by a subscription in cash and the use of the proceeds to repay the relevant debt. A debt for equity swap has the dual effect of reducing debt levels and therefore interest payment obligations, whilst increasing the company's capital base and so diluting the interests of existing shareholders. As a result, the company's gearing is improved at the same time as its debt service obligations are reduced.

Chapter 7

SCHEMES OF ARRANGEMENT AS A RESTRUCTURING TOOL

A INTRODUCTION

7.1 Whilst Chapter 6 focused on non-statutory and contractual restructuring processes, formal restructuring procedures under schemes of arrangement under the Companies Act 2006, s 895 (formerly the Companies Act 1985, s 425[1]) are increasingly used to force a contractual restructuring through to completion. This development is principally a result of the increasing complexity in capital structures for businesses that has emerged since the 1990s and in particular the growth of US-based investors in European high yield debt. The stakeholder position has become increasingly complex and therefore an increasing number of 'consensual' workouts will almost inevitably need to involve some sort of cram-down or the threat of such to enable a majority of creditors to execute a restructuring and overcome the objections of a dissentient minority. Companies Act 2006, s 895 (which supersedes the Companies Act 1985, s 425) is considered to be the most useful device under English law for achieving this[2]. As Asprey J articulated in the case of *Re Anglo-Continental Supply Co Ltd*[3], the purpose of the section is strictly limited in the sense that it does not confer powers and its only effect is to remove the need for an agreement by every member of a class in a restructuring whilst still procuring the validity of the relevant proposal where the requisite majority have approved it. In a restructuring context, schemes therefore facilitate rehabilitation by allowing the relevant majorities to execute a workout in which they can resolve the company's financial problems.

---

[1]   The Companies Act 1985, s 425 and the associated sections dealing with schemes of arrangement have now been restated in Parts 26 and 27 of the Companies Act 2006. See Part C of this chapter in this regard.

[2]   It should be noted that the procedural improvements to company voluntary arrangements ('CVAs') instituted by the Insolvency Act 2000, which are considered in the closing section of this chapter, have elevated CVAs as a more useful restructuring tool that can be used to facilitate a cram down.

[3]   [1922] 2 Ch 723.

B ADVANTAGES OF SCHEMES

Cram down

7.2 In many financing documents where unanimity is required (for example under the provisions of a bond indenture or pursuant to the entrenched rights provisions in a syndicated loan), it is possible that a significant majority of creditors will agree to the restructuring proposal, but that a minority are objecting or 'holding out' with respect to such a consensual restructuring. In these circumstances a scheme of arrangement has two functions: in the first instance the mere threat of a scheme to 'cram-down' the recalcitrant minority can procure a consensus without embarking on a costly scheme process and secondly if this threat of 'scheming' creditors does not achieve the requisite objectives the scheme can be fully executed to drive through the necessary restructuring. In the MyTravel restructuring for example, the threat of a proposed scheme to 'cram-down' recalcitrant convertible bondholders succeeded in bringing about a consensual deal. Under the proposed scheme (eventually modified) the business would be transferred to a 'newco' by the company pursuant to the Companies Act 1985, s 425 (as it was then) and the existing shareholders would be allocated 4% of the equity in the newco. The main creditor constituencies would be allotted 94% of the equity in newco following a conversion of their debt claims and the remaining 2% would be allotted to the convertible bondholders. However, the bondholder's debt claims would remain in the old MyTravel and would not otherwise be dealt with under the scheme. General creditors, customers and the Inland Revenue would have their claims transferred to newco. New working capital facilities and bonding lines would be made available to newco outside of the scheme.

Deferment of claims

7.3 As with MyTravel, most sophisticated schemes of arrangement that deal with complex capital structures will provide for a deferment of a company's liabilities through a moratorium established by the scheme, the reduction of an interest burden and the discharge of indebtedness in exchange for an equity interest as part of a debt for equity conversion. The use of schemes to effect a debt for equity swap has increased in recent years and the ease with which a scheme can compromise debts and allocate equity interests to creditors is a key attraction of them.

Establishing and identifying claims

7.4 Equally, a scheme may be used as a device for establishing a clear identification of a company's financial and other liabilities and a distribution of its assets, which, might otherwise be more costly and difficult to achieve in liquidation. Liquidators have different and far more rigid statutory rules to abide by in determining liabilities and the terms upon which a distribution can be made. A scheme on the other hand is driven by the will of the relevant majority of a class of creditors and affords more flexibility. The company does not have to be insolvent in order to undertake a scheme of arrangement and schemes are often used outside of an insolvency context.

Ability to imitate liquidation

7.5 Where schemes of arrangement are used in relation to a company that is technically insolvent, their purpose is to avoid liquidation and the associated costs by reflecting the returns that those creditors would otherwise achieve in liquidation. Schemes of arrangement are frequently used in the insurance sector for this purpose to accelerate distributions to creditors and a scheme can be used in conjunction with the administration procedure instead of using the CVA procedure.

Dealing with unknown and contingent creditors

7.6 Schemes are also a vital device for companies with a myriad of creditors, especially where all members of the potential class of creditors are not known to the company or if creditors have contingent claims and it would otherwise be very difficult to reach agreements varying each and every finance document on a purely contractual basis.

7.7 One of the main reasons for using a statutory restructuring procedure, such as a scheme of arrangement, is that the company is unable to identify and bind all of its creditors. This is particularly true where the company has issued bonds, which are held either in the clearing systems or in bearer form.

Ability to deal with bondholders

7.8 When a company is in financial difficulties it is not long before an ad hoc bondholder committee is formed. However, such ad hoc bondholder committees are inevitably unable to be specific about the value of the bonds they can speak for. They are also unwilling to commit that they will refrain from trading whilst negotiations are ongoing. Unless a company has certainty that it is dealing with a stable group of bondholders, which represent a sufficient number of bonds to make any changes or give any waiver it may require pursuant to the terms of the bond documentation, it will need to rely on some form of statutory cram-down procedure.

7.9 Recent case law on schemes of arrangement show that the courts understand the particular issues that dealing with such an uncertain group of bondholder creditors raises. In *Re Telewest Communications plc*[1], David Richards J confirmed that payment of the fees and costs of an ad hoc bondholder committee did not raise any class issues, so long as the payment was not made to 'buy' the vote. He also confirmed that the practice of obtaining voting agreements from the members of such an ad hoc committee did not raise any class issues. The court acknowledged that for Telewest there was much sense in securing votes in advance of the scheme meetings, so avoiding the waste of time and costs if bondholders who had indicated their support were simply to change their minds or sell the bonds without securing a similar undertaking from a purchaser. Voting agreements entered into by bondholders before the launch of a scheme would not cause class issues provided that the scheme creditor would not reasonably have voted differently in the absence of the agreement.

¹ [2004] EWHC 924 (Ch), [2005] 1 BCLC 752.

US Securities Act exemption

7.10 The new debt and equity securities which are issued to US bondholder creditors under relevant schemes can qualify under the US Securities Act of 1933, s 3(a)(10) exemption from SEC registration. Generally speaking, this exemption applies to any issue of securities in exchange for securities, claims or other non-cash consideration. In order to qualify for the exemption from the registration requirements of the US Securities Act of 1933 provided by s 3(a)(10), there must be a hearing on the fairness of the scheme's terms and conditions to the relevant scheme creditors, which all scheme creditors are entitled to attend in person or through representatives to oppose the sanctioning of the scheme, and with respect to which notification will be given to all scheme creditors. It is accepted practice to rely on the English court hearings to sanction a scheme for this purpose if the court has been advised that this is the intention in advance of the sanction hearings.

Recognition by the US courts

7.11 A scheme of arrangement will not be effective in the US unless it is recognised in the courts of that jurisdiction. The growth of US-based investors in European debt has made it increasingly important that the restructuring is effective in the US. Chapter 15 of the US Bankruptcy Code allows foreign debtors to seek relief in US Bankruptcy Court proceedings ancillary to a foreign reorganisation or discharge proceeding without the need for formal bankruptcy proceedings to be commenced in the US. Chapter 15 of the US Bankruptcy Code is therefore available to give schemes of arrangement full force and effect in the US and to make them binding and enforceable against each creditor compromised under a scheme.

7.12 An 'authorized representative' of the company must make the application under section 304 of the US Bankruptcy Code. Unlike in an insolvency procedure, a scheme of arrangement does not automatically vest the powers of a company in a particular 'authorized representative'. As part of the court process to implement a scheme, the English court can confirm the appointment of an 'authorized representative', for example one of the company's directors, and this will avoid the need for any further proof of appointment in the US procedure. This process was followed in Marconi and Telewest restructurings.

7.13 The scope of an order made under Chapter 15 of the US Bankruptcy Code can also extend to cover claims that would be barred by reason of the deeds of release referred to below, meaning that the order made under Chapter 15 of the US Bankruptcy Code can have a very wide-ranging effect.

Ability to deliver 'releases' through a scheme

7.14 It is increasingly becoming market practice in large multi-creditor restructurings for releases to be given by scheme creditors to the debtor (that is, the company whose debts are being compromised by the scheme), its advisers and the members of any creditors' committees and their advisers from any liability attaching to them in connection with the restructuring process. However, it is not considered contractually possible for a creditor under a scheme of arrangement to grant a release that third parties can enforce (because they are not party to the scheme). The practice has therefore developed for the scheme creditors to give the debtor the authority to enter into a separate deed of release on their behalf releasing the relevant third parties.

7.15 The enforceability of these deeds has not been tested, although they have been used in several schemes such as Ionica and Telewest, but where all creditors are in one class, it is important to ensure that their rights against the debtor are not treated differently. The concern is that if one creditor is giving up legitimate rights under the deed while another is not, they are being treated differently, which may raise both class and fairness issues.

7.16 In Telewest's case the release was particularly widely drafted. Although there were no known claims being released, the concern was that if one creditor claimed that the release did affect it unfairly, that could potentially cause a class issue on which the whole Telewest scheme could fail. Telewest got around this issue by providing that any claims made that were demonstrated not to apply equally to all creditors could be carved out of the release.

Litigation and temporary protection from creditors

7.17 One of the advantages of using a more formal process to restructure a company is that, although there is no statutory protection, the courts are more likely to give the company being restructured some protection from creditors' claims while a scheme is being prepared.

7.18 In *Sea Assets Ltd v PT Garuda Indonesia*[1], Thomas J exercised his discretion under Order 47 of the Supreme Court Rules (which preceded CPR) and granted a temporary stay of execution of judgment to give the creditors an opportunity to vote on a scheme of arrangement. A court will generally exercise its discretion in this way if (i) the judgment debtor is insolvent, and (ii) a scheme of arrangement has been set on foot for the main body of creditors and has a reasonable prospect of succeeding. In *Garuda*, although the scheme meetings had not yet been convened the preparation of the scheme was well advanced and had the support of the overwhelming majority of creditors.

¹ 27 June 2001, unreported.

7.19 The court has also shown willing (for example, in the Telewest restructuring) to enable a company in the process of restructuring to continue in business despite the fact that a winding-up petition was outstanding against it, by granting orders under the Insolvency Act 1986, s 127 to prospectively validate payments which it needed to make to implement the restructuring.

C RECENT LEGISLATIVE CHANGES

7.20 Companies Act 1985, ss 425–427 have been restated in Part 26 (arrangements and reconstructions) and Part 27 (mergers and divisions of public companies) of the Companies Act 2006 which came into force on 6 April 2008[1] as a result of the Companies Act 2006 (Commencement No 5, Transitional Provisions and Savings) Order 2007, SI 2007/3495. Part 26 of the Companies Act 2006 restates the provisions of the Companies Act 1985, ss 425–427 with some drafting amendments and consequential changes as a result of changes to provisions in other Parts of the Companies Act 2006[2].

[1] See the Companies Act 2006 (Commencement No 5, Transitional Provisions and Savings) Order 2007, SI 2007/3495. For transitional provisions and savings, see SI 2007/3495, arts 6, 9, 12, Schs 1–4.

[2] The Companies Act 1985, s 425(1) is to be replaced by the Companies Act 2006, ss 895(1), 896(1), (2). The Companies Act 1985, s 425(2) is to be replaced by the Companies Act 2006, ss 899(1), (3), 907(1) and 922(1). The Companies Act 1985, s 425(3) is to be replaced (with some changes) by the Companies Act 2006, ss 899(4), 901(3), (4). The Companies Act 1985, s 425(4) is to be replaced by the Companies Act 2006, s 901(5), (6). The Companies Act 1985, s 425(6) is to be replaced by the Companies Act 2006, s 895(2).

7.21 Companies Act 2006, ss 895–899 provide that where any compromise or arrangement is proposed between a company and its creditors or any class of them, or between the company and its members or any class of them, the court may, on the application of the company, or any creditor or member of the company or the liquidator[1], order a meeting of the creditors or class of creditors or of the members or class of members, as the case may be, to be called; and if a majority in number representing three-fourths in value of the creditors or class of creditors or members or class of members, present either in person or by proxy agree to the compromise or arrangement[2], and it is also sanctioned by the court[3], it will be binding on all the creditors or the class of creditors, or on the members or class of members, as the case may be, and on the liquidator and the contributories of the company. In a restructuring context Part 26 of the Companies Act 2006 provides a statutory device whereby a distressed company may enter into a compromise or arrangement with its creditors (or any class of creditor) which, provided that the necessary majorities of each class are obtained and the court sanctions the scheme, such majorities will bind the minority in each relevant class not accepting the proposal.

1   Companies Act 2006, ss 895 and 896 restate the Companies Act 1985, s 425(1) and (6) which grants the power for: a company; any of the company's creditors or members; or a liquidator or administrator (if the company is being wound up or an administration order is in force in relation to it), to apply to the court to sanction a compromise or arrangement, as well as providing for the convening of the relevant meetings by the court.

2   Companies Act 2006, s 899 restates the Companies Act 1985, s 425(2) which sets out the condition that must be satisfied before the court can sanction a compromise or agreement, namely if, at a meeting properly summoned, a majority in number representing 75% in value of the creditors or class of creditors or members or class of members (as the case may be), agree to the compromise or arrangement.

3   A scheme of arrangement must be sanctioned by the court and this is one of the features that distinguishes a scheme of arrangement from a CVA under Part I of the Insolvency Act 1986.

7.22 Due to the fact that a scheme of arrangement enables the court to sanction a compromise or arrangement between the company and its creditors without the consent of all creditors it is imperative that the strict statutory requirements are complied with. Indeed, adherence to the rules is critical because when sanctioned by the creditors and the court, the scheme will bind all members and creditors even if they did not have notice of the meeting.

7.23 Whilst a scheme of arrangement may be commenced on the application of a creditor or a class of them, the company must still be a party to the application and so a scheme cannot be used as a mechanism to implement an arrangement between the creditors merely as between themselves. In these circumstances the company will be a respondent with respect to the creditor's application.

7.24 The term 'creditor' is not defined in the Companies Act 2006, but the courts have given the expression its ordinary natural meaning so as to include all persons having pecuniary claims against the company notwithstanding that they are often difficult to quantify and irrespective of whether such claims are actual, contingent, unliquidated or prospective[1]. In order to vote at the meeting the creditor must still have such a pecuniary claim at the time of the meeting. In the case of bondholder creditors it will be necessary to determine the form of the bond and whether it is in a bearer or registered form and whether it has been structured through a trust in order to precisely identify the 'creditor'.

1   *Re Midland Coal, Coke and Iron Co* [1985] 1 Ch 267.

7.25 Foreign creditors whose relationship with the company is governed by a non-English law contract will not be prevented by English law governed schemes from taking action against the company with respect to assets located overseas or with respect to the original contract. It is of course different if the assets in question, with reference to which the creditor is contemplating action, are subject to the jurisdiction of the English courts.

D 'COMPROMISES' AND 'ARRANGEMENTS'

7.26 In the context of a creditor scheme, the terms 'arrangement' and 'compromise' are not defined. Whilst there has been a tendency for the question of whether the proposal is an arrangement or compromise to be conflated into the general exercise of the court's discretion to approve the scheme at the sanction hearing, it obviously makes much more sense as a practical matter for those initiating the scheme to understand the meaning and scope of those concepts so that schemes are not exposed to a subsequent and late rejection by the court. It is clear from the case law however that the court's jurisdiction is predicated on there being a compromise or an arrangement and that without this vital element the court will not have the requisite jurisdiction to sanction the proposal[1].

[1]   *Mercantile Investment and General Trust Co v International Co of Mexico* [1893] 1 Ch 484n, CA.

7.27 In *Sneath v Valley Gold Ltd*[1], the court suggested that the words be given their ordinary commercial meaning, such that in that case a compromise was equated to a settlement of a dispute. Similarly in *Mercantile Investment and General Trust Co v International Co of Mexico*[2] the court resolved that a compromise could be pursued because of the difficulty in actually enforcing rights or claims.

[1]   [1893] 1 Ch 477.
[2]   [1893] 1 Ch 484n, CA.

7.28 The cases in Australia and England and Wales have however accorded an 'arrangement' a wider meaning than 'compromise' in that an arrangement can simply mean to put affairs in order and does not necessarily imply a dispute. As the Victoria courts have commented '… almost any arrangement otherwise legal which touches or concerns the rights and obligations of the company or its members or creditors may come under this section'[1]. Similarly, in *Re Guardian Assurance Co*[2] it was held that the word 'arrangement' is not to be limited to something akin to a compromise. Hence the elements of dispute and an accommodation of that dispute need not be present as is the case for a compromise.

[1]   *Re International Harvester Co of Australia Pty Ltd* [1953] VLR 669 at 672 where Lowe ACJ concluded that 'arrangement' should be construed as liberally as possible.
[2]   [1917] 1 Ch 431.

7.29 Adopting the commercial approach recommended by earlier authorities, the court in *Re NFU (or National Farmers' Union) Development Trust Ltd*[1] held that an 'arrangement' for the purposes of a scheme involves some form of give and take and dismissed the notion that some form of confiscation can constitute an 'arrangement'. A scheme of arrangement that disenfranchised certain members of the company from voting on the affairs of the company in connection with livestock marketing therefore involved one or more of the interested parties agreeing to a relinquishment of all rights for no consideration which was not an arrangement in the court's view. An arrangement requires some form of concession, but not a complete loss of rights by one party for a consideration of questionable value[2]. This was indeed the position taken by the Court of Appeal in the case of *Mercantile Investment and General Trust Co v International Co of Mexico*[3] where the scheme purported to release security of fully secured debenture holders in exchange for preference shares. The court held that the nature of such a conversion from a fully secured position was not a compromise or an arrangement, but a voluntary relinquishment of significant priority rights. If of course there were to be difficulties in the way of enforcing secured rights, or the value of the security held by the debenture holders was of questionable value, such that the relevant majority of debenture holders could reach the conclusion that it was desirable to completely compromise their secured position, then it was a proposal that was capable of being characterised as a compromise[4].

1   [1973] 1 All ER 135. See the judgment of Brightman J at 140.
2   [1973] 1 All ER 135, [1972] 1 WLR 1548.
3   [1893] 1 Ch 484n.
4   *Mercantile Investment and General Trust Co v River Plate Trust, Loan and Agency Co* [1894] 1 Ch 578.

7.30 The scope of an arrangement is limited only by the imagination of those sponsoring the scheme and the commercial possibilities and could involve the merger of one or more companies involved in a restructuring, the separation of certain divisions within a company, or even a transfer of substantially the whole of a company's business and undertaking to a newco. However, in executing the arrangement the interests of all members and creditors whose interests might be affected will need to be taken into account[1] irrespective of whether the company is a going concern or is in the course of winding up.

1   See *Re Savoy Hotel* [1981] Ch 351, [1981] 3 All ER 646.

7.31 The Court of Appeal has also focused on the ingredient of reasonableness in any compromise or arrangement by declaring that:

'a compromise or agreement which has to be sanctioned by the Court must be reasonable ... A reasonable compromise must be a compromise which can, by reasonable people conversant with the subject, be regarded as beneficial to those on both sides who are making it. Now I have no doubt at all that it would be improper for the Court to allow an arrangement to be forced on any class of creditors, if the arrangement cannot reasonably be supposed by sensible business people to be for the benefit of that class as such.'[1]

1   Bowen LJ in *Re Alabama, New Orleans, Texas and Pacific Junction Rly Co* [1891] 1 Ch 213 at 243.

7.32 In cases where a creditor is likely to be repaid in full there can still be an 'arrangement' if it is clear that the provisions of the scheme will vary, at least to some extent, the bundle of rights and obligations which constitute the claims of that class against the company, such as the right to future interest or the commutation of claims at the time that the scheme is effective[1].

1   See the judgment of Neuberger J in *Re Osiris Insurance* [1999] 1 BCLC 182.

7.33 It should be noted that the English courts will not sanction any compromise or arrangement where the same is ultra vires the company[1], involves an unlawful or fraudulent scheme or the proposal knowingly conflicts with some provision of the companies legislation such as the conversion of issued shares into redeemable preference shares or which purports to evade the application of certain statutory procedures[2]. However, if the court does inadvertently sanction an ultra-vires arrangement or an arrangement that is in breach of other statutory provisions then the scheme will be binding on the company and the company will be unable to challenge the scheme on the grounds of capacity or any conflict with statute[3].

[1]   *Re Oceanic Steam Navigation Co Ltd* [1939] Ch 41, [1938] 3 All ER 740.
[2]   *Re St James' Court Estate Ltd* [1944] Ch 6.
[3]   See *British and Commonwealth Holdings plc v Barclays Bank plc* [1996] 1 All ER 381, [1996] 1 WLR 1, CA where an option agreement which constituted an unlawful return of capital and potentially unlawful financial assistance was entered into with a shareholder and formed part of the sanctioned scheme. The Court of Appeal upheld the option agreement despite the capacity issues and the conflict with other provisions of company law.

E COMPANIES THAT CAN BE SUBJECT TO A SCHEME

7.34 A 'company' that can be subject to a scheme under the Companies Act 2006, s 895 is defined in s 895(2)(b) as any company that can be wound up under the Insolvency Act 1986 or the Insolvency (Northern Ireland) Order 1989, SI 1989/2405. A 'company' that can be wound up under the Insolvency Act 1986 includes a company formed and registered under the Companies Act 2006, or under the Companies Act 1985, or an 'existing company' for the purposes of that Act[1].

[1]   Companies Act 2006, s 1.

7.35 An 'unregistered company' is also a company that is liable to be wound up under the Insolvency Act 1986 by virtue of s 221(1) of that Act. 'Unregistered company', for these purposes, includes any association or any company, except for any company that has been registered in any part of the UK under British companies legislation[1]. For practical purposes this means that unregistered companies are: statutory companies established by private Act of Parliament; foreign companies which have been carrying on business in Great Britain or have another relevant connection to the jurisdiction; or other bodies, eg unregistered friendly societies, for which provision for winding up is not made by specific legislation[2].

[1]   Insolvency Act 1986, s 220(1).
[2]   *Sealy and Milman: Annotated Guide to the Insolvency Legislation 2006/2007*, vol 1, p 240.

7.36 Therefore, subject to the provisions of the Insolvency Act 1986 and the Companies Acts a court may sanction a scheme in respect of an unregistered company. There is little statutory guidance on precisely when a court may do this. The starting point is the case law that deals with the winding up of an unregistered company.

7.37 The Insolvency Act 1986 does not prescribe when the courts will be justified in winding up an unregistered company – the courts have a discretion and the development of rules for the use of that discretion has been left to them. Case law establishes three preconditions which must be fulfilled before a court will exercise its discretion to order a winding up of an unregistered company[1]: (1) there must be a sufficient connection with England which may, but need not necessarily, consist of assets within the jurisdiction, (2) there must be a reasonable possibility that the order will benefit those applying for it, and (3) at least one of the persons interested in the distribution of the company's assets must be a person over whom the court can exercise jurisdiction[2].

[1]   At this point it is worth emphasising that in many cases the winding up of an unregistered company will in fact be the winding up of a foreign company.
[2]   *Stocznia Gdanska SA v Latreefers Inc (No 2)* [2001] 2 BCLC 116 at 140, CA, approving the formulation of Knox J in *Re Real Estate Development Co* [1991] BCLC 210 at 217.

7.38 The three preconditions, which are derived from case law relating to the winding up of companies, are not entirely helpful in the context of a scheme. This is largely because in the context of a scheme the company in question may not be insolvent. Lawrence Collins J in *Re Drax Holdings Ltd*[1] considered the principles which guide a court in determining its jurisdiction, and exercising its discretion, to sanction a scheme involving an unregistered company. He held that the three preconditions, referred to above, go to the discretion of the court to exercise its powers, rather than to its jurisdiction. Furthermore, the second and third of those preconditions need not be satisfied for the purposes of a scheme, because they do not go to the question whether a company is 'liable' to be wound up under the Insolvency Act 1986. Similarly, it is not necessary for the purposes of a scheme that the grounds for winding up in the Insolvency Act 1986, s 221(5) exist[2]. Lawrence Collins J reasoned that any other result would be odd and artificial, given that schemes of arrangement are used in many circumstances, which are not related to insolvency[3].

[1]   [2003] EWHC 2743 (Ch), [2004] 1 All ER 903, [2004] 1 WLR 1049, followed in *Re La Mutuelles du Mans Assurances IARD* [2006] BCC 11; and *Re DAP Holding NV* [2006] BCC 48.
[2]   *Re Drax Holdings Ltd* [2003] EWHC 2743 (Ch), [2004] 1 All ER 903, [2004] 1 WLR 1049 at [26].
[3]   [2003] EWHC 2743 (Ch), [2004] 1 All ER 903, [2004] 1 WLR 1049 at [27].

7.39 Nonetheless, there remains a limitation as to the exercise of jurisdiction over unregistered companies for the purposes of a scheme: the first precondition does apply and the court will not exercise its jurisdiction unless there is a sufficient connection with England[1].

[1]   [2003] EWHC 2743 (Ch), [2004] 1 All ER 903, [2004] 1 WLR 1049 at [29].

7.40 In the *Drax Holdings* case, Lawrence Collins J was able to find a sufficient connection with England on the facts: Drax Holdings was incorporated to raise finance to acquire a power station in Yorkshire; key finance documents were governed by English law and contained submissions to the jurisdiction of the English courts; assets charged under the finance documents included the power station in Yorkshire and shares in English companies[1]. Also, the proposed English scheme would make other schemes (in the Cayman Islands and Jersey) effective by making them binding on creditors who are subject to the jurisdiction of the English courts. To this extent, a connection with England came from the fact that an order of the English court was needed to give practical effect to anticipated orders abroad.

1   [2003] EWHC 2743 (Ch), [2004] 1 All ER 903, [2004] 1 WLR 1049 at [32].

7.41 Accordingly, a court may sanction a scheme in respect of an unregistered company if there is sufficient connection between the proposed scheme and England. Whether there is such a sufficient connection depends on the court's view of the facts presented to it. This was the decision reached by Lewison J in the case of *Re DAP Holdings NV*[1] where despite the provisions of the EU Insolvency Regulation[2] he held that the court had jurisdiction to sanction a scheme with respect to a Dutch company even though it did not have its centre of main interest or an establishment in the United Kingdom for the purposes of the EU Insolvency Regulation. The reasoning is that in determining whether a company can be wound up in the United Kingdom as a matter of principle, certain circumstances such as the potential existence of insolvency, which might otherwise trigger provisions under the EU Insolvency Regulation, should be disregarded[3].

1   [2005] EWHC 2092 (Ch).
2   Namely Council Regulation (EC) No 1346/2000, arts 1–3.
3   [2005] EWHC 2092 (Ch) at [11].

7.42 It should also be noted that non-United Kingdom insurance companies are capable of being wound up in the United Kingdom for the purposes of implementing a scheme of arrangement[1] even though credit institutions and insurance companies are subject to their own specific reorganisation and winding-up regulations[2].

1   The Insurers (Reorganisation and Winding Up) Regulations 2004, SI 2004/353, reg 5.
2   See the Credit Institutions (Reorganisation and Winding Up) Regulations 2004, SI 2004/1045 and the Insurers (Reorganisation and Winding Up) Regulations 2004, SI 2004/353.

F PROCESS AND PROCEDURE

7.43 The Chancery Division of the High Court issued a Practice Statement on 15 April 2002[1] which provides detailed guidance on the processes and procedures for implementing a scheme of arrangement. In addition, New Practice Directions came into force on 1 October 2007 relating to applications to court under the Companies Act 1985, s 425 and the Companies Act 2006, s 895.

1   Companies: Schemes of arrangement [2002] 1 WLR 1345) (Practice Statement) on the procedure to be followed on an application for a scheme of arrangement. It is expected that the procedure will be exactly the same for applications made under Part 26 (arrangements and reconstructions) of the Companies Act 2006.

The application hearing

7.44 The new procedure for initiating schemes is set out in paragraph 7 of the New Practice Direction to CPR 49. Before October 2007, applications for the sanction of the court for a compromise or arrangement were made first by a claim form seeking directions to hold a meeting and then a petition for the actual sanction. The New Practice Direction to CPR 49 dispenses with this application process and provides that all such applications will need to be made by a Part 8 claim form in the future. The claim form must seek:

(a)   directions for convening a meeting of creditors or members or both, as the case requires;

(b)   the sanction of the court to the compromise or arrangement, if it is approved at the meeting or meetings, and a direction for a further hearing for that purpose; and

(c)   a direction that the claimant files a copy of a report to the court by the chairman of the meeting or of each meeting.

7.45 At the initial court hearing, the court will convene the meeting(s) of creditors or members and will then adjourn the claim form until the meeting has been held. The claim form itself is to be resubmitted with appropriate amendments noting that the meeting has taken place. The court will also require a witness statement to evidence that the meeting has taken place. The final stage will be court sanction of the scheme.

7.46 The Practice Statement of 15 April 2002 requires that the same judge should be involved throughout the whole process to ensure consistency on the all important creditor class issue and in order to reduce time and costs. In larger schemes this is extremely helpful because it avoids the possibility of a judge at the sanction hearing making a determination that the incorrect meetings of creditors had been convened and therefore not sanctioning the scheme[1]. The initial claim form is still heard in chambers and the claim form should seek the order for convening meetings of the specific class(es) of creditors, give an indication of how and where the meetings will be held and identify a chairman for the meeting or one or more alternative chairmen.

[1]   In smaller cases where a registrar has approved the composition of the classes of creditor, a judge will not be bound by such a formulation at the main sanction hearing. Class composition is therefore an important responsibility of the company or creditor making the application.

Evidence

7.47 The claim form must still be supported by evidence and because most applications are made *ex parte* an affidavit will be used. Additional witness statements may support this, but in totality the evidence must contain sufficient detail on the composition of the classes[1]. It is the responsibility of the applicant to correctly identify the classes of creditor and whether or not more than one meeting of creditors should be convened, although the Practice Statement makes it clear that the court, when deciding whether to convene the meetings of creditors, should consider the constitution of the classes of creditors and whether one or more meetings should be convened. The evidence should also explain the reasons for the scheme and the structure and objectives of the scheme. All aspects of the company's statutory information must be specified including, in particular, details of its share capital.

1   The applicant has an ongoing responsibility to bring to the attention of the court, at the earliest possible opportunity, any issues which may arise relating to the constitution of meetings of creditors or which may effect the conduct of those meetings.

Composition of classes

7.48 Companies Act 2006, s 895(1) refers to a composition or arrangement with creditors 'or any class of them', and given the historic difficulty of the courts and practitioners in establishing classes it is slightly surprising that the Companies Act 2006 did not provide any guidance on the formulation of classes. Those establishing the relevant classes of creditors must therefore continue to have reference to the extensive body of case law. Establishing the classes accurately is of course crucial because creditors in specific classes are required to vote on the scheme at separate class meetings.

7.49 Historically, class composition was even more of a problem because the *Practice Note* of Eve J[1] effectively held that class composition was an issue for those initiating a scheme and that the court could give no conclusive guidance on class composition at the time of the initial application. The effect of getting class constitution wrong, as in the *Hawk* case[2], was to deprive the court of jurisdiction to sanction the scheme and this resulted in significant loss of costs, uncertainty and delays in executing schemes where classes of creditors had to be reformulated and meetings had to be convened.

1   *Practice Note* [1934] WN 142.
2   *Re Hawk Insurance Co Ltd* [2001] EWCA Civ 241, [2001] 2 BCLC 480, CA, where Arden J at first instance held that the different treatment of creditors' claims amounted to a weighting of their claims as 'unsettled claims', 'outstanding losses' or 'incurred but not reported claims', which in turn had different valuation mechanics and which ultimately gave creditors different rights which put them in different classes. Accordingly she refused to sanction the arrangement on the ground that the creditor's rights were sufficiently different to require their separation into more than one class.

7.50 As a result of the procedural difficulties posed by the *Practice Note* of Eve J, the effect of the *Hawk* case and the comments by Chadwick LJ in that case that the existing practices relating to class composition were defective and warranted re-examination, the Chancery Division of the High Court subsequently issued a Practice Statement on 15 April 2002[1] on the procedure to be followed with respect to schemes. The purpose of the Practice Statement is to enable issues relating to the composition of the classes of creditors and the summoning of the relevant class meetings to be identified at and resolved early in the proceedings so as to avoid the waste of time and costs associated with the court determining that the classes have not been properly identified at the hearing to sanction the scheme. The following changes in practice should be observed and these changes are paraphrased to reflect the new procedure for initiating schemes set out in paragraph 7 of the New Practice Direction to CPR 49, which came into force on 1 October 2007:

   (i) It is still the responsibility of those submitting the Part 8 claim form with respect to the scheme to determine the identity of the classes of creditors and therefore determine whether more than one meeting of creditors should be convened.

  (ii) Those submitting the Part 8 claim form in relation to a substantial scheme will now be listed before a judge (as opposed to a registrar). The same judge should be involved throughout the whole process.

 (iii) Those submitting the Part 8 claim form should bring to the attention of the court at the earliest possible opportunity, any issues which may arise relating to the constitution of meetings of creditors or which may effect the conduct of those meetings.

  (iv) The court, when deciding whether to convene the meetings of creditors, should consider the constitution of the classes of creditors and whether one or more meetings should be convened.

   (v) The court should consider giving directions for the resolution of any creditor issues brought to its attention by those submitting the Part 8 claim form with respect to the scheme, including directions to postpone a meeting of creditors until resolution of the matter in question.

  (vi) Directions for the resolution of a creditor issue may include orders giving anyone affected by the order a limited time in which to apply to vary or discharge the order.

 (vii) Creditors who feel they have been unfairly treated will still be able to raise objections at the hearing of the petition to sanction the scheme, but the court will expect them to show good reason why they did not raise the issue at an earlier stage.

1   *Practice Statement (companies: schemes of arrangement)* [2002] 3 All ER 96, [2002] 1 WLR 1345.

7.51 Bowen LJ formulated the classic test of a creditor class in the case of *Sovereign Life Assurance Co v Dodd*[1] where he held that a class 'must be confined to those persons whose rights are not so dissimilar as to make it impossible for them to consult together with a view to their common interest'[2]. The reference to 'rights' is one that encapsulates those rights to be released or varied under the proposal and the new rights that the scheme gives to those creditors whose rights are to be released or varied[3]. The corollary is also true under the Sovereign test in that where the rights of creditors are not sufficiently similar it will be necessary for the separate meetings of each specific creditor class to be convened. This will be the case even if a 'class' has only one member[4]. However, where there is more than one person in a class, the court has held that the attendance of a single member of that class will be insufficient to constitute a meeting of that class for the purposes of a scheme[5].

1   [1892] 2 QB 573 at 583, CA.
2   Chadwick LJ ([2001] EWCA Civ 241, [2001] 2 BCLC 480 at [31]) who gave the leading judgment in the *Hawk* case stated that it was now settled case law that this was the test which should be adopted to determine whether creditors fall into the same class.
3   *Hawk* case [2001] EWCA Civ 241, [2001] 2 BCLC 480 at [30] (Chadwick LJ).
4   See *RMCA Reinsurance Ltd* [1994] BCC 378.

[5]   See the judgment of David Richards J in *Re Altitude Scaffolding Ltd; Re T&N Ltd* [2006] EWHC 1401 (Ch), [2007] 1 BCLC 199.

7.52 Another way of expressing the Sovereign test is to question whether the rights of those to be affected by the scheme will be so affected by a single arrangement or whether the scheme can only in fact be executed in its entirety by a series of linked arrangements. In a scheme involving a number of linked arrangements separate meetings will be necessitated[1]. Dealing with the point that the different claims required different weighting and different valuation which might well lead to a composition to separate classes, Chadwick LJ in the *Hawk* case held that on a true understanding of the proposal the different weighting of potential claims simply necessitated the need for robust scheme provisions dealing with the valuation of individual claims. Pill LJ concurring with Chadwick LJ also added that a 'broad view' should be taken of the word 'class'.

[1]   *Hawk* case [2001] EWCA Civ 241, [2001] 2 BCLC 480 at [23] (Chadwick LJ).

7.53 In *Re Equitable Life Assurance Society*[1], the court held that the test is not whether the relevant class can consult together, but whether their rights are sufficiently similar to justify them voting in a single class. The earlier judgment of Neuberger J in *Re Anglo American Insurance Ltd*[2] suggests that the similarity or community of rights resulting in a specific class will be a question of degree in each case based on the specific facts which the court should construe carefully.

[1]   [2002] EWHC 140 (Ch), [2002] 2 BCLC 510.
[2]   [2001] 1 BCLC 755.

7.54 In the *Hawk* case Chadwick LJ does appear to put a gloss on the Sovereign test by articulating that the answer to the question of whether creditor's rights are sufficiently similar as to make it possible for them to consult together with a view to their common interest, depended in part on an analysis of the rights which are to be released or varied under the scheme and the new rights (if any) which the scheme gives to those whose rights are to be released or varied. It is submitted by Sykes[1], that the creditors by virtue of their different claims based on 'unsettled claims', 'outstanding losses' or 'incurred but not reported claims' had different interests especially as a consequence of a valuation of those claims which should have been sufficient to designate them as separate classes. Without such a designation Sykes argues that the protection afforded to minorities with specific interests is eroded because a larger majority within which their votes are pooled will bind them.

[1]   'The Hawk that muddied the waters', vol XII, PLC June 2001, p 6.

7.55 The courts have however continued to support the approach of Chadwick LJ in the *Hawk* case[1] and perhaps most notably Lloyd J in *Re Equitable Life Assurance Society*[2] held that creditors with possible mis-selling claims formed a single class even though technically it might have been possible to divide them into further sub-classes of claimant depending on the strength of their case. Lloyd J held that the strength of a claim was a matter of degree that did not affect the rights of the creditors so significantly that those rights were so dissimilar as to make it impossible for them to consult together with a view to their common interest. Whilst there is some merit in the arguments of Sykes, it seems clear that the courts are equally concerned creditors with substantially the same rights, but with slightly differing perspectives, should not constitute a minority that would form their own class so as to elevate them to the position where they can hold-out and prevent schemes. In order to alleviate concerns regarding minority prejudice the court will inevitably analyse the scheme provisions to establish how such minorities are treated especially in terms of valuation and settlement of their claims. Ultimately, prejudicial and adverse treatment of minorities should be cautioned because unfair shoe-horning of a minority into a single class may unfavourably affect the exercise of the court's inherent jurisdiction to sanction the scheme under the Companies Act 2006, s 899(1).

[1] *Re Telewest Communications plc; Re Telewest Finance (Jersey) Ltd* [2004] EWHC 1466 (Ch), [2005] 1 BCLC 772 and *Re MyTravel Group plc* [2004] EWCA Civ 1734, [2005] 2 BCLC 123.
[2] [2002] EWHC 140 (Ch), [2002] 2 BCLC 510.

7.56 The *Heron* case[1] is also highly instructive because it considers potential conflicts of interest and how this might impact on the composition of classes. In *Heron* certain of the banks that also held bonds had already signed into a consensual restructuring that gave them certain benefits. Other bondholders objected to their involvement in a class of bondholders on the basis that they were receiving benefits not generally available to that class such that there was a conflict of interest and a significant lack of community of interest. The Vice Chancellor Sir Donald Nicholls held that whilst the banks enjoyed a degree of additional benefits above and beyond other bondholders this was indeed a question of degree and on the facts of the instant case it was held that the benefit of security granted to the banks was granted to them in their capacity as banks and in any event was insufficient to disenfranchise those banks from the wider bondholder vote.

[1] *Re Heron International NV* [1994] 1 BCLC 667 Sir Donald Nicholls, VC.

7.57 Schemes are able to bind classes of secured and unsecured or only partially secured creditors, but it is imperative that the secured creditors are properly constituted in a separate class. Such a scheme can also be sanctioned where creditors are to be deprived of their security[1] although in many cases involving secured creditors the secured creditors will participate in the scheme as a separate class and will seek to ensure that their security remains unaffected under the scheme.

[1] *Re Alabama, New Orleans, Texas and Pacific Junction Rly Co* [1891] 1 Ch 213 and *Re Empire Mining Co* (1890) 44 Ch D 402.

7.58 Creditors with no economic interest need not be consulted and no separate meetings need be organised on behalf of such creditors. In *Re Tea Corpn Ltd*[1] it was held that it is not necessary to consult any class of shareholders who have no economic interest in the company. Vaughan

Williams LJ clearly stated that the votes of those who have no genuine economic interest can and should be disregarded:

'... if you have the assent to the scheme of all those classes who have an interest in the matter, you ought not to consider the votes of those classes who have no interest at all. It would be very unfortunate if a different view had to be taken.'[2]

1 [1904] 1 Ch 12.
2 [1904] 1 Ch 12 at 23. Mann J in his obiter judgment in *MyTravel* upheld the authority in *Re Tea Corpn Ltd* (see *Re MyTravel Group plc* [2004] EWHC 2741 (Ch), [2005] 1 WLR 2365, [2005] 2 BCLC 123 and Chapter 5 where the no economic interest is discussed in detail as part of the detailed assessment of valuation methodology in restructurings).

7.59 It is clear from the case the case of *In Re MyTravel Group plc*[1] that an assertion of no 'economic interest' will require the company to present clear and incontrovertible evidence to that effect. Mann J[2] also made it absolutely clear that class-related issues such as determinations as to who would participate in the scheme and be bound by it by reference to the no 'economic interest' argument could be dealt with at the practice directions stage when the company was seeking to convene meetings of shareholders and creditors for the purposes of approving the scheme. However, it is clear from his judgment that if the company is to raise the argument of no economic interest it would need to expressly raise the issue in its application. This would enable those contesting the submissions to deal with the point at the directions hearing and for the judge to deal with such a dispute in his directions. In the instant case he was completely satisfied that the company had raised the issue adequately in its application and that the bondholders having had the opportunity to prepare for the no economic interest submission should have prepared for and dealt with it.

1 [2004] EWHC 2741 (Ch); [2005] 1 WLR 2365; the Court of Appeal's decision is reported under a different case name *Fidelity Investments International plc v MyTravel Group Plc* [2004] EWCA 1734; [2005] 2 LCLC 123.
2 [2005] 1 WLR 2365, 2388–2392.

The directions sought

7.60 The directions sought by the applicant on the Part 8 claim form will normally extend to such matters as the method of giving notices of the meetings, the use of proxies and the form of class meetings. For example the court may direct that meetings are notified by advertisements in national newspapers. It should be noted that under the Companies Act 2006, s 896, the court has a wide discretion to summon the meetings in such manner as it directs.

7.61 Specifically the Practice Statement provides that the court should consider giving directions for the resolution of any creditor issues brought to its attention by the applicant, including directions to postpone a meeting of creditors until resolution of the matter in question. Directions for the resolution of a creditor issue may include orders giving anyone affected by the order a limited time in which to apply to vary or discharge the order. Clearly where a scheme involves some form of debt for equity conversion there will be a meeting of the relevant members or classes of members whose shareholder rights will be impaired by the conversion as well as the relevant creditors whose claims are to be converted into equity.

7.62 Directions on the work to be undertaken by the scheme sponsors to identify all known creditors might be sought as well as directions on the valuation of scheme claims. This valuation methodology may well be incorporated into the proxy forms and a process for valuing unliquidated claims could be subject to an application for directions.

Use of proxies

7.63 The form of proxy forms will usually be exhibited to the witness statement accompanying the Part 8 claim form. Proxies are often bespoke documents that have been created to enable creditors to quantify their claims and those administering the scheme to verify the value of that claim, even if it is a contingent claim. It is efficient to have one form of proxy covering all meetings and most registrars or judges will permit this unless it causes confusion. Specific proxies enabling the creditor to appoint a specific person are to be favoured although general proxies are permissible enabling any person to exercise the vote.

7.64 The form of proxies will usually be endorsed by the registrar or the judge to signify their approval. The registrar or the judge will also usually approve the time for their submission before the meeting although 48 hours prior to the meeting is the norm. The passing of the proxy to the chairman at the meeting will also suffice.

Explanatory statements

7.65 An explanatory notice providing detailed information about the background, reasons, objectives and terms of the scheme must be sent out with the notice to the creditors. In this regard the Companies Act 2006, s 897 restates the Companies Act 1985, s 426 which prescribes the details that must be contained in the statement that accompanies a notice convening a meeting of creditors or members. Specifically, the explanatory statement must explain the effect of the scheme[1]. If the notice summoning the meeting is given by advertisement it is essential that the advertisement states where and how creditors entitled to attend the meeting may obtain copies of such an explanatory statement for free[2]. The relevant creditor or member seeking to obtain the explanatory statement must be entitled (upon making an application in the manner prescribed by the advertisement) to receive a copy of the statement free of charge[3].

[1]   See the Companies Act 2006, s 897(2)(a).
[2]   See the Companies Act 2006, s 897(1)(b).
[3]   See the Companies Act 2006, s 897(4).

7.66 Explanatory statements have become mini industries in themselves, being drafted by a number of professionals including the company's account-ants, legal counsel and financial advisers, and whilst they may be regarded as too long and unwieldy, the need to provide detailed financial information and projections in order for creditors to make an informed decision is necessary. Explanatory statements usually open with a letter from the chairman of the company, but will explain the rationale for the scheme and its effect on creditors. They will also describe the nature of the company's business, set out the terms of the scheme and incorporate schedules of relevant and up-to-date financial information. One may question whether the level of detail provided on the larger schemes is absolutely necessary given the wording in the Companies Act 2006, s 897(2) which simply requires that the statement should explain the 'effect of the compromise or arrangement'.

7.67 Companies Act 2006, s 897(2)(b) also imposes further statutory require-ments on the content of explanatory statements and in particular requires that a statement of any material interests of the directors be included, whether this interest derives from the director's position as a director, creditor, shareholder or otherwise[1]. In addition, the Companies Act 2006, s 897(2)(b)(ii) requires that the effect of the compromise or arrangement on those directors be explained 'insofar as that effect is different from the effect on the like interests of other persons'.

1   See the Companies Act 2006, s 897(2)(b)(i).

7.68 Case law has also imposed further requirements on the content of explanatory statements, and given the need for shareholders and creditors to be able to understand schemes of increasing sophistication, it is not surprising that there is a requirement for statements to use language that enables the ordinary person unfamiliar with such matters to be able to exercise proper judgment. In *Re Heron International NV*[1] the Vice-Chancellor Sir Donald Nicholls, stated that the test was whether the contents of the explanatory statement were sufficient to enable the general body of creditors 'to reach a sensible decision on the pros and cons of the schemes(s)'.

1   [1994] 1 BCLC 667.

7.69 Clarity is an important point because in the case *Re Dorman Long & Co Ltd*[1] the court held that the explanatory statement was misleading and ordered the creditors' meetings to be reconvened and an adequate explanatory statement (properly explaining the effects of the scheme) to be resubmitted. In order to avoid the scheme being deemed to be misleading, and to meet the requirement of the court that the statement should contain all information reasonably necessary to enable the recipients to determine how to vote, explanatory statements have inevitably become longer. The increasing length of explanatory statements is also an inevitable result of the fact that most interested parties will now vote by proxy as opposed to attending a meeting and voting in person.

1   [1934] Ch 635.

7.70 The courts have repeatedly stressed the importance of a full disclosure of all known information such that interested parties vote on the basis of accurate and up-to-date information[1], for example, inadequate disclosure of matters relating to values of assets and shares has led to scheme meetings being reconvened[2]. Any material changes in the facts, especially the nature of the director's interests that affect the likely voting position of a creditor, should be disclosed, even if this information only transpired or otherwise became known after the explanatory statement was circulated[3]. Accuracy of information at the time of the meeting has been the primary concern of the courts.

[1]   See *Re Old Silkstone Colleries Ltd* [1954] Ch 169, [1954] 1 All ER 68 and the judgment of Slade J in *Re Jessel Trust* [1985] BCLC 119.
[2]   See the persuasive decision of the Australian courts in *Phosphate Co-operative Co of Australia v Shears* (1988) 14 ACLR 323.
[3]   See the judgment of *Re MB Group Ltd* [1989] BCLC 672.

7.71 In what is probably the leading case on the content and detail of statutory statements the Vice Chancellor Sir Donald Nicholls in *Re Heron International NV*[1] provided more clarity on how statements should explain the commercial effects that the scheme would have on a creditor. Essentially, those submitting explanatory statements need to take all reasonable steps to provide up-to-date financial information that explains to the creditor what he could reasonably be expected to recover under the scheme as opposed to his recoveries in a liquidation. Sections of an explanatory statement can be cursory, but must not in any event cause material prejudice to creditors. Courts may question whether the provision of more detailed information, in places, would achieve a different result, but on the facts of the instant case he was satisfied that this was not the case. The Vice Chancellor also confirmed that an explanatory statement will still be valid even if certain recipients of it have more information than others because of the quality of their professional advice or because of their proximity to the restructuring or prior involvement in it.

[1]   [1994] 1 BCLC 667.

The rights of debenture holders

7.72 In circumstances where the scheme affects the rights of debenture holders of the company, it should also be noted that the Companies Act 2006, s 897(3) requires that the statement must give the same explanation as respects the trustees of any deed for securing the issue of the debentures as it is required to give as respects the company's directors.

Navigating the uncertainty of the timetable

7.73 Schemes are sometimes perceived rather negatively due to the uncertainty of the timetable and the fact that the courts will only hear scheme petitions during the vacation if there are exceptional circumstances and counsel can certify that the matter is urgent. However, the courts have proven extremely helpful and flexible and will invariably agree a timeline or process with the company's counsel to provide a degree of certainty around the timetable. In any event further directions on timing can always be sought. In addition, the New Practice Directions which came into force on 1 October 2007 relating to scheme applications have streamlined the overall process.

The hearing of the Part 8 claim form for convening the meetings

7.74 The hearing of the claim form for convening the meetings is heard in chambers on an ex parte basis usually with only the company in attendance, unless of course the application has been made by a creditor, in which case the company will attend as the respondent. The company usually attends court with a draft order to be approved by the judge or registrar. If satisfied with the application the judge or registrar will initial the explanatory statement and proxy forms and will make the order in the form of the draft and will give directions for the subsequent sanction hearing.

7.75 It should be noted that the court does have an inherent jurisdiction to convene scheme meetings and in *Re Savoy Hotel Ltd*[1] it was held that the court should refrain from convening the meeting if it was clear that the holders of a majority of the votes were opposed to the scheme and that the convening of the meetings would serve no useful purpose.

1   [1981] Ch 351, [1981] 3 All ER 646.

Approval meetings

7.76 Companies Act 2006, s 899 requires that the scheme be approved by a majority in number representing 75% in value of the creditors or class of creditors at the meeting(s) summoned pursuant to the Companies Act 2006, s 896. The meetings should be held at a time and a place that is convenient to creditors which depending on the balance of convenience for the majority of creditors may be outside the UK[1]. The leading case on the conduct of scheme meetings is *Carruth v Imperial Chemical Industries Ltd*[2] and the judgment of Lord Russell is particularly helpful. The position of the courts is that the conduct of scheme meetings lies entirely in the hands of those who are present and constitute the meeting and that it therefore:

> '... rests with the meeting to decide whether notices, resolutions minutes, accounts, and such like, shall be read to the meeting or taken as read; whether representatives of the Press, or any other persons not qualified to be summoned to the meeting shall be permitted to be present, or, if present, shall be permitted to remain; whether and when discussion shall be terminated and a vote taken; whether the meeting shall be adjourned. In all these matters, and they are only instances, the meeting decides, and, if necessary, a vote must be taken to ascertain the wishes of the majority. If no objection is taken by any constituent of the meeting, the meeting must be taken to be assenting to the course adopted. It is not a case, as was suggested in argument, of those present at a meeting waiving rights of those who have elected not to attend; it is a case of those who have elected to attend regulating the conduct of the meeting, a question in

which those who have chosen to stay away have no voice. I am, however, far from assenting to the view that all that is necessary to constitute a valid resolution by a separate class of shareholders, or a valid separate meeting by a class of shareholders, is that a separate vote of the class be taken, in such circumstances to ensure that all members of the class shall have an opportunity of voting, and that no one who is not a member of the class shall vote. *Prima facie* a separate meeting of a class should be a meeting attended only by members of the class, in order that the discussion of the matters which the meeting has to consider may be carried on unhampered by the presence of others that are not interested to view those matters from the same angle as that of the class, and, if the presence of outsiders was retained in spite of the ascertained wish of the constituents of the meeting for their exclusion, it would not, I think, be possible to say that a separate meeting of the class had been duly held. In the present case, however, the deferred shareholders present, with knowledge that there were many in the room who held no deferred shares, and that it was proposed that no further discussion should take place, but that a vote on the resolution should be taken, raised no objection, or at all events no audible objection, of any kind. In these circumstances, they must be taken to have assented to the meeting being so conducted, and the resolution was accordingly a valid resolution, passed at a meeting of the deferred shareholders, within the meaning of [the articles]. I would like to add that in my opinion the question of convenience or inconvenience should not enter into consideration. Those responsible for convening a series of class meetings may find it more prudent to summon such meetings at longer intervals, or in different rooms, or even on different dates.'

1   See *Re RMCA Reinsurance Ltd* [1994] BCC 378.
2   [1937] AC 707, [1937] 2 All ER 422, HL.

Sanction by the court

7.77 Following the requisitioning of the meetings of the relevant class(es) of creditors and members if necessary, and the passing of the relevant resolutions by the requisite majorities of the relevant classes represented by three fourths in value of creditors in that class present and voting or represented by proxy, the company or creditor (if it initiated and sponsored the scheme) may apply to the court for a sanction of the scheme. Subject to court sanction, the scheme will succeed on this level of approval even though those actually voting in favour at the meeting do not constitute three-fourths of claims in actual value nor constitute a majority in number of the relevant class[1]. The reference to value is of course critical and this is calculated by analysing the relevant quantum of a creditor's claim under the valuation mechanisms incorporated in the scheme. There is of course considerable scope for abuse in terms of valuation methodology (particularly in relation to contingent claims) although discriminatory valuation provisions in the scheme may persuade the court not to grant final sanction[2]. Specifically, it is worth noting that if the court finds it impossible to determine creditor claims and to value them with at least a reasonable degree of certainty, then the court will be unlikely to sanction the scheme[3].

1   *Re Bessemer Steel and Ordnance Co* (1875) 1 Ch D 251.
2   See *Re British Aviation Insurance Co Ltd* [2005] EWHC 1621 (Ch), [2006] 1 BCLC 665.
3   *Re Albert Life Insurance Co* (1871) 6 Ch App 381, 40 LJ Ch 505.

7.78 It is vital that all relevant classes consent, but if sanction is not granted because one class dissents, but that class subsequently assents, the court may sanction the scheme on a further application being submitted to the court without requiring fresh meetings of the various classes that originally assented to the scheme[1].

[1] *Re United Provident Assurance Co Ltd* [1911] WN 40.

7.79 Court sanction of the scheme pursuant to the Companies Act 2006, s 899(1) is the all important second phase of the process and under the New Practice Direction to CPR 49 which became effective in October 2007, applications for the sanction of the court for a compromise or arrangement no longer need to be made by a petition and can be made by means of an amended Part 8 claim form. The claim form must provide all relevant administrative information in relation to the company such as its date of incorporation, its objects, registered number and address, details of its share capital and particulars of the scheme by reference to its objectives and effect. The amended Part 8 claim form should also attach a detailed witness statement from the chairman of the relevant meetings confirming the results of the meetings and any relevant issues relating to the voting and the receipt of proxies. Copies of all proxies, evidence of proof of posting the notices, a copy of the explanatory statement and scheme document and a copy of a draft order sanctioning the scheme should also be attached to the amended Part 8 claim form.

7.80 The sanction of the court is not a formality[1] and dissenting creditors can raise objections at the sanction hearing as to why the scheme should not be sanctioned. The court 's function is not merely to rubber-stamp the scheme and to provide a cursory check that the majority have been acting *bona fide*[2], although the conduct of those attending the meeting will of course be very relevant. The court's sanctioning discretion is unfettered, but in exercising this discretion the court will take into account whether all of the statutory conditions under the Companies Act 2006, ss 895–900 have been observed[3] and in particular whether the meetings were properly convened and con-ducted, whether the class summoned to the meeting was fairly represented by those who attended[4] and those voting acted legitimately and in a *bona fide* manner without coercing a minority in order to promote interests that are adverse to the class that they purport to represent[5]. The final consideration is whether the arrangement could be considered by an intelligent and honest businessman acting in his own interest to be one which he could reasonably approve[6].

[1] See the judgment of Lord Hoffmann in the Privy Council in *Kempe v Ambassador Insurance Co* [1998] 1 WLR 271 at 276.
[2] Re *English, Scottish and Australian Chartered Bank* [1893] 3 Ch 385.
[3] *Re Dorman, Long & Co Ltd* [1934] Ch 635.
[4] Bowen LJ in *Re Alabama, New Orleans, Texas and Pacific Junction Rly Co* [1891] 1 Ch 213 at 245 commented that it would be 'most unjust to bind creditors or classes of creditors by three fourths in value of those who attend a particular meeting, unless you have secured that the meeting shall adequately represent the entire body'.
[5] See *Re Wedgwood Coal and Iron Co* (1877) 6 Ch D 627 and *Re British Aviation Insurance Co Ltd* [2005] EWHC 1621 (Ch), [2006] 1 BCLC 665 for a modern elucidation of these principles.

⁶ Lindley LJ in *Re Alabama, New Orleans, Texas and Pacific Junction Rly Co* [1891] 1 Ch 213 at 239.

7.81 In challenging a scheme at the sanction stage on the basis that the meetings were improperly conducted and that votes were improperly recorded by the chairman of the meeting, Lewison J in *Re Linton Park plc*[1] held that those mounting the challenge will need to present cogent evidence to the court to demonstrate that there had been a failure to comply with the statutory requirements. Equally an allegation that a member of a class had a collateral interest that should result in it being disenfranchised on procedural grounds was serious and again strong, cogent evidence would need to be presented. Unless evidence of the motives and interests of all those voting in a class were considered, it was impossible for the court to conclude that the financial interests of one class member had influenced the vote.

[1] [2005] All ER (D) 174 (Nov).

7.82 Following the issue of the Practice Statement on 15 April 2002 by the Chancery Division of the High Court, it will be far more difficult to make a submission that the classes were improperly constituted because this issue is considered in far more detail at the originating stage and in all likelihood will have already been considered by the same judge now sanctioning the scheme. The judge will inevitably question why those challenging the composition of the classes did not do so at an earlier stage given the provisions of the Practice Direction which require interested parties to bring to the attention of the court at the earliest possible opportunity, any issues which may arise relating to the constitution of meetings of creditors or which may effect the conduct of those meetings.

7.83 This practice was also endorsed by the first instance decision of Mann J in relation to an assertion that any relevant creditor had no 'economic interest' so as to enable those proposing a scheme to dispense with the participation of such a creditor in it. It is clear from the case that an assertion of no 'economic interest' will require the company to present clear and incontrovertible evidence to that effect[1]. Mann J also made it absolutely clear that class-related issues such as determinations as to who would participate in the scheme and be bound by it by reference to the no 'economic interest' argument could be dealt with at the practice directions stage when the company was seeking to convene meetings of shareholders and creditors for the purposes of approving the scheme. However, it is clear from his judgment that if the company is to raise the argument of no economic interest it would need to expressly raise the issue in its application. This would enable those contesting the submissions to deal with the point at the directions hearing and for the judge to deal with such a dispute in his directions. In the instant case he was completely satisfied that the company had raised the issue adequately in its application and that the bondholders having had the opportunity to prepare for the no economic interest submission should have prepared for and dealt with it.

[1] In the hearing before Mann J this evidence was constituted by a detailed witness statement from Miss Margaret Mills a partner at Ernst & Young who made detailed reference to a complex liquidation model and a witness statement from Mr Peter McHugh the CEO of My Travel.

7.84 The question of whether a class was properly represented arose in the case of *Re Cape plc*[1] where David Richards J had to consider the impact of a low turnout of creditors at the meetings. The judge held that it was appropriate to rely on aggregate voting figures across the classes and whilst the aggregate figure was only 25% of claimants voting as opposed to 41% in the *Re Osiris Insurance* case and about 50% of total claims in *Re British Aviation Insurance*, he did not believe that this should undermine the validity of the scheme[2]. He acknowledged that there was likely to be a lower turnout when the claimants were principally 'future claimants', but he was comforted by the fact that the separate class of future claimants had overwhelmingly voted in support of the scheme[3]. It was also relevant on the facts of the case that all reasonable steps had been taken to simplify the explanation of the scheme and the proxies and that those promoting the scheme had not misled the creditors and on the contrary had taken significant steps to assist the creditors in reaching a decision[4]. Equally, there had been no organised objections to the scheme by a dissentient minority[5].

[1]   [2006] EWHC 1446 (Ch), 150 Sol Jo LB 858.
[2]   [2006] EWHC 1446 (Ch), 150 Sol Jo LB 858 at [26].
[3]   [2006] EWHC 1446 (Ch), 150 Sol Jo LB 858 at [27].
[4]   [2006] EWHC 1446 (Ch), 150 Sol Jo LB 858 at [28].
[5]   [2006] EWHC 1446 (Ch), 150 Sol Jo LB 858 at [29].

7.85 The question of whether the scheme is one that ought to be reasonably approved is a more unpredictable one and whilst there will inevitably be disadvantages in any scheme for a minority, the courts in responding to submissions of disadvantage have responded by focusing firstly on whether the class has been properly consulted and secondly whether the advantages to the majority acting reasonably and bona fide in supporting the scheme outweigh these disadvantages[1]. It is unlikely that in any scheme where the creditors interested in the company's property have voted emphatically in its favour, that the courts will allow a creditor to successfully oppose its sanction. However, where a class member has peculiar or extraneous motivations (as distinct from different rights of the type considered in the application of the class rules) the Australian courts have indicated that they will withhold approval. In *Re Chevron (Sydney) Ltd*[2] Adams J articulated the principle as follows:

> 'In so far as members of a class have in fact voted for a scheme not because it benefits them as members of the class, but because it gives them benefits in some other capacity, their votes would of course not reflect the views of the class *as such* although they are counted for the purposes of determining whether the statutory majority has been obtained at the meeting of the class.'

[1]   See *Re British Aviation Insurance Co Ltd* [2005] EWHC 1621 (Ch), [2006] 1 BCLC 665 and *Re Equitable Life Assurance Society* [2002] EWHC 140 (Ch), [2002] 2 BCLC 510.
[2]   [1963] VR 249.

7.86 In *Re British Aviation Insurance Co Ltd*[1], whilst the court accepted the principle in *Re Dorman, Long & Co Ltd*[2] that the courts should not substitute their own views for those of the meeting in determining whether the scheme is one that ought to be reasonably approved, Lewison J did accept that the conduct of reinsurers in supporting a scheme at the expense of certain insured parties was unreasonable because they had a clear motivation in ascribing very low values to claims of the insured parties so as to limit their reinsurance liabilities. It was also relevant that certain shareholders of the company would receive a substantial return of capital if the scheme succeeded against the interests of the insured parties who had direct claims against a solvent insurer. In essence a scheme that purported to return capital to shareholders in a solvent company in preference to satisfying the legitimate claims of creditors would not be sanctioned. This is also consistent with the principle noted by Chadwick LJ in the earlier case of *Re BTR plc*[3] when he indicated that the court would not sanction a scheme where those supporting it were promoting their own special interests, which were different from other independent and objective stakeholders in the same class.

1   [2005] EWHC 1621 (Ch), [2006] 1 BCLC 665.
2   [1934] Ch 635.
3   [2000] 1 BCLC 740, 747, CA.

7.87 In the case of *Re Home Insurance Co*[1], the court was invited by those challenging the scheme to adjourn its sanction of the scheme until the courts in another jurisdiction hearing matters related to the scheme had issued its judgment. Mann J held that the doctrine of comity was not relevant in such a case and that the scheme should be sanctioned because there was 'no material sense in which the activities which each court is conducting in its own jurisdiction can be said to trespass upon, or conflict with, the activities of the other'[2]. He confirmed that the obligation of the English courts was to only consider the schemes and their validity from the perspective of English law and that parallel proceedings in another jurisdiction on associated matters could not justify a deviation from this approach.

1   [2005] EWHC 2485 (Ch), [2006] 2 BCLC 476.
2   [2005] EWHC 2485 (Ch), [2006] 2 BCLC 476 at [15].

7.88 In rare cases the court may attach conditions to its sanction if it is not completely satisfied with the substance of the scheme or the procedures that led to the application for sanction. The court may make minor changes to the scheme[1] (without altering its substance)[2] or may require certain parties (particularly those constituting a majority) to provide the court with certain undertakings. In *Re Cape plc*[3] the court also imposed a condition that special shares be issued to a trustee of future claimants and that such trustee be able to appoint two directors with exclusive voting rights on certain key issues, and a prohibition on the company paying dividends in order to protect future creditors who may in the future suffer from asbestosis[4].

1   *Re Osiris Insurance Ltd* [1999] 1 BCLC 182.
2   *Re Hawk Insurance Co Ltd* [2001] EWCA Civ 241, [2001] 2 BCLC 480 at [52], per Chadwick LJ.
3   [2006] EWHC 1446 (Ch), 150 Sol Jo LB 858.
4   [2006] EWHC 1446 (Ch), 150 Sol Jo LB 858 at [33]–[34].

Effect of the order

7.89 Although the court's order is expressed to be binding on all relevant creditors in the relevant classes[1], it will not have any effect until a copy is filed with the registrar of companies[2]. In *Re Garner's Motors Ltd*[3] it was held that the scheme does not operate as an agreement between the parties affected, but that it has binding force by virtue of statute once sanction has been made and a copy of the order is filed with the registrar.

1   Companies Act 2006, s 899(3).
2   Companies Act 2006, s 899(4).
3   [1937] Ch 594, [1937] 1 All ER 671.

7.90   Once the scheme is validly existing it cannot subsequently be challenged or amended even by the agreement of the other affected parties and again this is due to the fact that the scheme derives its binding force by operation of statute[1]. The only exceptions to this used to be in relation to schemes procured pursuant to a fraud[2] or some other defect or irregularity in obtaining the court's sanction[3], but in *Re Cape plc*[4] David Richards J determined that the court has jurisdiction to sanction a scheme containing provisions that permitted limited amendments without the court's involvement providing that it is still fair and reasonable to sanction the scheme[5]. Given the likely longevity of the scheme over a 40–50 year period and the likely effect of legal, medical and financial changes that could impact the scheme, he resolved that it was essential or at least highly desirable to permit limited amendment provisions[6]. As such he commented that, 'it would be impracticable for a new scheme of arrangement to be proposed each time an amendment was required. In this case, arrangements, which did not allow amendments in such circumstances, could themselves be regarded as unfair'[7]. In order to protect future creditors from the effect of the amendment provisions in the scheme, the court imposed a number of conditions on the scheme which included inter alia restrictions on the declaration of dividends and board representatives with exclusive voting control on certain key issues. The court also imposed conditions to protect creditors[8].

1   This will be the case even if there has been a breach of company law as a result of the implementation of the scheme, see *British and Commonwealth Holdings v Barclays Bank plc* [1996] 1 All ER 381, [1996] 1 WLR 1.
2   *Soden v British and Commonwealth Holdings plc* [1995] 1 BCLC 686 at 700.
3   *Fletcher v Royal Automobile Club* [2000] 1 BCLC 331. The fraud may result in the scheme being completely unravelled unless it would have still been sanctioned irrespective of the fraud.
4   [2006] EWHC 1446 (Ch), 150 Sol Jo LB 858.
5   [2006] EWHC 1446 (Ch), 150 Sol Jo LB 858 at [30].
6   [2006] EWHC 1446 (Ch), 150 Sol Jo LB 858 at [31].
7   [2006] EWHC 1446 (Ch), 150 Sol Jo LB 858 at [32].
8   [2006] EWHC 1446 (Ch), 150 Sol Jo LB 858 at [33]–[34].

Examples of recent restructurings where a combination of formal and informal processes have been used

7.91   Many of the recent large restructurings, particularly those that have involved a debt for equity swap, have been implemented by a combination of formal and informal restructuring processes.

7.92 *Marconi plc and Marconi Corporation plc*: With certain specified exceptions, the Marconi schemes compromised all creditors. As not all of the creditors were known despite an extensive advertising strategy, it would not have been possible to effect this restructuring through a contractual procedure. Schemes of arrangement were used because this enabled the two Marconi companies to compromise unknown creditors, and a bar date was put into the schemes to ensure a drop dead date after which no further claims could be made.

7.93 One of the key advantages of the Marconi scheme was that it would bind scheme creditors regardless of whether their claims were present or future, actual or contingent, agreed or disputed and regardless of whether the creditors received 'actual' notice of the meeting. It also avoided certain cross defaults and insolvency defaults under, among other things, key customer and supplier contracts and licences that might have been triggered under certain other restructuring alternatives and ultimately avoided the potential damage to the business that might be potentially caused as a result of 'insolvency stigma' associated with formal proceedings under the Insolvency Act 1986.

7.94 The urgency of the restructuring and its implementation through the scheme also enabled certain reporting requirements under the UK Listing Authority's Listing Rules to be dispensed with. As a final point the scheme benefited from the US Securities Act of 1933, s 3(a)(10), which provides an exemption from the requirement to file a registration statement with the US Securities and Exchange Commission to effect the restructuring.

7.95 *Telewest Communications plc*: The Telewest restructuring involved a combination of formal and informal restructuring arrangements. Its senior secured bank debt was restructured contractually, but its high-yield bond debt was widely held, mainly in the US and unanimous consents were impossible to procure. Therefore the debt owing to bondholders and former bondholders was restructured formally using a scheme of arrangement under the Companies Act 1985. All other unsecured creditors were left in place (although as a result of a corporate restructuring, agreements with Telewest Communications plc were for the most part novated to another Telewest entity).

7.96 *British Energy Group plc and British Energy Holdings plc*: Part of the British Energy restructuring involved its main creditors reaching a contractual agreement on the terms of a debt for equity swap. However, in order to implement this restructuring and to bind dissentient minorities a scheme of arrangement was necessary to also bind all shareholders and bondholders.

7.97 *Queens Moat Houses plc*: Contractual agreements were reached with the various levels of debt, which were ultimately then capable of being refinanced or were purchased in their entirety by a third party. A shareholders' scheme of arrangement was used to complete the restructuring to ensure that the third party purchaser could acquire 100% ownership of the equity. If the shareholders had not voted in favour of the scheme, control would otherwise have been achieved by a business transfer agreement, the terms of which had been agreed and which the company was obliged to implement if the scheme had failed.

7.98 *MyTravel Group plc*: MyTravel was ultimately restructured contractually, but the threat of a restructuring using a scheme of arrangement that could be implemented without the consent of certain unsecured creditors enabled the deal to be done outside of a statutory restructuring procedure. Before launching a scheme of arrangement, MyTravel had been unable to reach an agreement with its bondholders, who would have been subordinated on a liquidation of MyTravel, as to the percentage of shares they would receive on a debt for equity swap. MyTravel commenced proceedings to implement a scheme of arrangement and during the course of those proceedings (before the scheme had become effective) reached an agreement with the bondholders, which allowed a deal to be implemented contractually.

G COMPARISON OF SCHEMES WITH CVAS

7.99 A company voluntary arrangement ('CVA') is a rescue procedure for a company in financial difficulties. A CVA is defined as 'a compromise or other arrangement' with creditors under Part I of the Insolvency Act 1986. A CVA is implemented under the supervision of an insolvency practitioner. The insolvency practitioner is known as the nominee before the proposals are implemented and as the supervisor afterwards. The arrangement will be binding on creditors (if the relevant majorities vote in favour of the proposals at properly convened meetings of creditors) and shareholders of the company.

7.100 It is arguable that schemes have a slightly broader reach in that jurisdiction can extend to foreign companies if they are a company which can be wound up under the Insolvency Act 1986 and there is a 'sufficient connection' to the United Kingdom. By way of contrast a CVA can only be used in relation to companies incorporated in the European Economic Area if the CVA is to be a main proceeding, as a CVA cannot be a secondary proceeding.

7.101 A CVA may involve less court involvement and there are certainly less documents to file at the court. Theoretically, this should mean that CVAs would be a popular, low cost option, however, a nominee (who must be a licensed insolvency practitioner) must still submit a report to court stating whether the meetings of creditors should be convened and a CVA can still be challenged on grounds of unfair prejudice or material irregularity following the CVA meetings. Schemes have become progressively more efficient as a process however and the Practice Statement of 15 April 2002[1] on the procedure to be followed with respect to schemes and the new procedure for initiating schemes set out in paragraph 7 of the New Practice Direction to CPR 49 which came into force on 1 October 2007, have assisted those promoting schemes significantly and have streamlined the court's involvement. All 'creditor issues' are now drawn to the attention of the court at the hearing to convene the scheme meetings.

[1]   *Practice Statement (companies: schemes of arrangement)* [2002] 3 All ER 96, [2002] 1 WLR 1345.

7.102 A scheme also has the potential advantage of being able to bind secured creditors providing that the secured creditors who are likely to be a separate class support the scheme. A CVA however is unable to bind any secured or preferential creditors without their consent.

7.103 In terms of voting, scheme creditors vote by reference to their class and despite the clarifications on class composition provided by the courts this is still a complex issue which can be subject to considerable court scrutiny at the first hearing. However, the modern practice of determining the classes at the first hearing and retaining the same judge throughout the scheme process has significantly reduced the prospect and indeed the costs of amendments to the scheme after documents have been prepared and filed. Creditors having 75% or more of the value of the claims in each class must also support the scheme. The potential inefficiencies outlined with respect to schemes (although minimised under current practice) are less of an issue with respect to CVAs as there is less pressure to formulate formal classes. The potential issue however with a CVA is that the resolution will be invalid if more than 50% of unconnected creditors vote against it.

7.104 In terms of a moratorium, case law supports the proposition that the courts will typically exercise their discretion to stay proceedings against the company when requested. In practice the court may even grant a stay before the first hearing where preparations to launch the scheme were advanced. With reference to a moratorium in a CVA a moratorium only applies to small companies although the courts may be likely to exercise discretion in the same way as schemes.

7.105 CVAs and schemes are indistinguishable in terms of the creditors that can be bound and as per schemes creditors can be bound now under a CVA (following the Insolvency Act 2000) irrespective of notice of the procedure. The only potential deficiency with a CVA is that secured and preferential creditors can never be bound without their consent and this restriction arguably does not apply to schemes.

7.106 Schemes and CVAs are both subject to challenges, but in different ways. A scheme can be challenged on the basis of the incorrect compositions of classes and that it is unfair or has a serious procedural defect, whereas a CVA can be challenged on the basis of a material irregularity and unfair prejudice.

7.107 It is becoming increasingly clear given the procedural improvements to CVAs introduced by the Insolvency Act 1986 that both procedures can be used to gain a tactical advantage depending on the circumstances. In any given case it will however be critical for creditors to understand the differences between CVAs and schemes so that they choose the correct procedure.

Chapter 8

THE IMPACT OF THE PENSIONS ACT 2004 ON RESTRUCTURINGS

A   Introduction
B   Why have pensions become so important in restructurings?
C   The importance of calculating the deficit
D   The moral hazard provisions
E   TPR Clearance statements
F   Restructurings involving multi-employer schemes
G   The impact of the Pensions legislation on restructurings and insolvencies
H   Conclusion

A INTRODUCTION

8.1 The impact of the Pensions Act 2004 on UK companies (and others operating in the UK or with a connection to a UK employer) is far reaching. The Pensions Act 2004 touches on many aspects of pensions law, but given the scope of the Pensions Act 2004 and the implications for corporate activity it has inevitably had a significant effect on corporate restructurings. One of the most controversial changes contained in the Pensions Act 2004 are the 'moral hazard' provisions. Since they came into force in April 2005, they have enabled the new Pensions Regulator ('tPR') to require certain third parties that are associated or connected with a company whose defined benefits pension scheme is under-funded to contribute to that scheme. TPR replaced the previous regulator the Occupational Pensions Regulatory Authority.

8.2 The Pensions Act 2004 sets specific objectives for tPR, namely:

(a)   to protect the benefits of members of defined benefit work-based pension schemes;
(b)   to resolve the risk of situations arising that may lead to claims for compensation from the Pension Protection Fund ('PPF');
(c)   to promote good administration of defined benefit work-based pension schemes.

8.3 Pension trustees, tPR and the PPF[1] are now key players in restructurings. One of tPR's initial goals was that pension trustees should start acting like any large unsecured creditor; specifically like a bank and experience has shown that they have done exactly that. This chapter also considers some of the solutions agreed by pension trustees to address pension deficit issues in restructurings.

[1]   The role of the PPF is considered in more detail in this chapter.

B WHY HAVE PENSIONS BECOME SO IMPORTANT IN RESTRUCTURINGS?

8.4 It is worth considering why pensions have become so important, given that in the last wave of restructurings around 2000–2002 they were scarcely mentioned. By way of background, it is only defined benefit pension schemes that are relevant to this chapter. Defined benefit schemes are those including a defined benefit promise – eg a pension based on a fraction of final salary or a career average (CARE) scheme. Defined contribution schemes (or money purchase schemes) – ie those with only defined contribution benefits – only pay out whatever the accumulated contributions allow and do not have deficits, save in unusual circumstances[1].

---

[1]   It can be a difficult question as to when benefits are 'defined contribution' or 'defined benefit'. See the (confusing) decision of the Court of Appeal in *Aon Trust Corpn Ltd v KPMG (a firm)* [2005] EWCA Civ 1004, [2006] 1 All ER 238, [2006] 1 WLR 97.

8.5 Primarily the change is down to three reasons. First, deficits grew enormously because of falling equity markets, low interest rates, declining bond yields and increased longevity of members. If equity prices are at high levels, and bond yields are favourable this will help shrink the deficits. However, deficits are still substantial, not least because of the increased longevity. Some of the so-called 'death tables' estimate that the average 40 year old woman will live to 100.

8.6 Another key reason for the elevated importance of pension liabilities in restructurings is the actual development of pensions legislation itself. Statute now creates legally enforceable debt obligations on the employers in relation to a relevant defined benefit scheme. As we will see in this chapter, the scheme-specific funding requirements under the Pensions Act 2004 have created an additional financial burden for employers/companies.

8.7 In addition, the methodology for calculating the statutory debt payable under the Pensions Act 1995, s 75 by an employer to a scheme in an insolvency (and various other circumstances) has dramatically changed. The old regulations calculated this debt using the Minimum Funding Requirement ('MFR') under the Pensions Act 1995. This formula assumed comparatively high levels of investment growth and interest rates, plus a modest mortality rate. Therefore, the MFR debt was generally small and often nil.

8.8 The situation has changed fundamentally with the implementation of the Pensions Act 2004, the introduction of the PPF and the new regulations regarding the debt on the employers on scheme wind-up or employer insolvency[1]. Under the changed regulations, the statutory section 75 debt is now calculated on a 'buy out bases'[2]. This is driven by the amount that an insurance company would charge to provide a policy securing the defined benefits in question. As one would expect, insurance companies typically apply conservative assumptions ie smaller asset growth rates and longer death tables. With the calculations running over decades, small changes make huge differences and the result can be an eye wateringly higher number. By way of example, the MFR deficiency on the Turner & Newall scheme was £19m in 2005 whereas the buy out debt was £850m ie over 40 times more[3]. The need to deal with such a deficit can obviously be a precursor for a major balance sheet restructuring.

[1]   See the Occupational Pension Schemes (Employer Debt) Regulations 2005, SI 2005/678, as amended. For previous regulations, see the Occupational Pension Schemes (Winding Up and Deficiency on Winding Up etc) (Amendment) Regulations 2004, SI 2004/403 and the Occupational Pension Schemes (Winding Up Deficiency on Winding Up and Transfer Values) (Amendment) Regulations 2005, SI 2005/72. For a more detailed history, see Chapter 25 of Pollard 'Corporate Insolvency: Employment and Pension Rights' (Tottel, 2007).

[2]   Also known as the section 75 debt.

[3]   Based on figures given in *Re T&N Ltd* [2004] EWHC 1680 (Ch), [2004] OPLR 343.

8.9   Third and finally, as mentioned above, the Pensions Act 2004 has brought in new 'moral hazard' provisions – financial support directions and contribution notices. These provisions are unprecedented in the UK and they have greatly widened the scope of who can be made liable for the pension deficit. As well as 'piercing the corporate veil' so that potentially any company in a group can be held liable, tPR can also potentially fix directors, shareholders, purchasers and even lenders with the pensions deficit. Whilst not an automatic liability and despite the fact that certain conditions must be met, plainly the risk of being liable for a large deficit claim is a serious issue for the various stakeholders in a restructuring and any purchaser of assets from a distressed company.

8.10   As we shall see, tPR has a statutory power to grant advance Clearance in relation to these moral hazard powers.

C   THE IMPORTANCE OF CALCULATING THE DEFICIT

Introduction

8.11   The Pensions Act 2004 vested in trustees and ultimately tPR wide-ranging powers to achieve the various objectives of the Pensions Act 2004 referred to above. What this means in reality is that the new pensions regime has created an extensive armoury of processes, powers and procedures to limit, control and reduce 'deficits' and to ensure that defined benefit schemes are properly funded and adequately supported. In this regard the bases for calculating a 'deficit' is all important:

(i)   For example (and as we will see in this section), the establishment of a 'statutory funding objective' for a scheme under the new legislation is designed to achieve an appropriate level of employer support and the identification of a possible '*deficit*' that might need to be subject to a recovery plan. As a result it is not always possible to restructure a company without simultaneously restructuring its defined benefit scheme.

(ii)   Equally, the statutory Clearance procedure by which tPR can give a Clearance statement to those persons concerned in a corporate transaction (including in particular restructuring transactions), is only applicable where there is a *'deficit'*. The guidance issued by tPR on when it will grant Clearance in relation to the moral hazard powers indicates that one test for when Clearance should be considered (it is a voluntary procedure) is whether or not the transaction in question will result in a material adverse change in the position of the pension scheme (or the support for it from the employers). The determination of financially detrimental may depend on whether there is a deficit on various measures.

8.12 Therefore, the pivotal question, (i) whenever the appropriate level of contributions or scheme funding is being considered, (ii) in any restructuring scenario when Clearance is desired, (iii) where the affordability of a defined benefit scheme is under scrutiny, or (iv) in any case where a balance sheet restructuring is being contemplated, is what is the 'deficit' and more specifically how and on what bases should it be calculated.

8.13 Determining the deficit is not straightforward and there are a number of bases upon which this could be done. In this regard it is interesting that in the revised Guidance from tPR published in March 2008 (the 'Guidance')[1], tPR expressly states that an employer-related event[2] will only be a Type A event (effectively requiring Clearance from tPR) if the scheme[3] has a relevant deficit. The question therefore is how do employers, financiers, pension trustees and other interested stakeholders assess whether there is a deficit, and on what bases is such a deficit to be calculated? The bases used to measure the deficit have been an issue of considerable debate and consultation. Under the original 2005 Guidance, tPR when applying the appropriate bases for calculating a deficit had drawn a distinction between circumstances where the trustees and indeed tPR have a duty to protect all pension benefits such as when the employer is on the cusp of insolvency, and scenarios where less protection of the pension benefits is required.

[1]   The revised Guidance published in March 2008 replaces the original April 2005 guidance and can be found at www.thepensionsregulator.gov.uk/guidance/Clearance/index.aspx. A consultation relating to the new Guidance was launched in August 2007 with submissions required by 30 October 2007.
[2]   An employer-related event: is an event in respect of an employer. See also paragraphs 31 to 62 of the Guidance. In addition, an 'employer' for these purposes is, as the context requires, an employer of persons in the description of employment to which the scheme in question relates.
[3]   A Scheme is, for the purpose of the Guidance and contribution notices and financial support directions, an occupational pension scheme, but does not include a scheme that only provides money purchase benefits.

8.14 The 2008 Guidance is now much more risk-based and far less principles-based and provides that in most cases the appropriate relevant deficit will be measured on the higher of:

1   FRS 17/IAS 19 bases;
2   the s 179 bases;

3   the bases of the 'technical provisions'; and
4   the 'ongoing bases'.

These measurements are each considered in turn.

1 FRS 17/IAS 19 as bases of calculating the deficit

8.15 In the current Guidance FRS 17/IAS 19 are described as the current accounting standards for retirement benefits, the primary objective of which is to ensure that a company's statutory financial statements reflect, at fair value, the assets and liabilities attributable to the employees' retirement benefits entitlement and any related funding. The FRS 17/IAS 19 deficit will be the amount reported in the latest available audited statutory accounts, unless the trustees and the employer agree that an updated amount is appropriate.

8.16 Previously, the 2005 guidance had indicated that in a risk-based scenario where it is unnecessary to protect all pension benefits, a sensible deficit trigger would be most appropriate. This was previously interpreted to mean that a FRS 17 calculation would in all likelihood be the most appropriate calculation[1]. This has now clearly changed under the revised Guidance where the relevant deficit will be the higher of FRS 17/IAS 19, the s 179 bases, technical provisions bases or an ongoing bases.

[1]   Indeed, at paragraphs 33 and 34 of the original 2005 Guidance, tPR stated that, 'We believe using FRS 17 would apply a higher test than protected liabilities (on average) and therefore moves to a full funding level. FRS 17 has the additional advantage of being audited and within a company's balance sheet. We therefore consider that, for the purposes of Clearance applications FRS 17 is currently the best way to measure the pension scheme deficit as a pragmatic, prescribed and readily available solution'.

8.17 The Accounting Standards Board issued Financial Reporting Standard 17 (FRS 17) on retirement benefits in November 2000, and whilst FRS 17 is a UK accounting standard, it has been modified considerably over time to become more consistent with IAS 19[1] which applies to all UK listed companies and those private companies voluntarily opting to adopt IAS[2].

[1]   See 'Amendments to Financial Reporting Standard 17' published by the UK Accounting Standards Board in 2006. The amended FRS 17 which was expressly stated to adopt IAS 19 became effective in May 2007.
[2]   Regulation (EC) No 1606/2002 of the European Parliament and of the Council of 19 July 2002 imposed International Accounting Standards on companies listed on a regulated market in the EU. International Financial Reporting Standards (IFRS) are standards and interpretations adopted by the International Accounting Standards Board (IASB) and are based on the International Accounting Standards. The Secretary of State for Trade and Industry enacted the Companies Act 1985 (International Accounting Standards and Other Accounting Amendments) Regulations 2004, SI 2004/2947 to implement the requirement for UK listed companies to adopt IAS. These Regulations came into force on 12 November 2004 and have applied to financial years beginning on or after 1 January 2005. As a result IAS will now apply to companies whose securities are trading on the Official List and to non-public companies that have opted to use IAS in both their individual and consolidated accounts.

273

8.18 The objective of FRS 17 and IAS 19 is to prescribe the accounting and disclosure for employee benefits (that is, all forms of consideration given by an enterprise in exchange for service rendered by employees). The principle underlying all of the detailed requirements of these standards is that the cost of providing employee benefits should be recognised in the period in which the employee earns the benefit, rather than when it is paid or payable.

8.19 FRS 17 and IAS 19 purport to ensure that all employers' financial statements will have to value all liabilities of a company with respect to employee benefits (and in particular pension obligations) and the assets set aside to meet them in a consistent way. FRS 17 and IAS 19 should create a broadly consistent measure across all corporates subject to the application of sensible mortality assumptions. Under FRS 17 and IAS 19 pension scheme assets are measured using market values[1] and pension scheme liabilities are measured using a projected unit method and discounted at an AA corporate bond rate[2]. The pension scheme surplus or deficit is recognised in full on the balance sheet and the movement in the scheme surplus or deficit is analysed into (i) current and past service costs which are recognised in operating profit, (ii) the interest cost and expected return on assets which are recognised as other finance costs, and (iii) actuarial gains and losses which are recognised in the statement of total recognised gains and losses.

[1]   The asset value of investments is to reflect their 'fair value' at the balance sheet date. Essentially, this means that shares, bonds, gilts, unitised securities and the like are valued at their mid-market price on that day. FRS 17 also contains rules for valuing (at an approximation to market value) assets like real property where the market price is not actually struck every day.

[2]   The distinctive feature of this is how it treats active members (employees who are still in pensionable service). Assumed liabilities to active members are based on their actual period of service (up to the end of the accounting year) and their expected final salaries when their pensionable service ends (typically in eight or ten years' time); it allows for their expected pay rises and promotions in the meantime.

8.20 The International Financial Reporting Interpretations Committee (IFRIC) of the International Accounting Standards Board (IASB) has issued an 'interpretation', IFRIC14, of IAS 19[1] that may lead to significant changes in the accounting treatment of pension scheme surpluses and deficits. In particular, schemes in deficit will become subject to the IAS 19 provision that limits the assets that can appear in company accounts to those that will be available to the company from reduced future contributions (or refunds). The practical consequence is that if a scheme's ongoing funding deficit exceeds its IAS 19 deficit, an employer may have to show the full amount of the funding deficit in its accounts, unless it can show that its future contributions will be reduced.

[1]   See Press release: IFRIC issues interpretation on IAS 19 – defined benefit assets and minimum funding requirements, IASB, 5 July 2007 (www.iasb.org/NR/rdonlyres/696C67B5-E7CB-4703-B63D-B8DCA9FC7014/0/PRIFRIC14.pdf).

8.21 FRS 17/IAS 19 has historically been perceived as advantageous bases because it is a measure that will ultimately reduce the level of distributable reserves on an employer's balance sheet, which in turn will reduce the prospects of a company with a large deficit paying a dividend. FRS 17 and IAS

19 do not however encapsulate the buyout cost of benefits and in that sense there is an inappropriate treatment of pensioners. Similarly, FRS 17/IAS 19 permits the use of a wide range of mortality assumptions that are not required to be disclosed under those accounting rules, but which may have a significant impact on the calculated level of liabilities and therefore give raise to potential inconsistency.

2 Section 179 bases

8.22 The s 179 bases refers to the Pensions Act 2004, s 179 and is the PPF's valuation bases for a scheme's deficit. It is also used for the purpose of calculating the risk-based pension protection levy. In order to be eligible for entry into the PPF, schemes must pay an annual risk-based levy to the PPF. In order to determine how much that levy should be, the PPF requires each scheme to undergo a PPF valuation. This valuation is also known as a section 179 valuation because the Pensions Act 2004, s 179 sets out what such a valuation must entail. Essentially the valuation is based on the estimated cost of securing scheme benefits by applying specific mortality rates and discount rates. The section 179 bases is also used to determine eligibility of a scheme to enter the PPF.

3 Technical provisions as bases for determining a deficit

8.23 A calculation of the deficit based upon the technical provisions is arrived at by applying the methods and assumptions usually agreed by the trustees and employer as set out in Part 3 of the Pensions Act 2004, of the amount needed at a particular time to make provision for the scheme's liabilities. Technical provisions are individual to each scheme. The technical provisions will not yet be available for every scheme. Further information relating to the technical provisions can be found in the scheme funding section on the regulator's website.

8.24 This alternative bases for calculating a scheme deficit is also known as the 'scheme specific funding bases'. This is derived from the Pensions Act 2004, s 222, which introduced a new statutory funding objective, which replaces the MFR. In meeting its statutory funding objective a defined benefit scheme will arrive at an appropriate level of 'scheme specific funding' which will ensure that the scheme has 'sufficient and appropriate assets to cover its technical provisions'[1]. A scheme's technical provisions determine the amount required to provide for its liabilities based on a 'prudent' choice of detailed actuarial and economic assumptions and an appropriate discount rate reflecting the risk of adverse changes. The technical provisions also incorporate mortality tables and demographic assumptions, which must be based on prudent principles having regard to the scheme's own circumstances[2]. In effect the technical provisions therefore result in the calculation of an amount expressed in actuarial terms that equates to the current discounted capital value of the future stream of liabilities[3].

---

[1]   See the Pensions Act 2004, s 222(1).

2   See the Occupational Pension Schemes (Scheme Funding) Regulations 2005, SI 2005/3377, reg 5(4)(a).
3   The actuary must certify the calculation of the technical provisions; see the Pensions Act 2004, s 225.

4   *The ongoing deficit*

8.25   The 'ongoing deficit' is the funding shortfall revealed in the most recent valuation undertaken under the scheme's trust deed and rules. Prior to the introduction of the scheme specific funding regime (see further below), scheme valuations were done in the manner prescribed by the trust deed and rules of each individual scheme (such a valuation would reveal the 'ongoing deficit' of a scheme). The trust deed and rules of a scheme could prescribe eg that the valuation be done by the actuary alone, by the actuary in consultation with the trustees or by the actuary in consultation with the company and the trustees, etc. Therefore, to determine who calculates the ongoing deficit in a particular scheme, it would be necessary to look at the trust deed and rules of that scheme. How the ongoing deficit would be calculated would again depend on the rules of the particular scheme, the approach of the relevant actuary, etc.

8.26   Many schemes will now have done their first valuations under the new scheme specific funding regime as all triennial valuations with an effectual date after 22 September 2005 had to be done under the new regime. As such the 'ongoing deficit' is unlikely to be the relevant deficit for the vast majority of schemes.

How have deficits been calculated and applied in practice?

8.27   The above four bases of calculating a deficit are merely identified as the four options and for Clearance purposes the highest deficit under those options will prevail. In practice, restructuring negotiations between companies, financial institutions and pension trustees relating to the share of security (both pre and post insolvency) and the entitlement to disposal proceeds (both pre and post insolvency), have been based on the level of deficit and have become increasingly protracted resulting in more complex intercreditor arrangements. Recent cases have taken months to resolve and have specifically involved prolonged debates relating to the applicable deficit that should drive these entitlements to security and disposal proceeds in a restructuring.

8.28   These negotiations have increasingly focused on the quality of the employer covenant and the impact of the transaction on the credit of the contributing employers. More recently trustees have increasingly sought to recover proceeds at a level or share that would reduce the much higher section 75 deficit. This is in contrast to the typical aspirations of companies and their bankers who will conduct financial analysis of the company post-transaction to demonstrate that the employer covenant has not been materially impaired and in some cases will be improved, such that the company will be able to continue as a going concern following the execution of the restructuring transactions in question. This analysis is frequently shared with the pension trustees and their financial advisers to justify an offering by the banks and the company of security or disposal proceeds that is consistent with the lower quantum of the FRS 17/IAS 19 deficit. This results in the company making a lower level of contribution to the deficit, thereby increasing its immediate liquidity and ability to make investment and the bank's security position being enhanced and the prospects for facilities being repaid improved. The prospects of convincing the pension trustees that the employer covenant has improved will potentially increase if the employer event or the transaction in question involves a disposal that reduces gearing and also reduces the deficit at least in part.

8.29 The new 2008 Guidance has purported to clarify some of these issues and has provided some insight into likely future practice. The Guidance stipulates that there are certain circumstances where the appropriate measure for the relevant deficit will differ from the higher of the FRS 17/IAS 19, s 179, technical provisions or ongoing deficits calculation[1]. Where the event is 'significantly detrimental' to the scheme's ability to meet its liabilities, including where there is a significant weakening of the employer covenant, then the Guidance provides a degree of flexibility and stipulates that trustees and employers may judge that using the highest of FRS 17/IAS 19, s 179, technical provisions or ongoing deficits, as the bases for the relevant deficit, does not properly reflect the impact of the event. It is submitted however that in most cases where the deficit has been calculated by reference to the technical provisions and the scheme specific funding requirement can be determined, this should be the appropriate deficit yardstick.

[1]   See para 51 of the Guidance.

8.30 Where comparing the employer covenant both pre- and post-event has identified a weakening of the employer covenant, the trustees and employers (as intimated above) need to assess whether that weakening is 'materially detrimental' to the ability of the scheme to meet its liabilities. The judgement as to whether an event is materially detrimental can be made by reference to, and by a comparison of, a number of factors, which may include:

(a)   the amount by which the employer covenant is weakened;
(b)   the size of the employer after the event; for example, the net assets of the employer or wider employer group;
(c)   the size of the scheme; for example, the value of the assets or number of members; and
(d)   the amount of the scheme's relevant deficit.

8.31 This judgement will often be a complex matter, for which both employers and trustees may need independent professional advice.

8.32 The critical question in future cases therefore is more likely to be whether (based on the above) there is a weakening of the covenant that is materially detrimental to the ability of the scheme to meet its liabilities. Stakeholders such as financial institutions and companies still have considerable scope for arguing that this is not the case where they can provide compelling evidence and data to the contrary.

8.33 In other cases where it is judged that there is likely to be weakening of the employer covenant that will be materially detrimental to the ability of the scheme to meet its liabilities, the Guidance suggests that a higher bases would be appropriate[1] and this effectively enables trustees to negotiate a higher security cover for a higher deficit or to negotiate a more substantive share of disposal proceeds as a means of reducing a higher deficit. Similarly, where the FRS 17 deficit for the employer group cannot be allocated on a company-by-company basis, and technical provisions are not yet available, the Guidance suggests that trustees may consider that some other bases would be appropriate[2]. In both scenarios the higher bases for determining a deficit as noted in the Guidance will be the s 75 bases.

[1] See para 52 of the Guidance.
[2] See paras 53–54 of the Guidance.

8.34 Under the Guidance it should be noted that the deficit is only being assessed to establish whether a Clearance statement should be sought. It may be difficult to establish a deficit on the basis of the usual four tests outlined above, but if there is perceived to be a weakening of the covenant then the s 75 deficit test may intrude pursuant to the Guidance which will in turn make it easier for pension trustees to raise the point that a Clearance is required. Moreover, if the Clearance itself is to be framed on the basis that the s 75 deficit should be relevant in relation to the anticipated transaction, then the trustee's negotiating position in relation to security sharing and an entitlement to disposal proceeds will in turn be enhanced as the trustees' starting point for this negotiation will be that the s 75 deficit is the one that is in play.

The alternative s 75 bases for determining a deficit

8.35 Where there are reasonable doubts that the employer will continue as a going concern, where the scheme is in wind-up, or the event may result in scheme abandonment, then the s 75 buy-out bases applies.

8.36 As explained in the preceding sections, the section 75 buy-out debt is a measure of a deficit payable by an employer under a relevant defined benefit scheme[1] where:

(i)   an 'insolvency event'[2] occurs in relation to an employer in a single or multi-employer scheme on or after 6 April 2005[3];

(ii) on the voluntary winding-up of an employer participating in a single or multi-employer scheme, a declaration of solvency has been made in relation to the employer – ie a members' voluntary winding-up[4];

(iii) the winding-up of a single employer or multi-employer scheme[5] occurs;

(iv) an 'employment cessation event' occurs in relation to an employer participating in a multi-employer scheme[6].

[1] Eg excluding a scheme, which is not tax registered under the Finance Act 2004. For other exclusions see the Occupational Pension Schemes (Employer Debt) Regulations 2005, SI 2005/678, reg 4.

[2] See the Pensions Act 1995, s 75(4) and (6C)(a) cross referring to the Pensions Act 2004, s 121 and the Pension Protection Fund (Entry Rules) Regulations 2005, SI 2005/590, reg 5.

[3] Pensions Act 1995, s 75(4) and (6A)(a) as modified by the Occupational Pension Schemes (Employer Debt) Regulations 2005, SI 2005/678, reg 6.

[4] Pensions Act 1995, s 75(4) and (6A)(c).

[5] Pensions Act 1995, s 75(2) as modified by the Occupational Pension Schemes (Employer Debt) Regulations 2005, SI 2005/678, reg 6.

[6] Pensions Act 1995, s 75 as modified by the Occupational Pension Schemes (Employer Debt) Regulations 2005, SI 2005/678, reg 6.

8.37 The section 75 debt is normally calculated by reference to any deficit on a 'buy-out' bases; that is, a bases which reflects the cost of securing benefits by the purchase of annuities. The debt is not preferential and must be calculated by the scheme actuary. Since 2 September 2005, the employer debt is calculated on an annuity buy-out bases in all cases, except if a withdrawal agreement is entered into in a multi-employer scheme[1]. Effectively this means that the calculation of the deficit is driven by the amount that an insurance company would charge to provide the defined benefits in question. As one would expect, insurance companies typically apply conservative assumptions i e smaller asset growth rates and longer death tables.

[1] See the Occupational Pension Schemes (Employer Debt) Regulations 2005, SI 2005/678, reg 5, the Pensions Act 1995, s 75A and the Occupational Pension Schemes (Employer Debt) Regulations 2005, SI 2005/678, Sch 1A.

8.38 Although the application of the section 75 buy-out bases would appear to be limited to the scenarios outlined above, a number of trustees in recent restructuring cases have purported to apply the section 75 deficit calculation where there is a reasonable basis for concluding that the employer will continue as a going concern and there is insufficient evidence or a weakening of the employer covenant. This is unjustified and can derail restructuring negotiations with other stakeholders.

8.39 The relevant deficit as determined under the Guidance is merely a trigger for Clearance of a transaction affecting a relevant employer by tPR and is not an indication that employers and trustees should only fund schemes to this level. If there is no relevant deficit, this is not an indication that the employer-related event is not detrimental to the scheme only that the employer-related event is not a Type A event. Any identified relevant deficit does not restrict the trustees', the employer's or the regulator's duties, powers and obligations. The determination of the relevant deficit under the Guidance is designed to give clarity to the market as to when an employer-related event might be a Type A event, but it does not dispense with the need to ensure that a scheme achieves satisfactory scheme funding.

Achieving satisfactory scheme funding

8.40 The trustees, having taken advice from the scheme actuary, must set out their strategy for achieving the statutory funding objective as outlined above. This strategy for achieving long-term satisfactory scheme funding must be recorded in a written statement of funding principles[1] setting out the trustees' decisions on the methods and assumptions used for calculating the scheme's technical provisions and a plan for eliminating any shortfall in funding over a specified period. It is possible for the trustees to record any specific funding objective (over and above the statutory funding objective) that they view as necessary in addition to the statutory funding objective. The written statement of funding principles must also generally (see below) be agreed with the employer and as part of this process the trustees and the employer will agree a schedule of contributions that the employer has to pay to the scheme over a five-year period (or, if longer, the length of the recovery plan)[2]. The scheme actuary must also certify the schedule.

[1]   See the Pensions Act 2004, s 223(2).
[2]   See the Occupational Pension Schemes (Scheme Funding) Regulations 2005, SI 2005/3377, reg 10(2).

8.41 Periodic actuarial valuations of a scheme's assets and pension liabilities and the schedule of contributions are vital in determining whether or not a scheme is meeting its statutory funding objective and calculating the level of scheme specific deficit. In this regard the Pensions Act 2004, s 224(1) provides that the scheme actuary must conduct full funding valuations at effective dates that are not more than three years apart. At each effective date the written statement of funding principles must also be reviewed[1]. In addition the trustees must obtain annual updating reports from the actuary summarising changes over the year in the scheme's assets and liabilities and the technical provisions.

[1]   See the Occupational Pension Schemes (Scheme Funding) Regulations 2005, SI 2005/3377, reg 6(3)(a).

8.42 If the valuation reveals a shortfall such that the scheme has insufficient assets to meet its future liabilities pursuant to an application of the technical provisions, the trustees must generally agree a 'recovery plan' with the employer. This will set out the additional contributions that the employer will have to make over a specific period in order to reduce the scheme's funding deficit[1]. The recovery plan and a summary of the results of the most recent valuation and the schedule of contributions must be communicated to tPR within a 'reasonable period'[2]. The need for a recovery plan and the sources of capital for funding it are becoming important issues in many restructurings.

[1]   See the Pensions Act 2004, s 226.
[2]   See the Pensions Act 2004, s 229(1).

8.43 Due to the fact that tPR has required recovery plans to be set aggressively so as to reduce the funding shortfall as quickly as the employer can reasonably afford[1], and in any event to set a date when half the deficit can be eliminated, this has made restructurings much more difficult to execute.

The trustees should as a matter of best practice obtain the actuary's advice on the risk of the recovery plan not eliminating the deficit as expected.

[1]   See paragraph 101, Code of practice 03: 'Funding Defined Benefits', published by tPR. At www.thepensionsregulator.gov.uk/pdf/codeFundingFinal.pdf.

8.44 The length of the recovery period depends on the trustees' assessment of the strength of the employer's covenant and its business plan. Although trustees have been encouraged by tPR to remain cognisant of the employer's viability there are examples of corporates effectively being forced into collective and prolonged negotiations with their bankers and trustees in order to accommodate an overtly aggressive recovery plan. The propensity for a recovery plan to result in a restructuring scenario is also increased by tPR's requirement that trustees should consider the nature and value of any security that the employer can provide. Where the employer has granted a negative pledge to its financiers this will not be possible without their consent. The trustees also need to consider their ability to pursue the employer for the section 75 debts if the scheme winds up and this in turn will facilitate a degree of contingency and insolvency planning by the trustees. The trustees will also need to take into account committed expenditure of the employer and the likely level of the risk-based funding levy that the employer will have to pay to the PPF over the recovery period. These further factors may well render the recovery plan a heavily negotiated process. As trustees begin to appreciate the risks for the employer and the schemes of an overly aggressive recovery plan, experience has shown that a sensible outcome resulting in a deferral of contributions quite often occurs.

8.45 As intimated, the scheme specific funding principles (actuarial bases, statement of funding principles, recovery plan, etc) need to be agreed between the trustees and the employers[1]. In default of an agreement within 15 months of the effective date of the valuation, tPR has power to fix the provisions[2]. The Pensions Bill 2008 currently before Parliament will, if enacted, also give power to tPR to reopen scheme specific funding even if the trustees and the employer have agreed it.

[1]   See the Pensions Act 2004, s 229.
[2]   Pensions Act 2004, ss 229(5) and 231.

8.46 The legislation provides that the trustees can fix the scheme specific funding provisions on their own (subject to consultation with the employers) if the scheme deed and rules give power to the trustees to fix employer contributions and the employer has no power under the rules to reduce or suspend them[1].

[1]   Occupational Pension Schemes (Scheme Funding) Regulations 2005, SI 2005/3377, Sch 2, para 9.

8.47 The interrelation between the statutory scheme funding provisions and the terms of the trust deed and rules can be complex and legally unclear[1].

[1]   See Warren J in *British Vita Unlimited v British Pension Fund Trustees Ltd* [2007] EWHC 953 (Ch), [2008] 1 All ER 37.

D THE MORAL HAZARD PROVISIONS

Aims and objectives

8.48 The statutory funding obligations (scheme specific and section 75) are obligations only on the relevant employers (or former employers) and are unsecured and (in the main[1]) non-preferential debts. As such, absent any specific agreement on security or guarantees (and these are becoming more common), the scheme (and its trustees) is dependent on the strength of the relevant employers. This is potentially subject to abuse by corporate structures, which could result in increased defaults and hence claims on the PPF (at the expense of the other UK defined benefit scheme, whose levy payments would increase).

[1] Some pensions debts are preferential – see Schedule 4 to the Pension Schemes Act 1993, but only (in relation to employer contributions) to a limited amount, less than £4,500 per active member for tax year 2006/7. See Chapter 9 of Pollard 'Corporate Insolvency: Employment and Pension Rights' (Tottel, 2007).

8.49 The moral hazard provisions in the Pensions Act 2004 are aimed at discouraging the abuse of corporate structures and abusive transactions to avoid pensions liabilities. The timing of the introduction of these provisions was tied to the creation of the PPF. The PPF is modelled on the Pension Benefit Guaranty Corporation in the US and is a fund established to compensate members of an eligible defined benefit scheme[1] if the employer becomes insolvent and the pension scheme is underfunded. The level of 'protected benefits' provided by the PPF is subject to various limits. The PPF is funded by a levy on defined benefit pension schemes. The moral hazard provisions are intended to reduce the risk of employers abdicating responsibility for their pension liabilities and transferring them to the PPF, particularly in a restructuring or where an employer is distressed and on the cusp of insolvency. As such the new regime has the consequential objective of seeking to keep the levy imposed on pension schemes by the PPF commercially sustainable.

[1] See the Pensions Regulator (Contribution Notices and Restoration Orders) Regulations 2005, SI 2005/931, reg 3 for details of excluded schemes (eg one which is not tax registered). This also applies in relation to FSDs – see the Pensions Regulator (Financial Support Directions etc) Regulations 2005, SI 2005/2188, reg 3.

8.50 The moral hazard provisions consist of two separate mechanisms that can be used by tPR to seek to plug pension scheme deficits:

(a)   contribution notices ('CNs'); and
(b)   financial support directions ('FSDs').

8.51 The intention behind FSDs is to ensure that there is adequate financial support from all group and connected entities for an ongoing pension scheme. So far, only one FSD has been issued[1] (and no CNs), but it is envisaged that tPR will use them to ensure that those entities with resources provide suitable backing to prevent a pension scheme from being unable to meet its liabilities. It is envisaged by way of contrast that a CN will be used as a means of dealing with pension scheme liabilities that have crystallised. Connectivity and the concepts of associates or connected persons are examined in more detail in this chapter.

1   See the determination in relation to Sea Containers, described on tPR website and below.

Contribution notices – Pensions Act 2004, ss 38–42

8.52 TPR may (if it considers it reasonable to do so) require a person 'connected with' or 'associated to' an employer to contribute up to the whole of the pension scheme deficit if tPR considers that he has deliberately acted or deliberately failed to act (or knowingly assisted in that act or deliberate failure to act[1]) with the main purpose of avoiding or, otherwise than in good faith, reducing pension liabilities[2]. TPR can specify that the recipient of the notice must pay either the whole or a specified part of the deficit[3]. The act or failure to act must have occurred on or after 27 April 2004 and within six years of the notice[4]. The relevant person must have been connected to or associated with an employer in relation to the scheme in that same period[5].

1   Pensions Act 2004, s 38(6)(a).
2   Pensions Act 2004, s 38(5).
3   Pensions Act 2004, s 39.
4   Pensions Act 2004, s 38(5)(b) and (c).
5   Pensions Act 2004, s 38(3)(b) and (6)(b).

Financial support directions – Pensions Act 2004, ss 43–51

8.53 TPR may direct (if it considers it reasonable to do so) that associated and connected persons must put financial support in place to meet the pension liabilities of an employer[1]. An FSD may be made where:

(a)   the employer is found to be 'insufficiently resourced' to fund pension liabilities; or

(b)   the employer is a 'service company'.

1   Pensions Act 2004, s 43(2).

8.54 A company will be insufficiently resourced under (a) above where it has insufficient assets to meet 50% of the estimated section 75 buy-out deficit in the scheme and another company in the group is able to meet the difference[1]. A company will be a service company under (b) above if its turnover, as shown in its latest available accounts, is 'solely or principally derived from amounts charged for the provision of the services of [its] employees' to other group companies[2].

1   Pensions Act 2004, s 44(3) and the Pensions Regulator (Financial Support Directions etc) Regulations 2005 (SI 2005/2188), reg 6.
2   Pensions Act 2004, s 44(2).

8.55 An FSD cannot be made against an individual if the employer is a company[1].

1   Pensions Act 2004, s 43(6).

8.56 TPR must also consider it reasonable, in all the circumstances of the case, for the FSD to be issued[1] and tPR can issue a CN if there is non-compliance with an FSD[2].

[1]   Pensions Act 2004, s 43(5).
[2]   Pensions Act 2004, s 47.

8.57 The financial support must remain in place for the life of the scheme[1]. It must take a form approved in a notice issued by tPR falling within the Pensions Act 2004, s 45(2) – ie joint and several liability of all group companies or a guarantee from the holding company or some other form of legally enforceable agreement of the relevant parties[2].

[1]   Pensions Act 2004, s 43(3)(b).
[2]   Pensions Act 2004, s 45(2) and the Pensions Regulator (Financial Support Directions etc) Regulations 2005, SI 2005/2188, regs 13 and 14.

8.58 On 5 February 2008, the Pension Regulator's Determination Panel (a statutory body set up by the Pensions Act 2004 to exercise the relevant regulatory powers of tPR) (the Panel) issued its first FSD under the Pensions Act 2004, s 43, against Sea Containers Limited (SCL), the Bermudan parent company of its London-based UK subsidiary Sea Containers Services Ltd (SCSL). The Panel was able to make the determination after SCL withdrew its appeal against tPR's earlier decision to issue the FSDs. SCL must now provide financial support to two pension schemes belonging to SCSL for the life of the schemes.

8.59 SCSL, a UK 'service company' and a wholly-owned subsidiary of SCL, is the principal employer of two UK final salary pension schemes (the Schemes). In September 2006 it was understood that the Schemes had a combined pension deficit estimated to be around £133mn on a section 75 buy-out bases and SCSL was said to have limited assets, consisting of mainly inter-company balances within the corporate group. After growing concern that SCL was not committed to the Schemes (they had made no formal proposals to address the pension deficit) and that the Schemes would continue to be under-funded, the trustees approached and enlisted the services of tPR. Initially tPR sent an informal letter to SCL noting that no proposals had been made to address the deficit and that it had the power to order an FSD to be issued. This was followed on the 19 October 2006, however, by a formal warning notice of tPR's intention to issue an FSD. The formal warning notice was sent four days after SCL had declared itself insolvent and had filed for Chapter 11 bankruptcy protection with the US Securities and Exchange.

8.60 In the proceeding months, both the SCL and the trustees of the Schemes made representations to tPR, discussions were held with the Panel and on 12–13 June 2007 a Determinations Panel hearing took place which focused on whether it was 'reasonable' for tPR to impose FSDs on SCL. It is a requirement of the Pensions Act 2004, s 43(5)(b) that tPR must consider it reasonable in all the circumstances for a FSD to be issued. On 18 June 2007, tPR issued formal determination notices confirming its intention to issue

FSDs, requiring SCL to underwrite SCSL's liabilities under the Schemes. SCL was given 28 days to appeal to the Pensions Regulator Tribunal. An appeal was submitted and later withdrawn.

8.61 The Sea Containers case is a useful indication of tPR's views on the factors that make it 'reasonable' to issue FSDs. In this case it was 'reasonable' to issue FSDs because of some of the following factors:

(a) SCSL as the principal employer of the Schemes was wholly owned and controlled by SCL;

(b)   SCL received 'the value of any benefits directly or indirectly' from SCSL. These benefits included:
    (i)   the services of SCSL – these services were recorded on SCSL's balance sheets but no actual payments were received from SCL; and
    (ii)   SCSL's purpose and position within the group structure – SCSL benefited the group of which SCL was the parent by allowing the group to trade from Europe but still receive tax advantages from the Bermudan tax regime;

(c)   SCL was closely connected to the Schemes and many of its officers acted as trustees;

(d)   SCSL was insufficiently resourced whereas SCL had substantial assets; and

(e)   FSDs can be issued in cases of insolvency and it was reasonable to issue a FSD in this case where SCL had entered into insolvency proceedings in the US by filing for Chapter 11 bankruptcy.

8.62 In practice it may be difficult for any holding company that has a 'service company' (as defined in the Pensions Act 2004), such as SCSL within its group structure, to argue that it does not obtain some kind of direct or indirect 'benefit' from that subsidiary. This factor was deliberately framed widely by the Panel during the Panel hearing and may have far-reaching implications in the case of future corporate transactions.

8.63 During proceedings, SCL's counsel argued that SCL would be placed in an 'impossible position' should the US bankruptcy court refuse to recognise tPR's claim. Although the Panel conceded that it could affect a demand for payment following non-compliance (see below), it was not a justification for refusing to grant the FSD in the first place.

8.64 The Panel were of the opinion that tPR's moral hazard powers were 'likely to be of particular significance in insolvency situations'. It should be noted, however, that the FSDs did not give the trustees of the Schemes 'super priority' in the event of insolvency. The FSD made the trustees unsecured creditors ranking equally with all other unsecured creditors of SCL.

8.65 Although unlikely, considering that SCL has withdrawn its appeal, it should be noted that if SCL fails to put arrangements into place to fund the Schemes in accordance with the FSDs then tPR has the power to issue a section 47 CN for a specific sum, anything up to the full amount of the estimated section 75 buy-out deficit. As discussed above, in a situation where SCL is prevented from making such arrangements by the US bankruptcy court, the Panel hinted that it might be unreasonable to issue a CN. SCL is a Bermudan entity, which in itself adds further complexity. Once a CN is issued, this becomes a statutory debt, which can be pursued through the civil courts. It is yet to be seen how an overseas jurisdiction will react to a judgment debt, which derives from a decision made by tPR.

8.66 The Sea Containers case is a useful indication of tPR's views on the factors that make it 'reasonable' to issue FSDs, however, it is still unclear whether it will be possible to use past 'precedents' in an argument with tPR over its powers. During the determination hearing in June, the Panel rejected SCL's attempt to draw comparisons with previous dealings that tPR had been involved in. If you add this to the fact that the details of past cases may never be reported in the public domain, it will remain very difficult for employers to draw comparisons.

8.67 The outcome of the case has shown that tPR truly is a force to be reckoned with and has placed pensions considerations firmly at the centre of all corporate transactions and insolvency proceedings. It may encourage scheme trustees to adopt a firmer line in negotiating scheme funding or during corporate transactions.

Whom do the moral hazard provisions affect?

Connected persons and associates

8.68 A CN or an FSD may be issued against persons who are (or have been in the relevant period) connected to or associated with the employer of a pension scheme. The terms 'connected person' and 'associate' are imported from the Insolvency Act 1986, ss 249 and 435[1]. This is a double-edged sword: on the one hand, these are terms with which those in the insolvency field need to be familiar; however, these terms are also complicated and extremely broad.

[1]   Pensions Act 2004, s 51(3).

8.69 The position at present can be summarised as follows:

(a)   where there is a corporate employer, an individual (including a director and his relatives) cannot be issued with an FSD;

(b)   an individual, eg a director (including a shadow director) and his relatives, can be issued with a CN if tPR considers it reasonable – this will depend on a number of factors, including any benefit derived by the individual from the relevant company;

(c)   parent companies are potentially liable to be issued with a CN – even if they merely omit to prevent the steps taken by a participating employer that lead to a weakening of the employer's ability to fund its pension scheme (for example, delays in making contributions); and

(d)   shareholders are potentially liable for an FSD if they have a large stake (more than a third voting stake) in a participating employer (directly or indirectly)[1]. It is this possibility that has caused considerable concern within the private equity community since liability can be traced through the corporate tax structures back to the various funds that sit behind leveraged buy-out vehicles.

[1]   Definition of 'associate' and 'control' in the Insolvency Act 1986, s 435(6) and (10).

8.70 Concerns can arise for banks, etc that take security over shares (eg in an employer subsidiary), which could give them voting control in some circumstances[1].

[1]   See the correspondence between tPR and the Financial Markets Law Committee in April and May 2005 on this issue (see Issue 104) on their website: www.fmlc.org/papers/Issue104PA.pdf.

8.71 There is power for regulations to be issued in respect of partnerships and limited liability partnerships.

Insolvency practitioners

8.72 Limited carve-outs relating to who can be issued a CN offer some protection to insolvency practitioners who may have been party to an act or failure to act with the main purpose of avoiding pension liabilities. To fall within the carve-out, the insolvency practitioner must have been 'acting in accordance with his functions as an insolvency practitioner'[1]. For the purposes of the carve-out, an insolvency practitioner means a person acting as an insolvency practitioner as defined in the Insolvency Act 1986 – ie a liquidator, provisional liquidator, administrator, administrative receiver or nominee or supervisor under a voluntary arrangement[2].

[1]   Pensions Act 2004, s 38(3)(c).
[2]   Pensions Act 2004, s 38(11) cross-referring to the Insolvency Act 1986, s 388.

8.73 The carve-out does not apply to fixed charge receivers or Law of Property Act 1925 receivers who, depending on the nature of their appointment (for example, if over a controlling interest in the shares of an employer), may be exposed to liability for CNs[1].

[1]   See the comments made by the Financial Markets Law Committee in their paper issued in December 2005 on the issue of receivers (see Issue 104) on their website: www.fmlc.org/papers/Issue104PA.pdf. This was updated in a letter dated 7 February 2007 (also on their website).

8.74 There is no equivalent specific carve-out for insolvency practitioners for FSDs for two reasons. First, there is no prospect of an FSD being issued against an insolvency practitioner where the relevant employer is a body corporate[1]. Second, as the risk only arises for an insolvency practitioner if he is an associate of an individual employer (ie he is related to the employer), professional rules of conduct ought to prevent an insolvency practitioner from taking an appointment over an individual employer to whom he or she is related. However, care should be exercised where an appointment is taken over a person (for example, a sole trader or partnership) who is an associate of an individual employer.

[1]   Pensions Act 2004, s 43(6).

Nominee directors

8.75 The position of 'nominee' directors, that is, persons appointed to the boards of companies to represent the interests of private equity investors, must also be carefully considered. As mentioned above, tPR has the power to issue CNs (but generally not FSDs) against individual directors. This will most likely be in situations where the director has knowingly assisted in or been party to an act or deliberate failure to act with a main purpose of preventing the recovery of a section 75 debt (or preventing it becoming due). To protect themselves from personal liability directors will need to be fully apprised of the financial circumstances of the companies to which they are appointed, and carefully consider the impact of their actions or omissions on the ability of the pension scheme to meet its liabilities.

8.76 Directors and officers ('D&O') insurance cover, if available, should be sought to cover this risk and any pre-existing cover should be carefully reviewed to ensure that the risk of incurring liability under a CN is not excluded. To the extent the risk is not carved out under existing policies, experience has shown that insurers have carefully re-examined their position when those policies are renewed.

8.77 Those appointing the director may also be at risk, for example if they have given an indemnity to the director or if the nominee is also an employee or director of the appointor (because the appointor will then be an associate of the director[1] and so connected with the employer[2]). As one of the matters tPR is to consider when determining whether it is reasonable to impose liability on a person is that person's financial circumstances, those with 'deep pockets' may find themselves especially at risk.

[1]   Insolvency Act 1986, s 435(4) and (9).
[2]   Insolvency Act 1986, s 249.

Chief Restructuring Officers (CROs)

8.78 CROs and company 'doctors' who are brought in to assist a company in financial difficulties may face potential liability under the moral hazard provisions. The risk arises if a person is appointed to the board of directors (for example, as chief restructuring officer) or takes an equity stake. They will, however, have the protection afforded by the requirements and concepts of 'reasonableness' considered below. As we mentioned above in the context of nominee directors, D&O insurance, if available, should be sought to cover this risk and any pre-existing cover should be carefully reviewed.

The importance of reasonableness in the context of issuing CNs and FSDs

8.79 A CN or FSD can only be issued where tPR considers it reasonable to do so. The Pensions Act 2004 prescribes a number of matters that tPR must consider in determining reasonableness for this purpose, which are summarised below in the context of both CNs[1] and FSDs[2].

[1]   Pensions Act 2004, s 38(7).
[2]   Pensions Act 2004, s 43(7).

Contribution notices

8.80

(a)   The degree of involvement in the act or failure to act of the person to whom the CN would be addressed.
(b)   The relationship that person has or had with the employer, including whether the person has 'control' of the employer.
(c)   Any connection or involvement the person had or has had with the pension scheme.
(d)   If the relevant act or failure was a notifiable event, whether the person had failed to notify tPR.
(e)   The purposes of the act or failure to act (including whether a purpose was to prevent or limit loss of employment).
(f)   The person's financial circumstances.
(g)   Other matters prescribed in regulations (none have been prescribed to date).

Financial support directions

8.81

(a)   The relationship that person has or had with the employer, including whether the person has 'control' of the employer.
(b)   The value of any benefits received directly or indirectly by that person from the employer.
(c)   Any connection or involvement the person had or has had with the pension scheme.
(d)   The person's financial circumstances.
(e)   Other matters prescribed in regulations (none have yet).

Department of Work and Pensions proposals in relation to CNs and FSDs

8.82 On 14 April 2008 the Department of Work and Pensions (DWP) issued a press release highlighting new powers for tPR in relation to CNs and FSDs. DWP is consulting on making amendments to provisions in the Pensions Act 2004 that allow tPR to issue financial support directions (FSDs) and contribution notices (CNs) against connected third parties (eg non-employers).

8.83 The consultation confirms and provides more detail on many of the changes that were announced in DWP's statement on 14 April 2008. In parallel with the DWP's consultation, tPR has also issued a statement confirming the circumstances in which it will use these proposed extended powers and the impact that these changes will have on the Clearance regime. The DWP's consultation closes on 20 June 2008.

Extending the circumstances when CNs can be issued

8.84 At present, a CN may be issued by tPR if there is behaviour, which is intended to prevent the recovery of a debt from an employer to a pension scheme, or at preventing a debt becoming due. While this is a key power for tPR, experience has shown that there are acts that present risks for member benefits which may not trigger the issue of a CN. The example cited in the press release is of a disposal of significant company assets, which could seriously undermine the ability of the company to meet the pension promises it has made. The Government has therefore proposed that CNs may be issued where 'the effect of an act is materially detrimental to a scheme's ability to pay members' current and future benefits, in order to cover situations such as this'. The previous need to show a 'main purpose' to avoid a debt will no longer apply. In addition there will no longer be an 'otherwise than in good faith' requirement for issuing CNs.

8.85 The DWP press release also contains a proposal for tPR to be able to issue CNs based on a series of acts or failures to act (to be backdated to 27 April 2004). Currently tPR can only issue CNs in relation to an isolated act or failure to act. There will however be a statutory defence to the above-extended powers where a party can demonstrate that they could not reasonably have foreseen that their actions could have a materially detrimental effect on the security of members' benefits. Importantly, the proposed changes make it clear that the moral hazard powers will not be frustrated by 'bulk transfers' of members between pension schemes.

Extending the circumstance when FSDs can be issued

8.86 It is proposed that tPR will be able to consider the resources of the whole group of companies when determining whether to issue a FSD when there is an under-resourced employer. Currently tPR has to identify a single entity which is sufficiently resourced to provide financial support before it issues a FSD.

Changes that will have effect from 2004

8.87 The proposal to allow the issue of CNs based on a series of acts will have retrospective effect to 27 April 2004. This retrospective effect of the legislation is likely to heighten the concerns of certain parties liable to a CN for their historic practice and conduct in relation to certain transactions that have had an impact on defined benefit schemes. However, tPR has confirmed that in relation to the proposed powers to issue a CN based on a series of acts, it will not withdraw a Clearance that has already been given. If a Clearance statement has been issued in relation to an individual transaction, then that transaction could not form part of a 'course of conduct' triggering the issue of a CN.

Changes that will have effect from 14 April 2008

8.88 The remaining changes are expected to have retrospective effect from 14 April 2008. However, tPR has confirmed that for the periods between 14 April 2008 and the date the legislation comes into force it will only use its proposed extended powers to issue CNs and FSDs where at least one of the following features is present in the transaction:

(i)   the employer or pension scheme is moving to another jurisdiction;

(ii)   the operating company is being split from the pension scheme without appropriate mitigation for the pension scheme;

(iii)   the assets are being split from the operating company without appropriate mitigation for the pension scheme;

(iv)   scheme assets and liabilities are transferring to another scheme which did not have adequate support from an employer;

(v)   a scheme is being run for profit without adequate account being taken of member interests; or the business model predominantly passes risk to scheme members, but high investment returns would benefit investors.

8.89 The DWP believes that the above features characterise the business models, which are the target of these proposed extended powers.

Clearance

8.90 TPR has stated that its approach to Clearance will not change as a result of the proposed changes and the Clearance guidance still applies. Moreover, tPR has also confirmed that if a Clearance statement has already been granted, it will continue to bind tPR, unless the circumstances of the case have changed in a material way or were not fully or accurately described in the Clearance application. According to the DWP consultation, tPR does not envisage any extension to the time taken to grant Clearance as a result of the proposals.

8.91 Since the DWP's statement outlining the new powers issued on 14 April 2008, there has been concern as to the potential reach of the amended CNs and FSDs, in particular that they might frustrate legitimate corporate transactions. The DWP's consultation document emphasises that this is not the intention. It confirms that the particular focus of the Government's attention is business models that may sever the link between the pension scheme and the employer in order to operate schemes for a profit.

8.92 However, under these proposed changes tPR will still potentially be able to use these changed powers in wider circumstances. While the DWP's and tPR's statements may go some way to mitigating concerns, it is likely there will be a period of uncertainty, perhaps resulting in an increase in applications for Clearance. In the three years that tPR has been in operation, there has already been a significant shift in its practice on Clearance. Connected parties should be cautious about relying on policy statements, which may well change in future.

E TPR CLEARANCE STATEMENTS

Introduction

8.93 There were initial fears that the CN and FSD regime would stifle corporate activity, especially in restructurings where there is often a sizeable deficit, thereby hampering attempts to rescue businesses. The Pensions Act 2004 therefore contains[1] a formal Clearance procedure whereby parties can seek from tPR a statement that their proposed transaction will not fall foul of the moral hazard provisions. Broadly, the relevant parties negotiate with the pension trustees and reach agreement[2]. This is submitted to tPR (who should have been kept abreast of the situation) for Clearance. If successful, tPR gives Clearance confirming that it will not issue an FSD or CN (as appropriate) in respect of the specified transaction. This gives protection to the applicants from being held liable for the pension deficit as a result of the cleared transaction. The Clearance is not absolute. It will cease to be binding on tPR if the relevant circumstances change in a material way[3].

[1] Pensions Act 2004, ss 42 and 46.
[2] Agreement with the trustees is not strictly a condition for Clearance, but in practice tPR will look for this and Clearance without trustee agreement is likely to be more difficult to obtain and to take much longer.
[3] Pensions Act 2004, ss 42(5) and 46(5).

8.94 'Events' qualifying for Clearance include transactions, agreements, decisions, other acts and failures to act. If one refers back to the section, which assesses who the moral hazard affects, it is clear that applications may be made by those parties who could be subject to a CN or FSD in relation to a scheme. As intimated, this could include the employer and those connected or associated with the employer. Parties that may become an employer, or become connected or associated with an employer (for example a purchaser), may also wish to apply for a Clearance statement.

The role and approach of tPR

8.95 In the revised Guidance from tPR published in March 2008 (the 'Guidance')[1], tPR has stated that it will adopt a risk-based approach and will focus resources on schemes where there was a risk to the security of the members' benefits[2]. TPR's preferred outcome is an appropriately funded scheme with a solvent employer and in order to procure this tPR has stated that it will deploy its resources in a risk-based manner, targeting risk in a proportionate, responsive, flexible, pragmatic, consistent, transparent and reasonable way. Simultaneously, tPR will seek to protect members' benefits and reduce the risk of calls on the PPF, while at the same time recognising commercial activity and business needs[3]. It is conspicuous that tPR does not state that it will seek the same balance in its dealings with other financial stakeholders and creditors of the employer.

[1] The revised Guidance published in March 2008 replaces the original April 2005 guidance and can be found at www.thepensionsregulator.gov.uk/guidance/Clearance/index.aspx.
[2] 2008 Guidance, paras 15–17.
[3] 2008 Guidance, para 17.

8.96 The power to issue CNs and FSDs whilst significant are only part of tPR's approach to ensuring that schemes are properly funded and that deficits are properly addressed. Indeed tPR may wish to appoint an independent trustee[1]. A Clearance statement only relates to the applicants, the relevant scheme and the events described in the application and the granting of a Clearance statement does not have any impact on the regulator's powers, other than the inability to issue contribution notices or the power to issue financial support directions (as applicable) where a transaction has been subject to Clearance.

[1] See the Pensions Act 1995, s 7. Independent trustees were appointed in a case involving Telent and this was upheld on appeal within tPR to its Determinations Panel – see the determinations section of tPR's website. The Pensions Bill 2008, currently before Parliament will, if enacted, expand tPR's power to appoint independent trustees by removing the requirement for this to be 'necessary' and replacing it with a requirement for this to be 'reasonable'.

8.97 For the Clearance to be of any value, full disclosure must be made by the parties seeking it[1]. Clearance applications are made on a standard form (which asks the applicant to provide details of any deficit in the scheme on a section 75 buy-out bases, on an FRS 17/IAS 19 bases, on an ongoing bases and on the PPF bases). If an applicant does not appear to be connected or associated with an employer, tPR may ask that applicant to explain why an application would be appropriate.

[1] As mentioned above, a Clearance is not binding on tPR if circumstances change materially, so this is a reason for making sure that tPR is properly informed when the application is made. Knowingly or recklessly providing tPR with information that is false or misleading in a material particular is a criminal offence: Pensions Act 2004, s 80.

8.98 Ordinarily, tPR will not expect trustees to sponsor an application relating to their scheme and it will not usually be appropriate for a trustee to apply for a Clearance statement[1]. While some corporate trustees may be connected or associated with employers, it will not usually be appropriate for any trustee to apply for a Clearance statement because of the conflicts the application would create between the trustee's duties to members and the trustee's personal interests as directors or even shareholders[2]. In most cases, corporate trustees will not have any assets (other than the scheme assets), so the practical risk of contribution notices or financial support directions will be minimal. Most directors of corporate trustees as well as individuals will not be connected or associated with an employer as a result of their trusteeship. As part of an application, the trustees will however be asked to comment on whether or not they support the application and to explain why and there is a section on the application form that confirms their views[3].

[1]   2008 Guidance, paras 22–23.
[2]   2008 Guidance, paras 121–123.
[3]   2008 Guidance, paras 121–123.

8.99 If the trustees become aware of an event that they believe could be a Type A event as described more fully below, they should raise their concerns with the employer and other relevant parties to the event, in order to ensure that appropriate mitigation is considered and to ascertain whether an application is being considered. Where an application is not being considered and the trustees are concerned that no mitigation is being offered, or that mitigation is inadequate, they should consider contacting tPR[1].

[1]   2008 Guidance, paras 112–114.

8.100 It is helpful that tPR has developed an efficient Clearance procedure, which can be fast tracked for urgent cases. TPR has proved to be extremely adept at considering Clearances for complex transactions on a commercial timetable and in certain instances has been able to consider and respond to an application for Clearance within 48 hours.

8.101 TPR's objectives are to protect pension scheme members' benefits, to promote good administration of pension schemes and to reduce situations that may lead to claims from the PPF. Many of tPR's permanent staff have been recruited from banks and law or accounting firms, especially from the restructuring field. TPR likewise has secondees from those organisations. This means that case officers are generally familiar with restructurings and well versed with current practice. They also are keen to facilitate commercial solutions and encourage informal discussions, even on a no-names basis, so as to promote an open dialogue with tPR. This works well so that parties can realise early on what is likely to be acceptable in the situation. The fact that only one FSD (in the case of Sea Containers Limited referred to above) has been issued to date is in part testament to the success of the Clearance procedure and the way that parties have responded to the new regime.

8.102 It is a question for those exposed to a CN or FSD whether Clearance should be sought. Clearance is not mandatory and it is designed to provide more certainty to affected parties. The 2005 guidance was helpful in that its principles-based approach created a satisfactory degree of certainty. It indicated the types of events it would be concerned about, and in relation to which an application for Clearance should be considered. The 2005 guidance termed those events that created the most significant risks for schemes and members 'Type A events', but in addition it outlined two other types of events: 'Type B events' and 'Type C events'[1]. Type B events were those not effecting the pension creditor, for which tPR had indicated Clearance was not necessary and Type C events comprised events that pointed towards a deterioration in the employer's covenant, which tPR had indicated it may choose to monitor with respect to pension schemes it considered to be 'at risk'.

[1]   2005 Guidance, paras 49 onwards.

8.103 The new regime under the 2008 Guidance dispenses with a principles-based approach and relies on a risk-based approach which focuses resources on schemes where there is a risk to the security of the members' benefits. The 2008 Guidance now dispenses with Type B and Type C events and only refers to Type A events which are 'all events that are materially detrimental to the ability of the scheme to meet its pensions liabilities'[1], and it is only in relation to these events that tPR expects to receive an application.

[1]   2008 Guidance, para 24.

Identifying Type A events

8.104 The first stage in the new regime is for employers and trustees to assess the relevant restructuring transactions and to determine whether they are 'detrimental events'. Detrimental events are defined in Appendix C of the 2008 Guidance as 'an event that could be detrimental to the ability of the scheme to meet its liabilities as well as some events that are directly detrimental to members' benefits'. Employers and trustees are assisted in determining whether an event is a detrimental event by paragraph 26 of the Guidance, which provides that a detrimental event will have one or more of the following effects, either immediately or in the future:

- it prevents the recovery of the whole or any part of the employer's s 75 debt;
- it prevents the employer's s 75 debt becoming due or compromises the s 75 debt;
- it reduces the amount of the employer's s 75 debt which would otherwise become due; or
- it weakens the employer covenant, because:
  - (i)   it has an impact on the ability of the employer to meet its ongoing funding commitments to the scheme, or an impact on those commitments; or
  - (ii)   it reduces the dividend that would be available to the scheme in the event of employer insolvency.

8.105 Having determined that the event or restructuring transaction is detrimental, employers and trustees must assess whether that detrimental event is a Type A event, by determining whether the event is an employer-related event or a scheme-related event[1].

[1]   2008 Guidance, paras 25–26.

Employer-related Type A events

8.106   An employer-related event will only be a Type A event if the scheme has a relevant deficit[1]. As intimated earlier in the section entitled 'The importance of calculating the deficit', this will be determined by using the highest of FRS 17/IAS 19, s 179, technical provisions or ongoing deficits as the bases for the relevant deficit. Higher bases may however be appropriate to calculate the relevant deficit where the event is significantly materially detrimental to the scheme's ability to meet its liabilities, including a significant weakening of the employer covenant[2]. In this situation the Guidance suggests that s 75 buy-out bases is likely to be more appropriate where there are ongoing concern issues, the scheme is in wind up or there is scheme abandonment[3]. Having determined that the scheme has a deficit it is then relevant to go to the final stage of determining whether the event related to the employer itself is a Type A event. This is done by:

(i)   comparing and contrasting the pre- and post-event employer covenant; and
(ii)   assessing whether there is any weakening of the employer covenant to such a degree that the event could be considered to be materially detrimental to the ability of the scheme to meet its liabilities.

[1]   2008 Guidance, para 24.
[2]   2008 Guidance, paras 49–50.
[3]   2008 Guidance, paras 51–54.

8.107   In assessing the employer covenant, it is necessary to analyse the employer's legal obligations to the scheme and its financial position (both current and prospective)[1]. In responding to the next question of whether there has there been a weakening of employer covenant, it is necessary to consider where the pension creditor sits in the statutory insolvency waterfall and to consider the employer's long-term viability and future. If trustees don't feel they have necessary skills to assess this, then they should consider obtaining independent professional advice. Professional advice might well inform the next question as to whether the weakening is 'material'. In making this assessment the Guidance provides that the factors to consider include:

(i)   the amount the employer covenant is weakened;
(ii)   the size of the employer after event;
(iii)   the size of the scheme; and
(iv)   the size of the scheme's deficit.

[1]   Appendix A to the 2008 Guidance provides more detail on how to assess the employer covenant.

8.108   A non-exhaustive list of employer-related events is provided in the Guidance. Many of these will be relevant in a restructuring scenario and they include changes in priority, a return of capital, changes to the group structure, changes in control of the group and particular the employer, business and asset sales from the employer or wider employer group (particularly where the transaction is not at arm's length for fair value, where the sale proceeds are not retained by the group or the whole/part of an operating business is sold) and a corporate event that would reduce sustainable cashflow for the group's funding commitment to the scheme[1].

[1]   2008 Guidance, paras 56–58.

Scheme-related events

8.109 If a 'scheme-related event' is detrimental to the ability of a scheme to meet its liabilities, or is directly detrimental to members' benefits, and such detriment is material, then it will be a Type A event. This will be the case irrespective of whether or not the scheme has a relevant deficit[1]. When assessing any event, employers and trustees should also refer to the guidance on the 'Abandonment of defined benefit pension schemes', on tPR's website. The method for assessing whether a scheme-related event is a Type A event varies, depending on the event, however it is important to consider both the immediate impact in scheme and members' benefits and the event's possible impact into the future, which can of course be complex. On this basis independent professional advice for the employer and the trustee is often appropriate.

[1]   2008 Guidance, para 24.

8.110 The Guidance[1] stipulates that certain scheme-related events will always be Type A events and many of these will be relevant in a restructuring scenario. The examples in the Guidance inter alia include compromises of the s 75 debt or apportionment (under scheme rules or a scheme apportionment arrangement conducted under the Occupational Pension Schemes (Employer Debt) Regulations 2005[2]), unless any resulting increases in the s 75 debt are immediately payable by an employer who can afford the increased debt or there is no net reduction of the employer covenant.

[1]   2008 Guidance, paras 65–66.
[2]   SI 2005/678, as amended by the Occupational Pension Schemes (Employer Debt and Miscellaneous Amendments) Regulations 2008, SI 2008/731 which were laid before Parliament on 14 March 2008 and which are expected to come into force on 6 April 2008.

Mitigation

8.111 Where the employers and trustees have identified a possible Type A event, they should consider and agree the most appropriate mitigation. The level and type of appropriate mitigation will vary, depending on the nature, circumstances and impact of the event or the restructuring as well as the funding level of the scheme, taking into account the relevant deficit. The Guidance requires that the appropriate mitigation should be identified for each Type A event and issues a reminder that any mitigation agreed does not restrict in any way the trustees', the employer's or the regulator's duties, powers and obligations in relation to scheme funding.

8.112 The Guidance cites various different types of mitigation, but examples include seeking additional employer contributions, placing funds such as disposal proceeds into escrow which can be paid into the scheme in certain scenarios, employers procuring letter of credit/guarantee from banks to guarantee contributions or deficits, a joint and several liability of the wider employer group, negative pledges on the grant of security or the disposal of certain assets or operating companies to preserve employer assets or perhaps performance thresholds whereby trustees and employers may agree financial thresholds for the employer that, if breached, would have to be reported to the trustees. These performance thresholds are unlikely to be sufficient mitigation alone for any detrimental event, but in combination with other forms of mitigation would act as an early warning for trustees of any deterioration or change in the employer's financial circumstances and provide an early opportunity for dialogue. They might effectively provide, or indeed preserve, a seat for the trustees at the restructuring table.

Information provision to tPR

8.113 Experience has shown that tPR has been alerted to troubled pension schemes not only by his own investigations, but also by a combination of the following:

(a)   A duty imposed on persons who are closely connected to a pension scheme (for example, employers, trustees, auditors and other advisers) to notify tPR as soon as reasonably practicable (ie whistleblow) if they believe that a duty, imposed by virtue of an enactment or rule of law, relevant to the administration of the scheme has not been or is not being complied with and the failure to comply is likely to be of material significance to tPR in the exercise of any of its functions[1].

(b)   A duty imposed on trustees and employers to make reports to tPR if certain prescribed notifiable events occur[2]. The events that will trigger this duty include compromising a pension scheme debt, receipt of advice that the employer is trading wrongfully, any breach of a banking covenant by the employer, a significant change in the employer's credit rating, a decision to cease carrying on business in the UK and a decision by a controlling company to relinquish control of the employer – see further below[3].

(c)   Information supplied to tPR in support of an application for a Clearance statement (see below for a detailed discussion of Clearance statements).

[1]   Pensions Act 2004, s 70.
[2]   Pensions Act 2004, s 69.
[3]   The Pensions Regulator (Notifiable Events) Regulations 2005, SI 2005/900.

8.114 A breach of either duty without reasonable excuse will be punishable by a civil penalty at the instance of tPR[1].

Challenging tPR's decision

8.115 Persons who are affected by a determination of tPR (for example, persons against whom a CN or an FSD have been issued) and who wish to challenge it can refer the determination to the Pensions Regulator Tribunal. The Tribunal, which was also created by the Pensions Act 2004, will have the power to confirm, vary or revoke determinations made by tPR.

8.116 Persons who wish to challenge tPR must act quickly: references to the Tribunal must be made within 28 days of the relevant determination. As a matter of principle there is nothing to prevent a determination of tPR being the subject of judicial review proceedings. However, judicial review is a remedy of last resort and therefore the applicant must first exhaust all other available remedies. As a consequence it will be extremely difficult to obtain permission to apply for judicial review of a determination of tPR. The refusal of Clearance is not a matter which can be appealed to the Pensions Regulator Tribunal. So the only way to challenge this would be by a judicial review application.

Notifiable events

8.117 The Pensions Act 2004 requires employers to notify tPR of any 'notifiable event' in relation to a pension scheme[1]. This notification requirement is designed to allow tPR the opportunity to assist, or intervene, before a call is made for compensation from the PPF.

¹ Pensions Act 2004, s 69 and the Pensions Regulator (Notifiable Events) Regulations 2005, SI 2005/900.

8.118 'Notifiable events' include:

(a)   any decision by the employer to take action which will, or is intended to, result in a debt which is or may become due to the scheme not being paid in full;

(b)   receipt by the employer of advice that it is trading wrongfully, or circumstances being reached in which a director (or former director) of the company knows that there is no reasonable prospect that the company will avoid going into insolvent liquidation;

(c)   any breach by the employer of a covenant in an agreement between the employer and a bank or other institution providing banking services, other than where the bank or other institution agrees with the employer not to enforce the covenant;

(d)   two or more changes in the holders of any key employer posts within the previous 12 months;

(e)   a change in control; or

(f)   ceasing to trade in the UK.

F RESTRUCTURINGS INVOLVING MULTI-EMPLOYER SCHEMES

Introduction

8.119 The Occupational Pension Schemes (Employer Debt and Miscellaneous Amendments) Regulations 2008 (SI 2008/731) (the Amending Regulations) were laid before Parliament on Friday 14 March 2008 and are expected to come into force on 6 April 2008. These regulations amend the current Occupational Pension Schemes (Employer Debt) Regulations 2005 (SI 2005/678) (the Employer Debt Regulations) which regulate what employers in single and multi-employer schemes must do to meet the employer debt when severing their relationship with their pension scheme. Transitional arrangements will allow the original Employer Debt Regulations to apply to certain arrangements already agreed or under negotiation until 5 April 2009.

8.120 The Amending Regulations make a number of fundamental changes to the way in which debts triggered under the Pensions Act 1995, s 75 are calculated and provide new options for addressing those debts.

8.121 As stated earlier in this chapter, the Pensions Act 1995, s 75 provides that a debt (based on the buy-out deficit) is triggered on an employer at the time when it (broadly) ceases to employ active members in a multi-employer defined benefit pension scheme. The ceasing employer's share of the debt is based on the amount of the scheme's liabilities attributable to employment with that exiting employer. The debt is also triggered when an employer suffers an insolvency event or when a defined benefit scheme winds up. In any restructuring where there is a severance of a contributing employer from the scheme, for example as a result of its disposal or insolvency, the Amending Regulations will be relevant. Of course if on a disposal the purchaser assumes the full liabilities of the existing employer and its covenants if sufficient, this will be acceptable to the trustees.

Key changes

Allocation of debt

8.122 Under the Amending Regulations, the exiting employer's share of the debt is the 'liability share' unless an alternative is agreed. The 'liability share' is similar to the default allocation mechanism under the former regime and is based on liabilities 'attributable to employment' with the exiting employer. This amount is now determined by the trustees (rather than the actuary under the former regime) after consulting the actuary and the relevant employer.

8.123 Where trustees are:

(i) unable to determine the exact liabilities attributable to the exiting employer; or

(ii) are able to do so only at disproportionate cost,

the Amending Regulations give guidance as to how liabilities should be allocated. This is useful where, for example, the employer has not kept detailed records of intra-group transfers.

8.124 Under the Amending Regulations the allocation options are as follows:

(i)   if the exiting employer was the last employer of a person, all liabilities of that person are attributed to that employer;

(ii)   liabilities in respect of any member which cannot be attributed to any employer are attributed in a 'reasonable manner' to one or more employers (which may or may not include the exiting employer); and

(iii)   if the trustees are unable to determine whether the exiting employer was the last employer and liabilities cannot be attributed to any other employer, those liabilities are not attributed to any employer and they become 'orphan' liabilities.

Options for dealing with section 75 debts

8.125 There are now four options for dealing with a section 75 debt.

1   *Scheme Apportionment Arrangement (SAA)*
This allows trustees to consent to the exiting employer paying the 'scheme apportionment arrangement share', which can be less than the default 'liability share'. This new arrangement also needs to be reflected on the face of the rules. The remaining employers must be able to meet the 'funding test' (see below).

2   *Regulated Apportionment Arrangement (RAA)*
This is similar to a SAA, but is only relevant where the trustees are of the opinion that there is reasonable likelihood of the scheme entering an assessment period for the PPF in the next 12 months or an assessment period has already started. It requires a notice of approval to be issued by tPR and the PPF must not object to the proposal. This will be the most relevant option in the case of a restructuring or insolvency.

3   *Withdrawal Arrangement (WA)*
This regime does not require tPR's approval. Trustees can agree with an employer that a lower debt (based on the scheme funding deficit rather than the buy-out deficit) is payable, with the difference being guaranteed by another employer(s) in the scheme or a third party. The 'funding test' must be met (see below) and the trustees must be satisfied that the guarantors have sufficient financial resources to be likely to be able to pay the guaranteed amount when required.

4   *Approved withdrawal arrangement (AWA)*
This option requires tPR's agreement but can be used where the exiting employer proposes to pay less than the scheme funding amount share of the debt. TPR must be satisfied that it is reasonable to approve the arrangement, having regard to such matters as it considers relevant, including:

    (i)   the potential effects of the employment-cessation event on the method or assumptions for calculating scheme's technical provisions;

    (ii)   the financial circumstances of the proposed guarantor;

    (iii)   the amount of the liability share (if it had applied);

    (iv)   the amount of the AWA share; and

    (v)   the effect of the proposed AWA on the security of members' benefits.

THE 'FUNDING TEST'

8.126 To meet the 'funding test', the trustees must be reasonably satisfied that when the arrangement takes effect, the remaining employers (ie those to whom the section 75 liability has been apportioned) will be reasonably likely to be able to fund the scheme so that it will have sufficient and appropriate assets to cover its technical provisions (taking account of any change in the technical provisions necessary as a result of the arrangement).

8.127 Trustees may consider the test met if, in their opinion, the remaining employers are able to meet the relevant payments as they fall due under the schedule of contributions, taking account of any revision necessary. Where there is a SAA, trustees must also be reasonably satisfied that there is no adverse effect on security of members' benefits as a result of:

    (i)   a material change in legal, demographic or economic circumstances that would justify a change to method and assumptions; or

    (ii)   a material revision to an existing recovery plan.

Existing schemes containing an apportionment rule to provide for an alternative allocation mechanism

8.128 Many employers and trustees have amended scheme rules to provide for an alternative allocation mechanism to ensure that minimal or reduced debts are triggered on employers ceasing to have active members, usually attributing responsibility to the principal company or other employers continuing to participate in the scheme. The 2006 case of *L v M Ltd*[1] confirmed that agreeing in advance to allocate the section 75 debts in this way would not prejudice the scheme's eligibility for the PPF. This approach is no longer possible under the Amending Regulations as other options have been introduced for dealing with a section 75 debt (such as the SAA). However, there are transitional provisions for schemes, which have already introduced such a rule. An existing apportionment rule can continue to apply in relation to a specific trigger event (eg employer-cessation event) which occurs before 6 April 2009 (ie a year from when the Amending Regulations come into force) where:

    (i)   an agreement between the employer and trustees is entered into before, on or within 12 months after 6 April 2008 (ie up to 5 April 2009) on the basis that a scheme's apportionment rule will apply after the 6 April 2008 in relation to a specific employment-cessation event, or in relation to a debt arising as a result of the commencement of winding-up of the scheme;

(ii)   the scheme's apportionment rule was in force before 14 March 2008; and

(iii)   the transaction to which the agreement related was considered before that date by the managing body (i e the board) of at least one of the parties to the agreement or of a connected or associated person of such a party.

¹   [2006] EWHC 3395 (Ch), [2007] PLR 11.

8.129 If a rule amendment has not been executed before 14 March 2008, it is now necessary to comply with the requirements of the Amending Regulations, i e use a SAA or one of the alternatives.

Involvement of tPR

8.130 TPR needs to approve a WA (i e when guarantors are used) where the amount being paid is less than the exiting employer's share of the scheme-funding deficit. He also needs to approve a RAA (relevant where the trustees are of the opinion that there is reasonable likelihood of the scheme entering an assessment period for the PPF in the next 12 months or an assessment period has already started). TPR's updated Clearance guidance (March 2007) suggests that consideration should be given to obtaining Clearance for a SAA or WA.

8.131 The Amending Regulations require that a guarantor under a WA (as well as a AWA) notify tPR of a notifiable event.

Calculating assets and liabilities

8.132 The value of assets under the Amending Regulations is to be determined, calculated and verified by the trustees. The trustees must use the value attributed to the assets in the latest scheme accounts unless the trustees decide, having consulted the employer, to carry out an updated assessment. The liabilities, which are to be taken into account, are to be determined by the trustees, however, the amount of the liabilities is to be calculated and verified by the actuary.

8.133 If a section 75 trigger event occurs while a transfer out is being carried out, the section 75 calculation will take account of the assets and liabilities attributable to those members unless the receiving scheme has received the assets of the full amount agreed by them as consideration for the transfer (a similar rule applies in relation to a transfer in).

8.134 When calculating the liability share, WA share or AWA share, liabilities (and corresponding assets), which are to be transferred out of the scheme, can be discounted where the transfer takes place within 12 months of the employment-cessation event (or longer if so approved by tPR in an AWA situation).

8.135 Former employers can still be liable under the Amending Regulations, as similar rules continue to apply as under the existing regime. The provisions confirming when an employer is not liable as a former employer (eg because there was no deficit at the time of the cessation) are however extended under the Amending Regulations to trigger events applying to employers in relation to frozen schemes (ie those with no active members).

Grace period

8.136 If an employer ceases to employ active members (but before, on, or as soon as possible and in any event within one month after it does so), it may give the trustees a 'period of grace notice' that it intends during the period of grace (which may be up to 12 months) to employ at least one person who will be an active member of the scheme. This will ensure that the section 75 debt will not be triggered. This can only apply, however, to a scheme where the employer 'is not aware of any intention for it to become a frozen scheme' during the grace period.

8.137 During the grace period, the (ex-)employer is treated as an employer for section 75 purposes and no debt is triggered on its ceasing to employ active members. However, if it does not employ any active members by the 12-month deadline, a debt will be due from the cessation date.

8.138 The grace period is terminated if, at any point, the employer no longer intends to employ any active members or if it suffers an insolvency event. In either case, the debt will be due from the cessation date.

Amendment to reflect an apportionment arrangement

8.139 Under the Amending Regulations, trustees have a statutory power for the purposes of the Pensions Act 1995, s 68(2)(e) to amend scheme rules 'after consulting such employers in relation to the scheme as they think appropriate' to provide for an employer's share of the difference under one of the options (SAA, WA, etc) to be attributed in a different proportion from that which would otherwise apply by virtue of the liability share.

G THE IMPACT OF THE PENSIONS LEGISLATION ON RESTRUCTURINGS AND INSOLVENCIES

8.140 As indicated, the Pensions Act 1995, s 75 effectively deems a debt to be due from an employer to the pension scheme in certain circumstances.

8.141 Under the revised regulations in force from 2005, even if the employer is in liquidation the amount of the section 75 debt will be based on the cost of securing all the liabilities of the scheme by buying matching annuities from insurance companies (the 'buyout' bases). As intimated, and as evidenced by the Turner & Newell example cited above, the difference between the sizes of liability as calculated historically by reference to a statutory minimum funding requirement (obliging a scheme to maintain a minimum level of assets to meet its liabilities) and a buyout liability could be enormous.

8.142 When the financial condition of an employer is precarious, the fact that the potentially greater section 75 buy-out debt is triggered by the commencement of formal insolvency proceedings may have a bearing on a director's decision to continue to trade. The directors might conclude that, properly having regard to the interests of the company's general body of creditors, it is in the best interests of the creditors as a whole for the company to avoid formal insolvency proceedings so that those claims are not diluted by a claim made by the pension scheme that is valued on the buyout bases. Directors here face a potential conflict. They may run the risk of personal liability (under a CN) if they act, otherwise than in good faith, to prevent a section 75 debt becoming due.

8.143 The combined effect of the new regulations and FRS 17/IAS 19 (which requires companies to show any scheme deficits (calculated on the FRS 17/IAS 19 bases) on their balance sheet) and the impact of s 75 will be to increase the prominence of defined benefit schemes that are in deficit or are underfunded. This will further differentiate the financial stability of employers that contribute to defined benefit pension schemes from those that do not.

8.144 This has had two consequential effects on the insolvency and restructuring market. First, companies that have a primary liability (that is, as employer) to defined benefit schemes that are in deficit on a buyout bases have been forced to restructure or, in the worst-case scenario, commence insolvency proceedings. At the very least, such companies have found it harder and more costly to raise debt and have been forced down a restructuring path.

Effect on restructurings

8.145 Restructurings need to be planned carefully if they are to avoid triggering a buyout debt under section 75 or the risk of participants being issued with CNs or FSDs. In particular, care must be taken where it is proposed as part of a restructuring that employees be transferred, companies wound up or value extracted from the group (for example, by way of payment of a dividend or the grant of security). This will be an issue even where the company's pension scheme has no deficit on an ongoing basis because tPR is concerned with ensuring there is potential funding in place in the future for the (much) higher buyout bases required under statute in certain situations.

8.146 There are, however, certain steps that can and have been taken as part of a restructuring to minimise the moral hazard risk:

(a) **Purpose:** purpose is a key part of the CN test. Care must therefore be taken in minuting the purpose of decisions that might weaken the strength of the participating employer's ability to fund the pension scheme. Purpose will be assessed with the benefit of hindsight and past experience with insolvency and tax legislation is that it is notoriously difficult to assess.

(b) **Clearances:** where a restructuring involves, or might affect the financial position of, a participating employer of a defined benefit pension scheme, the parties to the restructuring should consider seriously the need to seek a Clearance statement prior to completion. No doubt the need for full disclosure of the details of the proposed transactions will be time consuming and costly; however, a failure to do so may render the Clearance worthless.

(c) **Use of formal restructuring tools:** schemes of arrangement under the Companies Act 1985, s 425[1] and company voluntary arrangements ('CVAs') under Part I of the Insolvency Act 1986 may be used to implement a restructuring proposal. A scheme and a CVA can bind trustees of a defined benefit pension scheme to a compromise of the pension scheme debt if the trustees are parties to it. However, the decision by scheme trustees to seek to compromise a pension scheme debt gives rise to a duty on the employer and the scheme trustee to notify tPR of the proposed compromise[2]. This might lead to a review of the proposed transaction by tPR. Unless a Clearance notice is obtained in respect of the compromise it is possible that tPR might issue a CN or FSD in respect of any deficit. As a result of the compromise of a scheme debt the scheme might also be excluded from being eligible later to join (and obtain protection from) the PPF.

[1] The Companies Act 1985, s 425(1) is to be replaced by the Companies Act 2006, ss 895(1), 896(1) and (2). The Companies Act 1985, s 425(2) is to be replaced by the Companies Act 2006, ss 899(1), and (3), 907(1) and 922(1). The Companies Act 1985, s 425(3) is to be replaced (with some changes) by the Companies Act 2006, ss 899(4), 901(3) and (4). The Companies Act 1985, s 425(4) is to be replaced by the Companies Act 2006, s 901(5) and (6). The Companies Act 1985, s 425(6) is to be replaced by the Companies Act 2006, s 895(2). The Companies Act 2006, ss 895–935 are to come into force on 6 April 2008 (SI 2007/3495). For transitional provisions and savings, see SI 2007/3495, arts 6, 9, 12, Schs 1, 4.

[2] This is likely to be a 'notifiable event' under the Pensions Act 2004, s 69, discussed above.

8.147 The impact of the Pensions Act 2004 can be seen in a variety of restructurings. In the restructuring of a major listed furniture company for example where it was necessary to deal with two defined benefit pension schemes operated by the group, the restructuring outcome was radically different to the one that may well have transpired pre-Pensions Act 2004. The existence of deficits required tPR Clearance for a re-financing of £185m of unsecured debt with £150m of secured debt.

8.148 The pension trustees initially requested that the security be shared equally between them and the incoming financiers. Given the nature of the new financing (asset-backed lending) this was commercially unacceptable to the incoming lenders and threatened to prevent the re-financing, which potentially prevented the wider restructuring of the group from taking place. A very limited time was available within which to conclude the re-financing before a potentially value damaging covenant breach arose under the existing unsecured lending.

8.149 The agreement reached with the pensions trustees and the incoming financiers which was cleared by tPR was innovative in that it gave first ranking asset and share security to the asset-backed lenders in exchange only for a first charge over the share capital of the most valuable company in the group ('ValuableCo') being granted to the trustees. The trustees also received second ranking security from other members of the group. In this way, the trustees agreed to align their beneficiaries' interests with the future enterprise value of the group's main business so as to facilitate a financial rescue package. The trustees' ability to enforce their security was limited to circumstances where the secured lenders enforced against ValueableCo's assets or where that company failed to reach an EBITDA threshold that was set very low. This case is a clear example of how pension trustees under the auspices of the regulatory supervision of tPR are changing the nature and process of the restructuring of UK corporates, which have a defined benefit scheme.

8.150 Before the PPF was established, there were several cases where companies in financial difficulties compromised the employer debt due to the trustees of their scheme when the scheme was wound up. These were generally known as Bradstock compromises. The High Court accepted in *Bradstock Group Pension Scheme Trustees Ltd v Bradstock Group plc*[1] that, while it was not possible to contract out of the employer debt legislation, it was possible to compromise a debt once it had arisen. From the trustees' perspective, it was in the interests of the scheme members to enter into a compromise if the potential recovery to the scheme was greater than the potential recovery if the company became insolvent.

[1] [2002] EWHC 1461 (Ch), [2002] ICR 1427.

8.151 Since 6 April 2005, if an insolvency event occurs in relation to an employer, and the scheme enters into an assessment period, the PPF exercises all powers to compromise an employer debt[1]. If trustees enter into a legally enforceable compromise of an employer debt before an insolvency event, and the scheme has insufficient assets to meet the liabilities on the PPF bases, this can prevent future PPF entry[2].

[1] Pensions Act 2004, s 137.
[2] PPF Entry Rules, reg 2(2).

8.152 There have been cases since 6 April 2005 where, with the agreement of tPR, the trustees and the PPF, a scheme has entered the PPF as part of a restructuring exercise under which the employer emerges free of its pension liabilities. Often this has been achieved through a 'pre-pack' arrangement, under which the company is put into administration and the pension liabilities are then compromised by the PPF as part of a CVA. If the compromise potentially produces a greater recovery to the PPF than the alternatives (a non-pre-packed sale), and saves jobs, tPR is likely to give Clearance, with the PPF taking an equity stake in the surviving company.

8.153   Until the case of *L v M Ltd*[1], the problem with the current legislation was that trustees would not be willing to compromise an employer debt if it potentially barred PPF entry. Accordingly, the only way to enter into a Bradstock compromise since 6 April 2005 was to put the company into insolvency. Often this destroyed value, and it would have been preferable to enter into a similar arrangement without the company being put through an insolvency procedure.

[1]   [2006] EWHC 3395 (Ch), [2007] PLR 11.

8.154   This is what was achieved in *L v M Ltd*. With the approval of tPR, it was agreed in advance that a new employer would be admitted to participation into a single employer scheme. This new company then employed a couple of employees for a limited period. An apportionment rule was inserted into the scheme rules, permitting the trustees to allocate the debt differently than under the normal statutory formula. The old employer (with the bulk of the employees) then ceased to participate, and, under the new allocation rule, a £1 debt arose against it. Once the debt was paid, the old employer was treated as a former employer for employer debt purposes, and was not liable for any part of the statutory debt on the subsequent winding up of the scheme. The whole of the debt then fell onto the new employer, and the scheme could enter the PPF.

8.155   The trustees were understandably concerned that the arrangement should not bar PPF entry. Warren J held that, given the overall framework of the legislation, a narrow construction should be placed on regulation 2(2) of the PPF Entry Rules. This provision only barred entry into the PPF where a legally enforceable agreement was entered into, the effect of which was to reduce the amount of any debt that was already due, not one which may have been due in the future. Accordingly, by entering into the agreement, the trustees would not prevent PPF entry in the future.

8.156   It is understood that the agreement increased the PPF's overall recovery in this case (in comparison with the alternatives), saved jobs, and should not make any difference to the members as they will receive compensation from the PPF.

8.157   It should be possible to use this method in restructuring situations where the company genuinely cannot survive, if it has to continue to meet its pension liabilities. Neither the trustees nor the Regulator are going to approve such an arrangement if it is possible that the employer can meet its pension liabilities over an extended recovery period.

8.158 The Department of Work and Pensions consulted in Autumn 2007 on revised Employer Debt Regulations under section 75. If enacted, these may make the use of allocation rules or withdrawal arrangements more legally certain.

Impact on groups of companies and investors

8.159 A parent company or equity investor that holds more than one-third of the voting shares in a participating employer (or its parent) is an associate of the employer and will be, therefore, at risk of being issued a CN or an FSD in respect of any scheme deficit or underfunding. It is possible that those acting in concert for the purposes of the City Code may also be 'associates' for the purposes of the Act.

8.160 The potential for cross-contamination of pension liabilities between investments held by private equity investors was raised in consultation on the Pensions Bill and has fortunately been somewhat mitigated in the Act through the introduction of requirements of reasonableness. However, the risk to equity investors of being subject to a CN or FSD has certainly affected investor conduct and in particular the conduct of private equity firms in many LBO restructurings.

Impact on formal insolvencies and members' voluntary liquidations

8.161 TPR cannot issue a CN to an insolvency practitioner unless, in being a party to an act or a deliberate failure to act with the main purpose of avoiding pension liabilities, that insolvency practitioner was not acting in accordance with his functions as an insolvency practitioner.

8.162 Provided that an administrator or liquidator is properly carrying out his officeholder functions, there should be little risk of personal liability. This sits well with the approach taken by David Richards J in *Re T&N Ltd*[1], decided in July 2004. On the administrators' application for directions, it was held that the administrators' primary duty to act in the best interests of creditors justified their decision to withdraw associated participating companies from the T&N group pension scheme even though to do so would put the scheme into deficit on a buyout bases (although, crucially, at the time of withdrawal the buyout liability had not been triggered). Richards J referred to the then Pensions Bill in his judgment.

[1]   [2004] EWHC 1680 (Ch), [2004] OPLR 343.

8.163 The relatively strong position of insolvency practitioners may mean that there are more pre-packaged sales out of formal insolvencies where previously the cost of appointing an insolvency officeholder outweighed the benefits.

8.164 When used as a restructuring tool, the issues highlighted above will apply equally to members' voluntary liquidations ('MVLs'). Indeed, as a result of the impact of the increased buyout liability on pension scheme deficits and FRS 17/IAS 19 it is possible that there may be a reduction in the use of MVLs. In particular, in group situations where the group has an underfunded pension scheme, directors of non-participating companies may find it difficult to satisfy themselves that the company is and will continue to be solvent in view of the risk of a CN or an FSD being issued against the company. For the same reason, parent companies that would typically offer some support to such a company may be increasingly reluctant to do so. One option may be to seek a Clearance from tPR, as analysed in the earlier part of this chapter.

Practical restructuring solutions

8.165 So in practice how are pensions being addressed in restructurings? Perhaps obviously, the answer depends on the situation and, particularly, what value is available. Historically, the pension deficit has been unsecured and therefore ranked ahead of shareholders, alongside other unsecured creditors, but behind secured lenders.

8.166 Where there is value for shareholders, the pension trustees will drive a hard bargain. This is understandable, as why should the shareholders, who rank behind, be paid first? For example, in the Marconi/Ericsson corporate sale, according to press reports, £185m of the £1.2bn purchase price paid by Ericsson went to clear the FRS 17 deficit (the accounting deficit calculation used in annual accounts). A further £490m was paid into escrow to protect the pension deficit – the concern being that the post-sale Marconi covenant was weakened such that it might be unable to meet any future payments to the scheme. This amount was insufficient to cover the buy out deficit on the scheme. Nonetheless, the pension trustees and tPR also agreed to £577m being returned to Marconi shareholders – which shows their recognition that had the deal not been able to generate reasonable value for shareholders, it would not have gone ahead and the proceeds would not have been available for the scheme. In addition, money can be withdrawn from escrow and paid to the shareholders if the pension scheme becomes over funded. This avoids money being trapped in the pension scheme if, say, interest rates rise and assets grow beyond expectations. It also gives the shareholders the prospect of more value, subject to what happens to the deficit.

8.167 Another way to address deficits is to reduce the liability through amending the benefits. British Airways is perhaps the highest profile example, where amongst other things BA is trying to increase the retirement age for pilots from 55 years. Changing the investment strategy of the pension trustees can also work to decrease the deficit. Clearly pension trustees are often going to invest conservatively, but the pension trustees who remained in equities following the downturn around 2000 have done a lot better than some who moved into bonds. Whilst these can be effective solutions to a deficit problem, they both take time, which is often a luxury people can ill afford in restructurings.

8.168 In a restructuring situation and faced with a temporary cash squeeze, pension trustees will consider rescheduling pension payments but, like a bank, they will want to verify independently the crisis and the alternatives. Under the new regime, pension trustees will generally instruct separate lawyers and financial advisers to analyse and test what is proposed by the company or the purchaser. Like other commercial parties, they will consider the full range of options for obtaining value for the pension scheme or, if that is not possible, to protect the pension deficit as best they can.

Taking security and guarantees

8.169 The pension trustees may independently request security be granted for the liabilities of the group to the scheme, and will almost certainly do so if previously unsecured bank debt is being secured as part of the restructuring. The security can either be equal ranking or over a separate asset pool. Security can be granted to financial creditors jointly or separate assets may be isolated and secured in favour of the financial creditors or indeed the security trustee. On a number of complex cases detailed intercreditor arrangements have been established to create a security trust over the relevant pool of secured assets and to prioritise the competing claims of creditors and the pension trustee. In many cases the claims have ranked equally and rateably on insolvency, but on other transactions separate arrangements have been agreed in connection with pre-insolvency scenarios such that bank debt with a much earlier maturity can logically and indeed legitimately be discharged from disposal proceeds generated by the group outside of insolvency.

8.170 An exception to any requirement for pari passu security is where new money is being advanced to address an immediate liquidity need (but not if, say, to pay off other existing unsecured creditors). Pension trustees have generally agreed to this new money being given first ranking security ahead of the pension deficit.

8.171 In certain restructuring scenarios it is likely that various of the group companies will be participating employers in the pension scheme or have financial obligations under the scheme as scheme obligors. Depending on the group structure, there may be an element of structural subordination here, even though all the claims are unsecured. Indeed, certain financial creditors may well be at a disadvantage because they do not have any guarantee claims against the same group companies where the pension liabilities sit. In essence the financial creditors will seek entity equality in these circumstances and it is interesting to consider whether group companies can create parity between their pension trustee creditor and their financial creditors where it is commercially beneficial to do so as part of an initial phase of restructuring or as part of a wider restructuring, without infringing the moral hazard provisions under the Pensions Act 2004.

8.172 It is possible that the subsidiary companies that are to grant the proposed guarantees could seek to refuse to enter into them on the basis that the moral hazard provisions would apply, and that Clearance would not be granted, but it is submitted that such a view is incorrect[1].

[1]   In the absence of a shareholding by any of the financial creditors of a third or more in the capital of a company in the group, and the absence of any employee or director of one of the financial creditors also being a director (or shadow director) of a company in the group, no CN could be served on any of the financial creditors. However, this is likely to be of little consolation to directors concerned about their personal liability for the liability of their company.

8.173 Whilst one of the directors of the relevant subsidiaries granting the guarantee could in principle be open to receipt of a CN, this is also unlikely because in addition to the requirement for the issue of a CN of an act or failure to act, a particular state of mind (inherent in the concept of 'main purpose') is required. The question as to whether the proposed guarantees would render parties liable to a CN therefore depends on the 'main purposes' of the act or failure to act.

8.174 On the basis that the 'main purpose' requirement presupposes a state of mind whereby there is a positive desire to achieve the results of avoiding or, otherwise than in good faith, reducing pension liabilities, then it is unlikely that a CN could be issued on the directors. On an objective analysis of such proposed guarantees, it is at least arguable that there would be no such desire if the proposed guarantees are being put in place as a response to commercial pressures and a desire to retain the support of financial creditors. Any peripheral result of reducing pension liabilities is not the main purpose and the directors could avail themselves of the good faith defence.

8.175 In this regard, an analogy may be drawn with the construction of the test for 'preferences' under the Insolvency Act 1986, s 239, which refers to a 'desire' to produce a preference. It was held in *Re M C Bacon Ltd*[1] that a company will only fall foul of this section if it 'positively wished' to improve the position of a creditor in the event of its own insolvency. The court in that case indicated that a person was not to be taken as desiring all the necessary consequences of its actions. Applying similar reasoning here, the financial creditors could run an argument that the proposed guarantees do not involve a 'main purpose' of preventing a debt from being paid in full – as required by the Pensions Act 2004[2] – even if that were to be a possible result of the proposed guarantees being put in place. On this basis, the financial creditors could seek to provide comfort to the directors of the relevant subsidiaries that they would not be subject to receipt of a CN if the proposed guarantees were granted.

[1]   [1990] BCC 78, 87, Ch D.
[2]   On the basis that there is no suggestion of bad faith, it is head (i) of 'main purpose' that would be relevant here.

8.176 In this regard it would assist in denying the application of the moral hazard provisions if the boards of the relevant subsidiaries noted in minutes of their meetings:

(a)   that the purpose of granting the proposed guarantees is to maintain the group as a going concern and preserve the ability of the holding company or the subsidiaries to contribute to the scheme;

(b)   a belief that the grant of the proposed guarantees will have this effect; and

(c)   a belief that there is no alternative course of action open to them to achieve such effect.

8.177 If the directors of the relevant subsidiaries, despite the above arguments, are concerned that they might be at risk of receiving a CN, they can of course seek Clearance from tPR, by satisfying tPR that the act (or failure to act) does not satisfy the test for a CN. It is a question for the directors whether Clearance should be sought. Clearance is not mandatory and it is designed to provide more certainty to affected parties.

8.178 TPR's 2008 guidance on Clearance indicates the types of events it would be concerned about, and in relation to which an application for Clearance should be considered. None of the example Type A events would be applicable since tPR 2008 Guidance only cites the example of the granting or extending of a fixed or floating charge, and does not suggest that additional unsecured obligations in the form of guarantees would fall within the category of Type A events[1]. However, tPR emphasises that the spirit of the guidance must be taken into account as well as its specific wording, in particular where the guidance does not explicitly cover the circumstances in question. The guidance states that tPR will wish to know about all events having a materially detrimental effect on the ability of a pension scheme to meet its liabilities.

[1]   It should be noted that CNs and FSDs might still be possible even though the event of granting a guarantee is not a Type A event. However, the fact that the grant of a guarantee is not listed as a Type A event is likely to go the reasonableness of imposing a CN or an FSD.

8.179 The intended effect of the grant of the proposed guarantees would be to create additional obligors to whom the financial creditors could have recourse, correcting their structural subordination in the relevant financing structure. If insolvency of the holding company occurred immediately after the grant of the proposed guarantees, such grant would have had a materially detrimental impact on the potential recovery of the pension creditor, such that it could amount to a Type A event. However, the common objective of the proposed guarantees is to avoid a situation where either the holding company or the relevant subsidiaries enters insolvency. This factor would support an argument that the grant of the proposed guarantees should not be construed as a Type A event within either the letter or the spirit of the guidance, and perhaps more importantly within the terms of the Act.

8.180 Three further factors may militate in favour of the conclusion that tPR should not in principle be concerned about the proposed guarantees:

(a)   if the debt sought to be guaranteed by the relevant subsidiaries was borrowed by the holding company in order to finance the subsidiaries in the first place: from an economic perspective, tPR should therefore not be concerned about guarantees of the debt extending from them;

(b)   if going forward it would be possible to make the relevant subsidiaries primary obligors by acceding as borrowers to the loan facilities; in such case, when a revolving loan matures on the next rollover date, the subsidiary can be required to issue a utilisation request (funding itself directly). In principle this debt pushed down to the subsidiaries would not amount to a Type A event; by analogy, tPR should not be concerned about the issue of the proposed guarantees, which would effectively create the same liability by another means, albeit allowing more flexibility on the part of the group; and

(c)   to the extent that the holding company has on-lent to the subsidiaries, these intercompany loans would amount to assets on the balance sheet of the holding company; in the event of an insolvency of the holding company, the financial creditors could pursue such debts as intercompany claims on a *pari passu* basis with the scheme liabilities owed by the relevant subsidiaries. As such, tPR should not be concerned about the issue of the proposed guarantees, which would not necessarily create liabilities that do not already exist.

8.181 The conditions for a potential grant of an FSD would need to be considered. If one were granted against the non-employer group companies would it mean that their financial position was such that the grant of any guarantees resulted in potential insolvency?

8.182 Given the potential uncertainty of a company's ability to grant a guarantee it is noteworthy that the draft 2007 guidance does refer to unsecured obligations as potential notification events.

Action, which will, or is intended to, result in a debt not being paid in full

8.183 In this context the word 'will' imports certainty rather than mere possibility. Given the lack of certainty that the proposed guarantees would result in the failure of any debt to be paid in full, we believe the 'will' criterion is not fulfilled. Furthermore, some kind of desire (for a debt not to be paid) is arguably required for the 'intention' wording to come into play. It can therefore be concluded that a reasonable argument could be run that the decisions to grant the proposed guarantees would not amount to 'notifiable events' under this head.

Wrongful trading; no reasonable prospect of avoiding insolvent liquidation

8.184 It would be unlikely that this head of 'notifiable events' is likely to apply to the circumstances under consideration. However, it is possible that this head of 'notifiable events' may come into play if the proposed guarantees are *not* granted, and this is perhaps a point that can be put to the directors of the subsidiaries in the event that they do not co-operate in the restructuring and seek to refuse the grant of the proposed guarantees.

Breach of banking covenant

8.185 The breach of banking covenants that has already taken place, or may take place before or in connection with the granting of the proposed guarantees, have been or will be (at least in the short term) waived by the financial creditors. On this basis, this head of 'notifiable events' is not relevant for present purposes.

Implications of a notifiable event

8.186 Even if the directors of the subsidiaries consider that a 'notifiable event' has occurred, this in itself would not prejudice the directors; notification simply puts tPR on notice that it may wish to consider assisting or intervening in the scheme. It is a separate question whether a CN or an FSD may be issued, in relation to which the directors should gain some comfort from the arguments set out in the section above. Indeed, it is not necessarily adverse for the purposes of the restructuring if the directors conclude that a decision to grant the proposed guarantees would amount to a 'notifiable event', as this would make the practical process of seeking Clearance as part of the restructuring more straightforward.

Trustee powers

8.187 There may be action that the trustees of the pension scheme might be able to take in relation to the granting of the proposed guarantees (independently of tPR). It is possible that the relevant subsidiaries could seek to refuse to issue the proposed guarantees in light of such potential action.

8.188 What actions are available to the scheme trustees will depend on their powers under the scheme documentation. In principle, following the grant of the proposed guarantees, it is possible that they would be able to:

(a) consider increasing the contributions payable by the employer;
(b) move to a more cautious investment strategy than that currently in force; or
(c) (in an extreme case) wind up the scheme, triggering a full buy-out contribution from the employer.

8.189 However, there would be no obligation, under the general law, on the employer to notify the scheme trustees that they were granting the proposed guarantees. Any such obligation would only arise by virtue of specific agreement to this effect with the scheme trustees. Some companies have agreed formal information sharing arrangements with the trustees.

Serious distress

8.190 A different approach is needed where the company cannot be refinanced or restructured with the ongoing pension liability – in other words the company is in serious distress and facing insolvency. Here, the PPF comes into play. The PPF was established to pay compensation to members of eligible defined benefit pension schemes, when there is a qualifying insolvency event regarding the employer and where there are insufficient assets in the pension scheme to cover PPF levels of compensation. If on assessment by the PPF the scheme cannot be rescued, the PPF assumes responsibility for paying the scheme members (to the statutory protected levels) and takes over the assets of the pension scheme, including becoming the company's creditor.

8.191 For scheme members below normal pension age as at the assessment date, the statutory protected benefit levels are, broadly, 90% of entitlement with a cap of a little under £30,000. By contrast, a scheme member over the relevant normal pension age is entitled to a full pension. There are special rules for ill-health pensioners. This creates a cliff edge where a few days age difference can have a dramatic effect on a scheme member's statutory PPF entitlement.

8.192 Unstructured insolvency processes are value destructive – contracts get terminated, customers leave, employees are poached, etc. Where a balance sheet restructuring is required, creditors often agree a debt for equity swap to maximise value. Pension trustees cannot hold more than 5% of their assets by value as shares in their employer company (or an associate)[1], but the PPF can. This has enabled the PPF to take shares on a debt for equity swap, with the company/business being released from the deficit and able to continue trading with a restructured balance sheet.

[1]   Pensions Act 1995, s 40.

8.193 The PPF first agreed to take equity in July 2005 in the high-profile Heath Lambert administration. The Heath Lambert scheme had a £210m deficit. The administration was an insolvency event, which effectively led to the pension scheme transferring to the PPF who then had the buyout deficit claim against Heath Lambert. In the ensuing restructuring, the underlying Heath Lambert businesses were transferred to a new company, in which the PPF took shares. At the time, the PPF's actions were criticised by some. The Financial Times called it dangerous and flawed and described Heath Lambert as being 'sloughed of its pensions debts'. The FT wrongly saw the process as an easy panacea. A qualifying insolvency event was required and the PPF only agreed after taking extensive advice and because it decided that it provided a better outcome for the PPF than a full insolvency. Commercially the transaction provided more value to the PPF than leaving the Heath Lambert businesses in an unplanned insolvency.

8.194 A similar situation arose in respect of Pittards plc, the gloves and saddle makers. The Pittards pension scheme had a £33m deficit and entered the PPF through a CVA. In return, the PPF received 18.5% of the equity and Pittards agreed to pay £3m over five years, secured over a factory. Further, if the factory were sold before 2026, the PPF would get any windfall gain up to £6.8m. Interestingly, under the Pittards CVA, all other liabilities were paid and Pittards plc continued, freed of the pensions deficit. So why did the PPF agree to this? As a PPF spokesman explained, 'This company was clearly going bust ... we got involved to maximise the assets of the scheme'. This statement and the combination of equity, secured debt and a windfall payment show again how the PPF acts commercially. Provided the PPF is getting more than it would have done in insolvency, then it will do a horse trade to agree the terms of a deal which can include a wide range of options to give value.

8.195 Most recently a new innovative solution has evolved through the Polestar restructuring whereby a pension scheme deficit can be transferred off a company's balance sheet without an employer insolvency event. The Polestar Group was seriously financially distressed with over £1bn of debt, much of which was secured. The pension deficit of around £130m FRS 17 and over £300m on a buyout bases was unsecured. In insolvency, the pension scheme would have effectively got nothing.

8.196 The secured creditors and Polestar agreed a restructuring whereby a significant proportion of secured debt would be removed from the balance sheet. The restructuring was designed to avoid the value destruction of an insolvency event in the operating employer company. However, without an insolvency event, the pension scheme could not go into the PPF. After extensive discussions, a creative solution was agreed whereby the Polestar pension scheme and deficit was transferred to a separate SPV company ringfenced away from the Polestar Group. TPR gave Clearance and this, together with certain amendments to the pension deeds and other steps, insulated the purchaser and the ongoing Polestar Group from the historic pension deficit. In exchange, Polestar agreed to pay the pension scheme a total of £45m over 12 years.

8.197 This benefited all the stakeholders, including the pension scheme. However, this solution will not be possible in all situations. Critically, in Polestar a lot of secured debt was being written off, the pension deficit was unsecured, and the pension scheme effectively would have received nothing in insolvency.

8.198 In the case of *L v M Ltd*[1], mentioned above, a similar SPV transfer was recently approved by the court. An apparent difference in this case however, was that the transfer was to be followed by an insolvency event in the SPV. This would enable the pension scheme to enter the PPF, but without an insolvency event in the former employer.

1   [2006] EWHC 3395 (Ch), [2007] PLR 11 (Warren J).

H CONCLUSION

8.199 There has been a dramatic shift in the importance of pension trustees in UK restructurings. They have become key players, increasingly acting like other major creditors. However, the fears of stifling restructurings have proved unfounded. Far from being 'the living dead', the pension trustees, tPR and the PPF have embraced innovative alternatives that benefit all stakeholders. Whilst pension deficits remain a major issue in many restructurings, creative ways to preserve value have developed and more are evolving.

Chapter 9

RESTRUCTURING AND DIRECTORS' DUTIES

A INTRODUCTION

9.1 When the Companies Act 2006 ('CA 2006') received Royal Assent on 8 November 2006, it represented the culmination of many years of corporate law review the aim of which had been to establish a company law that was fair, modern and effective. The majority of the CA 2006 will have come into force by October 2008, although some parts will have been implemented before then[1] with others coming into force by the end of 2007[2]. The provisions relating to directors' duties came into force on 1 October 2007. Further consultation has recently been issued on how the CA 2006 should apply to existing companies[3]. Secondary legislation will be required to support some of the provisions of the CA 2006.

[1] See the CA 2006, s 1300 for further details; and the Companies Act 2006 (Commencement No 1, Transitional Provisions and Savings) Order 2006, SI 2006/3428 which lists those provisions of the CA 2006 effective (and the provisions of the 1985 Act to be repealed) on 1 January, 20 January and 6 April 2007.
[2] See Margaret Hodge's statement available on the DTI website, dated 28 February 2007, in which she announced the Companies Act Implementation timetable.
[3] See www.berr.gov.uk/consultations/page37980.html for a copy of the DTI's Implementation of Companies Act 2006 Consultative Document, February 2007.

9.2 The CA 2006 spans an impressive 1300 sections and 16 schedules. As with any legislative reform (especially one of this size), there will inevitably be a period of uncertainty faced by companies, directors and other interested parties. In a pure restructuring context, restructuring practitioners will have a key role to play in offering clarity where at all possible and devising effective ways of working with the legislative changes.

9.3 With this in mind, this chapter attempts to raise awareness of some of the changes introduced by the CA 2006, which are of relevance to the restructuring industry. In particular, the chapter analyses the provisions relating to directors' duties which are of critical importance to the restructuring process and finishes by looking at certain risks that confront directors undertaking a restructuring, including in particular the risks of fraudulent and wrongful trading and the possibilities of disqualification as a director. Of course the development of the concept of shadow directorship ensures that these risks can potentially apply to other stakeholders who are involved in a restructuring including in particular shareholders, other investors, parent companies, financiers and advisers.

B DIRECTORS' DUTIES

Statutory statement

9.4 Prior to the CA 2006, the rules governing directors' duties came from several sources. The general duties owed by directors to their companies were governed by the common law and have developed over many years in case law. The Companies Act 1985 (in particular Part X) sets out additional rules. The aim of the CA 2006 is to make the law in the area of directors' duties more consistent, certain, accessible and comprehensible. In view of this, the CA 2006 introduces a statutory statement of directors' duties described as 'general duties' which are intended to codify the existing common law and equitable rules and to a significant extent rewrite Part X of the Companies Act 1985. Where particular fact patterns dictate, the courts will almost certainly need to take into consideration common law case precedents, and in this important respect the common law relating to directors' duties remains relevant.

9.5 Although the statement of general duties has been described by the government as a codification of the existing law, it is not framed in exactly the same terms as the existing law. Much of the language in which the general duties are framed is different from the more archaic language used by the common law and this may lead to differences in approach when the new laws are applied in practice in the restructuring arena.

9.6 There are seven general duties in the new statutory statement as follows:

1 A duty to act in accordance with the company's constitution, and to use powers only for the purposes for which they were conferred. This replaces existing, similar duties.
2 A duty to promote the success of the company for the benefit of its members. This replaces the common law duty to act in good faith in the company's interests.
3 A duty to exercise independent judgement. There is no exact equivalent of this duty at common law. However, directors historically have been under an obligation not to fetter their discretion to act or to take decisions – this aspect of the general duty replaces this obligation.
4 A duty to exercise reasonable care, skill and diligence. This replaces the existing duty of care and skill.
5 A duty to avoid conflicts of interest (except where they arise out of a proposed transaction or arrangement with the company –see below). At

present, if a director allows his personal interests, or his duties to another person, to conflict with his duty to the company then, unless shareholders consent to the conflict: (i) the company can avoid any relevant contract, and (ii) he must account to the company for any 'secret profit' he has made out of the arrangement. The new duty replaces this old common law rule.

6   A duty not to accept benefits from third parties. There is no express duty to this effect at common law. It appears to derive from the current duty of fidelity, the duty to act in the company's interests and the rule dealing with conflicts of interest.

7   A duty to declare to the company's other directors any interest a director has in a proposed transaction or arrangement with the company. Historically, a conflict of interest arising out of a transaction or arrangement with the company has been dealt with by the general common law rule on conflicts of interest described above. In the future, such a conflict will be covered by this new duty of disclosure.

9.7 The most novel and interesting provision under the CA 2006 is the new duty set out in the statutory statement which obliges a director to 'act in the way he considers, in good faith, would be most likely to promote the success of the company for the benefit of its members as a whole' (CA 2006, s 172(1)). This duty is to be carried out with regard to a series of matters, including the likely long-term consequences of their decisions, the interests of employees, the impact of the company's operations on the community and the environment, the need to foster the company's business relationships with suppliers, customers and others, the desirability of maintaining a reputation for high standards of business conduct and the need to act fairly as between members of the company (CA 2006, s 172(1)(a)–(f)).

9.8 While the introduction of these additional factors has provoked much debate and a degree of concern for restructuring professionals who customarily advise directors of financially distressed companies, the government's expressed intention is not to impose additional bureaucratic burdens on companies. Rather, consideration of the matters listed in CA 2006, s 172 (while not exhaustive) is supposed to reflect current best practice. Most companies are therefore unlikely to need to make significant changes to present procedures in relation to directors' decision making, provided that they consider at least the factors listed above in reaching a decision.

9.9 Given the government's assurance, there is a strong argument that companies should not significantly change their procedure for documenting decisions. The CA 2006 does not require the board minutes to record that the factors were considered, although some companies may decide they want to include a reference to having considered the factors to evidence that they did this. The GC100 (the Association of General Counsel and Company Secretaries of the FTSE 100) has also published a paper on directors' duties which sets out its view on best practice guidelines for public companies' compliance with the law. The GC100 suggested that where a factor such as the impact on a supplier or a customer, is particularly relevant or sensitive to a decision, companies may wish to address this in board papers.

9.10 What is clear is that advisers should ensure that the directors (and those responsible for the production of board and other supporting papers) have had the new requirements explained to them generally so that when they come to a particular decision they take the factors set out in the CA 2006 into account. As indicated above, the consideration of such factors is unlikely to be revolutionary and should already accord with the best practice adopted by many public companies and other small and medium-sized enterprises. In deciding whether to include a more detailed record of discussions on a particular matter in board minutes, the directors should also take into account any general policy they have adopted in relation to record keeping and potential litigation.

9.11 In certain restructuring scenarios, perhaps where the company is operating on the cusp of insolvency pending a resolution of its financial position with its creditors, the relevance and application of the statutory factors (as explained below) does diminish. However, in the context of the new statutory framework, the board of a distressed company may still be more likely to wish to refer specifically in the minutes to a particular factor or even record a discussion about it. Where a factor is specifically pertinent in a restructuring such as reaching a strategic decision to effect a disposal of a non-performing business by way of example, a discussion on the effect on the employees (including logically their defined benefit pension scheme) or the likely long-term consequences of the directors' decisions on the impact of the company's operations, would still be recommended.

Distressed companies

9.12 Whilst the CA 2006 creates new duties and factors for consideration it should be noted that as the company becomes increasingly distressed, the duty to promote the success of the company for the benefit of its members is expressed to have effect 'subject to any enactment or rule of law requiring directors, in certain circumstances, to consider or act in the interests of creditors of the company' (CA 2006, s 172(3)). Under the existing common law, when a company's financial position has deteriorated to the point where its solvency is in question, the focus of the directors' attention must shift away from the shareholders towards protecting the interests of creditors. This is the position classically set out in *West Mercia Safetywear Ltd v Dodd*[1] and it would seem that the expressed intention is not to change this.

[1]　[1988] BCLC 250.

The importance of the statutory factors and the decision to stop trading

9.13 When a company is in trouble, should the directors in considering the interests of creditors continue to have primary regard to the various factors set out in CA 2006, s 172(1) or are they only relevant when the directors are looking to promote the success of the company for the benefit of its members?

9.14 The directors are in a difficult position because under the new legislation they could potentially make a determination that they should be taking into account the other interest groups and that they should delay filing for insolvency where to do so would impact adversely on the company's employees, the community, the environment or any of the other interests to which they believe they are to have regard. Perversely, this could expose them to claims for wrongful trading where the company was clearly insolvent at the time[1].

[1]   The section of this chapter on wrongful trading examines this conundrum more fully.

9.15 Alternatively, the directors of a company may decide to continue trading for a period in order to improve returns for creditors but, ultimately, with a view to filing for insolvency. In so doing, they would be minimising the potential loss to creditors and, at the same time, reducing the likelihood of a wrongful trading action. However, what if, in continuing to trade, it is harder for the employees to find alternative work when the company eventually files for insolvency – for example, if the directors decide to trade up until Christmas (as they might well do in a retail business)? Is this something the directors should be having regard to in considering the interests of creditors?

9.16 It is suggested that the factors relevant to promoting the company's success under CA 2006, s 172(1) are not directly relevant at a time when the directors need to take the interests of creditors into account. Such factors are only required to be considered in relation to the exercise of the duty in that subsection. There appears to have been no intention to change the existing law governing how directors should exercise their duties when a company approaches insolvency.

9.17 However, under the common law, it is difficult for directors to know precisely when creditors' interests are to intrude and to be preferred over the interests of shareholders in any given situation, as there is no neat dividing line. The section of this chapter on wrongful trading makes this point abundantly clear. Directors are not, currently, expressly required to take into account the matters that they must do under CA 2006, s 172(1) (even though it may be best practice to do so). There is, then, clearly scope for future conflict where it is unclear to the directors whether they fall within the territory of the new duties in CA 2006, s 172(1) or (3) much and the new matters that they have to take into consideration under CA 2006, s 172(1)(a)–(f). As the company's financial position deteriorates, the directors take on an increased risk of being accused of taking these matters into account at a time when creditors claim they should have been protecting the creditors' interests. Directors may find it more difficult to navigate the so-called 'twilight zone' as a result of the legislative changes made to directors' duties as a result of the CA 2006.

9.18   The proposed statutory statement of directors' general duties is likely (at least initially) to cause some confusion and concern for directors when a company is nearing insolvency. Directors are likely to require substantial advice as to whom their duties are owed in such circumstances, how to discharge them and which statutory factors they are to take into account. There might also be an impact on director and officer liability insurance if it leads to increased litigation.

Independent judgment

9.19   Fears have been expressed that the new requirement for directors to exercise 'independent judgment' may prevent individual directors (particularly, non-executives) from relying on the judgment of others, especially restructuring advisers and Chief Restructuring Officers, in areas in which they are not expert. The government confirmed in debate that directors will continue to be able to do this – and to delegate matters to committees – provided they exercise their own judgment in deciding whether to follow particular advice or to accept someone else's judgment on a matter.

Conflicts of interest

9.20   In many restructurings, particularly of former leveraged buy-out transactions, it is not uncommon for directors to negotiate their own so-called 'carry' as part of the turnaround negotiations or to negotiate their own extensive remuneration for delivering value back to the creditors. During the last five years as more leveraged financings have undergone a restructuring there have been many cases where a restructuring plan that is clearly in the best interests of creditors and, which on reflection would best serve the new statutory factors set out in CA 2006, s 172(1)(a)–(f)), has been undermined by the directors concentrating on and quite often maximising their own position.

9.21   Similarly, on transferring assets to a new divisional company as part of a reorganisation or even entering into complex arrangements with a 'newco' as part of a debt-for-equity swap, directors may well have a shareholding and a directorship in the new subsidiary or the newco that could be relevant to the new provisions dealing with conflicts of interests and accepting benefits from third parties under the new CA 2006 when they come into force.

9.22   The CA 2006 does impact on the interests of the directors in connection with certain of the mechanics of a restructuring outlined above. Several provisions deal with conflicts of interest and their disclosure and they are all scheduled to commence in October 2008. These distinguish between: (i) interests in transactions and arrangements with the company (which must be disclosed but need not be approved), and (ii) all other conflicts (which will normally require approval).

9.23 In relation to conflicts other than those arising in connection with a transaction or arrangement with the company, the CA 2006 contains a broad duty to avoid situations where a director has an interest that conflicts, or may conflict, with the company's interests. In particular, this applies to the exploitation of any property, information or opportunity – whether or not the company could have taken advantage of it and, it seems, whether or not the property, information or opportunity was available to the director because of his directorship. Two new safe harbours are provided: (i) where the situation 'cannot reasonably be regarded as likely to give rise to a conflict', and (ii) where the matter has been authorised by the directors. Board authorisation can be given only if:

(a)   in the case of a private company, it is not invalidated by the company's articles;

(b)   in the case of a public company, the articles expressly permit authorisation of conflicts by the board;

(c)   any quorum requirement is met without counting the interested director(s); and

(d)   the matter is agreed without counting any vote cast by the interested director(s).

9.24 It would also be prudent to assume that interests of anyone connected with a director will be taken into account in deciding whether or not a director has a conflict. The categories of 'connected person' have been broadened, and will include:

(i)   family members (including spouse or civil partner, anyone with whom the director lives as a partner in 'an enduring family relationship', children and stepchildren (both the director's own and his partner's) and the director's parents);

(ii)   bodies corporate to which the director is connected (detailed rules determine when this will be the case);

(iii) trustees of a trust of which the director (or a family member or a body corporate with which he is connected) is a beneficiary; and

(iv)   a director's business partner.

9.25 Logically, this will cause a director of a distressed company to consider his position equally carefully where the 'equity' in the restructured group is to be held by a family member or a family trust.

9.26 The CA 2006 also precludes a director from accepting a benefit from a third party (which although rare may include direct remuneration from a creditor) unless the acceptance of the benefit cannot reasonably be regarded as likely to give rise to a conflict of interest. This new provision would mitigate against giving existing directors of distressed companies equity in a distressed hedge fund as part of their remuneration, unless of course this was properly disclosed to the company and the benefit could not reasonably be regarded as likely to give rise to a conflict of interest.

9.27 It is likely that the new provisions will cause the greatest difficulty for directors and especially turnaround directors and Corporate Restructuring Officers ('CROs') who sit on more than one board. Government ministers suggested in parliament that a general authorisation by each board in relation to each other directorship held by one of its number will 'frank' any subsequent conflicts that arise as a result, if the authorisation powers conferred on the directors by the articles are wide enough to allow them to do this. If not, any such conflict must be expressly authorised as it arises. Some difficult situations arising for directors can therefore be foreseen, especially where they are unable to disclose the circumstances of a particular conflict because they are subject to a duty of confidentiality to another company.

9.28 It is not clear to what extent the new formulations under the CA 2006 regarding directors' personal interests changes the existing law, particularly given the scope for board approval of potential conflicts. However, it is anticipated that it will be possible to deal with any differences in approach through the articles of association and by taking practical steps, such as:

(a)   observing their existing common law obligations, such that when a company's financial position has deteriorated to the point where its solvency is in question and creditors interest's intrude, the focus of the directors' attention shifts away from their own rewards, incentives and remuneration and their shareholders' position towards protecting the interests of creditors[1]. This in turn will minimise their own personal liability from both shareholder action under the new CA 2006 and under the existing provisions under the Insolvency Act 1986 and the Company Directors Disqualification Act 1986;

(b)   ensuring that where a director wants to take on a new directorship or other position (even within the same corporate Group) in a company undergoing a restructuring, this is considered and, if thought appropriate, authorised by the board, which should consider what should happen if an actual conflict arises in the future and whether the authorisation should be subject to any conditions;

(c)   considering existing directorships and other positions in the same way this is particularly relevant to CROs;

(d)   renewing the company's approach to benefits received from a third party – board guidance on the circumstances in which acceptance cannot reasonably be regarded as likely to give rise to a conflict will be helpful; and

(e)   advising all directors that if a specific conflict arises, particularly in sensitive areas (for example, if it relates to an important area of the company's business or to a possible disposal), he should seek independent advice – if it is not possible to disclose the conflict and obtain approval, it may be necessary for the director to absent himself from relevant board discussions.

[1]   *West Mercia Safetywear Ltd v Dodd* [1988] BCLC 250.

Disclosure of interests in transactions with the company

9.29 As far as interests in transactions or arrangements with the company are concerned, although a director is not under any obligation to avoid such an interest, where one arises it must be declared.

9.30 Two separate provisions require such an interest to be disclosed: the first (one of the general duties) applies where a director is interested in a transaction or arrangement that the company is proposing to enter into; the second (part of the replacement for Part X of the Companies Act 1985) applies where a director is interested in a transaction or arrangement that has already been entered into. As with the other provisions dealing with conflicts, neither comes into force until 1 October 2008.

9.31 It is not clear why the two situations have been separated out in this way. There are some differences between the two sections – the most important being that breach of the first has only civil consequences (potential unenforceability of the transaction and a duty on the director to account for any profits), while breach of the second is a criminal offence by the director who fails to make the required disclosure. Although breach of the former renders the transaction voidable at the company's option, breach of the latter (despite being a criminal offence) is unlikely to lead to the unenforceability of the transaction in question (this, at least, is the position in relation to the provision it will replace).

9.32 A director is expected to declare interests of which he is aware or 'of which he ought reasonably to be aware'. As with the provisions on conflicts, it should be assumed that interests of anyone connected with a director will be taken into account. As at present, a director can give a general notice of an interest in another company or firm, or that he is connected with certain people.

9.33 Once these new provisions come into force, companies as a practical matter should ensure that:

(a)   all interests are notified as soon as the director becomes aware of them, in the manner described in the CA 2006 (at a board meeting, by notice in writing to the other directors or by a general notice);

(b)   steps are taken to make sure that anyone connected with a director is aware of the disclosure obligations and is asked to notify the director if a potential conflict arises; and

(c)   directors are reminded regularly of their notification obligations.

C SHAREHOLDER LITIGATION

Derivative actions under the CA 2006

9.34 The CA 2006 introduces a new statutory right for shareholders to sue directors, in the company's name in order to recover loss that the company has suffered as a result of the directors' negligence, default, breach of duty or breach of trust. At present, shareholders have only very limited common law rights, subject to the fulfilment of strict conditions, to bring actions in their company's name. Under the new provisions, shareholders will be able to bring proceedings in the company's name against the directors in a wider range of circumstances than at present. They will also be able to claim against third parties implicated in any breach (again, in the company's name).

9.35 The new statutory right – or 'derivative action' – will undoubtedly make it easier for shareholders to take directors to court. Considerable concern has been expressed that this, taken together with the statutory statement of duties (particularly the detailed list of factors to which directors are to have regard) will lead to significant risks for directors. As intimated above in the section on conflicts of interests, directors who over-play their own incentive scheme at the perceived expense of shareholders are perhaps most at risk from these types of derivative action, but until the case law develops there is also a risk that disgruntled activist shareholders will use the veiled threat of a derivative action as a much wider negotiating tool in a contentious restructuring.

9.36 The government has made some effort to respond to these concerns by introducing a two-stage process for derivative claims. First, a disgruntled shareholder will have to apply to the court for permission to make the claim. If the court considers that the evidence filed by the applicant does not make out a prima facie case, it will be required to dismiss the application ex parte at this stage. If an application survives this process, it will enter the second stage, during which the court will decide, based on the evidence of both sides, whether the claim should be allowed to proceed. At this stage a range of factors will be taken into account – including the views of independent shareholders with no personal interest in the matter. Public companies may find it helpful to approach institutional shareholders for support. Only if the claimant is successful will the claim progress to the third stage – a full trial of the issues.

9.37 These changes – when looked at against the background of the courts' significantly increased powers of proactive case management, and the obligation on parties in dispute to litigate as a last resort – go some way to improving the likely position of companies and their boards. They should also reduce the risk that the new provisions will lead to a significant increase in time consuming and expensive 'nuisance' litigation in relation to claims against directors that are ultimately unsuccessful. Boards that take the steps outlined in this chapter should be able to minimise these risks still further. However, there is still a risk that activist shareholders and pressure groups in a restructuring scenario will seek to use the new procedures at least to create publicity and put decisions of public company boards under even greater scrutiny. Directors may want to have in place a response plan if legal action is threatened.

Directors and officers insurance

9.38 Directors will also want to consider whether company insurance arrangements need to be revised in light of the potentially increased risk of shareholder litigation referred to above. The costs of dealing with and defending shareholder litigation could be significant for both the company and its directors.

9.39 If the court refuses leave to continue an action brought by a shareholder, the shareholder will bear the cost of the application. However, this is unlikely to include all the costs incurred by the company and the directors in dealing with the claim. If the court gives permission for the action to continue, the company may be ordered to reimburse the costs incurred by the shareholder in bringing the action. In these circumstances, the company may have to bear the burden of funding both the shareholder action and the directors' defence. Appropriate insurance cover should be able to help relieve this burden.

9.40 Directors will want to ensure that, in addition to any award of damages against them, the costs and expenses of dealing with and defending shareholder litigation fall within the scope of directors and officers insurance offered. Companies should review the wording of their policies and check the extent of their cover in relation to shareholder litigation (and any exclusions from cover) with their insurers.

D WRONGFUL TRADING

The concept

9.41 Wrongful trading is trading without any reasonable prospect of avoiding a liquidation which leaves creditors unpaid. In particularly distressed restructurings, where there is potentially no value for shareholders left in the company, the wrongful trading provision from a purely doctrinal perspective dictates that the directors owe their primary duties to creditors. Ironically, the relevant provision under English law, Insolvency Act 1986, s 214 does not even use the words 'wrongful trading', this is a description that is only employed in the title to the section. As one notable academic has correctly noted 'the trading that offends against section 214 is, perhaps, better referred to as 'irresponsible'[1].

[1] See an excellent article entitled 'Wrongful trading and the liability of company directors: a theoretical perspective' by Andrew Keay, Professor of Corporate and Commercial Law and Director of the Centre for Business Law and Practice, School of Law, University of Leeds, delivered at the Society of Legal Scholars Conference at the University of Sheffield on 13 September 2004.

9.42 As a provision that was designed to correct the weakness of the fraudulent trading[1] regime the Insolvency Act 1986, s 214 was designed to control more effectively corporate trading abuses. By implication it does inevitably impact significantly on the restructuring process and experience shows that it does force directors into conducting a more rigorous and robust assessment of their companies' health. As such 'regulating directors through the use of s 214 was an attempt to stop directors from externalising the cost of their companies' debts and placing all of the risks of future trading on the creditors'[2].

1   Insolvency Law Review Committee 'Insolvency Law and Practice (the Cork Report)' (Cmnd 858, 1982) paras 1776–1778.
2   See Andrew Keay p 3.

9.43 Specifically, liability for wrongful trading under the Insolvency Act 1986, s 214 arises in relation to a person who is or has been a director (or a shadow director[1] or de facto director[2]) of a company, in circumstances where:

(a)   the company has gone into insolvent liquidation;
(b)   at some time before the commencement of the winding up of the company, that person knew or ought to have concluded that there was no reasonable prospect that the company would avoid going into insolvent liquidation; and
(c)   that person was a director of the company at the time (Insolvency Act 1986, s 214(2)).

1   The Insolvency Act 1986, s 214(7) provides that for the purposes of this section, a 'director' includes a shadow director. A shadow director (defined in the Insolvency Act 1986, s 251) is, in relation to a company, a person in accordance with whose directions or instructions the directors of a company are accustomed to act (other than someone who provides advice only in a professional capacity). Also see *Re a Company No 005009 of 1987* [1989] BCLC 13, [1989] 4 BCC 424. The concept of shadow directorship and the risks for creditors, shareholders and other stakeholders in becoming shadow directors is considered in further detail in this chapter.
2   A de facto director is a person who claims and purports to be a director of a company and is also held out by the company as such, but is never actually or validly appointed. Accordingly, a de facto director and a shadow director are quite different. See *Re Hydrodam (Corby) Ltd* [1994] 2 BCLC 180, [1994] BCC 161.

Important introductory points

9.44

- There may be wrongful trading even though the company does not incur further debts during the restructuring process. An obvious example is where directors allow a company's assets to be depleted (eg by an unnecessary increase in salaries).
- As a practical matter, directors should bear in mind that their conduct during the restructuring process is likely to be judged with the benefit of hindsight. They should also be aware that they will not be able, unless criminal liability is in issue to rely on a right of silence based on the risk of self incrimination during any subsequent investigation by a DTI inspector and/or an examination of their conduct by an administrator, liquidator or administrative receiver. This is the case notwithstanding the provisions of the Human Rights Act 1998. Directors will therefore need to shape and take advice on their conduct during a restructuring accordingly, since ultimately they will be required to answer questions

even where this could result in a civil action against them in respect of directors disqualification, wrongful trading or even fraudulent trading.

- A company goes into insolvent liquidation if it goes into liquidation at a time when its assets are insufficient to pay its debts and other liabilities, including contingent liabilities and the expenses of the winding up (Insolvency Act 1986, s 214(6)). The test of insolvency applied by s 214(6) is on a 'balance sheet' rather than a 'liquidity' basis. This may be contrasted to the Insolvency Act 1986, s 123(1)(e) and (2) definition of 'inability to pay debts'.

- It is not possible to make an application to court, while the company is a going concern, for approval of specific proposed actions. This was unsuccessfully proposed by the Cork Committee[1].

- Executive and non-executive directors may be held liable if the liquidator pursues them for wrongful trading. Only a liquidator can do so. No other party (such as a receiver or a disgruntled creditor) has standing to sue.

- Wrongful trading under the Insolvency Act 1986, s 214 should be distinguished from fraudulent trading under the Insolvency Act 1986, s 213, the latter requiring an intent to defraud the creditors of the company or another fraudulent purpose. No intent (fraudulent or otherwise) is required for a director's conduct to be determined as wrongful trading.

[1]   'Insolvency Law and Practice (the Cork Report)' (Cmnd 858, 1982) paras 1798–1804.

Directors' defence and the concept of no reasonable prospects

9.45 The court will not declare a director liable for wrongful trading if it is satisfied that, after he knew or should have concluded that there was no reasonable prospect of avoiding an insolvent winding-up, the director took *every* step with a view to minimising the potential loss to the company's creditors (assuming him to have known that there was no reasonable prospect that the company would avoid going into insolvent liquidation) as he ought to have taken (Insolvency Act 1986, s 214(3)).

9.46 It should be noted that the wording of the Insolvency Act 1986, s 214(3) is that the director 'took *every* step'. A proposed amendment of this provision to 'every reasonable step' was expressly rejected in Parliament.

9.47 In a restructuring scenario therefore, the key question for directors is not simply whether the company is at a point in time insolvent, but rather whether there is a reasonable prospect at the relevant time that the company can trade out of its existing financial turmoil to ensure its future survival. The 'reasonable prospects' test is however a meaningful one and it prevents the directors from adopting a 'something will turn up' attitude where, objectively speaking there is no real prospect of saving the company from insolvent liquidation. In these circumstances creditors would be prejudiced unless the directors took *every step* to minimise losses.

9.48 In connection with the requirement to minimise the company's losses, should the directors conclude that there is no reasonable prospect of avoiding insolvent liquidation, resignation from the board will not protect the directors because once they have reached the conclusion that there is no reasonable prospect of avoiding insolvent liquidation every step must be take to minimise creditor losses and the directors will normally need to decide without delay which form of insolvency proceedings is most appropriate, unless a short period of controlled trading will improve the position of creditors. Whilst the directors are considering the 'reasonable prospects of avoiding insolvent liquidation', measures to safeguard the interests of creditors and a degree of contingency insolvency planning during the restructuring process will typically be appropriate.

9.49 Ultimately therefore, during the restructuring process the directors must monitor carefully on a continuing basis both the current financial position of the company and its prospects for the future, especially in the light of the attitude and support of the company's shareholders, other potential investors, its creditors and any achievable financing alternatives.

Circumstances in a restructuring that may indicate that directors knew or ought to have concluded that liquidation was (or was not) inevitable

9.50 *Unsustainable financial position*: As demonstrated by accounting, financial and trading records which the company maintained or should have maintained. The trigger date may be the date when records were disclosed or the date when they should have disclosed the position.

Late statutory accounts: If auditors have not delivered accounts the directors should be proactive in procuring their delivery. In a restructuring scenario where the company is on the cusp of insolvency it is insufficient for directors to acquiesce in accounting delays. By definition, the directors should consider their position even more carefully if auditors have resigned. Directors must keep the records that are necessary to prepare the company's accounts since failings in this regard will accentuate criticism against the directors and a finding that they did not take all steps to acquaint themselves with their financial position in circumstances where it later transpires that they ought to have known insolvent liquidation was inevitable.

Failure to maintain bank reconciliations and debtor books: Adverse inferences will inevitably be drawn against directors where they are unable to reconcile bank statements or debtor books or they have been issuing or retaining un-presented cheques. The authors have experienced large public companies that have been unable to reconcile their accounts or their debtor books or calculate their work-in-progress and in these circumstances the directors are increasing their risks under the Insolvency Act 1986, s 214.

Flawed trading systems: companies that have undertaken fixed price contracts with uncontrolled costs or who have a fixed income that precludes profit are obviously exacerbating the s 214 risks for their directors. Whilst the restructuring and turnaround strategy will inevitably be designed to terminate such a flawed trading strategy it does create a rather uncertain twilight zone for directors.

Optimistic trading projections: It is a feature of certain restructurings at least in the early phases that trading projections are untruthful, misleading and very rarely met. In these situations, directors may simply be emasculating the problem or being economical with the truth when dealing with creditors, thereby increasing their risks. Directors should not assume that even old established trading partners will wait indefinitely for payment.

Capital base: In *Re Purpoint Ltd*[1], Vinelott J said that he had some doubts as to whether a reasonable director would have permitted the company to have commenced trading at all because of critical factors such as the lack of a capital base and the fact that the only assets of the company were purchased from borrowings or funded by hire purchase.

Creditor pressure: Where the company's bankers return cheques unpaid or the finance director is keeping payment cheques in his draw pending the outcome of rescue discussions, the directors need to consider their position extremely carefully as this will almost certainly create negative evidence in a potential s 214 proceeding. Similarly, a reduction in facilities, the loss of credit insurance and creditor pressure manifesting itself by court proceedings or landlord's distraint should focus directors on their s 214 risks and the actual viability of the restructuring.

Inability to service and repay maturing debt: The courts have treated this kind of predicament as an indication that the directors ought to have known that they should not be taking on additional credit and would be unable to avoid an insolvent liquidation. Judges will view negatively cases where it was evident that the company was going to have to rely on all of its trade creditors and the bank being almost indefinitely willing to allow their indebtedness to remain outstanding if it was to continue to trade.

Professional advisers: A failure to heed the advice of their professional advisers, especially auditors and financial advisers, will be construed negatively by courts when assessing liability under s 214.

Second guessing the best interests of creditors: In one case[2], the company held a large quantity of perishable fruit in storage on behalf of its most significant customer and creditor. The directors' 'fine sentiments' that they should carry on business in order to realise the fruit, since by virtue of their specialist knowledge they felt that they were in the best position to protect the creditors' interests by obtaining the best price, 'would carry more conviction if [the creditor] had been given an opportunity to decide for itself if it wanted to avail itself of [the company's] marketing expertise'.

Continuing to purchase: Purchasing goods and services or even accepting them as agent for onward sale, at a time when the company is in severe financial difficulties without a viable rescue plan, will heighten the s 214 risks for the directors.

Failure of a rescue plan: Where creditors, shareholders and new investors fail to discuss a plan then the directors may need to act decisively. Where there is a genuine ongoing dialogue regarding a restructuring plan the directors should be entitled to continue trading especially where that plan will enhance liquidity or otherwise improve the financial position of creditors. There does however come a time in any restructuring discussions when the directors have to consider objectively the realistic prospects of its implementation.

Unforeseen circumstances: Directors should always plan for contingencies and should build in sufficient sensitivities into their projections and cashflows so that they are able to accommodate creditor pressure throughout the restructuring and turnaround phase and avoid an accusation that they ought to have known about certain specified liabilities that affected the company's solvency. In restructuring scenarios bankers are always seeking clarification that the directors can meet contingencies and downsides in trading and given their s 214 risks, directors are well advised to continuously make their own independent assessment in advance. Properly minuted board meetings reflecting the directors' views and setting out the steps to be taken to protect creditors are imperative.

Directors' knowledge: Liquidator litigants will argue that directors had a close and intimate knowledge of the business and consequently, even in the absence of actual figures, had a shrewd idea of the true position. Directors should anticipate this and should conduct themselves accordingly in a restructuring. For example directors may well seek to demonstrate that their knowledge led them to realistically believe that they could implement a turnaround and return the company to profit.

1   [1991] BCLC 491, [1991] BCC 121.
2   *Re Produce Marketing Consortium Ltd (No 2)* [1989] BCLC 520.

Standard of directors' conduct

9.51 The facts which a director of a company ought to know or ascertain, the conclusions he ought to reach and the steps which he ought to take are those which would be known or ascertained, or reached or taken, by a reasonably diligent person having both:

(a)   the general knowledge, skill and experience that may reasonably be expected of a person carrying out the same functions as are carried out by *that* director in relation to *the company*[1]; and

(b)   on a subjective basis the general knowledge, skill and experience which that director has (Insolvency Act 1986, s 214(4)).

1   The reference to the functions carried out in relation to a company by a director of the company includes any functions which he does *not* carry out but which have been entrusted to him (Insolvency Act 1986, s 214(5)). The result is that omission is as culpable as commission so that failure to act will be equally penalised.

9.52 This test effectively combines two independent subjective and objective tests and prima facie the director will be liable if he fails *either* test.

9.53 The courts have observed that '... the director in question is to be judged by the standards of what can reasonably be expected of a person fulfilling his functions and showing reasonable diligence in doing so ...'[1]. A director will therefore be deemed to be armed with a reasonable degree of competence to enable him to judge the company's position. It is also the case however, that an experienced and/or well qualified director is judged by his own high standards. For example, it could be expected that a director who is a qualified accountant will be assumed to have a greater appreciation of financial information.

[1] *Re Produce Marketing Consortium Ltd (No 2)* [1989] BCLC 520 at 550.

9.54 It should be noted that even this objective criteria (in part (a) of the test) is based on a 'reasonable' director of *that* company. It follows that the general knowledge, skill and experience required of a director of a small company with simple accounting procedures will be exceeded significantly by that of a director of a large sophisticated company with complex affairs and systems. The court has however stated that certain minimum standards are assumed to be maintained (such as to cause accurate accounting records to be kept and to satisfy statutory filing and accounting requirements)[1]. There is no statutory or case law distinction modifying the test for non-executive directors. As a consequence non-executive directors will need to be equally involved in the restructuring process and they may well be more risk averse thereby requiring more comfort on cashflow and trading projections.

[1] *Re Produce Marketing Consortium Ltd (No 2)* [1989] BCLC 520.

9.55 In deciding whether the requisite knowledge is to be imputed to a director, the court will have particular regard to the professional advice given to the directors[1].

[1] In *Re Purpoint Ltd* [1991] BCLC 491, [1991] BCC 121 the accountants' warning given on 28 May 1997 was identified as a point at which the directors certainly ought to have known that there was no reasonable prospect that the company could avoid going into insolvent liquidation. See also *Re DKG Contractors Ltd* [1990] BCC 903 at 912H.

9.56 In considering the conduct of directors and the degree of risk that they should be permitted to undertake, this will inevitably be closely linked to the level of financial difficulties experienced by the company. Indeed, it has been recognised by the Australian courts under similar Australian legislation that the degree of financial instability and the degree of risk are interrelated and that the latter must be determined by the former. Hence, the more obvious it is that the creditors' interests are at risk, the less risk to which the directors should expose the company[1].

[1] See *Kinsella v Russell Kinsella Pty Ltd* (1986) 4 ACLC 215 at 223.

9.57 Directors of UK companies should however take a degree of comfort from the fact the courts have displayed a degree of understanding of the pressures confronting directors at the relevant time they were making trading decisions. In *Re Continental Assurance Co of London plc*[1] Park J had to consider what the directors had done in the twilight period before the winding-up when they were alleged to have breached the Insolvency Act 1986, s 214 and he was satisfied that the directors had available to them sufficient financial information, even though the systems were slightly dated and the quality of the record-keeping systems could have been improved. Park J noted that typically the cases where directors have been found liable have involved directors who have 'closed their eyes to the reality of the company's position, and carried on trading long after it should have been obvious to them that the company was insolvent and that there was no way out for it. In those cases the directors had been irresponsible, and had not made any genuine attempt to grapple with the company's real position'[2].

[1]   [2001] BPIR 733.
[2]   [2001] BPIR 733 at 769.

9.58 Similarly, in the case of *Re Brian D Pierson (Contractors) Ltd*[1] it was reiterated by the judge that it was necessary to take into account the standard of the reasonable businessperson and that this type of person would be 'less temperamentally cautious than lawyers and accountants'[2]. The court clearly acknowledged the position of a director and that typically an approach to business involves a degree of risk. Directors can take a degree of comfort from the fact that the courts have not applied hindsight or second guessed directors in their critical decision-making period before the onset of insolvency. In *Re Sherbourne Associates Ltd*[3], Judge Jack QC expressed the view that one should not readily accept that 'what has in fact happened was always bound to happen and was apparent'[4].

[1]   [2001] 1 BCLC 275.
[2]   [2001] 1 BCLC 275 at 305.
[3]   [1995] BCC 40.
[4]   [1995] BCC 40 at 54.

9.59 Andrew Keay summarises the position under English law adopted by the courts when he states that ... 'Judges have sought to achieve a balance between the protection of bona fide creditors, on the one hand, and ensuring that directors (on behalf of their companies) are not totally discouraged from taking appropriate business risks on the other. The very paucity of cases where liquidators have succeeded contradicts the assertion that judges are going to be set against directors'[1]. He also points to his assessment of the UK cases and empirical evidence in Australia to demonstrate that it is really only the directors of small closely-held companies that are subjected to legal proceedings. In the Australian research 91% of the claims were brought against directors of private companies[2].

[1]   See Andrew Keay p 11.
[2]   See P James, IM Ramsey and P Siva 'Insolvent Trading – An Empirical Study' (2004) 12 Insolv LJ 210.

Extent of directors' liability

9.60 A director will be personally liable to contribute to the assets of the company if it goes into insolvent liquidation and he ought to have realised that there was no reasonable prospect of avoiding this and he did not take every step to minimise the potential loss to creditors.

9.61 The courts have said that the Insolvency Act 1986, s 214 is aimed to be compensatory (to the company's creditors) rather than penal[1].

[1]   *Re Produce Marketing Consortium Ltd (No 2)* [1989] BCLC 520.

9.62 Whilst it is important to bear in mind that the required contribution from the directors is left entirely to the court's discretion, it appears that the contribution will normally be the amount of loss suffered by the company from the time the director knew, or ought to have concluded, that there was no real prospect that the company would avoid going into insolvent liquidation.

9.63 For the sake of completeness the implications of the Company Directors Disqualification Act 1986[1] should be mentioned in the context of the Insolvency Act 1986, s 214.

- In certain circumstances, a court may, in addition to declaring a director liable to make a contribution to the assets under the Insolvency Act 1986, s 214, *also* disqualify a person from, inter alia, being a director of a company or in any way, whether directly or indirectly, being concerned or taking part in the promotion, formation or management of a company for a specified period.
- In respect of a company which has entered formal insolvency, the administrator, administrative receiver or liquidator *must* inform the Secretary of State for Trade whether or not he is aware of any matter which might make a director unfit to be concerned in the management of a company.
- If a matter is brought to court, the court is obliged to make an order if it is satisfied that a director's conduct (either taken alone or together with his conduct as a director of any other company or companies) makes him unfit to be concerned in the management of a company.
- Schedule 1 to the Company Directors Disqualification Act 1986 lists the matters to which the court shall have regard to determine the unfitness of directors.

[1]   See the Company Directors Disqualification Act 1986, s 10.

Directors' action list – practical guidance

9.64 The following guidance and steps must be considered/taken when a company's solvency is in question:

- It is unlikely to be sufficient that the directors take steps to minimise the loss of certain creditors and not others. The directors of a company must act in the interest of all creditors not individual creditors[1].
- Seek professional advice: the board should seek appropriate legal and accountancy advice on a regular basis to ensure it is complying with its responsibilities. An individual director can seek his own advice if he is not happy with what the board is doing.
- To resign or not to resign: resignation is normally the worst thing a director can do. This is because wrongful trading applies to directors and former directors. A director who has resigned is not in a position to assist the company in minimising its loss to creditors. This is the only defence to wrongful trading.
- Board meetings should be held regularly and be fully minuted: regular meetings evidence the directors' intent to consider all possibilities to minimise loss to creditors. The individual role and responsibilities of each director should be clearly understood and minuted. The minuting of meetings is the evidence that the directors have complied with their duties. These actions are critical during this period.
- The directors should not incur liabilities which there is no reasonable prospect of meeting them: the greatest risk of liability arises from incurring new debt without any real prospect of being able to pay it. All new liabilities need to be carefully scrutinised.
- Following on from the latter point, banks and other liquidity providers providing overdraft facilities and revolving credit lines (especially on structured finance transactions) in the absence of any agreement to the contrary, should not be seen as facility providers of last resort. As such, in circumstances where the solvency of the borrower company is fundamentally in doubt even regardless of the existence of the facility, the borrower should consider carefully whether it should make additional drawings. In particular the incurrence of a liability to one creditor in order to partially defray a liability to some other party would be gravely prejudicial to the first creditor if the borrower company had no reasonable basis to believe that you could repay the amounts drawn under the facility.
- The decision whether to stop trading: this must be kept under review at all times. If there is no hope of a successful restructuring/rescue, trading may have to stop immediately to avoid incurring liabilities which cannot be met. However, a premature decision to stop trading may be equally dangerous. For example, losses to creditors may be minimised by completing work in progress which would otherwise be valueless. This is particularly relevant where the completion of a long-term capital intensive project is necessary before any value can be recovered from the cashflows the project is expected to generate.
- Review of dubious transactions: when a company's solvency is in question, the review of any transaction which might be perceived as preferential or at an undervalue must be conducted with particular care. A director who authorises a transaction which is subsequently reversed may be held to be in breach of his duties to the company.

- Directors (even if they believe that they could procure a better return for creditors) should refrain from acting as quasi receivers or liquidators as this is not their function.
- Liability for wrongful trading is a ground for director's disqualification: wrongful trading is taken as evidence of unfitness to act as a director. Disqualification may follow liability for wrongful trading.
- It is very important that the risk of wrongful trading is put in context. The taking of appropriate action at an early stage, with professional advice, greatly minimises the directors' exposure. For directors who have acted prudently in this way, the risk becomes more remote.

[1] See *Kuwait Asia Bank EC v National Mutual Life Nominees Ltd* [1991] 1 AC 187, [1990] 3 All ER 404, PC.

E FRAUDULENT TRADING

The provision

9.65 The Insolvency Act 1986, s 213 sets out the fraudulent trading provision under English law. It provides:

(1) if in the course of the winding up of a company it appears that any business of the company has been carried on with the intent to defraud creditors of a company or creditors of any other person, or for any fraudulent purpose, the following has effect.

(2) the court, on the application of the liquidator may declare that any persons who were knowingly parties to the carrying on of the business in the manner above-mentioned are to be liable to make such contributions (if any) to the company's assets as the court thinks proper.

9.66 The section applies to any person who was 'knowingly party', not just directors, so professional advisers and family members that have participated in the fraudulent trading are equally exposed to liability[1]. It should also be noted that the contribution may include a penal element.

[1] See *Re Gerald Cooper Chemicals Ltd* [1978] 2 All ER 49, [1978] 2 WLR 866.

The meaning of fraud

9.67 The courts have stated that defraud and fraudulent purpose mean real dishonesty, according to current notions of fair trading among commercial parties. It involves real moral blame. Case law has recognised fraudulent trading where there was an intent to incur credit without a reasonable prospect of being able to repay the company's creditors. More recent case law suggests that recklessness whereby directors 'gamble' with creditors' money will also suffice to evidence an intent to defraud.

9.68 In consequence, if the company continues to carry on business and incur debts at a time when there is to the actual knowledge of the directors no reasonable prospect of the creditors receiving payment of their debts when due or shortly thereafter, it is in general a proper inference that the directors are carrying on the company's business with intent to defraud. Equally, where the directors can be shown to have been indifferent as to the consequences of continuing to trade where there was a real risk that the continuation would result in loss to creditors, it is in general a proper inference that the directors are carrying on the company's business with intent to defraud.

9.69 The Court of Appeal had the opportunity to consider the scope of liability under the Insolvency Act 1986, s 213 in the case of *Morphitis v Bernasconi*[1] where a company had undertaken a restructuring due to an onerous property lease. Professional advisers and the directors devised a scheme whereby the business would be transferred to a newco on an expedited basis in November 1993 to avoid an imminent winding-up petition. Under this scheme the liabilities of existing trade creditors would be discharged with the unfortunate exception of the landlord. Following the eventual insolvent liquidation, the liquidator brought a s 213 action against the solicitors who settled and the directors on the basis that the directors had deceived the landlord by promising a payment that they knew would never be made. The Court of Appeal accepted that whilst a business may have been carried on with an intent to defraud creditors even where only one creditor is shown to have been defrauded, it was not automatic that a single fraud on a creditor meant that the business was being carried on with the intention of defrauding creditors for the purposes of s 213.

[1]   [2003] EWCA Civ 289, [2003] Ch 552, [2003] 2 WLR 1521.

9.70 The court reiterated that a s 213 claim was a class claim that had to be brought by a liquidator for the benefit of the creditors as a whole. Individual creditors had recourse under the general law. The court was not satisfied that the business had been conducted with an intention to defraud creditors or even to defraud the landlord. What was at the forefront of the directors' minds was a rescue of the business as a going concern and limiting their liability under the Insolvency Act 1986. Whilst it was not strictly necessary to consider the issue the court also decided that the contribution from a person pursuant to s 213 should not be penal: the ability to punish a party for fraudulent trading is however separately preserved under the Companies Act 1985, s 458[1]. As a final point the court stated that there has to be a nexus between the loss caused and the fraudulent activity.

[1]   The Companies Act 1985, s 458 is to be replaced by the Companies Act 2006, s 993(1)–(3) on 6 April 2008 (SI 2007/3495). For transitional provisions and savings, see SI 2007/3495, arts 6, 9, 12, Schs 1, 4.

9.71 Fraudulent trading has a long history, but it has proved largely ineffective because of the need to prove dishonesty. Indeed, in most large scale restructurings such an intention is extremely rare given the veracity and integrity of directors and it is obviously far more likely that well intentioned directors will contravene the wrongful trading provisions as opposed to the fraudulent trading provisions. There are however exceptions even in public companies and the conduct and behaviour of the directors in the very public collapse of Versailles plc are testimony to that.

Additional penalties

9.72 In addition, by the Companies Act 1985, s 458, every person who was knowingly a party to the carrying on of the business of the company with the intent to defraud creditors of the company or creditors of any other person would be guilty of a criminal offence and liable to imprisonment and/or a fine whether or not the company was insolvent or was in the course of being wound up.

9.73 In a recent case[1] the appellant had been charged under the Companies Act 1985, s 458 with 'knowingly carrying on a business for a fraudulent purpose'. The 'carrying on of the business' consisted of the submission of accounts to the Revenue and the subsequent negotiations around fiscal issues. The fraudulent purpose was particularised as being to 'conceal the theft of monies to which [the appellant] was not entitled, these monies being amounts of corporation tax which were withheld or incorrectly funded'.

[1]   *R v Leaf* [2007] EWCA Crim 802, [2007] 2 All ER (D) 52 (Apr).

Funding proceedings

9.74 Liquidators will always seek the views of creditors prior to pursuing s 213 and s 214 claims, as the costs will significantly dilute creditors' dividends. If there are sufficient funds in the estate, loans from creditors can be made available to the liquidator to fund such claims with such loans being repayable in priority as an expense of the liquidation. It is also possible for a liquidator to agree a conditional fee with the legal advisers that conduct such claims on his behalf. It should be noted however that s 213 and s 214 claims and other statutory claims are not assignable[1].

[1]   See *Re Oasis Merchandising Services* [1998] Ch 170, [1997] 1 All ER 1009.

9.75 There are of course a number of difficulties in bringing any proceedings under ss 213 and 214 and the Companies Act 1985, s 458. These really relate to proof and the collection of evidence, especially under ss 213 and 458 where it is necessary to show an 'intention to defraud'. With specific reference to wrongful trading it has been said that 'there are a number of problems that have dogged s 214, including the difficulty experienced by liquidators in getting funds to run proceedings and determining from what date wrongful trading commenced, as well as lack of certainty in relation to the meaning of elements of the section, such as 'what constitutes a director taking every step so as to minimise potential loss to company creditors?[1]'

[1]   See Andrew Keay p 4.

F DISQUALIFICATION OF DIRECTORS

The main provisions

9.76 The Company Directors Disqualification Act 1986 enables a court to impose a 'disqualification order' upon a person. Such an order would prevent that person without leave of the court, *inter alia*, from being a director of a company or from in any way, whether directly or indirectly, being concerned or taking part in the promotion, formation or management of a company (which has been widely interpreted to include being a management consultant or giving advice on the financial management or reconstruction of a company). Given the impact for professional directors of a disqualification order, experience has shown that the risks posed by the legislation do occasionally affect the conduct of directors in a restructuring. Both economically and from the perspective of their reputation, directors will want to avoid any prospect of proceedings under the Company Directors Disqualification Act 1986. Contravention of a disqualification order involves a criminal offence and can render the person liable for the debts of the company.

9.77 The court may make a disqualification order against a person in the following circumstances:

(a)   If it appears to the Secretary of State (from an insolvency practitioner's report or from information or documents obtained under various statutory provisions) that it is expedient in the public interest to do so, he may apply to the court for an order to be made on grounds that a person's conduct in relation to a company makes him unfit to be concerned in the management of a company. Typically, this will be as a consequence of an investigation by the DTI Disqualification Unit following an insolvent liquidation and the issue of a negative 'D' Report[1].

Whilst this is likely to focus the minds of directors undertaking difficult restructurings where the outcome is uncertain, the courts as with wrongful trading cases have been reluctant to apply hindsight to directors' actions and have applied the standards of a reasonable businessperson confronted by the financial circumstances at the time[2]. In determining 'unfitness' the court is required to have regard to certain matters relating, broadly, to breaches of duty in relation to that company and, where that company has become insolvent, the person's responsibility for the insolvency of the company. Unfitness in this context does of course require more than commercial misjudgement and misfortune and it will be rare for properly advised directors in a conventional restructuring to even approach this standard.

If the director is unfit then the court must make a disqualification order. A maximum disqualification period of 15 years is available.

(b)   If he is convicted of an indictable offence in connection with the promotion, formation, management or liquidation of a company, or with the receivership or management of a company's property[3]. Again, a maximum disqualification period of 15 years is available.

(c)   If he is persistently in default in relation to statutory provisions requiring accounts, returns or other documents to be filed with or notice given to the registrar of companies, persistent default being conclusively proved by three defaults in the previous five years. A five-year maximum disqualification period exists under this ground.

(d)   If in the course of a winding up of a company it appears that he has been guilty of fraudulent trading under the Companies Act 1985, s 458 (see above) or that he has otherwise been guilty while an officer of a company of any fraud in relation to a company or of any breach of his duty as such officer. A similar maximum disqualification period of 15 years is available for this fraud-related ground.

(e)   If he is or has been a director (including a shadow director) of a company which has at any time become insolvent (whether while he was a director or subsequently) and his conduct as a director of that company (either alone or together with his conduct as a director of any other company) makes him unfit to be concerned in the management of a company. Under this limb a maximum disqualification period of 15 years is available, but a minimum disqualification period of two years also applies.

(f)   If the court makes a declaration that a person is liable to make a contribution to a company's assets in relation to fraudulent or wrongful trading[4] (see above) then a 15-year disqualification period is available.

1   See the Company Directors Disqualification Act 1986, s 6.
2   See the judgment of Lewison J in *Secretary of State for Trade and Industry v Goldberg* [2004] 1 BCLC 597 at 613.
3   See the Company Directors Disqualification Act 1986, s 2.
4   See the Company Directors Disqualification Act 1986, s 10.

9.78 Proceedings against a director must be commenced within two years of the relevant insolvency unless the leave of the court is obtained. Due to the fact that proceedings can be protracted and expensive disqualification can be made by consent under the so-called '*Carecraft Procedure*'.

G SHADOW DIRECTORS

Introduction – why is shadow directorship relevant?

9.79 In large workouts where the influence of shareholders and creditor constituencies is strongly felt and those stakeholders strive to manage and direct both the negotiations and the restructuring outcome in a manner that promotes their economic interests, there are inevitably going to be situations where such stakeholders are actively involved in the future direction of a company's business. Caution and care need to be exercised however, in order to ensure that the promotion of those interests does not transform and manifest itself as real influence over a company's board such that the stakeholder becomes a 'shadow' director.

9.80 In a restructuring scenario the four main categories of stakeholder that are exposed to the risk of shadow directorship are influential investors and shareholder (actual and potential) that are actively involved in a company's business; parent companies in a corporate group are at risk where the parent (or one of its directors) directs the affairs of a subsidiary; the third class are advisers who cross the Rubicon and begin to issue directions (as opposed to advice) that are acted upon by boards; and finally financial creditors have exposure when they are heavily involved in restructuring negotiations when a company is facing financial difficulties – especially if they are encouraging a company to adopt a particular restructuring plan and the board become accustomed to acting on the instructions of those creditors.

9.81 In this introductory section on shadow directorship, one should distinguish between de jure directors (properly appointed in accordance with the company's articles and company law), de facto directors who are persons operating and acting as directors without having been validly appointed at all[1] and shadow directors who are merely 'persons in accordance with whose directions or instructions the directors of a company are accustomed to act'. These distinctions are critical because de jure and de facto[2] directors have the full weight of fiduciary duties and obligations now imposed by the CA 2006.

1   Jacob J in *Secretary of State v Tjolle* [1998] 1 BCLC 333, set out the requirements for de facto directorship as follows '… it may be difficult to postulate any one decisive test. I think what is involved is very much a question of degree. The court takes into account all of the relevant factors. Those factors include at least whether or not there was a holding out by the company of the individual as director, whether the individual used the title, whether the individual had proper information (eg management accounts) on which to base decisions and whether the individual had to make major decisions and so on. Taking all of these factors into account, one asks "was this individual part of the corporate governing structure," answering it as a kind of jury question'.
2   See *Re Canadian Land Reclaiming and Colonizing Co* (1880) 14 Ch D 660, 670.

9.82 As regards shadow directors the position of whether they have any broader duties under the new CA 2006 is more convoluted. The duties of directors enacted in the CA 2006 apply to shadow directors in a qualified manner because s 170(5) provides that '[t]he general duties [in sections 171 to 177] apply to shadow directors where, and to the extent that, the corresponding common law rules or equitable principles so apply'. Further, s 170(4) provides that '[t]he general duties shall be interpreted and applied in the same way as common law rules or equitable principles, and regard shall be had to the corresponding common law rules and equitable principles in interpreting and applying the general duties'.

9.83 This of course takes you all the way back to the common law with respect to shadow directors and the case of *Ultraframe (UK) Ltd v Fielding*[1] and others which held that the mere fact that a person falls within the statutory definition of a shadow director is not enough to impose on him the same fiduciary duties as are owed by de jure and de facto directors unless such shadow activity extends to specific assets in which case there may be a fiduciary duty on the part of the shadow director in relation to that asset. There is little doubt that the duty to exercise reasonable care in s 174 will apply to shadow directors because this also seems consistent with *Ultraframe (UK) Ltd v Fielding*.

1   [2005] EWHC 1638 (Ch), [2005] All ER (D) 397 (Jul), Lewison J, dated 27 July 2005.

9.84 For stakeholders in a restructuring the risks of de facto directorship are even more profound because a de facto director is a person who does the sort of things that a normal director does and being on an equal footing in the 'notional boardroom'. Wrongful and fraudulent trading liability as well as other statutory and fiduciary duties attract to such a person.

9.85 When one considers the scope of a shadow director's liability the fact that such a person has the potential benefit of being shielded from the new statutory statement of duties will not exactly be a significant comfort since a shadow director is (i) subject to the Company Directors Disqualification Act regime, and (ii) personally liable for 'wrongful trading' if the company goes into insolvent liquidation (Insolvency Act 1986, s 214). By way of example, in an insolvency, this can result in a parent company being held liable for the debts of a subsidiary, ie effectively the corporate veil is pierced. What is more, a person can be liable for a breach of the wrongful trading regime and can be exposed to disqualification, even though the person was blissfully unaware that he was a shadow director.

Who is a shadow director?

9.86 The definition and parameters of shadow directorship is key because it will determine the extent to which shareholders, investors, financiers and advisers will be found liable for company debts and for actions of de jure and de facto directors. It is worth initially noting the case of *Re Bulawayo Market and Offices Co Ltd*[1] which clearly established that a body corporate could be appointed a director and that there is nothing in the statutory definition of shadow director to exclude a body corporate.

[1]   [1907] 2 Ch 458, [1904–7] All ER Rep 759.

9.87 Technically, a shadow director is 'a person in accordance with whose directions or instructions the directors of a company are accustomed to act (but so that the person is not deemed to be a shadow director by reason only that the directors act on advice given by him in a professional capacity)' (Company Directors Disqualification Act 1986, s 22(5), Insolvency Act 1986, s 251 [and Companies Act 1985, s 741[1]]).

[1]   The Companies Act 1985, s 741(1) has been replaced the Companies Act 2006, s 250. The Companies Act 1985, s 741(2) and (3) has been replaced by the Companies Act 2006, s 251(1)–(3). The Companies Act 2006, ss 250 and 251 came into force on 1 October 2007 (SI 2007/2194).

9.88 A liquidator alleging shadow directorship or the Secretary of State (in disqualification proceedings) will have the onus of proving on the balance of probabilities to the commensurate level of cogency, that a person is a shadow director.

9.89 In applying these provisions the courts have interpreted a shadow director as a person who exercises real influence over a board of directors.

This 'real influence' may be over just one area of a company's business, and need not be over all of it. Generally, there must be a pattern of real influence and a single act is not sufficient. The potential shadow director can be an individual person or a company, and can be located outside England. Professional advisers are excluded unless as indicated they cross the Rubicon and cease being mere advisers and issue directions and instructions that are customarily acted upon.

9.90 For many years the leading case on shadow directorship was *Re Hydrodam (Corby) Ltd*[1] where Millett J held that the positions of de facto and shadow director do not overlap and are in fact mutually exclusive. A de facto director purports to be and assumes the role of a director even though he is not properly appointed. Conversely a shadow director does not claim or purport to be a director so he cannot be a de facto director. Millett J formulated a logical process for determining whether a person was a shadow director: firstly the actual and de facto directors had to be identified so it could be tested whether the putative director purported to direct those people; it then had to be proved that those directors acted in accordance with those instructions and directions and finally that they became accustomed so to act. It was specifically held that whilst the parent company may well have been a shadow director and had liability under s 214 it was not axiomatic that the directors of the board of that parent were also shadow directors because they sat on its board and passed resolutions at its board meetings[2].

[1] [1994] 2 BCLC 180, [1994] BCC 161.
[2] This was subsequently reinforced in the case of *Secretary of State for Trade and Industry v Laing* [1996] 2 BCLC 324 where *Re Hydrodam* was cited with approval and the court held that an individual's own actions must constitute him a shadow director.

9.91 Essentially Millett J characterised shadow directorship as a 'pattern of behaviour in which the board did not exercise any discretion or judgment of its own, but acted in accordance with the directions of others'[1]. This judgment accords with Millett J's earlier submission that the defining characteristic of a shadow director is that the shadow knows that he or she is the controlling mind of the company and the 'appointed directors do as they are told, not because they choose to but because it is their function'[2].

[1] [1994] BCC 161 at 163.
[2] *Re Unisoft Group Ltd (No 3)* [1994] 1 BCLC 609, [1994] BCC 766.

9.92 The point that shadow directorship emerges via a pattern of behaviour was also made by Harman J in *Re Unisoft Group Ltd (No 3)*[1] who observed that the language 'accustomed to act' in the statutory provisions 'refers to acts not on one individual occasion but over a period of time and as a regular course of conduct'[2].

[1] [1994] 1 BCLC 609, [1994] BCC 766.
[2] *Re Hydrodam (Corby) Ltd* [1994] 2 BCLC 180, [1994] BCC 161.

9.93 In the case of *Secretary of State for Trade and Industry v Deverell*[1] the Court of Appeal made a number of further observations about the statutory definition of a shadow director some of which have been perceived to be inconsistent with Millett J's analysis in *Re Hydrodam*:

(a) The definition should not be strictly construed. He stated that the term is used in many different statutes and the interpretation therefore needs to take into account the many contexts in which it appears[2].

(b) The purpose of the legislation was to identify those (other than professional advisers) with real influence in the company's corporate affairs. This influence however did not have to cover all of the company's affairs or activities. Therefore requests or action in respect of any particular issue would be sufficient even if nothing was indicated, for instance about other significant business issues of the company.

(c) Whether an act or communication was to be classified as a 'direction or instruction' had to be objectively ascertained by the court in the light of all the evidence. The understanding or expectation of either the donor or the recipient of the instructions is not directly relevant and it will simply be sufficient to show the consequences of the instruction on a 'before and after' basis. To require proof that the de jure directors understood communications from the shadow directors as a direction would impose too difficult a burden on the plaintiff.

(d) Non-professional advice could potentially come within the statutory definition, but it was tacitly recognised that good advice that is followed because it is good advice is not instruction or direction.

(e) Somewhat surprisingly, the court held that a person could still be a shadow director even though the board had not adopted a subservient role to him or had not surrendered its discretion. He stated:

'it will no doubt be sufficient to show that in the face of directions or instructions from the alleged shadow director, the properly appointed directors or some of them cast themselves in a subservient role or surrendered their respective discretions. But I do not consider that it is necessary to do so in all cases. Such a requirement would be to put a gloss on the statutory requirement that the board are accustomed to act in accordance with such directions or instructions'[3].

---

1 [2001] Ch 340, [2000] 2 All ER 365.
2 This aspect of the judgment is justifiably challenged by Chris Noonan and Susan Watson in 'The Nature of Shadow Directorship: Ad hoc Statutory Intervention or Core Company Law Principle' principally on the basis that the uses of the concept of shadow directorship have unique statutory aims and objectives that should require more deliberate formulation of the concept in each context (see [2006] JBL 763–798 at p 765).
3 See *Secretary of State for Trade and Industry v Deverell* [2001] Ch 340 and the judgment of Morritt LJ at 354.

9.94 Conceptually and practically the most difficult aspect of Morritt LJ's judgment is the fusion of the concepts of de facto and shadow directorship. Whether this was borne out of a determination to see Hopkins and Deverell, the two individuals in question, disqualified on the basis that he could classify them as shadow directors is unclear. Indeed on the facts it is submitted that had the Secretary of State applied for disqualification on the basis of de facto directorship he would have been successful.

9.95 The fusion is potentially unhelpful because as Chris Noonan and Susan Watson correctly articulate[1]; if there is no requirement that the shadow director exercises influence over the de jure directors then shadow directorship may embrace certain types of de facto directorship. It will be therefore much easier to become a shadow director because inevitably if there is no requirement in terms of qualification that a person exerts any control or influence then persons who participate in board level discussions or discuss details of a restructuring with a board and who express views which are adopted by a board will risk being a shadow director. The DTI certainly believe that the threshold has been lowered and has interpreted the judgment as greatly widening the scope of persons who may be deemed to be shadow directors[2].

1   See their excellent article 'The Nature of Shadow Directorship: Ad hoc Statutory Intervention or Core Company Law Principle' [2006] JBL 763–798 at p 778.
2   See DTI Press Notice p/2000/56.

9.96 This last feature of Morritt LJ's judgment also appears to displace the requirement in *Re Unisoft* that there be control over acts of at least a governing majority of the board not just some of the directors, before a person could be designated a shadow director. This may not have been an intentional point in his judgment.

9.97 In applying the *Deverell* principles the court in *Ultraframe* did not think that the attendance of the putative shadow director at board meetings, his request for a relocation, his sole signature on a bank account, his assertion that he was 'running the company', decision to change suppliers, elevation to company secretary or his take-up of debentures from a company was sufficient to fix the person with shadow directorship as it still did not demonstrate that the board was accustomed to acting on his instructions or directions. The court held that this occurred later at which point he had become a de facto director when he had an equal voice with the de jure directors.

9.98 Lewison J held that in determining whether a person had become a shadow director it is necessary to look at all the various matters cumulatively. Unless and until the board do something in conformity with the putative shadow director's instructions, the question of shadow directorship does not arise. The mere giving of instructions does not make a person a shadow director, instructions must be translated into action.

9.99 In restructurings the risks of shadow directorship are relevant at all times. However, it is of particular concern where a company is financially distressed. This is for three main reasons: (i) in the lead up to an insolvency, interested parties often play a greater role than usual in the business of the company (eg in assisting in a restructuring plan), (ii) if a liquidator is appointed, he must report to the DTI on any shadow directors, and (iii) only a liquidator can bring a claim for 'wrongful trading'.

9.100 The case of *Re Tasbian Ltd (No 3)*[1] provokes interest because it provides some indication as to how a restructuring adviser can become contaminated by the legal status of a shadow director. In this case a Mr Nixon was appointed as a consultant to Tasbian by its finance company Castle which also held 99% of the shares in Tasbian. Nixon was an accountant who advised Castle on the financial position of Tasbian and its recovery strategy. Prior to the receivership of Tasbian its assets were transferred to a company called Hartbrook – a shell company formed by Tasbian for this purpose. The fact that Nixon monitored trading, assisted the board, operated Tasbian's accounts and advised on key issues such as the transfer of employees to Hartbrook supported the proposition that he had become so influential as an adviser that Tasbian's directors had become accustomed to acting on Nixon's instructions and directions. In some ways the case is a salutary lesson for company side advisers and CROs where the advice goes beyond professional advice such that they become the controlling influence.

1   [1991] BCLC 59, [1992] BCC 358, CA.

9.101 The position of banks and other creditors as potential shadow directors has always generated a great deal of concern. On almost every highly negotiated restructuring where workout bankers are monitoring trading and cashflow on a daily basis and are having considerable input on the restructuring and turnaround plan, bankers will be concerned about the risk of shadow directorship. It is probably an academic point, but whilst technically it might actually be the bank manager or restructuring banker that is the shadow director the bank in question would almost certainly be vicariously liable for the acts of its agents and employees.

9.102 In the US case in the context of deepening insolvency which can potentially establish a third party liability that is analogous to wrongful trading, the Delaware courts in the case of *Re Exide Techs*[1] declined to dismiss a complaint alleging that a bank syndicate had structured its loans in a way that allowed the lenders to exercise significant control over Exide and its subsidiaries, and that, by continuing to fund Exide after it was technically insolvent the lenders caused the company to fraudulently continue its operations at the expense of other creditors. Lender control was at the heart of the Exide complaint and it shows the potential at least for a common law based system to impose liability on a lender as a shadow director.

1   299 BR 792 (Bankr D Del 2003).

9.103 In *Re M C Bacon Ltd*[1], where an allegation of shadow directorship was made against National Westminster Bank plc, Knox J refused to strike out the application and accepted that as a matter of law that a bank is plainly capable of becoming a shadow director. However, the case failed on its facts and the claim of shadow directorship was abandoned after nine days of evidence. The case was sufficient however to cause a degree of alarm for bankers involved in English law governed restructurings.

1   [1990] BCC 78.

9.104 As intimated, the *Deverell* case (where the de jure directors were accustomed to following the advice of the purported shadow directors) has also been perceived as a potentially problematic case for banks involved in finely balanced restructuring negotiations. It raises the spectre that banks exercising some influence, but not dominance over strategy and other matters like disposals, capital expenditure, liquidity and general cash management, where the board is heavily involved, are increasing their shadow director risks.

9.105 The conventional wisdom and indeed the current English law does afford banks more protection in that banks are entitled to protect their own interests. Banks should be clear that a certain path is a condition of further financial support and credit approval and that the terms are driven by commercial necessity as opposed to any intention that the directors become accustomed to acting in accordance with directions or instructions from the lenders. Responses to bank requirements and terms should always be requested from independent boards who should understand clearly that they are considering bank terms as a matter of contract and in order to procure a restructuring that is in the best interests of the company, but perhaps more importantly the creditors as creditor interests intrude during periods of financial distress.

9.106 In the case of *Re PFTZM Ltd*[1], the representatives of a major creditor became involved in weekly discussions with the board of the debtor for just over two years. The court held that the representatives had become involved in board discussions as a result of the thrust of the insolvency of the debtor. Their involvement was directed at rescuing value in their capacity as creditors and defending their position and this had not constituted giving directions to the board of the debtor. Much of the discussions focused on the terms upon which credit would be extended and continued and the directors of the debtor were at liberty to make their own choices and decisions in this regard.

[1]   [1995] 2 BCLC 354, [1995] BCC 280.

9.107 In a leading article that significantly eased the anxieties of restructuring bankers Millett J (as he was then)[1] stated that he:

> 'brings good news to those who are bankers, and bad news to insolvency practitioners. I believe that the threat which some banks perceive of being held to have become a shadow director is almost entirely imaginary'[2].

[1]   'Shadow directorship – A real or imagined threat to the Banks', January 1991, Insolvency Practitioner 14.
[2]   'Shadow directorship – A real or imagined threat to the Banks', January 1991, Insolvency Practitioner 14 at page 14.

9.108 Millett J analysed the roles undertaken by banks in negotiating financial restructurings and indicated that the imposition of an independent business review, demand for security or a reduction in debt levels, requests for financial information and restructuring proposals and even the questioning of the desirability of and the examination of the case for strengthening existing management was all commonplace and a feature of commercial lending, the controls and implementation of which did not expose banks to shadow directorship. He accepted that:

> 'in doing all these things the bank may well expect its demands to be met, first because they were likely to be commercially sensible, and secondly because the customer has no option if it wants the facility continued. But that is not enough to constitute the bank a shadow director. The fact is that a bank has no business to be managing its customer's affairs, but it is entitled to attach conditions to the continuation of support. So long as it does nothing that a bank does not normally do in telling its customers what it requires if it is to continue banking facilities, and leaves the decision to the customer whether it will comply or not, in my view it cannot be held to have become a shadow director'[1].

[1] 'Shadow directorship – A real or imagined threat to the Banks', January 1991, Insolvency Practitioner 14 at page 15.

9.109 Despite these extremely sensible comments and reassurances from Millett J, the cases (particularly *Deverell*) show that care should be taken by all stakeholders in a restructuring to avoid shadow directorship. The key test is control over the board and therefore if the directors clearly continue to take independent decisions, then it is very unlikely that anyone will be a shadow director. Some practical points are set out below.

Dealing with the board/directors

9.110 Do not give directions or instructions (oral or written) to the board or to a director.

There is a critical distinction between 'recommendations' and 'directions/ instructions'. For example, a party should say 'our offer is that we will advance you more money if this business plan is adopted'. It should not say 'you must adopt this business plan'. The decision whether to accept the offer must be left with the directors.

Note that it is the board's responsibility to make its own decision after taking appropriate professional advice.

Be cautious about regularly participating in board meetings; consider explaining your position to a director who can report to the board.

If you attend a board meeting, consider if it is practicable to leave before the board takes any relevant decision.

It is common sense for decisions involving you to (especially where you represent a financial creditor): (i) explain your position, (ii) record that it is for the board to discuss this in light of appropriate advice, and (iii) record that the decision is for the board (not you) to take.

As a banker requirements or terms should always be presented as contractual terms of the credit as opposed to advice or directions or instructions.

Bankers should always request that the company's board perhaps through advisers should independently consider and respond formally to bank terms and requirements.

If applicable, make sure that board minutes record: (i) your attendance 'as an observer' or 'to explain a certain topic', and (ii) when you left the meeting.

Shadow directorship goes beyond board meetings. Where there is poor corporate governance, there is a heightened risk of shadow directorship being an issue. This is because the absence of a good documentary record of directors' decisions creates uncertainty as to how those decisions were taken.

General dealings

9.111 Do not sign a document on behalf of the company or become a signatory to the company's bank account.

In discussions with other parties, do not negotiate on behalf of the company.

Likewise, do not hold yourself out as acting for the company. Be careful about relaying messages on behalf of the company. If you must, make it clear that you are the messenger.

Finally, it is important that the risk of being a shadow director is put in context. It is rare for a court to hold that a person has been a shadow director and there have only been a handful of cases in just over 20 years since the Insolvency Act 1986. If the appropriate action is taken, the potential to become liable as a shadow director is greatly minimised. The risk becomes particularly remote if there is a full documentary record showing that you have acted prudently in this way. Other commentators like David Millman[1] have observed that the *Deverell* case and 'advances in substantive law will never compensate for the financial and procedural obstacles presented in insolvency litigation. Proving the existence of a shadow directorship in a claim for wrongful trading, for example, will still remain a speculative venture for any liquidator'[2].

[1] 'A fresh light on shadow directors' [2000] Insolvency Lawyer, pp 171–172.
[2] 'A fresh light on shadow directors' [2000] Insolvency Lawyer, p 172.

Chapter 10

RESCUE RIGHTS ISSUES

A INTRODUCTION

10.1 In a rights issue existing shareholders are invited to subscribe for further shares in the company in proportion to their existing shareholdings. Rights issues are typically launched to enable companies to grow at a rate faster than can be funded from current profits in circumstances where the company is already highly geared relative to its aversion to uncertainty and the short-term cost that is attributable to leverage. To the extent that the expansion augments the value of the business for the benefit of the equity, the benefit is shared pro-rata amongst the existing holders.

10.2 A rescue rights issue involves the same offer to existing shareholders to subscribe for shares in proportion to their existing shareholdings, but in many ways it involves staring down the opposite end of the telescope. Rescue rights issues serve to de-leverage a company by rebalancing its debt to equity ratio, in circumstances where the lenders themselves may not be prepared to undertake a debt for equity swap, and there may be no other source of equity capital for the company. In distressed companies, where the lenders are very concerned at debt levels, a rights issue may be the only way to inject new capital, calling upon the existing shareholders to provide it. In this sense the rights issue has the aura of a 'rescue' about it.

10.3 In order to persuade shareholders to provide additional capital to a distressed company, they must be convinced that continuing with the status quo, and relying upon the company trading out of its current problems, present more of a risk to their equity than providing new finance. A rescue rights issue usually has to offer a vision of recovery and the promise that a return to profitability will eventually be fulfilled. Any rescue rights issue must therefore be attractive to investors and in order to achieve this it should ideally be coupled with a change of strategy[1].

10.3 Rescue rights issues

[1] Andrew Wyllie, the chief executive of Costain plc, when speaking about the company's rights issue stated 'the Company's balance sheet was weak for many years. This is a bundle of necessary refinancing that will deliver the next phase of our strategy'. (Financial Times, 15 September 2007.)

10.4 If a company needs to recapitalise in this way, it is usually because an existing strategy or business plan has been flawed and the company has experienced a period of under-performance. In addition, other alternatives will not be available and a capital raising through a bond or other debt issue is likely not to be feasible on the grounds of the interest burden and the incremental leveraging effect.

10.5 Experience has shown that companies undertaking a rescue rights issue have to be sensitive to the message given to investors, and have to be candid about the background and context for the equity capital raising. They will also need to have well constructed answers to the inevitable questions from investors, analysts and the media. The company may well have approached its significant shareholders for undertakings of support.

10.6 Investors supporting a rescue rights issue are inevitably keen to establish that it is a definitive solution to the company's problems and that management have identified, and are in the process of resolving, the issues that have necessitated the capital raising. In almost all cases involving public companies, this will require a detailed explanation in the public documents of the reasons for, and anticipated effects of, the capital injection, and a convincing narrative in order to enable shareholders to conclude that the restructuring plan will remove the need for further requests to them, or to the market, for funding, and will rebalance the company, ultimately returning it to increased profitability and growth.

B TIMETABLE

10.7 In common with all rights issues, the timetable for a rescue rights issue will depend upon whether or not a general meeting of the company will be required. This would be necessary where the company has insufficient authorised but unissued share capital (or, under the Companies Act 2006, where the concept of authorised share capital will be abolished, the company may need to amend its articles in order to overcome a restriction on the amount of shares that it may, and which its directors have authority to, issue), taking into account any shares reserved for future issue (such as under any share option schemes). In determining the number of shares reserved for future issue, it will also be necessary to take into account the terms of any options, warrants or convertible securities, since these instruments will usually contain anti-dilution rights requiring adjustments to be made as a result of an equity issue, so that the holder may be entitled to an increased number of shares upon exercise of the option or conversion of the instrument following the rights issue (and the increased capital that it creates).

354

10.8 Similarly, a general meeting will be required if the directors do not have sufficient authority, for the purposes of the Companies Act 1985, s 80, to allot the new shares. Under the relevant provisions of the Companies Act 2006 (ss 549–551, expected to come into force in October 2009), the provisions remain broadly the same. Although this authority can only be given in a general meeting, most listed public companies should have in place a general authority for the directors to allot shares (probably renewed annually at each annual general meeting) which, in accordance with Investor Protection Committee ('IPC') guidelines, should be limited to the lower of one third of the issued ordinary share capital of the issuer or the amount of unissued, but authorised, share capital of the issuer.

10.9 In addition, it may also be necessary to seek shareholder approval to the rights issue where, for example:

(i)   a new class of share capital is being created, which will be offered pursuant to the rights issue (requiring an amendment to the company's articles of association as well as the creation of the shares themselves within the company's share capital);

(ii)   a linked transaction (such as an acquisition which is being partially or wholly financed by the rights issue) itself requires shareholder approval as a Class 1 transaction pursuant to the Listing Rules; or

(iii) a linked transaction is with a connected or related party, requiring shareholder approval pursuant to the Companies Act 2006 (such as a 'substantial property transaction' between the company and a director (see CA 2006, s 190)) or pursuant to paragraph 11.1.7R of the Listing Rules.

10.10 Statutory pre-emption rights exist in relation to the issue of new shares in certain circumstances. A disapplication of such pre-emption rights may be undertaken as part of the rights issue process, notwithstanding the general principle that the new shares are offered, in any event, to the existing shareholders pro rata to their current holdings. Among other things, such a disapplication will shorten the rights issue offer period to 21 days (which is the requirement pursuant to paragraph 9.5.6R of the Listing Rules) from 23 days (the requirement under the Companies Act 1985, s 90(6) being 21 clear days). Such a disapplication would need to be approved by a special resolution (75% majority) of the members in general meeting, having, therefore, a potential impact on the rights issue timetable. Pre-emption rights, and their disapplication, are discussed in further detail below.

10.11 If a general meeting is needed, the timetable for the rights issue will be lengthened by the requisite notice period for the general meeting. The sections of the Companies Act 2006 which regulate notice periods for general meetings came into force on 1 October 2007, and provide, in s 360(2), that 14 clear days' notice of the general meeting is required, regardless of the types of resolutions (whether ordinary or special resolutions) that are to be proposed. In reality, the requirement for a general meeting may have a 16 clear day impact, assuming that the company's articles of association (as is conventional) state that a notice is deemed received 24 hours after being sent by first-class post. These statutory minimum notice periods are subject to anything in the company's articles, which may continue to require longer notice periods to be given, such as 21 days' (or clear days') notice (which may have a 23-day impact), and so the precise provisions in relation to notice periods, and the deemed service of notices, will need to be verified. Notices may be able to be provided electronically (for example, by being published on a company's website), provided that individual members have consented to such electronic communication and that they have been informed of the electronic publication of the notice. In practice, this may have little effect on the timing of the notice, particularly if notification of its electronic publication must be given in a different way (such as by post) – the precise requirements of the company's articles, and the extent of any consents given by members, will need to be checked.

10.12   The timetable will, of course, have implications for the timing of the receipt of cash funds by the company, and therefore the timing of the restructuring. This can present issues where new equity capital is required as a matter of urgency, although one might expect that the company has kept a consistent and close watch over its financial position in order to avoid such urgency. Any extension of the timetable may also have a cost implication, if it increases the duration of any underwriting obligations which are in place, and therefore the amount of underwriting fees and commission which are payable. Underwriting is discussed in further detail below.

C PRE-EMPTION RIGHTS

10.13   A rights issue is an issue of shares for cash and, accordingly, the pre-emption rights set out in the Companies Act 1985, s 89 will apply to that issue unless it has been, or is to be, disapplied pursuant to the Companies Act 1985, s 95. (In October 2009, the relevant provisions of the Companies Act 2006, in relation to statutory pre-emption rights, and their disapplication, are expected to come into force (ss 560–577). They broadly restate the existing law, and so the discussion below in relation to pre-emption provisions will continue to be relevant).

10.14   Under the Companies Act 1985, s 89, a company proposing to allot equity securities wholly for cash must first offer them to each holder of 'relevant shares' or 'relevant employee shares' (or 'ordinary shares' under the Companies Act 2006) pro rata to his existing shareholding. This means that the proportion of the equity securities offered to each existing shareholder must be equal (as nearly as practicable) to the proportion in nominal value held by him of the aggregate of relevant shares and relevant employee shares. Since December 2003, companies have been permitted to hold their own shares in treasury, and such treasury shares are excluded for the purposes of a pre-emptive offer under s 89. If, however, s 89 has been disapplied (as to which, see further below) then, although the rights to subscribe for shares may be allocated to the company, it should specifically exclude treasury shares from the scope of the offer since the Companies Act 1985 prevents a company from exercising such rights or from benefiting from trading in the rights nil paid.

10.15 Pursuant to the Companies Act 1985, s 90, the offer must be in writing and must state a period of not less than 21 days (from the date of service) during which it may be accepted. The offer may be submitted personally to the shareholders or by sending it by post to a shareholder's registered address (or, if he has no registered address in the UK, to the address in the UK supplied by him to the issuer for the giving of notices). Under the Companies Act 2006, s 562, the position will be broadly the same, although the offer may be made in hard copy or electronic form. In addition, the deemed date of service may vary under the new law, depending upon the method of service. Whilst offers sent by post are, under the Companies Act 1985, deemed to be made at the time at which the letter would be delivered in the ordinary course of post, offers made in hard copy form are, under the Companies Act 2006, deemed to be made when sent or supplied. Offers made in electronic form, or by the 'Gazette route' described below, are deemed to be made when sent or published, respectively.

10.16 In the case of a shareholder who has not registered an address in the UK and has not supplied the issuer with an address in the UK for the service of notices on him, the offer may be made by publication of a notice in the London Gazette. Under the Companies Act 2006, this 'Gazette route' is extended to those without registered addresses (or addresses for the service of notices) in the EEA, and the holders of share warrants.

10.17 For the purposes of establishing the identity of the holders of shares which are entitled to have a pre-emptive offer under the Companies Act 1985, s 89 made to them, the relevant statutory provisions make reference to the concept of a 'record date'; striking the share register on a particular date (within the 28 days prior to the pre-emptive offer being made), which will then constitute the register of members for the purposes of the offer.

D DISAPPLICATION OF THE STATUTORY PRE-EMPTION PROVISIONS

10.18 The statutory pre-emption provisions of the Companies Act 1985, s 89 do not need to be complied with where that section has been disapplied by the company, pursuant to the Companies Act 1985, s 95. The Companies Act 2006 contains similar disapplication provisions in ss 570 and 571. Such disapplication must be approved by the shareholders by way of special resolution (75% majority), if there is no general authorisation in the company's articles for the directors to be able to allot shares for cash without first making a pre-emptive offer. If statutory pre-emption rights are disapplied listed companies will also not be subject to the pre-emption requirements of the Listing Rules (paragraph 9.3.12R, Listing Rules), which require equity shares, which are proposed to be issued for cash, to be offered to existing shareholders on a pro rata basis (paragraph 9.3.11R, Listing Rules). The advantages (particularly in a rescue rights issue situation) of disapplying the statutory provisions are discussed below:

(i) *Timing*: the Listing Rules, and s 89, require that the offer of rights must be open for acceptance for at least 21 days. In circumstances where s 89 has been disapplied, the offer becomes open for acceptance, for Listing Rules purposes, on the date on which the nil paid rights (discussed further below) are admitted to trading, and closes 21 days later (even where the offer may only be capable of acceptance for part of the last day, which is the case where the rights issue is being made through CREST). In order to comply with s 89, however, neither the day on which the offer is made (that is, the day on which provisional allotment letters are posted, which is usually the same day on which the nil paid rights are admitted to trading), nor the final day of the offer period, can count towards the 21-day period, and so the offer may not be closed until the 23rd day after the posting date. In circumstances of distress, where every day is critical, extending the timetable (and, therefore, delaying the receipt of funds by the company) by only a few days may have significant consequences. A shorter offer period will also reduce underwriting commissions.

(ii) *Fractional entitlements*: where s 89 has not been disapplied, fractions of shares to which shareholders are entitled will be disregarded (and so the number of shares which are the subject of the offer will be rounded down). Where s 89 has been disapplied, shareholders' entitlements are still rounded down to the nearest whole number, but the fractions themselves can be aggregated and sold in the market for the benefit of the company.

(iii) *Overseas shareholders*: where s 89 has been disapplied, the issuer will have the flexibility not to offer the rights to certain overseas shareholders (notably those in the USA, Canada, Japan and Australia). This may be attractive where compliance with the securities laws of such jurisdictions would be onerous, time consuming and expensive (for example, by requiring a detailed public disclosure document, such as a prospectus or 'registration statement', to be produced). Instead of making the offer into such overseas jurisdictions, the nil paid rights attributable to such persons may be sold in the market for their benefit, as soon as possible after the commencement of nil paid dealings. In contrast, where the statutory pre-emption rights continue, the offer must still be extended to all overseas shareholders, regardless of the securities laws issues that this may present. In these circumstances, the offer to overseas shareholders is generally made by the issuer arranging for a notice to be published in the London Gazette (generally on the business day following the posting of the provisional allotment letters), rather than by sending an offer document directly to the shareholders in question.

(iv) *Convertible securities*: it may not be possible for the issuer to comply with s 89 where it has convertible securities in issue. For example, convertible loan instruments do not fall within the definition of 'relevant shares' (the holders of which must receive the pre-emptive offer under s 89), yet the terms of the relevant instruments may require that the holders should receive the rights issue offer. By contrast, convertible preference shares do fall within the definition of 'relevant shares' yet, if their terms did not entitle the holders to participate in a rights issue, s 89 would require them to be included. Similarly, since the terms of any convertible preference shares would likely require that the rights issue offer is made on an 'as if converted' basis, compliance with s 89 would need to assume that the preference shares were of the same nominal value and convertible on a one-for-one basis (which is unlikely to be the case).

E LIMITS ON DISAPPLYING PRE-EMPTION RIGHTS

10.19 Companies can, and frequently do, have in place a general disapplication of the provisions of the Companies Act 1985, s 89 (this is permitted by the Companies Act 1985, s 95, and will continue to be permitted by the Companies Act 2006, s 570). However, for listed companies, there are limits on the extent to which they can disapply statutory pre-emption rights, recommended and monitored by various investor protection committees, which set maximum limits on the nominal amount of shares which can be issued without complying with pre-emption requirements.

10.20 Most listed companies disapply the statutory pre-emption rights on an annual basis, at the same time as the directors seek to be granted authority to allot shares under the Companies Act 1985, s 80, and usually as part of the general business at the company's annual general meeting. Broadly, this general section 89 disapplication will permit the directors to make small non-pre-emptive share issues and rights issues (for cash), but which should nevertheless follow the pre-emption rules in the Listing Rules. It is, however, essential that the precise terms of an existing section 89 disapplication, and an existing section 80 authority, are verified at the outset. An existing section 89 disapplication will not cover a situation where the authorised share capital of the issuer has to be increased and/or a new section 80 authority obtained; an existing section 89 disapplication can only relate to an existing section 80 authority.

10.21 On 15 May 2006, the Pre-Emption Group published a Statement of Principles, to provide guidance to companies and investors on the disapplication of pre-emption rights. The statement is intended to take into account recommendations made by Paul Myners in his 2005 report on pre-emption rights, and will replace the 1987 Pre-Emption Guidelines. The statement emphasises the need for flexibility where a new equity issue on a non-pre-emptive basis would be in the interests of companies and their owners. While the same thresholds are retained for disapplication requests, which are likely to be non-controversial (5% of ordinary share capital in a year, 7.5% in a rolling three-year period and a discount of no more than 5%), it is stressed that shareholders on a case-by-case basis should consider requests, which might cause the company to exceed those levels. Companies should also communicate any intent to seek a non-pre-emptive issue as early as possible and non-routine requests should be made at an AGM only where the company is in a position to provide the necessary information, otherwise an extraordinary general meeting will be needed. The Pre-emption Group has also stated that it will monitor the application of the principles. These principles are likely to be of limited use to a company seeking to raise immediate funding by way of a rescue rights issue.

10.22 Following the passing of a resolution to disapply the Companies Act 1985, s 89, the company's annual report should include certain information about that disapplication, such as the actual level of discount achieved, the amount of cash raised (and how it was used), and the percentage of shares issued on a non-pre-emptive basis over the last year.

F THE PRINCIPAL STEPS IN A RIGHTS ISSUE

10.23 A rights issue, whether in the ordinary course or as a result of a distressed situation, will follow the same principal steps. Lawyers and bankers will be involved from the outset, to provide advice on both the technical and documentary steps of the rights issue, as well as advice on pricing. Banks will also be closely involved in the underwriting process, the sales and marketing process, and in dealings with the FSA.

10.24 The main stages of a rights issue, which are discussed in further detail below, are as follows:

  (i) preparation of issue documents (eg circular, prospectus);
 (ii) preparation and negotiation of the underwriting agreement, agreement among underwriters (if applicable) and the sub-underwriting letter;
(iii) application for listing and admission prior to the issue of the circular;
 (iv) pricing, board approval and signing in escrow;
  (v) offer of shares to shareholders using 'provisional allotment letters' ('PALs') (for certificated shareholders) or through the CREST system (for uncertificated shareholdings);
 (vi) sale in the market of the entitlements of overseas shareholders' and any fractional entitlements (provided that, as mentioned above, the statutory pre-emption rights have been disapplied);
(vii) trading of rights in 'nil paid' form (whilst the rights issue is open for acceptance);
(viii) acceptance of the offer by shareholders (or those who have acquired rights in the market) and payment of the subscription price;
 (ix) sale of any shares not taken up by shareholders (the *rump*) in the market, if a price at least equal to the subscription price and expenses can be obtained;
  (x) any shares not taken up by shareholders or sold in the market are left with the underwriters and/or sub-underwriters (the *stick*).

Some of the more complex principal stages in a conventional rights issue by a UK listed company are set out in more detail below.

Preparation of issue documents

10.25 A number of fairly technical documents will need to be prepared in order to launch, and successfully carry out, any rights issue. A company will need to engage appropriate advisers to assist with their preparation, including lawyers, bankers and reporting accountants. The main issue documents will include:

(a) *Press announcement*: The press announcement will announce the issue to the market (upon its launch), and should contain all material information – including, not least, the price and size of the issue, and the reasons for the company seeking additional funding from its shareholders. Of course, in the case of a company which has no other source of funding, and finds itself seeking cash from its shareholders as a last resort, the content, context and tone of this message will be critical.

(b) *Circular and prospectus*: A prospectus will be required to be prepared and published by the company, in order that an offer of shares (being 'transferable securities') to the public can be made pursuant to the rights issue. The contents of any prospectus must comply with the detailed requirements of the FSA's Prospectus Rules, and will, therefore, include detailed disclosure about the company and its financial position, together with any disclosure required as a result of the general duty of disclosure pursuant to the Financial Services and Markets Act 2000 ('FSMA 2000'), s 87A(2). This section requires the disclosure of all such information which, having regard to the particular nature of the shares and the issuer, is necessary to enable investors to make an informed assessment of the assets and liabilities, financial position, profits and losses, and prospects of the issuer (which is taken in practice to include its subsidiaries) and of the rights attaching to the shares to be issued. The directors of the company will also be required to take responsibility for the accuracy of the information set out in the prospectus, which typically gives rise to a thorough verification exercise.

In addition, a circular to shareholders will need to be prepared (on the assumption that a general meeting of the company is being convened), providing a clear and adequate explanation of the rights issue (and the background to, and reasons for, it) and explaining why the shareholders are being asked to vote at a general meeting. The contents requirements of Chapter 13 of the FSA's Listing Rules will need to be complied with and the FSA will generally need to approve the contents of the circular.

The circular will generally set out how the directors intend to deal with their entitlements under the rights issue (whether to take them up or not), and how they intend to vote at the general meeting. Obviously, a positive message from the directors as to their support of the rights issue will be expected from shareholders and potential investors alike. The circular will also contain the notice of general meeting, which may be required to increase the company's share capital, provide the directors with authority to allot the resulting shares, and disapply the statutory pre-emption rights, as discussed above.

(c)   *Provisional allotment letter*: A 'PAL' is the temporary document of title
by which the new shares are offered to shareholders holding shares in
certificated form (in advance of the shares actually being issued) and
will show a shareholder's entitlement to the new shares. The PAL will
normally constitute the offer of shares itself (together with the prospectus). However, a PAL does not need to be, and in practice is not, sent to
those shareholders who hold their shares in CREST. CREST shareholders will instead receive a credit to their stock account in respect of their
entitlement to nil paid rights (see below).

Since the new shares will typically be being offered at a discount to
their market price, the right to take up shares at that discounted price
itself has a value. Therefore, rights to new shares can be traded by
shareholders and, during the minimum 21-day period during which the
offer is open, this occurs 'nil paid'. Where such rights are represented
by a PAL, the PAL will also need to be transferred to any person
acquiring such rights in such a way and so they are, in effect,
themselves traded. Holders of shares in certificated form who take up
their rights will, in due course, have share certificates issued in place of
their PALs. The PALs have to comply with the FSA's requirements
relating to temporary documents of title (paragraph 9.5.15R, Listing
Rules).

Preparation and negotiation of the underwriting agreement

10.26 The underwriting agreement is a critical document for the company,
since it provides an effective guarantee that the company will receive the full
proceeds of the rights issue, whether or not its shareholders take up their
rights to subscribe for new shares, and whether or not such rights are sold in
the market (with the purchaser then taking up the right to subscribe for new
shares). This is achieved by a certain bank or banks (the *underwriting banks*)
agreeing to subscribe for shares which are not so taken up, ensuring that the
company will secure subscribers for all of the shares being offered and,
therefore, all of the proceeds of that subscription.

10.26.1 Generally, the underwriting agreement will be signed the night before
the circular and prospectus are published, and will be dated the following day.
However, sometimes an underwriting agreement is signed before the circular
and prospectus are published, at the same time as the announcement by the
company that it plans to launch a rights issue. This is done where a company
needs the certainty of an underwriting, including for market confidence
reasons, but does not have time to prepare a full circular and prospectus prior
to announcement (more likely to be the case in distressed situations). Such an
underwriting may be of a 'stand-by' nature, which generally means that it will
be at a low price (often the nominal value of the company's shares) or for an
amount other than the offer price, and the price will be subject to upward
revision (or will be set later on in the process). This will generally be cheaper,
in terms of underwriting commissions, than a full underwriting, although it
provides less certainty and so may not be suitable in all cases. Where a full
indemnity is provided, the indemnity banks will generally seek additional

termination rights in the underwriting agreement if material information is disclosed in the public documents, when they are produced, which was not set out in the press announcement. Clearly, this presents additional risks for the company.

10.27 An agreement to underwrite the rights issue clearly presents a risk for the underwriting banks since, to the extent that the rights issue is not successful, and not all of the rights are taken up by shareholders or 'renouncees' (those to whom the rights have been transferred, or renounced), the underwriting banks will be required to take up those shares – and pay for them. There is, therefore, a cost attached to the taking of this risk, in terms of the 'underwriting fee' which the underwriting banks will charge the company for entering into the underwriting arrangements. The more risky that the rights issue is perceived to be, the higher the underwriting fee will be.

10.28 The rationale for not underwriting a rights issue is, therefore, one of cost. However, in undertaking a rights issue, companies (and particularly companies on the brink of distress) are obviously keen to ensure that they receive the funds they require. The risk that a rights issue may not get away can be offset by the discount which the company offers when pricing the rights issue – if the issue is at a deep discount, which will likely be attractive to shareholders and other investors, then the risk that they will not take up their rights is lowered, and with it the need for an underwritten rights issue.

10.29 However, particularly in an economic downturn, and perhaps as a matter of prudence in any event, companies may prefer to transfer the market risk from themselves to their underwriting banks. A rights issue which is 'hard' underwritten – that is, with very limited room for the underwriting banks to manoeuvre themselves out of the deal – will enable shareholders, other investors, bankers, analysts and the market as a whole to assess the company's financial position on the assumption that the equity funding is already in place. Since an underwriting does involve real market risk for the underwriting banks over the entire period of underwriting (which will be at least as long as the time for which the rights offer is open), both lenders and investors are comforted by the stability that an underwriting brings.

10.30 Substantial or influential shareholders may have undertaken in advance to take up their rights and, in this event, the relevant shares will be carved out from the underwriting (and, therefore, have a downward impact on the price of the underwriting). However, it will be critical to ensure that the shareholders' undertakings can be enforced, are themselves 'firm' and do not contain extended circumstances in which the shareholders can refuse to take up their rights. For example, a company would not wish a market 'material adverse change' ('MAC') clause or a business MAC clause to be included, so as to maximise the certainty of the funding being delivered (though there may be a force majeure clause). The undertaking may well track the underwriting agreement in terms of the circumstances in which the shareholders are no longer bound by it being similar to the circumstances in which the underwriting banks are no longer obliged to take up the shares.

10.31 The underwriting agreement may well contain a 'MAC clause', allowing the underwriting banks to terminate the underwriting agreement if there is a material adverse change (either in the market generally, or in the business of the company, depending upon what has been negotiated) between the time the underwriting agreement is signed (usually the night before the rights issue is announced and launched) and the admission of nil paid rights.

10.32 Typical matters upon which the underwriting agreement will be conditional include shareholder approval of any relevant matters (such as an increase to the company's share capital or the disapplication of the Companies Act 1985, s 89) and the admission, in nil paid form, of the new shares to listing on the Official List and to trading on the London Stock Exchange. This second condition (often referred to as the 'admission condition') is critical to the underwriting banks (and the sub-underwriters, discussed below), as any underwriters will not wish to be obliged to acquire unlisted and untradeable shares if their underwriting commitments are called upon, since there will be no market on which they can be sold. The intention, of course, is for the underwriting agreement to be relatively free from conditions which the company does not think will be easily achieveable, since it wants the underwriting – and its rights issue – to be as certain as possible. However, as mentioned above, the underwriting banks will generally negotiate at least a MAC.

10.33 The company will be required to give certain warranties and undertakings to the underwriting banks in the underwriting agreement, breach of which may give rise to rights of termination (as well as a contractual or tortious right to damages, depending upon whether representations as well as warranties are provided). The company will typically also provide an indemnity against any losses to the underwriting banks arising in relation to the rights issue.

10.34 Underwriting fees, in the context of rights issues, can be higher than for other methods of equity capital raising, such as placings, because of the duration of the risk, the perceived scale of the risk (since there is a risk that the market simply will not 'buy' the rights issue, although this will ultimately come down to pricing) and the work involved. However, fee levels are not fixed and the underwriting banks' assessment of the risk will be a driving factor. Some deals could have fees of approximately 2% of the total equity funding being raised, but smaller or more risky issues could cost up to 5%. Issuers may seek to build in incentives into the fee structure, perhaps dependent upon the percentage of shares which are taken up by shareholders or renouncees, rather than underwriters. Such underwriting fees will be specified in the underwriting agreement, together with any other fees and expenses (such as advisory or documentation fees) which are payable by the company.

Sub-underwriting

10.35 Once the underwriting agreement has been executed and released from escrow, the underwriting banks are fully committed and will be obliged to subscribe for any shares not taken up (provided that the conditions to the underwriting agreement are fulfilled, though such conditions will be relatively limited). Typically, the underwriting banks will want to offload some of their risk by procuring 'sub-underwriters' – other banks or financial institutions, or institutional shareholders, which will agree to subscribe for a proportion of the shares which the underwriters themselves would be obliged to subscribe for if the shares were not fully taken up.

10.36 Therefore, when the rights issue is launched, the underwriters will seek to arrange such sub-underwriters. The sub-underwriters will be paid a fee for taking the market risk involved in their underwriting for the transaction period, but because their risk is (optically, at least) one step further removed from the issuing company, and will likely be (on an individual basis) a smaller risk in terms of the number of shares being sub-underwritten than the underwriting banks themselves, this fee is usually of a lower magnitude (possibly 1–2%). (In general terms, however, the underwriting banks will seek to lay off their entire risk in this way.) If there is a rump of shares left at the end of the process (not having been taken up), these sub-underwriters will acquire such shares at the rights issue price. To the extent that the sub-underwriters are institutional investors, rather than banks, this technique will ensure that the relevant rump of shares will end up with those institutions rather than with underwriting (or other) banks, which banks may simply want to sell out of the shares immediately, which will likely have a downward effect on the share price. If the rights issue is successful, and the sub-underwriters (or, indeed, the underwriters) are not called upon to subscribe, then they will each have received their fee as compensation for the risks taken. Sub-underwriting is typical on European rights issues, and will be particularly important in a rescue context, when the underwriting banks will be keen to ensure that their exposure is as limited as possible.

10.37 Sub-underwriting typically takes place with the issue of a letter to each sub-underwriter from the underwriters, which will set out the conditions of the sub-underwriting and the fees that will be payable. The conditions to the sub-underwriting should mirror the underwriting agreement so that there is no gap between the risk of the underwriting bank and sub-underwriter – if there is, there will be a risk that the underwriting bank will be exposed to the entirety of the underwriting obligations without recourse if the underwriting agreement has become unconditional, but the sub-underwriting letter has not.

10.38 As a legal matter, the underwriting banks will be liable to the company under the underwriting agreement whether or not the rights issue is sub-underwritten, and if any sub-underwriter fails to take up (or find the money for) its agreed participation. So the underwriters' ability to procure sub-underwriters is key, as is the ability of the underwriting bank to claim against a defaulting sub-underwriter.

Pricing and discounting

10.39 The evening before the rights issue is launched ('impact day'), the company will meet with its financial advisers and the underwriters to determine the issue price. As mentioned above, fixing the correct price is critical to ensure that the rights issue is successful – at sufficient a discount that it is attractive to shareholders and other investors, but not too heavily discounted such as to prejudice a positive market reaction. There will also be an element of risk weighing as regards the likelihood (and the cost) of the underwriting.

10.40–10.41 Historically, in rescue scenarios, the discount has been typically in an amount of between 30%–50% to the market price immediately prior to launch. More recently, over 60% of rights issues undertaken between March 2002 and March 2006 (which raised over £10m), were priced at discounts of more than 30%. Deep discounts of this nature have generally been connected to recent restructurings, which require greater certainty of success and support of shareholders.

10.42 There is an argument that deep discounting offers protection against market volatility and lowers underwriting fees as the underwriter is taking on less risk. Whilst deep discounting may appear to be value destructive, all shareholders on a pre-emptive issue have the opportunity to acquire the new shares at that price, or sell the rights for the perceived 'value' in the discount, so no value should be lost. In addition, the size of the discount on a pre-emptive issue has no effect on financial or accounting dilution. The beneficiaries of any discount are the current shareholders themselves. Moreover, under IAS 33, a pre-emptive discounted rights issue is treated much the same as a bonus share issue and earnings per share is adjusted accordingly.

Board approval and signing in escrow

10.43 Just prior to impact day, a board (or board committee) meeting takes place at which all the relevant rights issue documentation is approved. If no general meeting is to be held, the shares which are the subject of the rights issue are, subject to admission, 'provisionally' allotted to shareholders on the register on a specific record date (otherwise, this takes place immediately following the general meeting at which the relevant resolutions have been passed).

10.44–10.45 In cases where the statutory pre-emption rights (under the Companies Act 1985, s 89) have been disapplied, and as discussed above, the shares representing the aggregate of any fractional entitlements, and shares which would otherwise have been allotted to overseas shareholders, are provisionally allotted to the underwriting bank. The 'provisional' nature of the allotment relates to the fact that the subscription price for the shares has not yet been paid and that, for a period, such shares will trade in nil paid form. Where a rights issue is being conducted in accordance with s 89, with the overseas offer being made via the 'Gazette route', for example, fractional entitlements are generally not allotted so, in practice, the number of new shares to be issued will be less than the maximum number theoretically possible. This gives rise to an 'up to' number of shares being the subject of such a rights issue.

G IMPACT DAY

10.46 Before the markets open for business on impact day, the financial advisers, the underwriters and the company will confirm that no material adverse change has occurred overnight which might significantly affect the market and the rights issue (the 'overnight MAC' referred to earlier). This being the case, the rights issue will be 'live' and, to the extent not already released, the escrow over the underwriting agreement will be released.

10.47–10.48 This will give rise to an announcement obligation on the part of the company and, once the press announcement has been released (usually at 7.00 am), the underwriters will arrange the sub-underwriting, aiming for it to be completed by 3.00 pm on the same day.

H APPROVAL, FILING AND POSTING OF THE CIRCULAR

10.49 A company will wish to keep its rights issue timetable as short as possible, not least so that the underwriting commissions which are payable are kept to a minimum. For this reason, the public documents will ideally be posted on impact day; though this may be impractical, depending upon the number of shareholders to whom the information must be sent. The circular and prospectus must be approved by, and (in the case of the prospectus) filed with, the FSA (paragraph 3.2.1R of the Prospectus Rules). FSA approval must be obtained before the prospectus can be published. In addition, copies of the company's consolidated accounts must also be made available to the public for the duration of the rights issue (paragraph 24, Annex I, Prospectus Rules). The PAL (personalised for each shareholder and showing his proportionate entitlement to shares) will be posted to certificated shareholders at the same time as the circular, where no general meeting is required, or after the relevant resolutions have been passed by the shareholders, where a general meeting is required. This posting of PALs is subject to any overseas securities restrictions, however; the Gazette route must be followed where the Companies Act 1985, s 89 has not been disapplied.

Dealings commence

10.50 On the first trading day after the PALs are posted, the FSA and London Stock Exchange will each issue a statement that the new shares have been admitted to listing and trading – at which time admission becomes effective.

10.51 At this point, the admission condition – typically the last condition to the underwriting – becomes satisfied, the underwriting becomes wholly unconditional, and dealings commence, nil paid, in the new shares which have been provisionally allotted. These nil paid dealings will continue for a period of not less than 21 days (paragraph 9.5.6R, Listing Rules), during which time existing shareholders can trade their rights in the market, based upon the 'value' in the amount of the discount built into the rights issue (unless the rights issue is poorly received and the market price falls below the rights issue price).

Sale of overseas shareholders' and fractional entitlements

10.52 Where the Companies Act 1985, s 89 has been disapplied, overseas shareholders' and fractional entitlements are generally sold as soon as possible after dealings commence, nil paid, if an amount at least equal to the expenses of sale can be obtained. Any premium obtained in relation to each overseas shareholder's entitlement (subject to a minimum of £5.00) is accounted for to the relevant overseas shareholders. Any premium obtained in relation to aggregated fractional entitlements is paid to the company.

10.53 If the Gazette route is being used, or the company expressly reserves to the overseas shareholders the right to take up their entitlements if they can demonstrate that there would be no breach of securities laws, the entitlements of overseas shareholders are treated like any other entitlements – instead of being sold immediately, they are sold at the end of the trading period (assuming the overseas shareholders do not take them up), at the same time as any other shares not taken up. Fractional entitlements are generally not allotted where the Gazette route is followed.

Acceptance date

10.54 By the end of the nil paid dealing period, all shareholders or renouncees wishing to take up rights must have paid the (discounted) subscription price for the relevant shares. After the last date for acceptance, dealings become fully paid. Details of the mechanics of payment and acceptance (including through CREST) will be set out in the circular.

Sale of shares not taken up

10.55 If payment in respect of a provisional allotment has not been received by 3.00 pm (11.00 am where the rights issue is being made through CREST) on the last date for acceptance, the provisional allotment is deemed to have been declined. (There are limited circumstances in which acceptances received after this time may be accepted by the company (at its discretion), such as: (i) where the acceptance arrives in the first post on the day after the deadline, with a postmark no later than the latest time for acceptance; and (ii) a remittance has been received from an authorised person (for the purposes of FSMA 2000) prior to the deadline, with an undertaking to provide the completed PAL in due course).

10.56 At this stage, the underwriting banks and brokers will attempt to sell these shares (known as the 'rump') in the market, at a price at or above the subscription price (plus the expenses of sale). Two business days are generally permitted for this exercise, after which any remaining shares (the 'stick') will be taken up by the sub-underwriters or the underwriting banks, pursuant to the relevant underwriting (or sub-underwriting) arrangements. Where a premium is raised on the sale of the rump and the individual entitlement is £5.00 or more, it is paid to the provisional allottees that did not take up their rights. The sale of the stick will be at the subscription price, pursuant to the underwriting arrangements. In all cases, the company will receive the subscription price, ensuring that the equity funding it requires is received in full.

10.57 When selling the rump, the banks will act as agent of the company, in procuring subscribers, in order to avoid any charge to stamp duty or stamp duty reserve tax. Similarly, as regards any premium over the subscription price, the company will be keen to ensure that it does not acquire any beneficial interest. This is because any such premium received by the company would be treated as the proceeds of a share subscription, and so any return of it to shareholders may be viewed either as a return of capital, or as an income distribution (requiring reserves and possibly creating a tax charge for the shareholder).

Announcing the result

10.58 The Listing Rules require that the results of the rights issue must be notified without delay and, if any shares not taken up are sold, details of the sale (including the date and price per share). However, the company has a discretion to delay (for up to two business days) such notification of the results of the rights issue where there are underwriting arrangements in place and until such time as the underwriters' obligations are finally determined or have lapsed. This coincides with the period for selling the rump, described above.

10.59 The company must, however, ensure that it does comply with its legal obligations of disclosure (both under the Disclosure Rules and otherwise), and so should ask itself whether there might be circumstances in which the exercise of that discretion to delay would be 'unreasonable'. In an extreme case, this may be a risk; FSMA 2000, s 397 (in relation to misleading statements) may be relevant, and advice may need to be sought.

Chapter 11

CREDIT DERIVATIVES
AND RESTRUCTURING

A INTRODUCTION

11.1 Credit derivatives are used, among other things, to hedge the potential risk that borrowers might fail to repay their outstanding debt obligations (ie their bonds and loans). Credit risk is transferred from the buyer of protection to the seller. The market has been growing extremely rapidly, more than doubling every two years. The global market is predicted to reach $33 trillion in terms of outstanding notional amount by 2008 (see the BBA Credit Derivatives Report, September 2006), with London as the main global centre. Credit derivatives are a powerful mechanism for reducing the concentration of risk on financial institutions' balance sheets. Never before has there been a credit market where the provider of credit capacity is potentially so distant from, and unknown to, the borrower. This has implications for relationship banking and for the role that creditors play when borrowers run into financial difficulty. This section examines the evolution of restructuring as a credit event in an attempt to understand the interplay between the growing credit derivative market and the corporate restructuring process, and goes on to look at the impact of credit derivatives on restructurings more generally.

B THE MARKET IN CREDIT DERIVATIVES

11.2 Under a credit derivative, the value of the obligations to be performed by at least one party is determined by the creditworthiness of an agreed 'reference entity'. The simplest type of credit derivative is the credit default swap ('CDS'). Under a CDS, one party (the 'protection buyer') agrees to pay an amount (the 'premium'), either initially or periodically, to the other party (the 'protection seller'). The protection seller agrees to pay an amount to, or buy a debt obligation from, the protection buyer on the occurrence of specified credit-related contingencies (each a 'credit event').

11.3 Banks are by far the largest protection buyers with over 50% of global market share (see the BBA Credit Derivatives Report, September 2006). The major sellers of protection are also banks. However, hedge funds' share of the market is growing.

11.4 Typically in all financial markets, the information advantage lies with the banks or the major liquidity providers, as is the case in the credit derivatives market. Problems occur if a protection buyer has either some influence over the triggering of a credit event or is in possession of certain information regarding events within a company. According to Matt Wood-hams, global product manager for analytics at GFI, 'it is not a question of insider trading, more that buyers and sellers have a different rationale ... there may be a feeling amongst protection sellers that there is no downside for a lender agreeing to a restructuring if they have also bought protection'. (See GTNews.com, *The Moral Hazard: Credit Events*, 7 May 2003). This senti-ment was prevalent amongst protection sellers in the Conseco restructuring, discussed in this chapter.

11.5 To date, CDSs have mostly been taken out on well-known corporate (and sovereign) names. High-profile restructurings have of course occurred in this market including the Marconi restructuring and the Conseco restructur-ing.

C CREDIT EVENTS

11.6 Credit events are referable to the reference entity or certain or all obligations ('obligations') of the reference entity. When some event occurs that adversely affects the credit-worthiness of the entity, such as a failure to pay, a bankruptcy or a restructuring (a 'credit event'), the protection seller agrees that it will acquire ('have delivered') credit-impaired securities from the protection buyer ('deliverable obligations') at a pre-agreed price ('physical settlement'), or pay the difference between that price and their current value ('cash settlement').

11.7 Credit derivatives are usually documented under the International Swaps and Derivatives Association (ISDA) documentary framework. ISDA is the global trade association representing participants in the privately negoti-ated derivatives industry. ISDA requires (in most cases) that trades be confirmed by a confirmatory letter. There is a standard long-form confirma-tion published by ISDA for use with CDSs. ISDA also publishes standard Credit Derivatives Definitions which are discussed in detail in this chapter.

Restructuring as a credit event

11.8 Credit derivatives were originally intended to protect against major financial crises, such as payment defaults. Financial institutions embraced them as they were seen as a mechanism for reducing risk concentrations (thereby improving the stability of the financial system). However, restructurings often occur, at least in the context of loans, long before any default because companies would naturally prefer to restructure rather than default. Restructuring has been called a 'soft' credit event, meaning one that does not immediately cause default and allows reference entities to continue to trade, although their liabilities will naturally have different prices. There is arguably scope for restructuring as a credit event to be manipulated by protection buyers in order to receive cash windfalls.

11.9 Restructuring has been one of the most contentious credit events seen in the market. Europe and the US have different definitions. Many argue that there needs to be a drive towards standardisation in the documentation globally, though this was not achieved by the publication of the 2003 ISDA Credit Derivatives Definitions in May 2003.

11.10 The January 2003 report from the Working Group of the Committee on the Global Financial System (CGFS) suggested that market participants were a long way from an agreement on the issue of restructuring, stating:

> 'The restructuring question, in particular, remains unresolved. Indeed risk takers and risk shedders seem at present to be moving further apart. Some risk takers (insurance companies) appear to have concluded that including restructuring leaves them too exposed to opportunistic behaviour on the part of the banks shedding risk. On the other hand, many – though certainly not all – banks regard credit protection as incomplete without cover against restructuring.'

11.11 Paul Czekalowski, now global co-head of credit structuring at UBS, suggested that many in the market believed that restructuring should be removed from the list of credit events. Indeed a group of monoline insurers also approached ISDA to have restructuring eliminated from the list of credit events prior to the publication of the 2003 Definitions (See GTNews.com *The Moral Hazard: Credit Events*, 7 May 2003). Those looking for the removal of restructuring from the table of potential credit events have not had their way, however. Importantly, most bank regulators (including the Basel Committee) also take the view that CDSs must include restructuring in order to qualify as a credit risk mitigant for regulatory capital purposes.

11.12 At the end of June 2004, the Bank for International Settlements (BIS) announced a new capital framework for banks worldwide, known as 'Basel II'. Under this framework, credit derivative transactions must include restructuring as a credit event to get advantage of the full hedge. This is one new factor of many to be considered when parties to a credit derivative are considering whether restructuring is included as a credit event.

11.13 Restructuring is, however, an important credit event for a hedger of risk. If restructuring is chosen as a credit event, it introduces credit deterioration as well as credit default into the protection coverage. In practice, the value of restructuring as a credit event will depend on the likelihood that restructuring will be the trigger credit event, as well as the recovery rate upon restructuring.

11.14 If the credit derivative market is to provide its participants with the benefits they are seeking, its credit event definitions need to describe accurately the events they are trying to capture. Restructuring presents particular difficulties in this regard. It is difficult, though not impossible, to say when a restructuring begins or can be regarded as being in progress. As a result, the ISDA definition of restructuring has been reviewed and modified on a number of occasions. The first major review of the definition resulted from events following the Conseco restructuring in the US.

The Conseco restructuring

11.15 In August 2000 a US company, Conseco, Inc, restructured US$900m of its bank debts by extending their maturity by 15 months, in order to avoid an impending liquidity crisis. Because the restructuring involved a postponement of the repayment dates of the loans, it constituted a credit event, although the company remained solvent and there had been no payment default. The lenders were not perceived to have been adversely affected but that did not prevent some banks from declaring the restructuring as a credit event.

11.16 The unexpected outcome was that, by making it easier for Conseco to meet its payment obligations, the restructuring resulted in the loans trading at a higher price than the company's bond obligations. The bonds were therefore cheaper to deliver in physical settlement of the CDS than the loans. With restructuring loosely defined in ISDA documentation as a credit event, compensation payments in CDSs were triggered for Conseco's lenders. They proceeded to buy un-restructured, long-term poor quality Conseco bonds from the marketplace, which had dropped significantly in price, delivered them under a CDS and then demanded the full face value in return. This became known as the 'cheapest to deliver' option, a concept and terminology imported from the futures markets.

11.17 Holders of Conseco loans that had bought credit protection could deliver the lower-priced bonds rather than the loans they owned and make a windfall profit. The 'cheapest to deliver' option was considered unfair to protection sellers who considered that the losses they had made did not reflect the actual losses on the restructured loans because Conseco had become a healthier company as a result of the restructuring. They were aggrieved that banks could deliver bonds when they had put their contracts in place to hedge their loan portfolios. Protection sellers ended up holding the least favourable deliverable obligations.

Implications of the Conseco case

11.18   Conseco caused trepidation in the market as protection sellers felt they would be obliged to compensate for an event that is seen as routine happening in lending practice. Also, protection sellers feared that protection buyers had virtually nothing to lose by agreeing to a restructuring. There were fears of a 'moral hazard' as protection sellers considered that protection buyers that had been involved in the Conseco restructuring had a profit incentive to agree to it. Sellers questioned whether the situation had been manipulated.

11.19   Conseco led to protection sellers asking the following key questions:

(a)   whether restructuring should be a credit event;
(b)   how many lenders should agree to a restructuring to qualify as a credit event; and
(c)   what should a protection buyer deliver to a protection seller in the case of a physically-settled CDS.

11.20   This situation resulted in many US dealers not offering restructuring as a credit event. The London market continued to offer it, so a two-tiered market evolved, with different transaction pricing depending upon whether or not restructuring was included as a credit event. On average, there is a difference of 10–20 basis points between premium quotations for CDSs with or without modified restructuring. The Conseco restructuring and the result-ant polarisation of the market prompted the evolution of the ISDA definition of restructuring.

D   EVOLUTION OF THE ISDA DEFINITIONS

11.21   Since their publication in 1999, the 1999 ISDA Credit Derivatives Definitions have been tested on a number of occasions, particularly in relation to a number of high-profile credit events such as the Conseco and Marconi restructurings. Whilst as a general matter, they were found to be effective, issues arose which it was decided it would be best to clarify. This led to various iterations of the definition of restructuring as a credit event.

E   1999 ISDA DEFINITION OF RESTRUCTURING

11.22   The 1999 definition provided a certain level of objectivity by listing specific events that would constitute 'restructuring' in a CDS contract. These events were the following:

(a)   a reduction in the rate or amount of interest payable;
(b)   a reduction in the amount of principal;
(c)   a postponement of payment (interest or principal);
(d)   a change in ranking of priority (subordination); and
(e)   a change in the currency of composition of any payment.

11.23 To allow for negotiation of changes in interest rates or maturity extensions on bank loans under circumstances falling well short of severity of bankruptcy or payment default, the ISDA drafting committee introduced an exception to the definition that stated that events (a) to (e) would not be considered a restructuring if the event did not 'directly or indirectly result from a deterioration in the creditworthiness or financial condition of the reference entity'.

11.24 Following the Conseco restructuring, protection sellers strongly wanted the maturity of deliverable obligations to be subject to a limit. This was considered to be an appropriate means of protecting against the 'cheapest to deliver' option that sellers believed they had been exposed to in the Conseco restructuring. In 2001 ISDA published three supplements to the old definitions to clarify some issues which had arisen. These are referred to as the Restructuring Supplement, the Successor Supplement and the Convertible and Exchangeable Supplement. The approach adopted in the Restructuring Supplement became known as modified restructuring ('MR') because it modified the characteristics of the deliverables that settle the credit derivative transaction.

F THE SPECIFICS OF MR (THE CURRENT US STANDARD)

11.25 The underlying argument against restructuring as a credit event lies in the fact that such occurrences rarely lead to insolvency and equally rarely lead to an acceleration of the debt held by a company. This means, of course, that there can be quite large differences in the value of a company's long- and short-dated debt. Under the modified restructuring clauses, not only does there have to be a minimum number in agreement that a credit event has taken place, but limits have been placed upon the length of maturity of the debt that can be used for delivery after such an event.

11.26 By incorporating the provisions of the Restructuring Supplement relating to MR and checking the 'Restructuring Maturity Limitation Applicable' box in the standard confirmation the following applies.

11.27 If a protection buyer triggers after a restructuring credit event only, the maximum maturity of deliverables must:

(a)   be transferable to the protection seller without any requirement for consent; and
(b)   have a stated maturity that is not later than the earlier of:
    (i)   30 months after the legally effective restructuring date; and
    (ii)   the latest final maturity date of any restructured bond or loan,
    provided that such maturity can never be earlier than the scheduled termination date of the CDS contract (and, if it is, it is deemed to be the scheduled termination date of the CDS contract or 30 months following that date, as the case may be).

11.28 The deliverable obligation must be 'fully transferable' (consent not required) to an 'eligible transferee' (which contemplates a wide range of institutional market participants).

11.29 Restructuring credit events can only be triggered for obligations that (1) have more than three holders in the case of a bond or a loan, and (2) in the case of loans only, require at least a two-thirds majority to implement a restructuring. Under the 1999 ISDA definition of restructuring, a single party could trigger such an event. With MR, restructurings of bilateral loans are not triggers, though they are still deliverable if they otherwise meet deliverable obligation criteria.

11.30 Most US dealers adopted MR but European dealers did not. This is because the market in Europe is dominated by longer-dated bonds and consent-required loans, neither of which can be delivered under the modified restructuring definition. In 2003 a new version of definitions was published by ISDA and the amended definition of restructuring, known as modified modified restructuring ('MMR'), has primarily been adopted in respect of European credits.

G THE SPECIFICS OF MMR (THE CURRENT EUROPEAN STANDARD)

11.31 Where Modified Restructuring Maturity Limitation and Conditionally Transferable Obligation are specified as applicable in the confirmation and the buyer of protection triggers the contract in respect of which the only credit event is restructuring then:

(a)   the deliverable obligation must have a maximum maturity no later than the later of:
      (i)   the scheduled termination of the CDS contract; and
      (ii)   60 months (in the case of restructured bonds or loans) or 30 months (in the case of all other deliverable obligations) following the legally effective date of the restructuring; and
(b)   the deliverable obligation has to be transferable to any bank, financial institution, or other entity which is regularly engaged in or established for the purpose of making, purchasing or investing in loans, securities or other financial assets either (i) without consent, or (ii) with consent of the reference entity, not to be unreasonably withheld.

11.32 A restructuring credit event can only be triggered for obligations that (1) have more than three holders in the case of a bond or a loan, and (2) in the case of loans only, require at least a two-thirds majority to implement a restructuring.

H THE DIFFERENT ISDA DEFINITIONS OF RESTRUCTURING

11.33 MMR provides for a longer maturity cap for restructured bonds and loans than MR because it may be more common to see longer maturity extensions in the European market. In addition, it is more common for borrowers in Europe to restrict transferability of debt instruments to banks and financial institutions.

11.34 Since the adoption of the 2003 Definitions there are four choices relating to restructuring as a credit event (see www.credit-deriv.com, *ISDA promulgates new Credit Derivatives Definitions 2003*, 13 February 2003):

(a) trade without restructuring;
(b) trade with full restructuring, with no modification to the deliverable obligations aspect;
(c) trade with MR, as has been market practice in North America since the publication of the Restructuring Supplement in May 2001; or
(d) trade with MMR, a provision generally aimed to address issues raised in the European market.

11.35 Which definition is chosen depends on the nature of the market, the investment grade of the reference entity as well as the raison d'être for entering into the transaction. Default protection is not the only reason for entering into CDSs. According to one commentator 'many people use them to take a view on the widening and tightening of credit spread'. (See Michael Fuhrman, credit market specialist, GFI Group quoted in the article *Fools Gold* in the Banker, April 2004.)

I PRICING OF DERIVATIVES: CREDIT EVENTS UNDER ISDA AND RATINGS AGENCY DATA

11.36 It has been estimated that the probability of a credit event under ISDA is 30% higher than observed historically by the rating agencies, see Ernst & Young Financial Services Credit Derivatives 2003. This suggests that naïve use of agency data will underprice the derivatives. Credit events under the ISDA definitions may cover events that would not be considered default events by ratings agencies. It is a fear of many practitioners that banks with more sophisticated models and databases are able to price structures more accurately thus resulting in claims of 'moral hazard' especially from insurance companies.

11.37 The Conseco restructuring referred to above involved a deferral of maturities for three months, an increased coupon, a new corporate guarantee and additional covenants in favour of the lenders. According to the CGFS (see January 2003 report from the Working Group of the Committee on the Global Financial System) this made it unclear whether the lenders were disadvantaged by the restructuring. The rating agency Moodys did not define the events that occurred at Conseco as a default event. However, under ISDA documentation it was a credit event, so protection payments were triggered. This highlighted the fact that the scope for opportunistic behaviour seems to be greater in the case of restructuring than for other credit events (see Global Financial Systems report January 2003).

J THE ALTERED INTERESTS OF COVERED CREDITORS

11.38 As we have seen throughout this memorandum, restructuring is a non-judicial consensual process in which a business in financial difficulties and its main creditors participate. During the restructuring process, these parties aim to reach a consensus as to how to adjust the obligations of the business to their mutual benefit, and avoid the insolvency of the business. Additional or replacement loan facilities are often provided to the business beyond the term of its original facilities, and are sometimes made available in return for security (or greater security).

11.39 Where insolvency of a debtor is a credit event under a CDS that has been used to hedge the lender's credit risk under the loan, the lender will have a claim under the CDS in the event of, say, the debtor's failure.

11.40 A lender that has laid off part of its risk in this way may, at the least, be less co-operative than otherwise in the restructuring process, given its reduced economic interest in the success or failure of a rescue, and the possibility of recovering capital and leaving the relationship with the debtor if a credit event under the ISDA documentation occurs. (See *Credit Derivatives in Restructurings*, INSOL International, 2006.)

11.41 The behaviour of parties at the restructuring table may have a tendency to become unpredictable, if interests are altered in this way. 'You can have a creditor with GBP 100 million at stake who is relaxed about what happens because he has laid off all his debt exposure through credit derivatives while a GBP 10 million creditor who has not laid off any risk wants to put money in', notes Ian Powell, head of business recovery services at the accountancy firm PricewaterhouseCoopers. Quoted in the Financial Times, 11 February 2004 (*Credit default swaps join booming derivatives line-up*, Charles Batchelor).

11.42 Indeed, if a proposed restructuring contemplates the extension of new or replacement facilities beyond the period covered by a credit derivative taken out as a hedge for the original facility, a lender with such credit protection – in the possible absence of restructuring (of obligations) as a credit event under the derivative – is being requested to move from a covered to an uncovered position. This may be financially disadvantageous from the lender's point of view, especially if the price of cover in the market has increased. The lender may be less encouraged to turn the debtor's failing business around, and may even be incentivised to encourage failure of the business.

11.43 In relation to the mechanics of a restructuring, a hedge may, in addition, give rise to a reluctance on the part of the lender to incur costs such as a share of the expenses of a 'steering committee' (a committee of creditors acting as a sounding board for the lender leading the restructuring negotiations), or a share of the fees of such a committee's advisers. (See *Credit Derivatives: Current Legal and Regulatory Perspectives*, Simon Firth, Linklaters & Paines, July 1996, para 7.3.) A lender reluctant to incur the costs of a restructuring may still, of course, wish to share in the benefits of the restructuring, such as an increase in margin or a restructuring fee.

11.44 Further, even if a lender such as a bank is not averse to restructuring, it may not consider that it is in its best interests to disclose its derivative cover. Admitting that a bank's loan has been hedged by way of credit derivatives may be damaging to the bank's relationship with the particular customer.

11.45 Such lack of transparency will give rise to an asymmetry of information at the restructuring table, leading to practical difficulties in negotiating an agreement as to how a company is to be restructured. In particular, the relative exposures of creditors are used to determine issues such as risk sharing, voting and distribution of recoveries; if a particular creditor's true (lack of) exposure is not recognised until late in the process, such issues may be resolved inappropriately.

11.46 It has been suggested that the increasing use of credit derivatives such as CDSs may therefore lead to a reduction in the number of restructurings taking place, and a corresponding rise in the number of more formal workouts such as schemes of arrangement under the Companies Act 1985, s 425[1]. The extent to which this is true will of course depend on the use to which CDSs are put. As noted in this section not all credit derivatives are used to cover credit positions to which lenders are exposed.

[1] The Companies Act 1985, s 425(1) is to be replaced by the Companies Act 2006, ss 895(1), 896(1) and (2). The Companies Act 1985, s 425(2) is to be replaced by the Companies Act 2006, ss 899(1) and (3), 907(1) and 922(1). The Companies Act 1985, s 425(3) is to be replaced (with some changes) by the Companies Act 2006, ss 899(4), 901(3) and (4). The Companies Act 1985, s 425(4) is to be replaced by the Companies Act 2006, s 901(5) and (6). The Companies Act 1985, s 425(6) is to be replaced by the Companies Act 2006, s 895(2). The Companies Act 2006, ss 895–935 are to come into force on 6 April 2008 (SI 2007/3495). For transitional provisions and savings, see SI 2007/3495, arts 6, 9, 12, Schs 1, 4.

11.47 The flipside of the information asymmetry discussed above is asymmetry of information between the protection buyer and the protection seller, where the protection buyer, as originator of the underlying loan, has greater information as to the credit quality of the reference entity. Protection sellers may seek a premium against additional risks engendered by such asymmetry. Market participants have commented that the cost of protection by means of a single-name CDS is often higher than the equivalent cost of selling a loan in the secondary market. A protection seller could also attempt to require a protection buyer to retain the first share of any losses. CLOs (special purpose credit derivative vehicles that acquire loans with funds raised by issuing bonds or notes), for instance, generally include a first loss tranche of about 2–3% of the value of the underlying portfolio. Another way of reducing asymmetry problems is to involve independent third parties in initial credit assessments, subsequent credit monitoring, verification of credit events and assessment of loss severity. Any of these additional costs of buying protection may limit the value of credit derivatives to commercial banks.

11.48 The Marconi restructuring is a recent example of information asymmetry coming into play in practice. This restructuring involved a scheme of £340 of cash, £750m of new notes, and 99.5% equity in Marconi Corporation plc. It was established quite late in the initial refinancing phase (which took place in late 2001 and early 2002) that certain lenders did not want to participate in a rescheduling of debts which extended maturity dates beyond those of the original €4.5m facility, as they held derivative cover. Various solutions were put forward to resolve this problem, but the refinancing was eventually suspended by Marconi.

11.49 There is a strong counter-argument that such information asymmetry is likely to be rare in practice. This is an argument from reputational risk. It could be said that banks are unlikely to compromise their reputation by either refusing to disclose their derivative interests, or encouraging a debtor's insolvency. (See *Corporate Workouts, the London Approach and Financial Stability*, Peter Brierley and Gavin Vlieghe, Financial Stability Review, November 1999, page 178.) Nevertheless, the economic upside to a bank of the insolvency of a debtor will, at the least, be greater if the bank's risks arising from such insolvency are hedged by means of a credit derivative.

K PHYSICALLY-SETTLED DERIVATIVES IN A RESTRUCTURING

11.50 It is not uncommon for a Standstill agreement to require lenders not to assign, novate or transfer any obligations of the company being restructured. This may give rise to difficulties for lenders that have obligations under physically-settled credit derivatives.

11.51 Conversely, if physical settlement takes place before a Standstill agreement is implemented, the possibility arises of protection sellers under credit derivatives sitting around the table with the reference entity and its creditors, having received *physical delivery* of deliverable obligations. This might be beneficial for protection sellers, who will thereby have the chance to negotiate terms on the obligation they have received in settlement of the derivative.

11.52 However, physical settlement may give rise to a certain instability in the restructuring process, especially if settlement takes place and the stakeholders engaged in the process change substantially as a result. In practice, though, the greater practical issue during a restructuring (as was the case in the Marconi restructuring) may be as to whether a credit event has occurred in the first place. (See *Lessons from the Marconi restructuring*, Nicholas Frome and Claude Brown, IFLR, September 2003.) Numerous public announcements as to the development of Marconi's restructuring negotiations were released, and conflicting views pervaded the market as to whether these amounted to 'bankruptcy' or 'restructuring' credit events under the ISDA documentation. (See *Marconi reveals shortcomings of credit swap documents*, News Focus, IFLR, October 2002, discussing a difference in the positions taken by Linklaters and Clifford Chance on this issue.) In such a scenario, the identity of those ultimately bearing the risk of default will be unclear. Indeed, as parties engaged in the restructuring process will not necessarily have access to the derivative documentation, it may be difficult for them even to take a view as to whether a credit event has occurred.

11.53 Protection buyers may, though, seek to agree cash settlement rather than physical settlement, given that a squeeze of liquidity in the market for instance, may make it difficult for a protection buyer to obtain suitable deliverable obligations to deliver. (See *Credit derivatives 2002: Fundamentals and latest developments in credit derivatives documentation techniques*, Alessandro Cocco, (2002) 3 Derivatives Use, Trading & Regulation 267, 278.) Cash settlement mechanisms are continuing to evolve.

L THE RESTRUCTURING OF MARCONI

11.54 As outlined earlier in this section, the derivative cover of some of Marconi's creditors caused significant difficulties as they sat at the restructuring table. Analysing the Marconi scenario, Nicholas Frome and Claude Brown of Clifford Chance put forward a view that restructurings should be conducted in such a way that credit events under derivative contracts are clearly triggered. They suggest (though they note the disadvantages) that one or more of the following approaches could otherwise be adopted:

(a)   introduction of a debtor-in-possession reorganisation procedure with the benefit of a statutory moratorium;

(b)   allowing covered lenders to opt-out from the INSOL Principles and London Approach upon expiry of the cover;

(c)   standardisation of the transferability of bank debt after an event of default, by eliminating the need for consent of the borrower;

(d)   a mandatory extension to derivative cover in line with any extension to the underlying loan;

(e)   according priority of return (in any pay-back or insolvency) of extension cover for a covered lender, by treating it as either 'new money' or a loss-sharing priority granted to the covered lender if a credit event occurs after the original cover has expired; or

(f)   lending to special purpose vehicles of the borrower, thereby facilitating what Frome and Brown term a 'controlled' ISDA credit event, in circumstances that do not disturb the asset-holding and income-generating companies in the rest of the borrower's group; recourse to the rest of the group would be provided through guarantees.

11.55 It should also be pointed out in relation to paragraph (e) that insider dealing rules may apply to the purchase of additional cover.

11.56 There are clearly problems with these suggestions. In the first instance recommendation (a) is not particularly practical or likely given that Parliament declined to take the opportunity to introduce a procedure comparable to Chapter 11 during the debates on the Enterprise Act 2002. Similarly, the opt out of the London Approach and the INSOL Principles is not actually necessary given that they are merely non-binding standards of recommended practice. Paragraph (c) is not particularly compelling either given that the market standard position in most credit agreements is that lenders have an unfettered right to transfer following an event of default. The suggestion in (d) is also slightly incongruous given that this would seem to require a link between the cover and the hedged debt, thereby partially undermining the logic of purchasing the cover as a hedge in the first place. Finally in relation to (f) cross-default or cross-acceleration clauses in other facilities might kick in upon default, making this an impractical approach where other debt exists.

11.57 Moreover, only the latter four suggestions can be attempted by individual parties; the first would require legislation and the second would require consensus on the part of market participants generally.

11.58 Martin Hughes of White & Case suggests, in response (see *Derivatives must deal with restructuring quandary*, IFLR, December 2003) that the definitions in the ISDA documentation need to reflect more accurately the events that are to be captured. Although the Marconi restructuring was concerned with the 1999 edition of ISDA's definitions, Hughes contends that similar issues arise in relation to the 2003 Definitions. The approach of Frome and Brown, he comments, is one of the tail wagging the dog. A company having discussions with its creditors would then know where it stands. Hughes's solution may be one way of at least providing certainty of identity of the appropriate parties at the table, even if it does not eliminate information asymmetry and the problems arising from this.

M THE RESTRUCTURING OF MIRANT CORPORATION

11.59 A similar issue became apparent on the restructuring of Mirant Corporation, which filed for bankruptcy in the US in 2003. The following details on the restructuring of Mirant are drawn from the Wall Street Journal, 30 January 2004 (*Lenders to Ailing Firms Discover a New Reality: Bitter Disputes Replace Co-operation Among Banks; Mirant Offers a Preview*, Henny Sender). See also Bank Loan Report, 21 July 2003 (*Mirant's Failed Restructuring: Rumors Point to Citigroup*, John Hintze). Creditor discussions on how to restructure the company broke down at the eleventh hour, and this is believed to have surprised players in the market, on the basis that banks had lent to Mirant without collateral, and might therefore have been expected to attempt to arrange a settlement giving them rights ahead of other creditors.

11.60 When Mirant's financial problems became apparent, one bank is understood to have expressed scepticism about the company's restructuring proposals. Originally, many banks and bondholders are said to have considered this scepticism to be simply a negotiating tactic. It is thought that they later considered the opposition of that bank to have been influenced, at least in part, by CDS protection.

11.61 The bank in question has vigorously denied such rumours, and has argued that it could not in good faith support a business plan that it was convinced would fail immediately. It said that in its view, the flawed plan would leave creditors facing a lengthy, highly litigious second bankruptcy during which it would receive zero interest payments and disputed collateral with an unknown value.

N CONCLUSION

11.62 The behaviour of a protection buyer in the context of a restructuring is affected by the fact that its exposure to risk based on the financial instability of the borrower is hedged by credit derivative protection. The 2001 restructuring supplement and the 2003 ISDA Credit Derivatives Definitions aim to clarify what constitutes restructuring as a credit event and to protect against the so-called 'cheapest to deliver' problem that could arise where the reference entity's obligations had many maturities and prices.

11.63 The role of the definitions is crucial as credit event definitions need to describe accurately the events they wish to capture. If credit derivative transactions are properly documented, a company that needs to have difficult discussions with its major creditors may be more likely to know where it stands.

11.64 Protection sellers have many concerns. They feel that protection buyers, especially if they are the originator of the underlying debt obligation, may have greater information as to the credit quality of the reference entity. There may be claims of 'moral hazard' from protection sellers where protection buyers involved in a restructuring may have a profit incentive to agree to it.

11.65 ISDA has responded to these concerns with new variations on the definition of what constitutes a restructuring in 2001 and in 2003. Which form of definition is used in a transaction depends on several factors including the nature of the market, the investment grade of the reference entity and the reasons that each party is entering into the transaction. In response to these arguments is the opinion that the new and volatile credit derivatives market often misprices risk and banks could be paying way over the odds to transfer risk off their balance sheet, especially smaller banks who may be in danger of being fooled. (See *Fools Gold*, the Banker, April 2004.)

11.66 Protection buyers may be in a position to contribute to the triggering of a credit event leading to a payout under the terms of a credit derivative. Whilst the ISDA definitions in 2001 and 2003 aim to address these concerns, the concerns still exist.

11.67 However, it should not be thought that the credit derivative market is a constant hotbed of legal actions. In the main, the market functions very smoothly. Problems are likely to be solved purely because the one thing, above all else, that financial institutions dislike is uncertainty.

Index

References are to paragraph number.